Culture and Po...
in Early Stuart E...

Southampton
SOLENT
University

...designed to
...important new work on key historical
problems and periods that they encounter in their courses. Each volume is devoted to a central topic or theme, and the most important aspects of this are dealt with by specially commissioned essays from scholars in the relevant field. The editorial Introduction reviews the problem or period as a whole, and each essay provides an assessment of the particular aspect, pointing out the areas of development and controversy, and indicating where conclusions can be drawn or where further work is necessary. An annotated bibliography serves as a guide for further reading.

TITLES IN PRINT

The Mid-Tudor Polity c.1540–1560
edited by Jennifer Loach and Robert Tittler

Church and Society in England: Henry VIII to James I
edited by Felicity Heal and Rosemary O'Day

The Reign of Elizabeth I
edited by Christopher Haigh

The Reign of James VI and I
edited by Alan G.R. Smith

The Origins of the English Civil War
edited by Conrad Russell

Culture and Politics in Early Stuart England
edited by Kevin Sharpe and Peter Lake

The Early Stuart Church, 1603–1642
edited by Kenneth Fincham

Reactions to the English Civil War 1642–1649
edited by John Morrill

The Interregnum: The Quest for Settlement 1646–1660
edited by G.E. Aylmer

Absolutism in the Seventeenth Century
edited by John Miller

Britain in the Age of Walpole
edited by Jeremy Black

British Politics and Society from Walpole to Pitt 1742–1789
edited by Jeremy Black

Slavery and British Society 1776–1846
edited by James Walvin

Britain and the French Revolution
edited by H.T. Dickinson

Enlightened Absolutism
edited by H.M. Scott

Popular Movements, c.1830–1850
edited by J.T. Ward

British Imperialism in the Nineteenth Century
edited by C.C. Eldridge

Later Victorian Britain, 1867–1900
edited by T.R. Gourvish and Alan O'Day

The Revolution in Ireland. 1879–1923
edited by D.G. Boyce

Britain Since 1945
edited by T.R. Gourvish and Alan O'Day

Series Standing Order

If you would like to receive future titles in this series as they are published, you can make use of our standing order facility. To place a standing order please contact your bookseller or, in case of difficulty, write to us at the address below with your name and address and the name of the series. Please state with which title you wish to begin your standing order. (If you live outside the United Kingdom we may not have the rights for your area, in which case we will forward your order to the publisher concerned.)

Customer Services Department, Macmillan Distribution Ltd, Houndmills, Basingstoke, Hampshire, RG21 2XS, England.

Culture and Politics in Early Stuart England

EDITED BY
KEVIN SHARPE
and
PETER LAKE

MACMILLAN

First published 1994 by
THE MACMILLAN PRESS LTD
Houndmills, Basingstoke, Hampshire RG21 2XS
and London
Companies and representatives
throughout the world

ISBN 0–333–57850–3 hardcover
ISBN 0–333–57851–1 paperback

A catalogue record for this book is available from the British Library.

Typeset by Expo Holdings, Malaysia

Printed in Hong Kong

Contents

List of Figures

Preface and
Acknowledgements

In recent years there have been exciting developments in both
the historical and critical scholarship on the Elizabethan and
early Stuart period. For all the gesturing to the interdisciplinary,
however, these have proceeded, for the most part, distinctly and
in isolation. In the historiography of the period, revisionism and
the subsequent debates about revisionism have found little room
for consideration of the broad range of cultural texts that New
Historicist critics have been rereading as representations of social
and political arrangements and values. Still in too many courses
on early modern England the study of culture is either ignored or
relegated to a luxury topic outside the mainstream histories of
politics, religion and society. In Renaissance England, however,
cultural practices and texts – verbal and visual – not only reflected
but constructed political attitudes and arrangements. Any history
which ignores them is an impoverished political history of the
period.

Our volume therefore had its origin in a desire to reorient the
somewhat sterile debate over early Stuart England: to broaden the
questions we may fruitfully ask and especially the evidence we
should examine to elucidate that political culture in which any
satisfactory narrative or explanation of events must be situated. We
hope that the introduction and essays that follow may stimulate a
'cultural turn' in the historiography of Tudor and Stuart politics.

The field of early Stuart studies is notorious for sharp exchanges
and disagreements. We would therefore here like to record how
enjoyable and amicable an experience the composition of this volume has been. Scholars who disagree with each other, come from
different disciplines and, doubtless, ideological sympathies, will-
ingly offered contributions and responded to suggestions. Two
were even able to co-write the introduction. Co-operation, however, is not consensus. Indeed, rather than attempting to resolve
disagreements, we suggest that the quite different historical

interpretations of this period illuminate its own ambiguities and contradictions.

Whilst the essays that follow express their particular acknowledgements, as editors we would especially like to thank our contributors for the enthusiasm they have shown from the beginning and sustained throughout the period of compilation, colleagues with whom we have tried out early thoughts and approaches, and Vanessa Graham for her editorial counsel and care. And we would like to express our gratitude to the Institute for Advanced Study, Princeton, and the Humanities Research Center, Canberra, for providing environments and leisure in which early musings could mature into coherent projects and arguments.

K. S.
P. L.

Introduction

KEVIN SHARPE and PETER LAKE

At first sight a book of essays addressed to the relations between 'culture' and 'politics' in the age of Milton and Shakespeare, of the Petition of Right and the Civil War, would seem to need no justification. And yet, as we shall see, recent developments in the historical and literary scholarship on the period have rendered both 'politics' and 'culture' problematic categories and identified the relations between them as an area of some controversy.

Amongst historians 'revisionism' – a loose movement of rein-terpretation and re-evaluation aimed at many of the pieties of the old 'Whig' vision of a parliament- and principle-centred politics – has served to make the central political narrative of early seventeenth-century England controversial again. Under the sceptical gaze of revisionist historians many of the fixed points around which the 'story' of early seventeenth-century English politics was once organised have been shifted or altered almost beyond recognition. The result is that politics is back on the agenda as a legitimate and important subject of historical research and that political narrative is once more in favour as a mode of historical writing.[1]

A central feature of the revisionist project was to replace what one might term a principle-centred account of the politics of the period, in which political ideas and groupings fell more or less tidily into various bi-polar categories – government and opposition, crown and parliament, court and country, Anglican and puritan – with a narrative centred on the monarch and his or her court. This view of the period located the motor of political change in the day-to-day rivalries, the personal plots and factional intrigues that surrounded the person of the monarch. Here was a politics of patronage and place, of personal manoeuvre and rivalry. Parliamentary politics were seen as an epiphenomenon of court politics. The basic unit of political life was the court-based faction. As one might expect from its emphasis on the inward-looking politics of the court there was scant room in this account

1

of the period for ideological division. What was needed, rather than an attempt to capture the broad sweep of a principled, parliamentary politics leading inexorably towards Civil War and beyond to 'the making of modern freedom' (as one recent formulation has it)[2] was a renewed attention to the detail of day-to-day political manoeuvre. Careful narrative reconstruction of discrete events, of the political intentions and trajectories of particular individuals and groups was the order of the day. This approach was combined with an insistence that such narratives should be based on largely manuscript sources. Printed, literary texts were viewed with extreme distrust. The real course of politics was distinguished sharply from fictive discourses developed by contemporaries to describe it. Indeed, perhaps the most powerful version of the revisionist case was based on an analysis of the real, financial and material, causes of administrative and then political breakdown, causes which were in large part hidden from contemporaries and which their own categories of thought were unable fully to comprehend. In this interpretative world what was closed to contemporaries was clear to the modern historian; the line between the real and the represented was sharply drawn and well policed.[3]

Perhaps unsurprisingly, almost from the outset, this revisionism, as it came to be called, was accused of stripping ideology and ideas from our view of early seventeenth-century politics. Where once there had been an intelligible story organised around coherent principles and positions there was now only an interminable, almost antiquarian, narrative, a sort of 'Yesterday in Parliament' reconstructed from a peculiarly moth-eaten and episodic run of Hansard, and written almost entirely in terms of the absence of ideology and opposition and the presence of ideological consensus and political faction and interest in the politics of the period.[4]

That was always something of a caricature of the revisionist approach. It would be more accurate to say that the revisionists produced an alternative reading of the political culture of the day, centred on the relative homogeneity of political values and the practical and ideological difficulties of effective dissent or 'opposition'. However, in many instances that account of contemporary political culture was left implicit rather than rendered coherently explicit. In much, if not all, revisionist writing the reconstitution of the webs of meaning and assumption within which contemporaries conducted their political lives was a peripheral rather than a central concern.[5]

Certainly, the logic of their polemical engagement with what they took to be the existing 'Whig' orthodoxy led the first wave of revisionist scholars to stress the relative absence of 'ideology' in their version of the period. Accordingly, the first round of the debate between the revisionists and their critics tended to be couched in terms of the presence or absence of ideology and principle in early modern politics and of a potentially very unhelpful dichotomy between conflict and consensus. In this polemical universe the presence of 'ideology' in politics was assumed to be coterminous with a certain sort of conflict: conflict engendered by principled opposition to central strands of royal policy. It would not be going too far to claim, therefore, that in producing their rival accounts of the period both the revisionists and some of their opponents have remained trapped within a rather attenuated vision of the political and a somewhat impoverished account of the role and nature of ideology, of political culture, in structuring the political lives of contemporaries. They share a perhaps unwarranted confidence in the capacity of the historian to discern the represented from the real and to relate the two into a coherent account of the political activities of contemporaries.

At this point we need to turn to other parallel developments in the literary scholarship on the period. These, too, produced a fresh concentration on the domain of the political, albeit one conceived very differently from that implicit in the narrative austerities of recent revisionist historiography. Applying the insights of French structural Marxism and other more recent strands of social theory, various scholars have imported into the study of Renaissance literature a notion of politics that embraces all power relationships. ('Power', in this rhetorical universe, is an utterly pervasive, smothering phenomenon and, consequently, a potentially vague, even obfuscatory, term. Moreover, since all relationships are conceived as being, in some sense, power relationships, 'politics' emerges as a very broad catergory indeed.) These scholars have then sought to relocate the process whereby literary texts were produced, circulated and consumed within this broadened definition of the political sphere. This, in turn, has led to a renewed emphasis on the relationship between texts and the various (necessarily political) contexts in which they were written and read, produced and appropriated. Thus in certain circles the response to the renewed sensitivity amongst literary critics to the theoretical problems involved in the extraction of meaning from texts has been a turn or rather a return to historical context, or perhaps more accurately to a variety of more or less successfully historicised contexts, within which literary texts can be set, worked on and interpreted.

One aspect of this project has been a certain broadening of the concept of culture as it is employed in negotiating these dialogues between text and context. For if all relations are power relations and all texts are both produced and consumed within power relations, then the full range of contemporary culture, viewed as the maps of meaning and interpretation with which contemporaries navigated their way through the world and conferred meaning on their experience, became relevant to the interpretation of even the most rarified and seemingly arcane literary texts.

Central to this project has been an assault on the boundary between the represented and the real which played such a crucial role in the revisionists' repudiation of 'printed sources' and their return to manuscript-based narrative history. Many literary critics became fascinated by the cultural forms in and through which political power expressed and sought to reproduce itself. They stressed the ways in which the representation of the person and power of the monarch became a crucial means of exerting control over a society devoid of either standing army, police force or developed bureaucracy. This concern with 'the forms of power and the power of forms' became in some hands almost obsessive, producing a view of the period in which, in the words of David Norbrook, 'the court and indeed society as a whole comes to be seen as a work of art, scripted by a prince who is himself no more than an effect of discourse.' And yet such a sensitivity to the role of the symbolic and the imaginary in constituting the political field provides a useful corrective to the blithe confidence of many revisionist scholars in their own capacity to tell the difference between the real and the represented and, on that basis, to decide which sources to take seriously and which to marginalise.[6]

To take an example, in a recent book Conrad Russell felt able to pronounce Charles I an unpolitical man. Russell's was a verdict based on an apparently timeless and unproblematic concept of the political sphere and political competence. It was reached at the conclusion of an analysis of Charles's attitudes and style which largely ignored the vast range of cultural artifacts – court masques, portraits, poems, ceremonies – in and through which Charles articulated his view of politics and his own position as king.[7] The point to be made here is not just that historians should broaden the range of documents that they consult but that they need, as well, critically to examine and change the ways in which they approach even 'conventional' historical sources. Questions of canon, genre, reception, reader response are arguably just as applicable to the traditional materials of political history (parliamentary statutes, speeches and, still more, diaries and private letters) as they are to other, more obviously 'literary' texts.

The developments in the fields of history and literature sketched here took place at roughly the same time and, as David Norbrook has pointed out, they were both in some sense the product of the same ideological moment.[8] They share, moreover, certain central characteristics – a revalued sense of the personal nature of monarchy, of the significance of the person and personal preferences of the monarch and his or her court. They both tend, too, to emphasise the resultant cultural or ideological power of the court and the monarch and present a severely constricted account of both the capacity and indeed the propensity of contemporaries successfully to challenge or subvert the structures of power with which they found themselves confronted. However, that said, the two schools of thought developed largely independently of one another and for all the enthusiastic genuflection before the idol of the interdisciplinary that characterises the present academic scene, what would appear to be an interesting and fruitful conjunction between them has been little commented on or exploited. It is to that conjunction and that opportunity that this collection of studies is, in part, directed.

On the one hand, the widened sense of the political, the vision of the pervasive role of the ideological and the cultural in shaping, indeed, determining the political lives and intentions of contemporaries developed by certain literary critics cannot help but be of use to historians. For instance, a self-conscious expansion, a deliberate blurring of the boundaries, of the political sphere might prove to be of peculiar value to an historiography perhaps overconfident of its capacity to tell where the political and the ideological ended and where the administrative, the fiscal and the organically traditional and prepolitical structures of the local began.[9] Again, we might be able to recast the terms in which the debate between the revisionists and many of their critics is conducted. We can refuse the false choices between either the presence or the absence of ideology, between the dominance of the early modern political system by either consensus or conflict, with which much of the current literature tends to confront us. Taking as our starting point the revisionists' disruption of the comfortably familiar Whig narrative, we need consistently to interrogate and examine the norms and codes of contemporary politics; we need to problematise, from the outset, the way contemporaries saw themselves and the society and political system in which they lived.

If we include in our analysis a rather less sharply drawn line between the real and the represented than that characteristic of much recent historical writing, then we can widen enormously the range of questions and the types of evidence deemed appropriate for the study of early seventeenth-century politics. For, as a number of the authors in the current collection have pointed out, to restrict our search for the cultural materials, the traditions of thought and feeling in and through which contemporaries could construct themselves as political agents and construe and interpret their political environment, to formal treatises on law and politics, on the one hand, and the traditional manuscript sources of the narrative political historian, on the other, is to miss a great deal that was central to the conduct of contemporary political life and argument. Without our advancing any claim to comprehensive coverage, it is one of the aims of this book to show how a whole variety of sources, both verbal and visual, from high culture, – classical translations, court portraits, royal palaces, the very arrangement of the paintings in royal apartments, the conduct of chivalric ceremony in tiltyard and chapel – and from low – cheap pamphlets, scurrilous verses and libels – can all be brought to bear on questions crucial to the political history of early seventeenth-century England.

But if historians can benefit from some recent developments within literary criticism, so too can literary critics benefit from the revisionist and post-revisionist concern with political narrative. For the more both the production and consumption, the writing and the reading of literary texts is seen as the product of specific historical, and in particular political and polemical, contexts then the more necessary a close engagement with the materials of narrative political history becomes. As a whole series of the succeeding essays show, often only the most scrupulous attention to the attendant political circumstances will do if texts often of an apparently apolitical nature are to be historically interpreted. Thus Martin Butler's very close reading of various Jonsonian masques in terms of the immediate circumstances of both their composition and performance provides a prime example of the integral links between a genuinely contextual interpretation and command of the nuances of contemporary politics. David Norbrook's explication of the significance of the dedication of various parts of May's *Pharsalia* to a number of 'oppositionist' peers is an object lesson both in the complex exchanges of reputation and resonance that could characterise the apparently simple patron–client relationship and of the heuristic value of the closest attention to the interplay between text and immediate context.

II

What is being suggested here is neither the rescue of an unreflective English historical 'empiricism' by a theoretically informed and sophisticated American cultural criticism, nor the cure of a dangerous case of 'theory' with liberal doses of historically produced 'fact'. Rather we are suggesting an approach that builds on and incorporates a range of insights and approaches produced in recent historical and literary scholarship.

It was not the least of the achievements of recent work in both fields to have rejected many of the binary oppositions, the mutually exclusive categories with which the political history and political culture of the period were habitually analysed. Of these perhaps the most pervasive was the opposition between court and country.[10] The essays which follow, for all their different emphases and arguments, do not easily lend themselves to any simple application of that model. In the first place, as Malcolm Smuts has pointed out, in its broadest sense the court milieu embraced many noblemen and even ministers who spent much of their time on their estates in the country. Courtly artists like Jonson and Van Dyck belonged at least as much to metropolitan society as to the court.[11] Moreover the cultural and political resonance of the court – what the court meant – owed much to its representation and image, an image or images constructed by those outside its gates as well by those within. The court is best conceived here not only as a nexus of offices and office holders in attendance on the monarch, but also as a symbol or series of symbols. As such it elicited a whole series of responses – emulation, admiration, contempt and despair – in both the country and in Whitehall alike.

Much the same can be said of 'the country'. As an idyll and an ideal the country was composed af an amalgam of cultural materials and genres – classical topoi from Virgil's eclogues, pastoral literature and landscape painting – all of which, of course, flourished as 'courtly' genres. The country as a repository of organic harmony, natural virtue and order was eagerly appropriated as a symbol for a morally refurbished court, even as the very same images and symbols could be mobilised to criticise a 'court' pictured as a site of unnatural vice, greed and immorality. Country and court are best conceived as constructed, often polemically constructed, ideological terrains. As ideal types they were constructed out of very similar ideological materials or discourses, and contemporaries, both in Whitehall and beyond, habitually espoused, appealed to and manipulated images of both 'the court' and 'the country'.

This is not to deny that 'court' and 'country' could and often did articulate contrary or opposing values. Country innocence and purity were frequently contrasted with courtly avarice and corruption – but not least by those themselves within the courtly milieu. Thomas May, as David Norbrook points out in his essay, found the potential for praise of both monarchy and republicanism in Lucan; he was as 'self divided' as the text he translated. In the images of various noblemen constructed and praised by Ben Jonson's poems the values of court and country 'are in conflict not between individuals but within them'. His masques, too, often seem to be tensely pivoted between the two ideals.

Nobles and courtiers replicated courtly fashion in the country. Endymion Porter evidently built a gallery that was a reflection in miniature of the King's Whitehall collection. As John Peacock's essay demonstrates, at Theobalds and at Hardwick, the Cecils and the Countess of Shrewsbury respectively arranged family portraits with those of monarchs and princes to advertise, like a ruler, their dynasty and power. In London, on the other hand, the Covent Garden development, financed by the Earl of Bedford and designed by Inigo Jones, reconstructed the ideal rural parish in the capital.

Some historians have suggested that an opposition between verbal and visual culture, set up in large part by the Protestant Reformation, helped to constitute and maintain the division between court and country. Certainly, the first generation of Protestants, anxious to eradicate the superstitions of popery, were vigorous iconoclasts, and the reformed faith of the most committed Protestants (conformists as well as puritans) placed far greater emphasis on the word, both read and preached, than on the rituals and symbols of public worship.[12] However, extensive though the effects of iconoclasm may have been, they were never complete. The preferences of the Queen and the failure of the cause of further reformation ensured that. Stained glass and some pictures and images remained in many parish churches, and the early Stuart period witnessed a renewed enthusiasm for church decoration in some quarters.[13] The increasing vogue for funeral monuments, prominently displayed in parish churches, often at the behest of the most godly families, ensured that puritan iconoclasm never gave way to simple iconophobia. In the wider culture the effects of the more austere forms of Protestantism should not be overrated. Neo-Platonic philosophy depicted words as images; classical rhetoric stressed the need for a concretised, almost visual imagery, in speech; in Aristotle's *Poetics* both poetry and painting were alike concerned with mimesis, the representation of nature as an ideal to be attained.[14]

In early modern England text and image were interdependently conjoined in a number of prominent social and cultural contexts – in heraldic devices, emblems, seals, in masques, interludes and public rituals and ceremonies. The frontispiece to many books, with accompanying caption or verse, often sought to encapsulate the meaning of the text that followed. At a more popular level, the uneven spread of literacy ensured the prevalence of visual media. Illustrated broadsheets were a common form of satire. As Tessa Watt has shown, cheap, printed religious pictures, broadsheets and painted cloths were common decorations in alehouses and private houses.[15] Various popular inversionary rituals were in effect rich visual tableaux both displaying and containing social and gender roles and tensions. Even amongst 'the people' however, social and political values were very often represented through a mixture of verbal and visual genres.[16] The murder pamphlets discussed below were often illustrated with crude woodcuts and contained a language so visually evocative as to bear comparison with cinema. Chronograms and acrostic verses, as Alastair Bellany shows, turned words into memorable patterns on the page, and speech bubbles facilitated the reading of satirical woodcuts and broadsheets. Far from Protestant iconophobia having subordinated visual culture, throughout the period some of the most powerful expressions of popular anti-popery were to be found in scatalogical woodcuts depicting popes, cardinals and, latterly, Arminian bishops, as devils, depraved fornicators and ignorant fools.

Such observations suggest, too, that the division between élite and popular culture may have been drawn too sharply in some recent writing. It must be admitted that in the present volume there is no treatment of the sort of popular ritual and festivity in which some scholars have sought to identify the implicit meanings and structures of a genuinely autonomous popular culture lodged in the collective consciousness of the rural masses. Every genre or form discussed here, even – perhaps especially – the cheap pamphlets and rude libels discussed by Peter Lake and Alastair Bellany, were cultural commodities, self-conciously produced for an audience and, in most cases, for a profit, by literate and in some sense educated men, often cleverly mediating between a highly literate Protestant and classicising 'high culture' and the rather cruder taste of their audience. Whether, in early seventeenth-century England, the production and circulation of such commodities, the generation and appropriation of the various meanings they encoded, was so common a phenomenon as to call into question any notion of a popular culture hermetically sealed or largely autonomous from the culture of the literate middling and upper classes must in the present state of knowledge remain an open question.[17]

But certainly, when we examine the ways in which the various texts discussed below circulated, what is striking are the connections and parallels between 'high' and 'low' cultural levels. The playhouse, for example, drew artisans as well as gentlemen, and playwrights produced scenes to entertain the very different audiences that might attend the same performance.[18] Chivalry, that most apparently élite of concerns, had its popular as well as its élite heroes: Bevis of Southampton and not least Robin Hood. The accession day tilts and other court ceremonies and royal entries, soaked in arcane chivalric and classical imagery, drew large crowds. Dr Adamson's essay can profitably be read against William Hunt's recent piece on the genuinely popular resonance of chivalric ideas amongst ordinary citizens and apprentices in London.[19] In some of the murder pamphlets, ideas concerning providence, conversion and election culled from the arcana of literate Protestant, even puritan, culture were attached to brutally titilating accounts of crime. By the same token, one of Tessa Watt's sources for her cheap godly pamphlets was a collection made and preserved by a gentlewoman, and Margaret Spufford's study of the chap book literature, later in the century, was based on a collection made by Samuel Pepys.[20] If some ballads and libels can often surprise the modern reader with their sophistication of reference and allusion, James I took the genre seriously enough to reply to 'the raylinge rymes' produced by critics of his foreign policy with his own doggerel verse.

Moreover, building on the insights of Martin Ingram and others, it might be possible to see the structures and concerns of the culture of the élite paralleling and reflecting many of the concerns of 'the people'. As the articles by Bellany and Lake argue, as well as an élite preoccupation with threats to social and political hierarchy there was a corresponding popular concern with the fragility of order. No less than the culture of the literate and the godly, many of the forms of popular culture, like the charivari examined by Dr Ingram, existed to regulate and revalidate social and sexual norms through the identification and exclusion of deviant behaviour. The search for out-groups, for external, corrupting threats to order and unity, as a means to explain and to control crisis, provided a common theme in the mental world of university-educated divines and gentry and of their socially inferior and less educated contemporaries.[21]

In some popular song and verse we can discern an organic conception of the state (with the monarch figured as reason and head), notions which can also be found in much contemporary political and legal theory, medical treatises and metaphysical poetry. Again in some popular works (like the libels and poems discussed by Alastair Bellany) disease and sexual depravity functioned as cultural metaphors for social corruption and political conflict, just as they did in more sophisticated political treatises, sermons and parliamentary speeches.[22] Libels and ballads crossed social boundaries because, at some level, they deployed common moral vocabularies and legitimating (and delegitimating) languages. Thus, the vulgar invectives and libels against the Duke of Buckingham that circulated amongst the people replicated, albeit in a rather demotic form, the charges of his peers.

Many of the points made here in rather abstract form are summed up in the figure of Ben Jonson. Very much a courtly artist, Jonson never disguised his serious misgivings about courtiers, courtly culture and even kings. His greatest praise is reserved for those who, as Blair Worden puts it, were 'political failures or half failures', semi-detached from a court of which they were also a part. Despite his famous quarrel with Inigo Jones, Jonson also appreciated the necessary interdependence of verbal and visual genres, knowing that his masques required the body of the visual image as well as the soul of the word, that with regard to the claims of poet and architect 'either's art is the wisdom of the

mind'.[23] And the Jonson who was the friend of Selden and
Camden and who proved his classical learning in detailed foot-
notes to his plays was also the author of that most brilliant evocation of popular culture, *Bartholomew Fair*.[24]

Jonson embodies other of our themes and questions. Perhaps
more than any other figure he was engaged in a 'cultural translation' of classical genres and values to his age and circumstances.[25]
From the Roman but also from the Elizabethan past he constructed a moral code against which kings, nobles of ancient lineage
and parvenus should be judged. He moved easily across a variety
of genres, writing history as well as verse, pot poetry as well as
epigram, tragicomedy as well as burlesque. Political experience
and friendship undoubtedly shaped his writing, as much as reading formed his political values. And most self-consciously of his
contemporaries he fashioned a role for the artist that made him,
quite literally, the counsellor of kings. Jonson certainly belongs as
much to the history of Jacobean politics as to the history of
culture. Indeed, Jonson's whole career – from his origins in the
backstreets of Westminster, through his entry into the world of
classical learning at the feet of Camden, his success as both a popular playwright and a court poet and finally his attempt, through
such ventures as the heavily annotated folio edition of his works,
to parley his court connections into a form of cultural capital, a
status and authority partly social and partly cultural – sums up
much of what we have to say about the culture and politics of the
period.[26]

III

Thus, if we accept a good deal of this broadly revisionist rejection
of the polar opposites, the binary oppositions, that have sometimes been used to discuss the political culture of the period, what
categories and approaches are we left with to organize and interpret the politics and culture of the period? The approach suggested by several of the following essays centres on the identification
of certain strands of thought, congeries of concerns, catchwords
and symbols in and through which contemporaries could view,
describe and shape their political experience. These rhetorics or
discourses could be culled from a variety of sources. Three of the
chapters in this volume seek to explicate and recapture one such
rhetoric centred on the translation, interpretation and, in the

case of Thomas May, the extension of a Tacitean, neo-Stoic corpus of texts and the application of the values discerned and
extracted from those texts to contemporary politics. John
Adamson's essay attempts to construct a similar congery of
symbols and concerns organised around the concept of chivalry.
Leah Marcus's piece similarly seeks to recapture the range of
contemporary political resonances inherent in the various genres
of the pastoral mode.

This, of course, is to appropriate both a usage and an approach
pioneered and now rendered familiar by the work of J.G.A.
Pocock and other historians of political ideas.[27] However, where
Pocock's work was intensely text-based, both Adamson's and
Marcus's essays examine visual and iconographic as well as literary
sources and John Newman's piece similarly reminds us that the
deployment of classical motifs and associations could take an
architectural as well as a literary form – and one no less political
for being mute. Thus even as we adopt, from the history of
political thought, a notion of the political and cultural languages
or discourses of contemporaries as both an organising principle
and an object of study for our research, we need to remind
ourselves that the modes of expression through which those
languages and concerns were circulated, invoked and manipulated by contemporaries were not only or even primarily linguistic
or literary. In order to meet this situation we may need some sort
of melding or synthesis between notions of political language or
discourse developed by historians of political ideas and notions of
genre and motif more familar to art historians and literary critics.
Many of the strands of thought that will emerge from such an
approach, and the genres and forms in which they were expressed,
would not easily find inclusion in traditional histories of early
seventeenth-century political thought. But, as a number of our
authors claim, they represent central elements in the political
culture of the period, which political historians ignore at their
peril.

As a number of our contributors are also anxious to point out,
none of the discourses discussed above can be reduced to a simple
ideological programme, a single theory of government. Rather
they were all polyvalent, that is they could all be read or glossed in
very different ways, appropriated for very different purposes. Thus,
as John Adamson points out, chivalric imagery and values could, in
their most protestantised form, do sterling service in 'the
Protestant cause', helping to legitimate and further the self-image

of an aristocracy anxious to go to war on behalf of international
Protestantism, and consequently critical of the pacific and
seemingly pro-Spanish policies of James I. Yet, in a relatively short
space of time, those same chivalric modes could also be
appropriated by Charles I for very different purposes and then be
recycled yet again by certain aristocrats seeking to legitimate their
opposition to royal policy and evil counsel in the early 1640s. Both
Malcolm Smuts and David Norbrook make similar points about
the political resonance of Taciteanism. There was a monarchical as
well as a republican reading of the Tacitean corpus available and
often the same man could produce both, as political circumstances
and his own personal and polemical needs dictated.

Again all these three languages – the chivalric, the pastoral and
the Tacitean – were rooted in the court and could lend crucial
legitimating power to monarchical rule. Yet at the same time, in
certain circumstances and in certain hands, they could all be used
to produce powerful critiques of royal policy.[28] This was true of
several of the other ways of construing and interpreting contemporary politics. The image of the godly prince, legitimated ultimately by a strongly Protestant, and in some hands puritan,
eschatology certainly seemed to strengthen the hand of the
monarch, as a nursing father or mother of the church, a protector
of the Protestant cause, an absolute ruler untrammeled by the
dictates of any foreign authority. And yet at the same time should
the ruler fail to act in ways which seemed to accord with the
dictates of this world view, this same tradition of thought could be
mobilised to produce sharply critical analyses of royal policy and
even of royal authority itself.[29] Again, the natural law tradition,
within which so much contemporary political thinking and debate
was conducted, contained within itself both 'absolutist' and
'constitutionalist' tendencies, just as there was frequently a common law case to be made for the king as well as for his critics.[30]
Thus when contemporaries employed languages like these to
make even the most extreme and coherent case they were very
often employing ideological materials, words and their associations, which could lead in the opposite direction.

Thus as Kevin Sharpe, John Adamson and Malcolm Smuts all
point out in this volume, throughout the period various monarchs
and their cultural agents were engaged in a constant struggle to
appropriate and control these discourses, to subject them to
readings that rendered them supportive of the current tenor of
royal preference and policy. And yet, as those same authors also

show, the very polyvalence of the discourses involved always threatened to slip out of royal control, to allow other, variant readings and glosses which accorded rather less well with the prevailing orthodoxy.

The ambiguities inherent in this situation become all the greater when we remember that the moral standing, the cultural authority to which men like Ben Jonson and Inigo Jones laid claim were worked out within this space between complicity with the power of the prince and his courtiers and independence from it. Inigo Jones certainly believed that by representing the perfect harmonies of the cosmos in stone the architect no less than the statesman directed citizens to an emulation of order, while Jonson frequently asserted the partnership and even the identity of poets and princes. Such claims often met with seeming official encouragement. During James's reign Jonson was in high favour, a virtual poet laureate, and, under Charles, Van Dyck received a knighthood and, as John Newman describes, Inigo Jones served as architect to the Crown. And yet crucial to the maintenance of these men's image of themselves as the moral educators of princes and their subjects was an element of independence not always compatible with the closeness of their relations with the court. Both Martin Butler and Blair Worden explore the ambiguities of this situation in relation to Jonson's career and come to interestingly different conclusions. Where Worden's Jonson, as a great artist, manages to maintain a certain Olympian detachment and integrity, Butler's Jonson is far more mired in the circumstances of court politics and consequently far less able to control either the content or the reception of even his more avowedly critical works.

Things become yet more complicated when we realise that none of these discourses or rhetorics was mutually exclusive. Analyses which centre on individual rhetorics risk losing a proper sense of the way in which particular groups and individuals could arrange them in very different combinations or syntheses. After all, the ideological resonance of chivalric imagery was very different when it was combined with a militantly Protestant apocalypticism than when it was appropriated for the Garter ceremonies of a Laudianised Caroline court. The capacity of contemporaries for creative bricolage is best recaptured through studies of individual careers and corpuses of work. We need both attempts to discern and trace different rhetorics, congeries of concern, catchword and symbol, through a multiplicity of texts and contexts and more studies of the ways in which those same rhetorics could be combined, spliced together, brought into tension the one with another in individual texts and careers.[31]

By now some of the difficulties inherent in the approach being described here will have become apparent. Given the ambivalence, the polyvalence, of each of these discourses, how can we be sure that they did indeed represent coherent strands of contemporary thought? Might they not be merely constructs created from a variety of divergent texts by historians for their own interpretative convenience? What precisely was chivalric about Dr Adamson's chivalric tradition and what did that mean? Is this part of a distinctively 'baronial context' for the English Civil War or not? If strands from the same discourse could lead in both republican and monarchical directions, what value has Taciteanism as an explanation of political conduct or preference? Given their complexity and ideological ambiguity how can we avoid the conclusion that, rather than authentic and autonomous ways of looking at the world, of shaping experience, discourses such as these represented a series of masks, a rag bag of legitimations and arguments, amongst which contemporaries could rummage as they sought to justify inherently prudential political manoeuvres? And, if we go too far along that route, how do we describe the relationship between the manipulating subject and the manipulated discourse? Are we not back here with Professor Russell's timeless canons of political prudence and cunning?

These are not only questions of theoretical concern for the modern critic, they were also pressing practical issues for contemporaries. After all, the evil machiavel, cynically manipulating the masks of contemporary rhetoric and moral suasion to conceal and realise his own corrupt ends, was a stereotype of considerable contemporary currency.[32] This was a society obsessed with questions of rhetorical artifice and artificiality and with the occasions for dissimulation and concealment offered by rhetorical skill. Much contemporary religious polemic centred on the alleged hypocrisy and self-seeking of one's opponents. Both popery and puritanism were regularly portrayed as entirely self-seeking value systems that legitimated the barefaced pursuit of pleasure and self-interest under a thin veneer of piety.[33] The distinctions between good and bad counsel – the faithful courtier and the corrupt favourite – were crucial to the conduct of contemporary politics, but in practice it was often difficult to tell the two apart. This was a period in which the very projects, the get-rich schemes of courtiers and would-be courtiers, were justified (sometimes genuinely enough) in precisely the same rhetoric of the commonweal and the common good that was used in parliamentary and popular political discourse to denounce the corruptions of the 'evil projectors' and parasites who allegedly surrounded the court.[34] Lionel Cranfield, perhaps the greatest reforming Lord Treasurer of James's reign, was impeached for corruption by the House of Commons, but at the behest and with the connivance of that arch-courtier the Duke of Buckingham. The ironies inherent in contemporary politics were manifold. To use Kevin Sharpe's phrase, at times the difference between criticism and compliment was almost non-existent. Yet the claims of a man like Jonson to independence and integrity had to be maintained by his capacity, often in the tightest of political corners, to transmute the one into the other.

Often couched in more abstract language, issues such as these have become a preoccupation of much recent literary and cultural criticism. How far do historical subjects speak and constitute themselves through discourse and how far does discourse constitute and speak through historical subjects? How far can any producer of culture transcend or even subvert the relations of power within which his or her texts are created and consumed? Of late, questions like these have been the subject of considerable theoretical or, at least, theoretically informed discussion. And yet it seems that they might not, finally, yield to purely theoretical resolution. Perhaps they are best regarded as conundrums, areas of ambiguity, tension and difficulty both for the Stuarts and for us. As such, they can be investigated and their implications examined in case studies of particular historical moments, particular individuals and texts. As the following essays show, these are not only theoretical problems but also historical ones that can be met, in part, with the traditional methods and concerns of the historian.

But again, as the succeeding studies also illustrate, the result of such investigations will scarcely be agreement or unanimity. Given that the gravamen of this introduction has been the inherent ambivalence and ambiguity of the languages or traditions of thought in and through which contemporaries approached their political lives, it seems inevitable that historians, too, will subject the usage of contemporaries to a number of different glosses or interpretations.

For instance, on the one hand, it is clearly possible to stress the wide currency of the discourses discussed here, to assert their status as common languages, able both to express but also to contain a whole gamut of ideological tensions. On this view the early seventeenth century saw the apogee of the English Renaissance state. This was a period in which a blend of classical and Christian inheritances, thought and action, private and public life, learning and statecraft, literature and other discourses were melded into an organic system. The result was a synthesis rent with tensions and contradictions, tensions which were still somehow contained within the essentially hierarchical structures of English humanist culture. Here was a culture centred on the court, subject to considerable royal control and influence, but also able to sustain lively criticism of and dialogue about royal policy. Moreover, the circulation of cultural commodities – the common structuring assumptions and forms uniting high and low, élite and popular, literate and illiterate cultural levels – could be adduced to play down any natural cultural or social tensions dividing the rulers from the ruled or providing any very obvious cultural leverage for opponents of the regime to mobilise mass support. On this view, the organic unity or this culture was only shattered by the fact of civil war and the shock of regicide.[35] Here is a view of the period perceived if not through Ben Jonson's eyes then at least one in which Jonson figures as a normative, even paradigmatic, figure.

On the other hand, it is possible to stress the relative instability of many of the discourses discussed here. Such a view would emphasise the ease with which the dominant political discourses of the period could escape the calming glosses placed upon them by the agents of the royal will. With alarming speed they could be and were mobilised to produce rather sharp criticisms of royal policy and, even, alternative readings of the nature of legitimate authority and of the locus and nature of political virtue. Many of the traditions of thought under discussion were effectively shared validating languages, to which any political agent needed to be able to lay claim if he or she were to command the assent of con- temporaries. But these common rhetorics could be and often were put to widely divergent purposes. In this rendition of the period much emphasis would be placed on the capacity of contemporaries for creative synthesis, the often ostensibly unlikely combination of various strands of thought and feeling for particular polemical or political purposes. Here a rather less benign view of the court's ability to hear criticism addressed to it in a courtly mode would be combined with stress on the relative inability of the crown to control the variant readings that could be placed on the very discourses that were being enlisted to legitimate its own policies and power.

If we need to understand, from the inside, the cultural values and assumptions that lay behind the buildings of Inigo Jones, the chivalric rituals of the Knights of the Garter, the policies of the Laudian church, we also need to understand the interpretative frameworks within which such projects could appear to some contemporaries, by turns, threatening and ridiculous, laughable and sinister. In short, if attempts to write the history of the period through the eyes of William Prynne or John Pym must ultimately break down as partial and confining,[36] so too must interpretations that assume the perspective and typicality of Ben Jonson. Any satisfactory view of the period must, on this view refuse the spurious pleasures of an inherently misplaced search for the typical and the representative. This was a period in which many discourses jostled against one another, each multivalent and capable of almost infinite combination with the other cultural strands of the period. Using often the same or very similar cultural materials and assumptions, contemporaries were able to produce a number of different totalising visions of their circumstances. Rather than privilege one of these variant readings of the period as somehow typical or normal, and thus by implication marginalise other contemporary positions as somehow untypical or deviant, it is the role of the historian to document and imaginatively inhabit the cultural world in which these very different viewpoints were constructed and maintained. Such a decentred vision of the period has room for both conflict and consensus and allows a proper appreciation for both the power of discourse to determine and limit individual and group action, and of the capacity of contemporaries to produce, maintain and manipulate divergent views of their own situation, interests and identity and of the church and polity in which they lived.

Again, from this perspective, the cultural links between the élite and popular spheres could produce a relatively rapid circulation of political and religious messages between events and agents at the centre and popular opinion in the localities. In time of crisis, relative cultural homogenity could serve to induce rather than retard political polarisation. Given the failure of Crown and Parliament, king and Scots, to agree, the assumptions and obsessions about order and disorder, unity and disunity, the common search for scapegoats with which to account for political breakdown, noted above, might heighten rather than suppress political tension and conflict. The rapid circulation and easy plausibility of alarming and divisive messages about evil counsellors, popish or puritan plots and conspiracies, delivered in a cultural context in which unity and order were assumed to be in some sense of normal, and their absence cause for panic, was not, given crisis in the centre, conducive to peace, order and unity. Relative cultural homogeneity, need not, on this view, guarantee political stability, but could, in the right circumstances, bring about its opposite.[37]

Such differences of interpretation and emphasis, of course, echo many of the points at issue between revisionist historians and their earliest critics. It is being argued here that they do so within a rather more nuanced view of the cultural and rhetorical context within which contemporaries framed their political lives. But even if the view of the contemporary discursive field implied here represents some sort of advance on the way in which these issues have been canvassed hitherto, it is not an advance that brings a final end to these debates any nearer. But that recognition in itself may bring us closer to the culture and politics of an early modern England in which 'closure', the trapping of discourse in the vice of settled meaning, of firm polemical and political positions and alignments, was no more available to contemporaries then than it is available to us now.

1. Court-Centred Politics and the Uses of Roman Historians, c.1590–1630

MALCOLM SMUTS

Early modern England was a personal monarchy, whose politics centred around the court. Anyone who aspired to a role in national or international affairs had to look to the court for advancement, while even in local politics court influence often made a crucial difference. Political culture and discourse were profoundly shaped by these facts. The court produced its own culture, embodied in pageants, masques and occasional verse, while extending its patronage to poets and scholars throughout the kingdom. But it also affected ideas and cultural habits indirectly, simply by virtue of its pre-eminence. Country peers and gentry emulated court fashions; newsletters reported court gossip; authors of chronicles, plays and political treatises focused upon the dynamics of court politics.

By the late sixteenth century a varied and somewhat contradictory range of attitudes had developed towards the court. Panegyrics conveyed an ideal of order and virtue spreading outward, from the ruler through the court to the kingdom, promoted by the moral force of example more than by coercive authority. This ideal coexisted, however, with acid criticism of royal courts, as places where ruthless men sought to advance their own interests at the kingdom's expense. 'He that thriveth in a court must put half his honesty under his bonnet,' wrote the Elizabethan courtier, John Harington, 'and many do we know that never part that commodity at all, and sleep with it all in a bag'.[1] Samuel Daniel warned that

> ...Courts were never barren yet of those
> Which could with subtle train, and apt advice,
> Work on the Prince's weakness, and dispose
> Of fable frailty, easy to entice.[2]

21

Nor were kings themselves always spared, especially by historians and playwrights, who produced a stream of books and tragedies on tyrannical and inept monarchs between the 1580s and the Civil War.[3]

The weak rulers and tyrants portrayed in plays and books were normally foreign or historically distant. Since the humanist culture of this period emphasised the importance of applying the lessons of literature and history to contemporary politics, however, stories of fifteenth-century kings and Roman emperors sometimes acquired a pointed contemporary significance, especially during periods of tension.[4] Shakespeare's *Richard II* seemed politically innocuous when first written in the mid-1590s but the revival of a play about Richard on the eve of Essex's revolt was a highly provocative act.[5] The Privy Council took even greater umbrage over a prose history of Richard's deposition, John Hayward's *The First Part of the Reign of Henry IIII*, which appeared in 1599.[6] This work was among the first English examples of a style of 'analytic' history, influenced by the model of Tacitus and other ancient historians, which sought to expose the underlying causes of political events and the secret counsels of rulers.[7] Hayward's analytical approach disturbed the Council less, however, than the fact that he had dedicated his book to Essex and described Richard's reign in ways that seemed uncomfortably similar to Elizabethan politics. His story of a childless monarch unable to suppress a revolt in Ireland, who levied unpopular forced loans and ultimately lost the throne to a rebellious peer with a great military reputation, seemed 'to point to this very time', or so the Attorney General, Edward Coke, charged.[8] Hayward was twice imprisoned on charges of sedition and almost executed.

Over the next forty years historical analogies continued to be widely applied to court affairs, by poets and playwrights and men actively engaged in politics.[9] Perhaps the most provocative of such applications occurred in the Parliament of 1626, when Sir John Eliot compared the Duke of Buckingham to Sejanus, the notorious favourite of the Emperor Tiberius. The squalid story of the early Roman imperial court, as told by Tacitus and other ancient historians, provided a model for interpreting the career of Charles I's great minister.

This essay sets out to explore the development of such potentially subversive models of court politics in late Elizabethan and early Stuart England, by concentrating on the uses of Tacitus and other classical sources in shaping analyses of political behaviour.

In doing so it also seeks to challenge the widely held tendency among scholars to associate the crown's traditional dominance of politics with a culture emphasising hierarchical subordination, obedience and consensus, while associating ideological dissonance and conflict with the beginnings of parliamentary challenges to royal authority. It will be argued here that by the late sixteenth century political conflict, over issues as well as power and patronage, had become a normal feature of court life. A more sophisticated and critical political language, inspired by classical sources, initially developed within the context of a court-centred political system. Only in the Stuart period, and particularly in the 1620s, did that language spread well beyond Whitehall, helping to fuel parliamentary and public critiques of the Stuart court.

I

The role of conflict within court politics has been underestimated because historians normally associate the court with the power of a small group of privy councillors and royal attendants. This view contains an obvious element of truth but it is a partial truth that can obscure major features of early modern politics. Courts not only provided the setting within which monarchs lived in daily association with a few great ministers and personal servants. They were also focal points of fierce competition among the political élite for access to patronage and influence over royal policy.[10] The English court, moreover, was always polycentric, in the sense that its politics revolved not only around the royal privy apartments but also the large, independent households that privy councillors maintained in the London area.[11] Councillors frequently disagreed with each other and at times divided the court into rival interests. Policy debates and political rivalries were also shaped by the demands of lesser courtiers and provincial landowners seeking patronage, and by the flow of ideas and information provided by diplomats, spies and policy advisers employed by the crown and its great servants. Understanding court politics requires attention not only to the policies of the crown, but to rivalries within the royal entourage and efforts by people beyond the ruling group to gain access and influence.

This argument applies with particular force to culture. Most of the court's cultural patronage was dispensed not by the crown but by great courtiers, whose tastes and outlooks could vary considerably.[12] Equally important, culture developed not only through the dictates of court patrons but in response to initiatives by those seeking patronage, including professional writers and scholars, and gentry embarking on court careers. A humanist tradition developed under the Tudors, emphasising the importance, to men pursuing such careers, of training in languages, rhetoric and classical learning. Queen Elizabeth and leading ministers like Burghley were themselves products of that tradition, superbly trained in classical languages and literatures. The culture that developed in and around the Elizabethan court was never rigidly controlled, however. It was shaped partly by the Queen's predilections, but also by many people beyond the inner group, including scions of leading gentry families, like Sir Philip Sidney, and socially less elevated poets, scholars and intellectuals recruited into the royal service, among them Edmund Spenser, John Donne and William Camden.[13]

This tradition was also deeply affected by international trends. The court had always been a centre of cosmopolitanism, but in the late sixteenth century political conditions greatly reinforced the importance of certain kinds of international discourse. The assassinations, judicial murders and civic violence stemming from Europe's wars of religion provided a constant backdrop to English affairs, a terrible object lesson in what might happen, should a Spanish invasion or disputed succession destroy the Elizabethan peace.[14] These conflicts also formed an immediate context for court politics, since the foreign sponsorship of plots against the queen and the diplomatic and military demands of European affairs dominated the Council's agenda. Both the theory and practice of statecraft accordingly developed within an international setting. War and diplomacy involved members of the English court in European politics, leading some to develop working relationships with foreign leaders, especially members of the Dutch and Huguenot nobility and intelligentsia.[15] Elizabethans also read European books on politics, including tendentious Protestant accounts of recent events and manuals on the practice of politics, which aided efforts to make sense of international affairs.[16]

The 1570s and 1580s produced a particularly rich harvest of books on statecraft, often written in reaction to Machiavelli, who had come to symbolise a style of politics, divorced from religious and ethical convictions, which many writers blamed for Europe's troubles. Theorists attempted to counter Machiavellianism by arguing that it was ultimately counter-productive, since a politics devoid of religious and moral norms, in which power depended entirely on guile and force, would soon become so unstable as to threaten even the most resourceful prince. To restore stability in an age corrupted by Machiavellian practices, however, rulers could not simply fall back on conventional moral commonplaces. They needed somehow to reconcile a pragmatic and analytical approach to politics with an underlying commitment to fundamental religious and ethical norms.[17]

European interest in Tacitus developed within this context, especially through the work of the great Flemish scholar Justus Lipsius, who published a definitive edition of Tacitus's works and a highly influential treatise on politics that gave Tacitus pride of place among the classical and modern sources of political wisdom.[18] Against the background of civil war in his native Netherlands, Lipsius set out to provide a guide to politics in a corrupt and bloody environment. He turned to Tacitus and other writers of early imperial Rome because they described a world at least as debased as his own. Among these sources, Tacitus excelled in exposing the ruthlessness of politics at the imperial court, normally hidden by dissimulation, lies and flattery. He therefore became a surrogate for Machiavelli: a more respectable authority since, unlike the infamous Florentine, he did not advocate the amoral behaviour he described.

In England a fashion for Tacitus developed at Oxford in the 1580s and quickly spread to the court, especially the circle of the Earl of Essex. The key figures linking academic and courtly Taciteanism were Henry Cuffe, an Oxford professor of Greek who became Essex's personal secretary, and Henry Savile, Warden of Merton College, Oxford, Tutor in Greek to the Queen and an Essex protegé.[19] In 1591 Savile published the first translation of Tacitus into English, comprising four books of *The History* and *The Agricola*.[20] To these he added a short work of his own, *The Ende of Nero and Beginning of Galba*, filling a gap in Tacitus's extant works corresponding to the lost final chapters of the *Annals*. Savile also supplied an appendix on Roman military practices and a number of detailed scholarly notes. The volume began with an epistle of 'A. B. to the reader', which Ben Jonson later attributed to the Earl of Essex.[21] Even if we discount this attribution, Savile's volume provides suggestive evidence about the way Tacitus was being used in the Earl's circle.[22]

The historical narrative in that volume covers a particularly chaotic period of Roman history, beginning with the rebellion that toppled Nero and extinguished the Claudian dynasty, and proceeding through two years during which the Praetorian Guard and the legions of Gaul, Germany, Britain and the East fought each other for control of the Empire. Three emperors were deposed and murdered before the final triumph of Vespasian, a thoroughly unsympathetic character in Tacitus's account. *The Agricola* is a laudatory biography of Tacitus's father-in-law, a Roman military commander and sometime governor of Britain, who retired from politics to avoid provoking the jealousy of Vespasian's successor, Domitian, and died a short time later amidst rumours that Vespasian had poisoned him.[23] Savile's volume thus takes its place beside a large number of other publications of the 1580s and 1590s, describing the horrors of civil war and, by implication, the blessings of the sort of stability Elizabeth maintained in England. A. B. emphasised this point:

> In these four books of the story thou shalt see all the miseries of a torn and declining state...If thou mislike their wars be thankful for thine own peace; if thou dost abhor their tyrannies, love and reverence thine own wise, just and excellent Prince.[24]

On closer inspection, however, Savile's book does not really fit within the conventional Tudor tradition of works illustrating the evils of rebellion. Savile treats Julius Vindex, the originator of the rebellion against Nero, as a patriotic hero who acted 'to redeem his country from tyranny and bondage'.[25] He blames the civil wars on Nero's misrule and the underlying weaknesses of the Roman state:

> As in a body corrupt, and full of ill humours, the first pain that appeareth, be it never so slender, draws on the rest, discloseth old aches and strains, actuateth what else is unsound in the body: so in a state universally disliked, the first disorder dissolveth the whole.[26]

Rather than the evils of rebellion, the book deals with the process by which a weak monarchical state disintegrates under pressure.

By placing Vindex's rebellion at the front of his work and *The Agricola* at its close, Savile also bracketed Tacitus's narrative of civil war with stories of two noble and patriotic soldiers, who emerge as virtually the only admirable characters in the volume.[27] He thereby provided a classical counterpart to the chivalric ideals of honour and heroism, deriving largely from the model of Sir Philip Sidney, already prevalent within Essex's circle.[28] But in Tacitus military action is embedded in a complex and nasty political environment, requiring shrewdness and guile as much as courage. Sidney's *New Arcadia* also explored the relationship of military courage to political calculation.[29] Savile's Tacitean history, however, examines these issues at a level of detailed realism beyond the reach of even the most complex pastoral romance or chivalric epic. As a recent study has shown, Savile's description of the 'virtue' of Vindex has pronounced Machiavellian overtones, involving qualities of resourcefulness and energy that for a time allow him to control the course of events.[30] Political success depends not only on honour and heroism, but an ability to manoeuvre in a political world in which motives of fear, jealousy and self-interest normally motivate behaviour.

We cannot, of course, assume that Savile and Essex would have read the same meanings into Tacitus as modern readers. It is surely significant, however, that of all Tacitus's works, *The History* and *The Agricola* are most concerned with war and its relation to politics. Issues involving strategy and tactics, military discipline, and relations between rival commanders and their civilian superiors are so prominent in these books that a careful reader could scarcely have avoided them, especially one as concerned with military affairs as Essex.[31] Savile's appendix on Roman military organisation and terminology would have aided attempts to use Tacitus as a guide to ancient warfare. The study of Roman military history yielded important tactical innovations in late sixteenth-century warfare, especially in the Dutch army.[32] A few years later Essex revived the Roman practice of decimation – which Savile had discussed in one of his notes – to deal with troops in Ireland who had run from an inferior enemy force.[33] Savile emphasised the relevance of history to the training of military commanders in a Latin oration to the Queen at Oxford in 1592.[34] His Tacitus should be placed in this context, as a practical guide to war and politics, produced under a patron who aspired to become England's greatest general.

It is difficult to imagine how the story told in Tacitus's *History* could have applied very systematically to English politics in 1591. It would have been far more applicable to recent events in France, where the assassinations of the Duke of Guise and Henry III, the last Valois king, had created a chaotic situation not altogether dissimilar to that of the Roman Empire in A.D. 69. Essex led an army to France in the year that Savile's translation appeared.[35] The implicit justification of rebellion in *The Ende of Nero* and the description of the politics of civil war contained in the whole volume should thus be seen primarily within a European and French, rather than an English, setting.[36]

On a more general level, however, Savile's book provided a view of politics applicable to any court. His notes show that, like Lipsius, he read Tacitus as an author who revealed political realities hidden from uninitiated observers. A particularly long note explained the meaning of the crucial Tacitean phrase, *arcana imperii* (secrets of state). Tacitus commented that Nero's successor, Galba, disclosed a secret of state by allowing his troops to proclaim him emperor in the provinces, rather than at Rome. Savile explained that here 'are met the secret truths of appearances in affairs of estate. For the mass of people is guided more by ceremonies or show than matter in substance.' Reason and tradition both suggested that emperors should be made in the imperial city

> and so it had been always observed: but the truth was, and so much the secret imparted, that in substance it mattered not much where he were made, that afterwards could maintain it with arms, and with the good liking of subjects of the Empire. This secret Galba disclosed, and making his profit thereof against Nero, gave like occasion to other to practice the like against him.[37]

Savile concludes his note by remarking that Tacitus also referred to *arcana domus Augustae* or 'secrets of the court'. He does not immediately explain what these are, but *The History* and *The Agricola*, like virtually all Tacitus's writings, are full of the duplicitous activities of people near the Emperor. A note towards the end of *The Agricola* elaborates on a cryptic remark by Tacitus to provide a commentary on tricks of court politics. Tacitus stated enigmatically that Domitian's jealousy against Agricola was aroused by 'the most capital kinds of enemies, commenders'. Savile explained that although 'to hurt or disgrace by way of commendation ... seemeth a strange position at first sight', it is actually a common practice. He then described various strategies courtiers used to weaken rivals by commending or praising them, for example getting rid of a man by commending his qualifications for a job far from court.[38] The most dangerous sort of commendation, however, is that which arouses the sovereign's jealousy, especially:

> where the quality commended breed not only love but admiration ... among the people; as military renown, magnanimity, patronage of justice against all oppressions and wrongs, magnificence and other heroical virtues properly belonging or chiefly beseeming the Prince's person. And this being general to all in some measure, no Prince in the world having his mind so well armed against cunning but that some breach may be made at some seasons into it, yet there worketh both most speedily and most dangerously where the Prince ... is a witness to himself of his own weakness.[39]

In the course of the 1590s, as their frustration over setbacks at court increased, Tacitean attitudes came to colour the ways in which Essex and his followers perceived rival groups at court.[40] Taciteanism alone cannot, of course, explain the Earl's tactless behaviour or his paranoia toward rivals like the Cecils and Sir Walter Raleigh. Essex sometimes signally failed to heed the kind of shrewd advice that Savile's book provided and that others in his entourage reiterated. Thus he ignored Bacon's warnings that he should avoid provoking the queen's jealousy by his popularity and military leadership and accepted an appointment to Ireland in 1599 that contemporaries widely interpreted as an attempt by court rivals to remove him from the centre of power.[41] Savile's edition nevertheless suggests how Tacitus was used to construct a view of politics justifying Essex and condemning his court rivals. *The Ende of Nero* and *The Agricola* glorify the kind of bold and energetic military leadership that Essex advocated. Yet both works and, even more, *The History*, also show that in a debased state heroic 'virtue [is] the ready broad way to most assured destruction'.[42] The jealousy and duplicity of clever but small-minded men, intent on destroying all possible competitors, so dominates politics that true nobility is always perceived as a threat and attacked. Savile's juxtaposition of these works suggested a sharp dichotomy between the great man of action and the petty viciousness of civilian politicians. Essex assimilated that dichotomy to his own social and political prejudices, as a peer intent on pursuing an active military policy, bitterly resentful of the diplomatic caution and manoeuverings of courtiers of lesser birth. Tacitus thus came to reinforce a particularly dangerous aristocratic mindset.[43]

II

The 1601 rebellion destroyed the Earl and his political circle as a cohesive group at the English court, but the influence of Tacitus and the kind of readings of court politics associated with him had by then gained wider currency. An English translation of Lipsius's Tacitean political manual, *Six Bookes of Politickes or Civil Doctrine*, had come out in 1594. Richard Greneway's translation of *The Annals* and *The Germania* appeared in 1597, making nearly all of Tacitus's extant work available in English.[44] In the same year Bacon published the first edition of his *Essays*, a shrewd guide to politics influenced by Tacitus and Machiavelli.[45] Hayward's Tacitean history, *Henry IIII*, followed two years later. A fashion for satires patterned after the work of Juvenal and Persius, which developed suddenly in the late 1590s, among poets associated with the Inns of Court, further reinforced Taciteanism. These Latin satirists acidly described Roman society in roughly the period covered by Tacitus, complementing his depiction of a decadent age.

In the last years of Elizabeth the humanist intellectual and literary culture that flourished around the court was being transformed through the influence of classical models emphasising political treachery and a moral corruption associated with luxury and cultural sophistication. As this happened, competition for entry into the court reached new levels of intensity. The number of young men seeking positions there was greater than ever before, while the pressures of war finance and the old queen's parsimony and truculence resulted in a constriction of opportunities. The intensity of the factional struggle between Essex and his rivals further complicated the lives of lesser courtiers, who sometimes found it difficult to retain the patronage of one group without thoroughly alienating the other.[46] Taciteanism and Juvenalian satire provided languages capable of articulating the frustrations and cynicism these conditions produced.

We should not, however, equate complaints against the court with a fundamental aversion towards it, much less with political opposition to the crown. People reviled the court while continuing to seek advancement within it, so that anti-court prejudice became embedded within court culture. Perhaps the clearest example is Ben Jonson's work, in which satiric attacks provide a continuous counterpoint to praises of the king and Jonson's other patrons.

The interplay of praise and polemical attack is especially marked in three works produced around the time of James's accession – the Tacitean tragedy, *Sejanus*, and two pieces written for ceremonial occasions: a *Panegyre* addressed to the King at the opening of his first Parliament, and the verses Jonson contributed to James's first formal entry into London in 1604. Although *Sejanus* depicts the court of a tyrant while the other two works celebrate royal virtues, they have important features in common. Both *Sejanus* and the verses written for the London entry are buttressed by elaborate scholarly notes, reminiscent of those Savile supplied in his edition of Tacitus. The ceremonial works contain passages of invective plainly indebted to Juvenalian and Tacitean models and reminiscent of the bleak tone of *Sejanus*. Toward the close of the *Panegyre* Jonson introduces the figure Themis (Justice), who launches into a diatribe against corrupt English statutes, showing James:

> Where laws were made to serve the Tyran' will;
> Where sleeping they could save and waking kill;
> Where acts gave license to impetuous lust
> To bury Churches in forgotten dust,
> And with their ruins raise the Pandar's Bowers:
> When public justice borrowed all her powers
> From private chambers, that could then create
> Laws, Judges, Counselors, yea Prince and State.[47]

The London speeches include a comparable tirade concerning the victimisation of the poor and innocent by great men and their spies:

> Now innocence shall cease to be the spoil
> Of ravenous greatness, or to steep the soil
> Of raised peasantry with tears and blood;
> No more shall rich men (for their little good)
> Suspect be made guilty, or vile spies
> Enjoy the lust of their so murdering eyes:

> Men shall put off their iron minds and hearts
> The time forget his old malicious arts.[48]

Both passages reflect Jonson's Catholicism, since recusants were among the chief victims of Elizabethan spies, while the evil statutes Themis castigates were associated with the Reformation. But Jonson's evocation of a predatory style of politics, which destroys its victims through informers, false charges, corrupt judges and laws framed to serve tyranny, is plainly indebted to Tacitus.

In *Sejanus* Jonson borrows extensively from Tacitus, Juvenal and other classical sources to portray a court dominated by informers, false accusations and conspiratorial plots.[49] The virtuous characters can only fall back on 'the plain and passive fortitude/ To suffer and be silent' in an environment permeated by an ethos of ruthless political opportunism:

> He that will thrive in state, he must neglect
> The trodden paths that truth and right respect,
> And prove new, wilder ways; for virtue, there,
> Is not that narrow thing she is elsewhere.
> Men's fortune there is virtue; reason, their will;
> Their license, law; and their observance, skill.
> Occasion is their foil; conscience their stain;
> Profit, their luster; and what else is, vain.[50]

This Machiavellian ethic interacts with motives rooted in vanity, fear and the sort of envy that causes Tiberius to invite men born under especially prosperous astrological signs to his island retreat on Capri, so that he can have his slaves throw them off the cliffs.[51] Men and women exploit each other's ambitions and weaknesses for political gain, violating the bonds of married love, friendship and kinship. Political language invariably seeks to deceive; speaking the truth becomes an act of treason.

On one level portraying political vices in this way provided Jonson with a foil against which to set the wisdom and virtue of King James. *Sejanus*, however, exposes the manipulative, destructive features of court politics with a thoroughness implying a more complex relationship between political good and evil than a simple contrast of opposites. In this play the sort of political skills emphasised in the humanist tradition become tools of destruction. *Sejanus* vividly displays what Jonas Barish has called Jonson's anti-theatrical prejudice: his distrust of verbal agility and the manipulation of appearances in the service of illusion.[52] In the Renaissance, however, these were not simply theatrical qualities. Since Castiglione they had been regarded as quintessential traits of the courtier, while humanists argued that rulers must also learn to shape behaviour through words and appearances.[53] 'In all wise humane government,' wrote Bacon,

> they that sit at the helm do more happily bring their purposes about, and insinuate more easily into the minds of the people, by pretexts and oblique courses, than by direct methods; so that sceptres and maces of authority ought in very deed to be crooked at the upper end.[54]

Jonson defended his role as a court poet on the basis of similar ideas. 'Speech is the instrument of society,' he asserted in *Discoveries*, and those who master language can refashion social relations. Eloquence must be complemented by psychological insight, a true knowledge of virtues and vices. When poetry derives from such knowledge it becomes 'the absolute mistress of manners', and thus a fitting study for princes.[55] But in *Sejanus* eloquence and psychological insight become tools of exploitation. Tiberius describes Sejanus's talents in precisely these terms:

> I know him subtle, close, wise, and well read
> In man and his large nature. He hath studied
> Affections, passions; knows their springs, their ends;
> Which way, and whether they will work.[56]

He uses his knowledge to debase rather than to reform manners; but his skills are essentially those of the ideal humanist prince.

There is no easy solution to the problem posed by this kind of villainy. Sejanus reveals a potential for evil inherent, not in a particular system of government, but in political life itself. As critics have often pointed out, the play holds out no real promise of reform. Its virtuous characters seem hopeless in the face of more ruthless and imaginative adversaries. The Senate is fickle, cowardly and sycophantic; the Roman people figure in the action only briefly, as a demented mob that seizes Sejanus's body and rips it to pieces after his execution. His fall ultimately makes little difference, since Tiberius still rules and the equally vicious Macro takes his place as favourite.

The attitude underlying *Sejanus* finds parallels in other works produced by figures connected to the court in the years around 1600. F.J. Levy has shown that Bacon, in the 1597 edition of his *Essays*, conveyed the view that in politics 'all men wore masks' and success depended on skill at seeing through the disguises of others while dissimulating one's own intentions.[57] Greville's *Of Monarchy*, written between 1604 and 1610, approached politics from a more abstract, metaphysical standpoint. But Greville – who greatly admired Tacitus – also saw political life as mired in a fallen world 'of real ill and seeming good', in which all institutions have become so corrupted that government always depends on force and fraud.[58] Taciteanism had become one strand within a broader fascination with the ways in which men (and occasionally women) deceive and exploit each other in pursuing power.

III

The fashion for Tacitus and Juvenalian satire appears to have reached a peak around the turn of the century.[59] James I thought Tacitus overrated and agreed with the great French humanist Isaac Casaubon, who moved to England in 1610, that Tacitus's admirers implicitly 'accuse our present princes of tyranny, or would manifestly teach them the principles of tyranny.'[60] James's scholarly interests centred on theological controversy and patristic scholarship, and he encouraged others – including both Casaubon and Savile – to pursue the same subjects. Savile turned away from the study of ancient war and politics to produce a multi-volume edition of the works of the ancient Greek theologian, St James of Chrysostom.

Nevertheless Tacitus continued to enjoy a reputation in many circles as a masterful guide to politics. Joint editions of Savile's and Greneway's translations appeared in 1604, 1612 and 1622 and 1640; Prince Henry stated around 1610 that he heard 'Tacitus represented by everyone as a writer of admirable sagacity'.[61] The probing, analytical attitude towards politics associated with Tacitus had been widely assimilated. This outlook fed into the fascination with court news that is such a remarkable feature of the Jacobean period.[62] Interest in news derived partly from the practical need of people engaged in royal service to keep up with the shifting balance of factions at Whitehall. But newsmongering was also a cultural fashion, part of the sophisticated environment centring in London's western suburbs, which Jonson, Donne and others satirized.

The cynicism that had developed in the 1590s continued to flourish after 1603, partly because Robert Cecil and his allies consolidated the dominance of the Privy Council they had achieved after Essex's fall. Cecil's many enemies thus had reason to nurse their resentment. Retrospective analyses of the politics of the 1590s portrayed Cecil as a devious and treacherous politician and at his death in 1612 he was widely vilified.[63] Favours and money James bestowed on Scots courtiers added another source of jealousy.[64]

The letters written by Sir John Holles in the mid-1610s illustrate how one man seeking to break into the Jacobean court viewed its leaders. Holles had enjoyed a position in Henry's household until the prince's death. In early 1614 he attached himself to the following of Robert Carr, Earl of Somerset and rising favourite of the king, in the hope of gaining another post. Somerset's fall stranded him once again, however. As he resided in London, acting the part of 'a courtier', he produced a series of biting reports on factional infighting. He alluded to Tacitus in giving a sinister twist to a minor piece of news:

The last week one Smith my Lady Arabella's solicitor was made prisoner in the tower, wherefore I cannot learn. Some think this a prologue to further Tragedy, for Harry the seventh rested not till the Earl of Warwick, his wife's cousin germane forfeited his head, and the same course Harry the eight took with the old Countess of Salisbury. Neither was old Tiberius sorry, that Piso and Plancia poisoned Germanica, nor angry with Sejanus that Drusus could not digest his broth.[65]

He quoted him again when he feared that Somerset's fall might jeopardise his own safety: 'too late I find ... Tacitus his opinion confirmed, that safety dwelleth not in doing well or ill, but in doing nothing'.[66] Mostly he simply reported on the scramble for places and power, 'for courtiers merchandise is matter of state, what factions be up, what down'.[67] 'Forsooth there is a new favourite springing,' he wrote in May of 1615 about George Villiers, the future Duke of Buckingham: 'who makes much noise and great expectation, that all the fortune followers in that place seem to be distracted...It may be the King's affection, and others malice to the other [favourite, Somerset] will bring forth something in his behalf.'[68] A few weeks later, as Villiers's star continued to rise, he commented on courtiers' desertion of former patrons under pretences of 'neglects and injuries'. 'If the sun had shone still, these flies had still fluttered in the light, and now supposing change of weather, they creep to the warmer side of the hedge.'[69] Holles saw court politics in Tacitean terms, as a factious pursuit of personal advantage, shaped by jealousy, malice and fear.

Thanks to the letters of people like him, historians have at their disposal more unsavoury gossip about the court of James I than that of any previous English monarch. This fact has long biased the historical record, producing a picture of an age characterised by scandal, immorality, extravagance and sycophancy. This is, however, largely an illusion, created by the great increase in the volume of written news about court affairs and the mental habits shaping political discourse. The Jacobean court certainly had its faults, but so had the courts of previous rulers. Corruption and bloody factional contests were far worse under Edward VI, for example, than in the Jacobean period. The growth of a larger upper-class society in London, the development of a taste for news and the evolution of a political culture fostering close analysis of high politics meant that the court was subjected to far closer scrutiny than in the mid-Tudor period. Ironically the development of a political culture oriented towards service to the crown ended up making it more difficult to confine political discussion within narrow, courtly milieux or to preserve deferential respect for mysteries of state.

IV

Taciteanism and Roman history ultimately did far more, however, than reinforce diffuse cynicism about courtiers and politicians. In James's reign divergent attitudes towards the Roman past developed, reflecting differing views of contemporary England. As J.H.M. Salmon has recently shown, Taciteanism flourished, especially among surviving members of Essex's following and within the household of Prince Henry, who, like Essex, advocated strong anti-Habsburg policies and military preparedness.[70] This was not coincidental. Tacitus reinforced two attitudes characteristic of anti-Spanish militancy, both of which originated in the sixteenth century and persisted through the early Stuart period. One was a highly conspiratorial interpretation of Spanish methods and objectives, which Essex and others had advanced in Elizabeth's reign and which continued to flourish after the peace of 1604.[71] Paranoia towards Spain derived primarily from religious prejudice and anti-Spanish propaganda, widespread throughout Europe. But a Tacitean outlook, with its emphasis on the role of deception and conspiracy in politics, was highly compatible with fears of Spanish intrigues and infiltration of the English court.

Secondly, Tacitus and other Roman imperial writers associated prolonged peace with luxury, corruption and the decline of old Roman virtues. Savile had developed this view in his 1592 oration before Elizabeth.[72] In 1598 Essex associated resistance to high war taxation with luxury and the loss of virtue:

> Though her Majesty's treasure be drawn deep into and ... the poor husbandman by these late hard years past hath now scant left any means to live, yet if our sumptuous buildings, our surfeiting diet, our prodigality in garments, our infinite plate and our costly furniture of houses be considered England cannot be thought poor. Is England so base a state as that the people in it will not bestow some of their superfluous expenses to keep themselves from conquest and slavery?... Is this such a degenerate age as we shall not be able to defend England? No, no, there is yet some seed left of that ancient virtue.[73]

By 'that ancient virtue' Essex meant the spirit of medieval warriors but the phrase has strong Roman and Tacitean overtones.

After 1604 the long Jacobean peace became widely associated with growing luxury and vice. The mounting peacetime expenditures of the crown on pensions and expenses at court fed into this prejudice, creating an impression that money was being diverted from the kingdom's defence to supply corrupt and extravagant courtiers.[74] In the pamphlets of Thomas Scott in the 1620s, mistrust of the luxury and corruption caused by peace fused with a conspiratorial interpretation of Spanish politics and acute mistrust of English courtiers in a powerful indictment of James's policies.

It was also possible to use Tacitus and Tacitean methods to argue that military men threatened the state, as Robert Cotton did in a manuscript treatise surveying the impact of war upon England throughout the Middle Ages. Cotton turned the sort of conspiratorial analysis of political behaviour associated with Tacitus against warrior aristocrats.[75] 'Great men', he argued,

have been disposed sometimes to humour the waste of treasure
in their Princes, either to subject [their] power ... or to force
necessity to extend prerogative so far, until by putting all into
combustion, some may attain unto the end of their ambition...
Thus did the faction of Henry IV ... and the nobility under
Henry III.[76]

The enormous financial burdens of war had time and again
distorted English politics, impoverishing the people, encouraging
arbitrary uses of power and ultimately provoking rebellion.
In commenting on Richard II's reign, Cotton wrote: 'Thus
under grievous burdens did the State labour continually all his
[Richard II's] time, for his treasury being wastefully emptied by
war was, as Tacitus saith of Tiberius *Scelere replendum*, by which he
meant intolerable rackings of the people.'[77]

By and large, however, writers associated with the king and his
policies adopted a different approach to both the Roman past
and the interpretation of contemporary politics. The Tacitean
tradition focused attention on corruption and duplicity at the
centre of power, paying little attention to social and political
conditions beyond the imperial élite and those caught up in its
nefarious intrigues. James and his panegyrists, by contrast, tended
to stress the benefits to society at large of strong, stable royal
government. James never denied the potential for tyranny inherent in any monarchical state. But he preferred to discuss the
king's role as a mediator of conflict, a protector of traditional
rights and a constructive agent of change. Thus in *The Trew Law of
Free Monarchies* he asserted that it is a king's duty:[78]

to maintain the whole country, and every estate therein, in all
ancient privileges and liberties, as well against foreign enemies,
as among themselves: And shortly to procure the weal and
flourishing of his people, not only in maintaining and putting to
execution the old ... laws of the country and by establishing new
... and to maintain concord, wealth and civility among them.

Court panegyrics expressed this attitude by associating James
with Augustus, who had healed the wounds of civil war and
presided over a golden age of peace, prosperity and cultural brilliance. More generally James's view of kingship encouraged interpretations of history that portrayed kings as agents of constructive
change. In *Prince Henry's Barriers*, Ben Jonson pointedly contrasted

the destruction of war with the prosperity he attributed to the economic policies of Edward I and Edward III:

> To your first speculation, you may view
> The eye of justice shooting through the land
> Like a bright planet strengthened by the hand
> Of first and warlike Edward; then th'increase
> Of trades and tillage, under laws and peace,
> Begun by him, but settled and promoved
> By the third hero of his name, who loved
> To set his own a-work, and not to see
> The fatness of his land a portion be
> For strangers. This was he erected first
> The trade of clothing, by which art were nursed
> Whole millions to his service, and relieved
> So many poor, as since they have believed
> The golden fleece, and need no foreign mine,
> If industry at home do not decline.[79]

These verses echo a minute to the Council of 1610, in which James emphasised his eagerness to undertake 'such works and actions as may be an ornament to the present and future times, be it either in building, planting, opening rives or mines, or any other work of industry, tending to the increase of home-bred commodities or growth of foreign within the land'.[80] The politics of the court matter less in this view because attention is deflected to a wider field of action.

Edmund Bolton's *Nero Caesar or Monarchy Depraved*, published in 1623 with James's active encouragement, applied this outlook to an interpretation of Roman history in the Tacitean period.[81] Bolton argued that monarchy was such an effective form of government that it benefited the Empire even during the reign of vicious tyrants.[82] Republicanism had embroiled Rome in civil war. Under a monarchy 'the joints and compactures of the empire's fabric under an head were so supple and solid' that the state endured four hundred years with only brief periods of unrest.

> That sacred monarchy could preserve the people of Rome from final ruin, notwithstanding all the profanations, blasphemies and scandals of tyrannous excesses, wherewith Nero defiled and defamed it, is the wonder which no other form of government could perform.[83]

In the 1590s, on the other hand, Samuel Daniel had described the Empire as a degeneration from the Republic, which survived for four centuries only because of the strong foundations laid down under republican rule.

A subplot in Bolton's book dealt with the British story of Boadicea's rebellion. Here the author's sympathies lay unequivocally with the Romans. Before the Roman conquest, Britain was filled with petty, warring states whose 'endless iniquities' and conflicts caused the inhabitants 'to fly under foreign guards to avoid oppressions at home'.[84] The Romans brought peace and civilisation, benefits which greatly outweighed the loss of a liberty that had bred disorder. Tacitus, by contrast, stated in *The Agricola* that Roman civilisation had *corrupted* the ancient Britons, leading to 'provocations of vices, to sumptuous galleries and baths, and exquisite banquetings; which things the ignorant termed civility, being indeed a point of their bondage'.[85]

V

Bolton's treatise suggests how attitudes towards English constitutional issues had begun to shape readings of the Roman past, making Tacitus unacceptable in some circles because he seemed to undercut royalist ideals. It is important, however, to recognise that this was a relatively late development. Taciteanism had not entered English political culture as an expression of opposition, a form of protest against absolutism. It was initially an echo of a larger European ferment produced by the ideological and political chaos of the late sixteenth century, in which England's ruling élite was directly involved. A Tacitean language then developed primarily in association with the issues that dominated court politics, such as the relationship between religion and foreign policy, the proper role of aristocratic warriors in national affairs, and the impact of war and peace on the moral fibre of the nation. The significance of these issues, and the complexity of the debate that developed around them, has been obscured by a fixation on conflicts between crown and Parliament, and a corresponding preoccupation with formal constitutional theory.[86]

The influence of Tacitus and other classical sources did, none the less, contribute to a mental climate of anxiety over the survival of Parliament and other traditional liberties, amplifying alarm over such events as the attempt to marry Charles to a Spanish princess, the increasing dominance of Buckingham over the court and the arbitrary taxes of 1626 and 1627. The Roman history studied most intensively under Elizabeth and James I covered a period in which the old Republic collapsed and was replaced by an imperial state. It was, in short, a story of constitutional instability and subversion. Unlike both divine right and common law arguments, which conceived of political relationships in terms of eternal principles or immemorial precedents, the Roman model suggested that states were vulnerable to continuous historical change. In particular, Roman history showed how a decline in social cohesion and virtue, together with the conspiratorial actions of ambitious men, might subvert ancient constitutional forms, giving rise to despotism. Many Englishmen read the recent history of Europe in a similar light. 'In all Christian kingdoms', Sir Dudley Carleton told the Parliament of 1626:

> you know that Parliaments were in use anciently, by which their kingdoms were governed in a most flourishing manner until the monarchs began to know their own strength, and seeing the turbulent spirit of their parliaments, at length they, by little and little, began to stand on their prerogatives, and at last overthrew the parliaments throughout Christendom, except with us.[87]

The growth of monarchical power and destruction of republican forms might be interpreted in different ways, however, depending upon evaluations of imperial Rome. The Tacitean view saw the Empire as a tyranny characterised by moral corruption and a ruthless and conspiratorial style of politics. As a paradigm applied to English politics it fed nostalgia for the Elizabethan past – now widely regarded as a period more virtuous than the present – and acute paranoia about the designs of the Buckingham and other courtiers.[88] Yet it was also possible, as Bolton had shown, to interpret imperial rule as the salvation of Rome from the evils of factiousness and demagoguery. This view might easily buttress ideological support for a resort to prerogative measures.

Perhaps the clearest example of such a reading of Roman history appeared in 1632, under the title, *Augustus: Or an Essay of those Means and Counsels, whereby the Commonwealth of Rome was Altered and Reduced unto a Monarchy*. Published anonymously, it was probably written by Laud's chaplain, Peter Heylyn. This work based itself in a theory of constitutional mutation deriving from the Greek historian Polybius, which held that all states tend to degenerate through time until they become vulnerable to revolutionary change. In particular, the Republic had declined from an aristocracy to mob rule, 'the worst form of government', so that the rise of autocratic power in reaction became 'an inevitable necessity in Nature'.[89] Marius, Sulla, Pompey and Caesar had all attempted to bring this about but failed to establish a permanent change. Augustus succeeded because he recognised the importance of cloaking his new power in traditional forms, so that the people, who judge 'more by appearances than truth' would accept his rule. He therefore restored and preserved republican institutions, 'yet so that nothing was done without the privity of the Prince'.[90]

This analysis was plainly meant to apply to recent events in England. It implied that Charles ought to adjust the English constitution to control the incipient forces of democratic corruption, subordinating traditional institutions to the crown, so as to create a state that is constitutional in form but absolutist in substance. In 1627 Thomas Hobbes had argued along similar lines that Thucydides was a monarchist, since he admired Periclean Athens, which was a monarchy in substance though a democracy in outward form. Like Bolton – and like Thomas May's 1633 continuation of Lucan's *Pharsalia* – Hobbes sought to enlist the intellectual tradition of Greece and Rome behind a monarchist philosophy.[91] Treatments of Roman imperial history focusing on tyranny, moral degeneracy and court intrigue also persisted, however. In 1628 May's *Tragedy of Julia Agrippina* graphically portrayed the murderous intrigues and moral degeneration of Nero's court, laying particular stress on the destruction of noblemen by ruthless freedmen at court.[92] A few years later the most serious charge against William Prynne arising out of the publication of *Satiromastix* was that he had used the reign of Nero as a precedent justifying the violent overthrow of tyrants.[93]

Roman historiography thus not only provided a variety of precedents that could be used to justify resistance theory or absolutism. It also helped to nourish the seventeenth century's rich sense of the psychology of power and the dynamics of the struggles that the pursuit of power engendered. It showed how politics could be understood, not only in terms of abstract, formal principles of law and divinity, but as a product of the hidden goals and concrete actions of rulers and their associates. It also suggested that political change is related to broad cycles of social and cultural evolution, so that the preservation of liberty and stability were ultimately linked to a nation's military prowess and moral discipline. By doing so it helped link constitutional fears to concerns over religion, foreign policy and the enforcement of morality, both at court and in the country. If we want to understand how seventeenth-century minds thought about politics, and what their political life had to do with their culture, then this sort of historically grounded analysis deserves much closer attention.

2. Lucan, Thomas May, and the Creation of a Republican Literary Culture

DAVID NORBROOK

In September 1661, order was given to disinter the body of Thomas May from its prominent position in Westminster Abbey and rebury it outside. In 1650 he had been buried by the republican regime with all the honours due to the official historian of the Long Parliament. The act of expelling May from the Abbey formed part of a ritual expulsion of republicanism from the nation's political culture: twenty other men and women opposed to the royal cause were also reburied.[1] May is today best known from the satire 'Tom May's Death', a similar act of ritual expulsion which invokes the spirits of Chaucer and Spenser to drive him out of the Abbey. The poem brands May as a drunken, sordid apostate, driven into a specious cult of the Roman Republic by his resentment at being denied the post of poet laureate.[2] That view of May did not go unchallenged: down to the nineteenth century his history of the Long Parliament vied with Clarendon's. Though his Lucan translation did not equal the greatest verse translations of the period and was to be displaced by a new version by that staunch Whig Nicholas Rowe, his Latin sequel to the *Pharsalia* was regularly printed in editions of Lucan. Literary history from the later nineteenth century onward, however, has tended to be written by critics sympathetic to the royalist cause, and the sharply revisionist account in 'Tom May's Death' has become orthodox.[3] (Critics almost universally echo the satirist's familiar 'Tom', though they would be unlikely to speak of Clarendon as 'Ned Hyde'.)

The revisionist view assumes that monarchism was natural to Renaissance poets, that the republicanism of the mid-century was a fleeting aberration to be explained largely in terms of personal

45

grievances. But some contemporaries saw things very differently. Thomas Hobbes believed that one of the causes of the Civil War was the study of Greek and Latin literature: nurtured in their youth on texts which glorified liberty, the ruling élite were dangerously liable to forget the glories of monarchy.[4] Hobbes's particular concern was with the study of orators like Cicero: the leading poets of the literary canon, Horace and Virgil, had thrown their weight behind the regime of Augustus, and thus became appropriate models for court poets.[5] Yet there was one leading Roman poet who could become a focus for republican loyalties: Lucan, author of the *Pharsalia*. According to Hobbes's friend John Aubrey, it was the study of Lucan that 'made [May] in love with the republique, which tang stuck by him'.[6] If that is the case, perhaps what needs to be explained is not why May became a Parliamentarian but why he became a courtier. The evidence remains open to different interpretations, but some light can be thrown on the question if May's career is set in the broader context of the reception of classical literary and political cultures.

Recent literary theorists have forcefully reminded us that reading poetry is not a passive process, that texts are not simply passive containers for ideas and values: they are always potentially multiple in meaning, and the process of reception and interpretation is one of selecting meanings according to particular ideological standpoints. An important implication for cultural history is that we need to question a sharp distinction between the original texts produced in Renaissance England and the reception of classical texts: reading and interpreting the classics was itself an active process. Standard studies of the period's political thought note the absence of explicitly republican treatises, but fail to take account of the significance of the constant process of scrutinising and interpreting republican texts from the classical era. Scholarly editions poured from the presses in England and on the Continent each year, and their editors were commanding figures on the intellectual scene; but such texts do not register in conventional accounts of the period's literary production.[7]

If reading is an active process, however, we need to be cautious about describing texts as intrinsically republican: almost any text could be made to serve divergent political interests. And that, as will be seen, was the case with the *Pharsalia*. Such divergent interpretations responded to ambivalences in Lucan's own career, and a brief account of Lucan's political contexts needs to be given in order to situate the Renaissance reception of his poem.[8]

I

Renaissance and modern scholars agree in finding it difficult to give a wholly consistent reading of Lucan's political career; the scorn which 'Tom May's Death' directs at May's apostasy could equally be directed at Lucan himself by those sympathetic to the Empire. For Marcus Annaeus Lucanus (39–65 A.D.) had begun his literary career with the highest court connections. His uncle, Seneca the Younger, had acted as tutor to the Emperor Nero and became his leading counsellor and speechwriter in his first years of power. The opening lines of Lucan's epic of the Roman civil wars praise Nero highly, and some scholars have argued that they were written early in Nero's reign when there were still hopes that he would prove an ideal ruler. Lucan's grim warnings of the terrors of civil war could be read as a strong disincentive to rebellion. For a time Lucan enjoyed Nero's patronage. Since Nero fancied himself as a poet, however, he was always jealous of potential rivals, and he broke up a reading by Lucan of the first three books of the *Pharsalia*. This amounted to censorship: Lucan was to be deterred from continuing or publishing his poem. Lucan eventually became involved in a conspiracy to assassinate Nero, but he betrayed his co-conspirators, many of whom were killed. Lucan was allowed to take his own life, and he died reciting the dying words of one of his own characters.

It is possible, then, to construct an account of Lucan's career as one of personal grievance by one ousted from court favour. Such a reading, however, neglects significant ideological factors. Lucan had been brought up in a Stoic milieu whose members looked back nostalgically to the days of the Republic. Though they were generally pessimistic about the possibility of change, their hostility to the Empire would occasionally flare up into attempted tyrannicide. Lucan's poem communicates the stifled radicalism of this group. It translates that radicalism into literary terms, forming a specifically republican poetic. Lucan systematically challenges the generic conventions of Virgil's *Aeneid*, the poem that had consecrated the accession of the Augustan dynasty. For many literary scholars, in the Renaissance and today, the courtly Virgil provides the ideal of epic poetry: the foundation of Rome is presented as part of a divine scheme. Virgil's celebration of political stability and harmony is embodied in gravely melodious lines. If we apply such standards, Lucan is sadly lacking. But many of Lucan's alleged defects can be seen as conscious revisions of

Virgil's ideological norms. Lucan undermined the conventions of the Virgilian epic by rejecting any comforting mythological schema, expressing scepticism about the gods' existence, and complaining that if they did exist they had chosen the wrong side: they sided with Caesar against the virtuous Cato, who believed that all good men were as gods and who would himself be made a god if liberty were ever restored to Rome (i.128, ix.572–603). At the opening of the poem, in a passage modelled on Virgil's praise of Augustus in the *Georgics*, he looks forward to Nero's apotheosis in heaven, and cautions him not to sit anywhere other than the centre of the celestial sphere, or his weight will bring it crashing down. The poet then declares that as far as he is concerned Nero is in fact divine already, and he has no need to invoke a Muse because the Emperor himself is muse enough. Most Renaissance commentators saw this passage as ironic, ludicrously literalising the concept of imperial and divine *grauitas* in the image of Nero's divine bulk ruining the cosmos.

Lucan's hostility to myth led to much debate amongst classical and later critics as to whether he was not rather a historian than a poet.[9] Whatever the answer, Lucan certainly did not share Virgil's vision of Rome's destiny as gaining fulfilment under the Augustan peace: early in the poem an astrologer laments that it is useless to pray that the bloodshed will end because peace will only bring tyranny (i.669–70). Whereas Virgil's imperial epic centres on one central figure, Aeneas, who functions as a type of Augustus, Lucan's republican epic is suspicious of locating political salvation in an individual. As in Milton's *Paradise Lost*, a republican epic whose conception is indebted to Lucan, the most obvious hero is also the villain: Caesar is a single-minded and unified figure because he subordinates the interest of the state to his own private interest (iii.109, 168). Pompey, his chief opponent, is almost an antihero, liable to charges that he himself might become a tyrant if he won the war (ix.257–8). There is undoubtedly an ambivalent fascination with Caesar's heroic energy, but the poem questions the nature of true heroism: its repeated gory invocations of bloodshed lead to doubts about whether the war was worth fighting. Before the battle that gives the poem its traditional name, Pompey suggests that a less bloody way of proceeding could be found, but he is urged on by Cicero, the voice of republican integrity. In a double irony, Pompey proves himself as a hero in a republican mould by obeying the will of the Senate rather than following his personal impulses, but in doing so unleashes horrifying bloodshed and

dooms himself. Lucan emphasises the distinction between merely
personal allegiances and ideological commitment to a cause after
Pompey's defeat: from now on, he writes, the struggle will not be
merely a defence of the 'popular' Pompey but the perennial
struggle whose contenders are liberty and Caesar (vii.694–7, cf.
ix.257–8). Lucan thus combats a Roman mode of historical
revisionism, inaugurated by Augustus himself, which cast the
Empire's enemies as 'Pompeiani', motivated by personal rather
than ideological factors.[10] Long before the climactic battle, Lucan
has suggested that the individual protagonists are secondary to the
cause: Cato declares that liberty has already dwindled until only its
shadow is left – yet it is still worth fighting for that shadow
(ii.302–3). Lucan presents his own generation as shadows of those
shadows: after describing the defeat at Pharsalus, he complains
that it is unjust that his contemporaries, who are subject to tyranny, should be accused of cowardice: rather, the charge should
be transferred to those who failed to fight fiercely enough for
liberty (vii.642–5). Behind this reproach lies a sense of despair at
being unable to arrest inexorable historical processes: Destiny is
malign rather than benign.

Lucan's challenge to Virgilian norms extends to his style.
Where Virgil offers weightiness and a sense of benign destiny,
Lucan offers paradox, parody, and compulsive repetition. Lucan's
sense of a disharmonious universe is heightened by the uneven-
ness of the style, with abrupt shifts from elaborate hyperbole,
verging sometimes on self-parody, to the taut, aphoristic manner
that was considered more appropriate for epigram than for epic.
Renaissance educationalists urged their pupils to copy out such
aphorisms and memorise them, and Lucan was a valued quarry of
such wisdom. The kind of pointed effect for which Lucan was so
much admired can be best illustrated by the line in which the
narrator breaks off a description of Brutus who has disguised
himself as a common soldier during the battle of Pharsalia to try
to stab Caesar. The odious Caesar will indeed be killed by Brutus,
we are reassured, but not yet: 'Vivat et, ut Bruti procumbat victi-
ma, regnet' (vii.596: 'Let him live and, in order that he may fall as
a victim of Brutus, reign'). By sandwiching the prophecy of successful tyrannicide in the middle of a ritual formula of praise of
the monarch, Lucan destabilises courtly rhetoric, and the stabbing alliteration sharpens the sardonic edge. There is perhaps a
certain melancholy in the knowing slickness of the operation, an
acknowledgement that such verbal tricks may be all that is left for

Lucan's shadow-generation. Under the Empire, rhetoric as a means of overt political debate had given way to ornate ceremonial display, and the poem embodies this tendency as well as criticises it. To that degree, Lucan's can be said to be a courtly style; he became popular in the baroque era amongst writers who were far from republican in sympathy. Yet the poem's unfinished state testifies to the fact that Lucan did in the end translate his anti-tyrannical rhetoric into action.

II

In 1560 the poet Barnabe Googe recorded a dream vision in which Melpomene, the Muse of Tragedy, urged him to translate the *Pharsalia*. Under the more vigorous urging of Calliope, however, Googe turned to a different translation project.[11] About ten years later, Melpomene appeared to his friend George Turbervile: he had, he tells us, already embarked on a version of Lucan, but Melpomene declared that the task was beyond his skills and he should leave it to a greater poet like Thomas Sackville, Lord Buckhurst.[12]

In view of the account just given of Lucan's political sympathies, we may suspect that there were political as well as other motivations for the wariness about undertaking a translation which these poets so conspicuously deflected on to mythological figures. Yet the *Pharsalia* was certainly not regarded as a seditious text. Italian, Spanish and French versions had already appeared, and the Latin text formed a staple element in the English school curriculum, though its difficulty reserved it for more advanced pupils.[13] It was possible to glide over the problem of Lucan's republicanism by reading the poem quasi-allegorically, with Pompey as the representative of legitimate authority, whether monarchical or otherwise, and Caesar as a usurper. And the poem's passionate denunciation of civil strife permitted the conclusion that Rome was better under the peace of the Empire than the chaos of the civil war, even if Lucan himself had refused to draw such a conclusion. A work by the fifteenth-century poet John Lydgate, *The Serpent of Division*, which was heavily based on Lucan, had been published in 1559 as a warning against sedition, and a further edition appeared in 1590 along with a reprint of the Senecan tragedy *Gorboduc* (1559), in which Sackville and Thomas Norton presented a grim picture of civil strife. For Turbervile, the message

of Lucan was 'how discord bréedes decay'. Lucan was an important model for Samuel Daniel's highly negative portrait of
Bolingbroke's usurpation of power in *The Civil Wars*.[14]

And yet there were always problems in pushing such analogies
too far: Renaissance humanism tended to urge increasingly
specific readings of texts in their historical contexts, and the more
Pompey was seen as the representative of a specifically republican
political form, the harder it became to use the poem to buttress
monarchy. Attentive readers would not necessarily have come
away with a simple choice between monarchical order and republican anarchy: the order imposed by the emperors is the order of
death. In suggesting that Sackville would make the most appropriate translator of Lucan, Turbervile was perhaps implying that
his impeccable political connections would free him from any
aura of sedition. But the challenge of undertaking the first
English version was to be taken up instead by a figure notoriously
undaunted by accusations of unorthodoxy: Christopher Marlowe.
A line-by-line version of Book I was posthumously published in
1600. Some critics see it as a mere literary exercise produced in
his youth (its date is unknown); but Marlowe's choice of blank
verse, a metre relatively unusual for non-dramatic poetry, suggests
that he had higher ambitions, emulating the Earl of Surrey's
translations from Virgil to give England a republican epic to
match the imperial one. In view of the hesitations of Marlowe's
predecessors, we may question whether he regarded the task as
entirely 'politically sound'.[15] Certainly Lucan was circulating in
politically restive circles. One of the Earl of Essex's supporters,
Henry Cuffe, was a translator and admirer of Tacitus; and, according to one account, he helped to nerve Essex for his fatal rebellion in 1601 by citing a maxim from Lucan: if he had no friends as
a private individual, he would find many if he took up arms. That
verse, commented Isaac Casaubon, was fatal to Essex.[16]

Lucan's epic made its next appearance in English translation
at an extremely sensitive political moment. The author of the new
version, Sir Arthur Gorges, was a close friend of Sir Walter Raleigh.
Like Raleigh, he had frequently found himself in difficulty because
of his militantly anti-Spanish views and his outspokenness. He had
placed high hopes in the patronage of Prince Henry and gained
no further court favour after his death. The publication of his
Lucan translation became the occasion for a political statement.
In the dedication, it is true, Gorges's son Carew protests the
absence of political motivation: he had chanced to find the poem

amongst his father's papers and decided that it would make a
worthy present for his patron the Countess of Bedford. Such
claims of accidental publication in the Renaissance, however, are
not always to be taken at face value, the more so in this case since
Carew Gorges was only ten years old at the time. His dedication
praises the Countess of Bedford's patronage as living up to 'that
worthy blood of the *Sydneyes*, wherewith you do so neerely parti-
cipate'.[17] By this stage of King James's reign, Sidney had become a
symbol of a lost age not only of generous literary patronage but
also of strong resistance to Habsburg absolutism. The Countess of
Bedford, whose husband had taken part in Essex's rebellion, was
turning increasingly to religious and political interests, becoming
a patron of Calvinist divines at home and on the Continent, and
taking an active role in opposing the Spanish alliance of James's
later years.[18]

The countess was thus an appropriate patron for a book whose
publication signalled discontent with the current direction of
royal policies. The dedication was succeeded by a poem by Sir
Walter Raleigh, who in 1614 was languishing in the Tower. His
History of the World was called in that year for its irreverent comments about princes. At several points in his notes to the poem,
Gorges drew attention to Raleigh's enthusiasm for an expan-
sionist foreign policy, offering parallels with military episodes
such as the siege of Antwerp (77, note to ii.676–7), the loss of the
Mary Rose (114, note to iii.647ff) and expeditions to the West
Indies (199, note to v.620ff). Like many Renaissance humanists,
Gorges regarded classical texts as important in part because they
represented a storehouse of military wisdom, and Lucan was
widely celebrated for his skill in bringing military matters to life.[19]
Raleigh's champions of course wanted him to be released so that
he could take part in such exploits. Raleigh's commendatory
poem (sig. A4r) makes a direct link between Lucan's relationship
with Nero and Gorges's relationship to the English court:

> Had *Lucan* hid the truth to please the time,
>   He had beene too vnworthy of thy Penne:
> Who neuer sought, nor euer car'd to clime
>   By flattery, or seeking worthlesse men.

Nature, wrote Raleigh, had created Gorges's muse like Lucan's;
and he went so far as to suggest that he might resemble him in his
death too:

> Who with a manly faith resolves to dye,
> May promise to himselfe a lasting state[.]

It is not clear what Gorges felt about being cast as a possible martyr, but the other commendatory verses shared with Raleigh's a strong emphasis on the poem's political significance, linking Lucan's poetics with his anti-courtly standpoint. 'S.S.' writes that while Homer and Virgil 'did Poetize' in matter and style and therefore dimmed the deeds they celebrated, Gorges told the truth about Caesar and Pompey directly,

> S'deining [disdaining] their high atchieuements to defile,
> Or inter-lace with idle vanities...
> So farre aboue all feigners LVCAN shines[.]

'T.W.' gives a more specifically political cast to this truth-telling: Lucan has

> ... taught succeeding *Poesy*,
> That flatteries and fictions may delight,
> May please a Tyrant, wrong a rightfull King.

He contrasts Lucan's subject-matter with the dynastic fables retailed by

> ... the *Trojan* Theamers fit for schooles,
> Fabling of this and that in Heauen, Earth, Hell[.]

Lucan was indeed exceptional amongst classical poets in rigor-ously abstaining from mythological machinery – the kind of machinery which animated Jacobean court masques.

That demythologising tendency was visible in the poem's opening lines, where Lucan invoked the cult of the emperor as divine in terms so exaggerated as to suggest parody. Gorges con-fronts these problematic lines with two incompatible interpreta-tions in his marginal notes. On one reading, the passage is to be dated early in Nero's reign, and Lucan 'teacheth NERO how he should gouerne, by an Imagination of what is': this is the familiar humanist strategy of giving advice under a mask of praise. Another note, however, baldly declares that 'This is meere Ironicall flattery' (4). If the lines are relatively early, we can see Lucan as forming for Nero an image of the godlike virtue to which he hopes he may aspire; if they are late, we can read them as a more desperate strategy for the survival of Lucan and of the state, trying to raise Nero's sights above moral degeneracy and at the same time to cover the Emperor's suspicions of the rest of the poem by a public profession of orthodoxy.

This passage draws attention to the interpretive complexities we need to be aware of in reading Stuart court poetry. Gorges offers alternative accounts of Lucan, as a supporter of monarchy who wants to hold it up to its own best ideals, and as a closet republican seeking to undermine the credibility of monarchy by reviving the cult of liberty under a camouflage of praise. If Lucan spoke so strongly to men like Raleigh and Gorges it was perhaps because of that very ambiguity. And yet Gorges leaves his readers in no doubt about the poem's overall republican bias. In drawing attention to the ironical reading, he gives a respectable classical genealogy to an attitude towards the monarch's body very different from that propagated in mystical theories of 'the king's two bodies'. In his note to vii.213, where Lucan declares that the readers in whose minds he revives the memory of these battles will side with Pompey, Gorges comments: 'A pretty conceit of the Authors for those that shall read his booke' (270). The marginal note presents the book as a space in which Jacobean readers can become involved in a universal struggle between absolutist and republican values. Later in the book, after a lament for the devastation caused by the wars, Lucan makes another dynastic intervention, saying that at least the disaster has had a good consequence, that the Caesars will be made gods (vii.457). Gorges has no doubts about how to read these lines: 'This is spoken in derision of the Caesars that were so Deified and called *Diui*' (283). Later Gorges notes a speech in which it is declared that 'Rome [was] euer an enemy to Monarchy' (335) and comments on 'The Authors bitternesse in taxing *Caesar*' (344) and his 'loue to *Pompeys* merit' (355). 'Romes libertie' was 'buried with Pompey' (356).

Gorges' translation reflected a growing interest in Lucan. Its publication in 1614 was perhaps designed to cash in on interest throughout Europe in a new edition by the great Dutch statesman Hugo Grotius, who had visited London the previous year. Grotius found in the Roman poet an image of his own aristocratic republicanism, and he is said always to have travelled with a copy of Lucan in his pocket. Lucan, he declared in 1614, was a freedom-loving, aristocratic, and tyrant-hating poet; let the Dutch read it so that the more they loved the Spanish bard (he had been born at Cordoba), the more implacably they would hate the Spanish king.[20] An important edition by the English scholar Thomas Farnaby appeared in 1618, with commendatory verses by John Selden, and Farnaby's notes were added to later printings of Grotius's edition, later being joined by May's Latin supplement. By 1619 Lucan's popularity in England was great enough to provoke reaction. One 'A.D.B.' found it necessary to publish a defence of James's court, complaining at 'the peruerse petulancie of many *Poets*, which laid so many odious aspersions vpon Courts, as if no vertue had in them any residence'. The author rejected Lucan's claim (actually that of the wicked Photinus, viii.493–4) that men should depart from court if they would be pious: 'Let *Lucan*, then, in this respect, with all his lunaticke Companions go shake their eares'.[21]

Poetic attacks on the court in this period were focused on the Duke of Buckingham, who became the object of ferocious satires. When in 1628 John Felton assassinated Buckingham, there was a chorus of praise for his valour. One particularly fine epitaph described Felton's corpse hanging in chains and proclaimed that his would outlive courtly memorials.[22] The poem thus outlines an anti-courtly poetic as well as an anti-courtly political stance: a poem clandestinely circulated in manuscript is worth more than all the elaborate masques and architecture of the Caroline era because its allegiance is with liberty. The combination of a grotesque physical image, grim wit and soaring rhetoric is very much in the spirit of Lucan. In one manuscript collection of material about Buckingham, the poem, and the whole manuscript, concludes with a quotation from Lucan: 'Coelo tegitur qui non habet urnam.'[23] This comes from a climactic moment of the *Pharsalia* (vii.819) after Caesar has defeated Pompey's army and the conflict has become one not just for Pompey but for liberty in general. The battlefield is strewn with corpses, but Caesar malevolently refuses them burial. The narrator declares that his spite is ultimately in vain, for their spirits will ascend to the heavens and Caesar will soar no higher. Though the dead may be denied a pyre, in the end all things will be consumed by fire. The allusion could not be more pointed. Charles's action in denying Felton due burial resembles that of the tyrannical Caesar. Felton's action, by contrast, had aligned him with Brutus. The shift of attention from Buckingham to his living defenders has ominous implications: Charles himself, the quotation implies, may one day meet his Brutus.

It is not surprising that James and Charles displayed concern during the 1620s about the enthusiasm for tyrannicide being shown by some of their subjects. There was a growing interest in Tacitus's highly critical view of the Roman emperors, and one of Buckingham's clients, Edmund Bolton, set himself to counter this tendency. Bolton warned that 'the noble and other the ingenuous youth of this monarchy [are] taking harm by their unwary reading that historian (who is no friend to regality), and offered a monarchist commentary on Tacitus's *Annals*.[24] In 1624 Bolton published a new account of Nero's reign to supplant Tacitus's. He had submitted the book to James I before publication, and James may even have had a hand in its revisions.[25] Bolton's strategy was boldly to turn the republicans' arguments against them: he would agree that Nero was a sadistic tyrant, but use this as evidence not for popular power but for absolutism. The fact that good men refrained from resisting Nero revealed that '*No Prince is so bad as not to make monarckie seeme the best forme of gouernment*'.[26] Subjects should be all the more grateful to the king if he chose not to plunder and murder his subjects because he knew that their duty to God if he did so would be passive submission. Bolton denied subjects the right to attack evil rulers in writings or in action: their punishment must come from God alone.[27]

Bolton gave a strongly revisionist account of Lucan and his circle. He viewed Seneca as covetous and time-serving, and was prepared to praise Nero for his 'poëticall Genius'. Though Bolton acknowledged Lucan's gifts, he also condemned him as the 'shrillest trumpet of popular paritie, and the boldest decryër of monarckie'. Bolton pointed the contrast between his cowardice over the conspiracy and his 'immoderate praises' of Nero in Book I. The moral of his failed rebellion, Bolton argued, was that poets should not meddle in political affairs.[28] That Bolton was here thinking as much of his own time as of Lucan's is indicated by his aligning Lucan with 'popular paritie': Lucan's brand of republicanism was in fact self-consciously aristocratic, and much of the poem's odium against Caesar was directed against his courting of the masses and undermining the power of the senatorial class.

Bolton's revisionism was in fact relatively muted in comparison with his royal master's. For Bolton, the *Pharsalia* was to be condemned for its sympathy to the Republic; but as a young man, James had published a poem giving a sympathetic reading of one of Caesar's most notorious speeches. At a time when his troops are becoming sickened at the bloodshed, Caesar demands that

they fight on, and asserts that he can no more lose by their desertion than the sea would be threatened by the rivers' withdrawal of
their water (v.335–40). James interpreted these lines as an absolutist manifesto, showing that it is vain for subjects to resist their
sovereign, because they need him but he does not need them.[29]
While it was common for extracts from classical texts to be
invoked without regard for context, some of James's subjects must
have felt uneasy about this apparent admiration for the enemy of
Rome's liberties. With Lucan either becoming anathematised at
court or celebrated as a defender of absolutism, it is not
surprising that there were revivals of the view of Lucan as a bold
critic of monarchy. He makes an appearance in *The Tragedy of Nero*
(published, possibly in response to Bolton's work, in 1624), where
characters look back to 'the happie dayes/O'the common wealth'.
Interestingly, he is given an opportunity to answer the charge that
was made by his enemies against him and was soon to be made
against May: he hates Nero, Lucan insists, not just because the
Emperor has turned against his own poetry but mainly because
he is a tyrant and an enemy to virtue.[30]

III

It was in this highly charged political climate that Thomas May
embarked on his translation of Lucan. From what has been said of
the political context, it is hard to interpret this project as an
attempt to ingratiate himself with the court. As a young and strug-
gling professional writer, May was doubtless motivated in part by
the prospect of financial success. There was space for a new translation: Gorges's translation had already sounded old-fashioned by
the time it was published, and its octosyllabic couplets were not a
metre normally deemed appropriate for heroic verse. May seems
to have tested demand by publishing the first three books separately in 1626 before bringing out a complete version in 1627; the
demand was certainly there, and the translation went through
three editions by 1635. If the poem was a good financial prospect,
however, it was to a considerable degree because of the political
sensitivity of its subject-matter. Hobbes's claim that there was a
dangerous level of enthusiasm for classical republicanism in the
years leading up to the Civil War cannot be seen simply as wisdom
after the event: he was closely involved with poets and dramatists
during the 1620s, and in 1628 he published a translation of

Thucydides's history of the Peloponnesian War, an act which was designed to counter enthusiasm for democracy. Hobbes emphasised Thucydides's salutary conservatism: 'For his opinion touching the government of the state, it is manifest that he least of all liked the democracy... he most approved the regal government.' Hobbes saw the history as a warning of the disasters that ensued from a state dominated by rhetoric, where 'such men only swayed the assemblies, and were esteemed wise and good commonwealth's men, as did put them upon the most dangerous and desperate enterprizes'.[31]

May was moving in similar circles to Hobbes in the 1620s: he dedicated his translation to William Cavendish, second Earl of Devonshire, who had been tutored by Hobbes and to whose son Hobbes dedicated his Thucydides the following year. But May's presentation of his translation testified to the kind of enthusiasm for 'good commonwealth's men' that so alarmed Hobbes. In his dedication May countered the Augustan claim that the republicans were a mere personal faction, insisting that Pompey was 'the true serua[n]t of the publike State' rather than 'the head of a faction'.[32] May saw the Empire as an unfortunate though perhaps historically inevitable phenomenon. The Republic had grown corrupt because 'the greatnes of priuate citizens excluded moderatio[n]'; this meant that Rome 'could neither retaine her freedome without great troubles nor fall into a *Monarchy* but most heauy and distastfull'. The powers of the Empire were 'too absolute and vndetermined'. Each book apart from the first and the last carried a separate dedication, with a comment explaining why the book was suitable to the dedicatee. Thus Book II, where Brutus tries to dissuade Cato from taking up arms on the grounds that virtuous men must strive for peace and disinterestedness, is addressed to that 'noble Patriot' William Herbert, Earl of Pembroke, who was widely seen as a mediator between opposing factions at court. Book III, which ends with an account of war at sea, is addressed to Edmund Sheffield, Earl of Mulgrave, and recalls how in the days of the 'blest *Elizae*' he had seen the sea dyed with the blood of slaughtered foes. Book IV, which presents the valour and solidarity of Caesar's troops, is dedicated to Robert Devereux, Earl of Essex, who had exiled himself from James's court to lead military campaigns on the Continent. The fifth book, continuing the story of Caesar's military triumphs with special reference to a daring maritime exploit, is addressed to Robert Bertie, Earl of Lindsey, who was about to set sail with the fleet to liberate La Rochelle.[33]

Book VI, which May describes as the most poetical of the books, is addressed to the Earl of Devonshire (a political ally of Pembroke) as a lover of the Muses. Book VII, dealing with the climactic battle at Pharsalia at which

> Great *Pompey's* fortune, and the better cause
> Were all enforc'd to yeild to *Caesar's* fate

goes to Sir Horatio Vere, whose victory in defence of the Dutch cause at Nieuwpoort is seen as a comparable achievement.[34] May addresses Book VIII, which chronicles the death of Pompey, to Theophilus Clinton, Earl of Lincoln, with the declaration that these

> ... life-giuing lines by times to come
> Shall make that little, and vnworthy Tombe,
> That kept great *Pompey's* dust, more honor'd far
> Then the proud Temples of the Conquerer.

May's dedicatees had a high reputation as men of patriotic independence; and at the time the Lucan was published this independence had driven several of them into opposition to royal policies. Four of the men May addressed – Lincoln, Warwick, Essex and Devonshire – had recently refused to pay the forced loan imposed by Charles to fund his war with France. Essex had distanced himself from court ever since the scandal of his marriage's forced annulment so that his wife could marry the king's favourite, Somerset; he was a symbol of the kind of determined and efficient military support for the Protestant cause that seemed lacking amongst Buckingham and his courtiers. Essex's resistance to the forced loan had led to his being deprived of the Lord Lieutenancy of his home county.[35] Sheffield, though recently created an earl with a view to pacifying him, had strongly opposed Buckingham in the 1626 Parliament.[36] Lincoln was the most determined of all the campaigners, and was in political trouble at the time the poem was entered in the Stationers' Register on 12 March 1627 for circulating a pamphlet which accused Charles of seeking to 'suppresse Parliaments' and called on the people to take action without being daunted by fear of imprisonment.[37] In giving Lincoln pride of place as the patron of Book VIII, thus making him the custodian of Pompey's spirit, May was being extremely provocative. To some degree, he was also being prescient: of the surviving dedicatees, the majority – Lincoln, Warwick, Essex and Mulgrave – were to side with Parliament in the Civil War. The language of May's introductory address to Virgil echoed the terms of his dedications:

> Thou gott'st *Augustus* loue, he *Nero's* hate;
> But twas an act more great, and high to mooue
> A Princes enuy, then a Princes loue.[38]

This point was brought home by an engraving of Lucan's suicide.[39] May added a few lines to the end of the poem, which Lucan had not lived to finish, in which he gives an epigrammatic formulation of the republican position, challenging the Augustan marshalling of the gods to defend the Empire:

> *But he* [Caesar] *must liue vntill his fall may prooue*
> Brutus *and* Cassius *were more iust then* Ioue.[40]

In most surviving copies of the 1627 Lucan, the dedications to the individual books have been tampered with. Some have been cut out, sometimes with signs of great haste and damage to other pages. It is possible that these excisions were caused by an embarrassing misprint: the printer had rendered the recently ennobled Mulgrave's name as Mowbray.[41] Perhaps it was deemed impossible to excise one dedication without excising them all. But political caution on the part of the author or his dedicatees may also have been a factor. The year 1627 was a high point of political influence for those who were deeply suspicious of 'popularity' and dissension in the realm. Isaac Dorislaus, the nominee of Sidney's old friend Fulke Greville for the first Chair of History at Cambridge, found himself in trouble when he chose Tacitus as his topic. The series was discontinued after the second lecture, in which he declared that the Roman emperors had had no legitimate authority and that power had still rested with the Roman people.[42] May later acknowledged the effects of political pressure both in censoring and in compelling particular kinds of writing; of the outpouring of poems acclaiming Prince Charles's return from Spain in 1623 he commented: 'I suppose the like consent, *without any interposing authority*, hath not been often knowne' (emphasis added).[43]

Whether or not 'interposing authority' played a part, May began from 1627 to move closer to the dominant voices of Caroline panegyric. Within a few years May was offering a very different view of the Roman Republic. In 1628 he brought out a translation of Virgil's *Georgics*, the pattern for Lucan's eulogy of Nero, and he followed this with a version of the epigrams of Martial, who had written disparagingly of Lucan. And in 1630 there appeared a *Continuation* of the Lucan translation with a dedication to King Charles. This sequel marked a significant political shift: whereas the concluding lines which he had added to Lucan's incomplete ending in 1627 were unequivocally hostile to Caesar, the new version was less critical of Caesar than the original. The last book in particular, which takes the story up to the sensitive ground of Caesar's assassination, is hedged with reservations about the republican cause: the civil wars proved 'What horrid dangers follow'd libertie'.[44] The Romans had already lost

> ... that vnsafe prerogatiue
> Their libertie, and gladly would adore
> A safe and peacefull Scepter.[45]

This milder tone made it hard for May to treat the assassination of Caesar, with which the poem ended, in Lucan's spirit; he ends the *Continuation* with the comment that the attempt to regain liberty merely resulted in further bloodshed. Though space is given for the views of the republicans, the poem ends by presenting Caesar more as a martyr than a villain, and the historical pattern, which for Lucan is tragic, for May becomes providential. Augustus's accession was to be welcomed, not least because it favoured poetry:

> ... the Muse before lack'd power to clime,
> Or else disdain'd her highest notes to raise,
> Till such a Monarch liu'd to giue the Bayes.[46]

This was a strong hint from May the aspiring court poet to his monarch. Charles was to reward him by commissioning two historical poems; these poems, on the reigns of Henry II and Edward III, proclaimed on their title pages that they were 'Written... by his Majesties Command', and demonstrated the evil results when aristocrats escaped the control of the monarchy – a message very different to that implied by the Lucan dedications.[47] When Ben Jonson died in 1637, May could have been considered an appropriate candidate for the laureateship.

As May looked back on his career from the 1640s, it would have been his proximity to the monarchy rather than his desertion of it that constituted the apostasy. It is not that his Lucan translation in itself established him as a republican: the dedications testify to an admiration for a politically independent nobility, but not to a belief that such independence was necessarily incompatible with monarchy. The court could still be seen as a necessary forum for debate and patronage rather than an enemy of the 'country'. After all, the *Pharsalia* continued to appear and its publication had not hindered May's advancement – unless we read the shift of emphasis in the *Continuation* as a price he felt he had to pay. Moreover, while Lucan's admirers were branded by their enemies as flirting with 'popularity', Lucan's own republicanism was strongly aristocratic, and May seems to have been alarmed at the depth of popular fury unleashed by Buckingham's assassination: writing when he had nothing to gain by doing so, he declared that Buckingham's death had provoked 'such expressions, as indeed were not thought fit nor decent by wise men, upon so tragicall and sad an accident', and suggested that the personal rule of Charles might have been a divine punishment for the excesses of popular joy.[48] May here invokes not explicit constitutional programmes but questions of language and decorum: Buckingham's opponents unleash a kind of language that destabilises the social order. Charles's court did indeed appeal to many men of arts and letters because of its emphasis on decorum and elegance. Yet May concluded with hindsight that the elegance had been specious: men were deceived by the specious appearance of peace and prosperity into forgetting the struggle for liberty. A traveller from abroad 'would verily believe, a Kingdom that looked so cheerfully in the face, could not be sick in any part'.[49] The ideal court demanded a balance between elegance and decorum on the one hand and the demands of open and sincere speech on the other. May came to feel that the reaction against 'popularity' had led to an attenuated, superficial courtly language. Thus some of the greatest statesmen and councillors would 'ordinarily laugh at the ancient Language of *England,* when the word Liberty of the Subject was named'.[50] May suggests that the problem lay not so much in external censorship as in an inner self-censorship, a loss of spirit. Some men, he wrote, followed Thraseas Paetus in Tacitus who declared that there was no point in trying to speak out where resistance was futile.[51] But poets who aligned themselves with the monarch when liberty was in danger were betraying the nation's ancient language. A brief autobiographical document from the 1630s suggests that May came to feel that he was betraying himself. He had a very bad stammer, and he described the various professions which he was therefore denied. He could not turn to the public arenas of the law or of Parliament. The court offered a kind of refuge; but he then faced the difficulty that princes placed too much emphasis on grace and elegance of speech, not enough on inner substance, and May was found wanting:

> Princes themselves have learn'd but to admire,
> And praise the truest and most lasting frame
> As children doe their peacockes beauteous traine.
> Learning, that wants a Tongue, can truely tell
> How bootlesse 'tis to write though ne're soe well.[52]

May was perhaps reflecting his own experience when he wrote that from about the year 1636, with an escalating crisis in Scotland and growing polarisation, the zeal for liberty began to be recovered.[53] May's familiarity with Lucan would have predisposed him to a belief in the increasingly corrupting effects of royal power: Nero had started his reign in a manner worthy of Lucan's panegyrics but degenerated into a tyrant; when Charles showed signs of doing likewise, he could no longer be given the benefit of the doubt and it was necessary to stop him. There are signs that during the 1630s he changed his view of Charles and likewise of Roman history. He began work on a translation of the *Continuation* into Latin; and in the process he pared away his earlier extenuations of Caesar's conduct, bringing the poem's political standpoint closer to Lucan's own.[54] The act of translating his poem into Latin registered a shift from a courtly idiom towards a more severe Latinity, and from a royal audience to the international humanist republic of letters.

It is difficult to be certain that these changes were political in motivation, for the volume certainly retained the monarchist panoply of the English version, with a fulsome dedication to Charles. Several of the commendatory poems praised Charles for allowing the Roman liberty that had been stifled under Nero to be re-enacted under his rule. May's old friend, and strong royalist, Sir Richard Fanshawe, urged him to take his story up to the time of the Augustan peace.[55] According to John Aubrey, on the outbreak of the Civil War Fanshawe had a long discussion with May before departing to the court at Oxford: Charles's court had contained a diversity of opinions whose sharp polarisation was uncomfortable to many. Nonetheless, the polarisation could not ultimately be contained, and widely divergent readings of the *Pharsalia* emerged in the 1640s. The strongly royalist poet Abraham Cowley began an epic on the English Civil War which was closely modelled on the opening of the *Pharsalia*: here Charles was identified with Pompey as representative of the established government, while Caesar figured Parliamentarian usurpation.[56] Such an identification of Charles with Pompey, however, was hard to sustain, and Cowley abandoned his poem. For May, it was the Parliamentarians who were the true heirs of Pompey's spirit, and when he looked back on the 1630s from the 1640s he frequently saw through Lucan's eyes. His *History* opened with an allusion to the opening of the *Pharsalia*. When writing of the Scots' resistance to the liturgy imposed by Charles when they had already lost much of their presbyterian discipline under James, May alludes to a speech where Cato says it is still worth fighting for liberty even when it really died along ago (ix.204–5).[57] He likened Strafford's defection to the King to Curio's defection to Caesar (iv.814–19).[58]

It is perhaps possible to find a more profound though less easily definable debt to Lucan in the whole structure of his thought in his later writings, a resistance to readings of history in the courtly or Virgilian terms of panegyrics of individual princes, and an insistence on more impersonal mechanisms of power. (Here of course it is hard to separate Lucan's discourse from that of Seneca and Tacitus, writers who were also very important to him.[59]) The problems of courtly language were perhaps not ultimately separable from problems of political institutions. In a work published on the eve of the Civil War, May set out to defend the 'constitution of our English Monarchy', but he revealed some serious problems in that constitution. For example, a virtuous king might paradoxically be worse for liberty than a vicious one. Henry III, Edward II, Richard II – and, implicitly, Charles – had undermined liberty even though their moral character was not intrinsically evil. They were manipulated by favourites who diverted their attention from the public interest to private gratification. And the people, admiring the king's private virtue, might fail to see that his actions worked to their detriment, and be drawn to accept a diminution of their liberties. May quoted from the sixteenth-century resistance tract, the *Vindiciae Contra Tyrannos*, to illustrate the ways in which liberty might dwindle to a mere shadow.[60] Even the removal of a favourite from power, May later argued, might be counter-productive: looking on Buckingham as the only hindrance to the kingdom's happiness, the people had been too indulgent to Charles after his death.[61] In emphasising the gap between public and private virtues, May countered the logic of the Caroline masque, according to which the king brought public and private virtues into perfect harmony, embodying the good of the realm. Whereas masque writers presented these spectacles as mirrors in which the king might view images of good government, May declared that kings should be made to 'look their faces in so true a glasse as parliament' (6).[62] Unfortunately, kings were unlikely to relish this process, and there was an inherent dynamic in the tendency for monarchy to undermine the public interest: as Parliaments became less frequent and the people lost memory of former liberties, monarchs would become more tyrannical. Having delivered a disturbing critique of the notion of a harmoniously balanced constitution, May declared that the only remedy was 'a long Parliament' (8), one that lasted long enough to counter that structural dynamic and whose leaders would demonstrate unremitting 'constancie and magnanimitie' (11).

With a huge effort, May argued, it would still be possible to bring the ancient constitution back into harmony, and force the monarchy to represent the common good rather than its own private interests. But what would happen if the monarch refused to go along with that process? Then, presumably, the only recourse would be a republic. Once Parliament began to issue its own ordinances, May acknowledged, 'things were growne beyond any president of former ages'[63]; one conclusion might be that Roman parallels were more relevant than merely English traditions. Nonetheless, May seems to have had reservations about the eventual establishment of the Republic, refusing to narrate the regicide itself in a revised version of his history.[64] He had, however, provided the regime not only with a legitimising historical narrative but also with a point of reference for a republican cultural politics; for the first time a republican reading of the *Pharsalia* could gain official sanction. The republicans regarded Lucan as very much their own poet: quotations from Lucan abound in Algernon Sidney's *Discourses*.[65] Marchamont Nedham, who became a leading spokesman for the Republic, composed May's epitaph which proclaimed him as 'Lucanus alter plusquam Romanus' – another Lucan, excelling the Roman one.[66] As has been seen, Lucan's own political consistency had been open to question, and Nedham's claim that he excelled the Roman perhaps did not entirely banish the vestiges of uncertainty about his career. For the royalists after the Restoration, however, the issues were clear-cut enough, and May's memorial was destroyed along with the brief phase of republican literary culture which it had commemorated.

3. Ben Jonson among the Historians

BLAIR WORDEN

In the summer of 1605 Ben Jonson was in prison for the third (and last) time. The cause was the play *Eastward Hoe!*, which he had written with George Chapman and John Marston during the previous autumn, and which had earned 'the anger of the king' by mocking his Scottish manners and favourites. Describing the episode fourteen years later, Jonson remembered being told that the three prisoners would have 'their ears cut and noses'. He recalled too that on the day of their release, when he 'banqueted all his friends', his mother told the company that she had prepared 'strong poison' for her son and herself, to be taken 'if the sentence had taken execution'.

Jonson named two of the 'friends' who had been present at the banquet: William Camden and John Selden.[1] Here is a scene to give us pause. Jonson, the English dramatist whom his seventeenth-century countrymen admired above all others, turns for company, at a charged moment of his life, to the two foremost English historians of his time: Camden, whose *Britannia*, first published in 1586, had become and would long remain the most respected and influential source for the history of those islands, and whose *Annals* of the reign of Queen Elizabeth, written under James I, would become the definitive study of it; and Selden, whose studies – legal, medieval, biblical, classical – would make him a giant of seventeenth-century scholarship. We shall find that Jonson, Camden and Selden had common political perspectives. We shall also find that they shared political anxieties, which throw a grim light upon the public life of late Elizabethan and of Jacobean England.

The three writers were not of an age. Camden, Jonson's teacher at Westminster School, was born in 1551, Jonson in 1572, Selden in 1584. Camden was the master, Jonson and Selden the disciples. That a playwright – and poet – should have been friendly with historians is not a matter for surprise. Dramatists and poets and

67

historians mingled freely. They liked to meet at the London
house of the antiquary Sir Robert Cotton, who had been Jonson's
contemporary under Camden at Westminster. The house was 'a
rendezvous of all good and honest spirits', and 'seemed a kind of
university'.[2] Jonson was close to Cotton, who, through his involvement in Camden's researches, became in Camden's words 'the
dearest of all my friends'.[3] Camden wrote verse and was commended to James I by Jonson, a little audaciously, as a 'poet'.[4] His
historical writing is suffused with theatrical metaphors and with a
sense of the dramatic.[5] Samuel Daniel, poet, playwright and
historian, counted Camden among his closest friends,[6] and was
termed by Camden 'our Lucan' after the Roman poet who, like
Daniel, had related the story of his nation's civil wars in verse.[7]

Around the end of the sixteenth century, English historical
writing and English drama came of age together. As Daniel's
career reminds us, historical and dramatic writing could seem
alternative and complementary means of recovering the lessons of
the past. History, like drama, was conceived as an exercise of the
imagination, in which historians, like dramatists, asked themselves
what a given character would have said or done in a given situation. Like dramatists, historians invented speeches for their
characters (a rule to which Camden is admittedly a significant
exception[8]). Of course, the two genres were not held to be iden-
tical. Jonson was mocked by John Marston for his failure to
distinguish, in his tragedy *Sejanus his Fall*, between the office of a
'poet' and that of a 'historian'.[9] Yet the two were intimately connected in Jonson's mind, and not in his alone. The duty of historians and poets alike, he thought, was to excite their readers to
imitate virtue and renounce vice. A generation earlier Sir Philip
Sidney's *An Apology for Poetry*, pursuing the same ethical goal, had
relegated history, which is tied to what has been, beneath poetry,
which explores what might be. The capacity of poetry for imaginative delight equips it, thought Sidney, for a role of moral
instruction to which history, 'captived to the truth of a foolish
world', is unequal. Jonson, by contrast, believed that moral
instruction can be enhanced by the faithful re-creation of the
past. The accuracy of detail for which he laboriously strove in his
Roman tragedies, *Sejanus his Fall* and *Catiline his Conspiracy*,
answered to the demands of an influential school of Renaissance
critical theory, which argued that tragedy is most authentic,
perhaps only authentic, when it represents historical truth before
an audience which already knows the story.[10]

Sejanus his Fall, which was published in 1605, had been registered for publication in the autumn of 1604, the time when
Eastward Hoe! was written. The Roman play had been first performed at some point between March 1603 (when Queen
Elizabeth died) and March 1604: probably between December
1603 and February 1604.[11] The text of that performance does not
survive. We know that it contained material by a second author,
but we do not know who he was. The revised, published version is
Jonson's alone. Its account of the suppression of Roman virtue
and liberty under the corrupt Emperor Tiberius and his evil
favourite Sejanus reflects the anxieties about modern politics
which Jonson shared with William Camden and John Selden. In
Jonson, and perhaps in Camden too, those anxieties were at their
sharpest in the last years of Queen Elizabeth's reign, the time
when *Sejanus his Fall* was conceived and when at least some of it is
likely to have been written. Jonson probably began work on the
play in 1601, after the failure of his 'comical satire' *Poetaster*, when
he resolved to 'try/ If Tragedy have a more kind aspect'. During
the next two years, when he apparently withdrew from company,
he pursued 'something come into my thought,/ That must, and
shall be sung, high and aloof'.[12] Jonson was deeply hurt by the
failure of *Sejanus his Fall* on the stage, as he would be later by the
hostile reception of *Catiline his Conspiracy* (though both works
would be successes on the printed page). No doubt his pride in
his Roman tragedies showed a misunderstanding of his dramatic
gifts, which lay in comedy. Yet their earnestness offers valuable
clues to our understanding of him.

The earnestness is intimately bound with Jonson's responsive-
ness to parallels between past and present. To his generation the
detection of such parallels, and particularly of parallels between
ancient Rome and modern England, had become a habit of mind.
The parallels could be disturbing. In 1604 a honeyed tribute to
the memory of Queen Elizabeth by the Speaker of the House of
Commons contained an unexpected sting. The Queen having
died, 'Virtue is now no treason, nor no man wisheth the reign of
Augustus, nor speaketh of the first times of Tiberius':[13] the times,
that is, before the ascendancy of Sejanus, times which the victims
of imperial tyranny had longingly recalled. In 1626, early in
Charles I's reign, the MP Sir John Eliot was sent to the Tower for
comparing the Duke of Buckingham with Sejanus. The same
parallel was obviously intended in the widely read *The Powerfull
Favorite, or the Life of Aelius Sejanus,* published two years later. That

is not to say that Jonson's *Sejanus his Fall* is a *pièce à clef*. Tiberius is not Queen Elizabeth. The play can be most intelligibly read as a warning against tyranny, not as an accusation of it. Even so, its contemporary relevance would have been unmistakable to its readers.

II

Ben Jonson's historical reading was careful, wide, and often arcane. In publishing the texts of his Roman plays he kept his readers copiously informed of his many sources. He did not merely read and use history. He wrote it. He wrote a section of Raleigh's *History of the World*.[14] He nearly completed a history of the reign of Henry V, a work which fell victim, together with books and notes borrowed from Sir Robert Cotton and John Selden, to the fire that destroyed Jonson's library in 1622.[15]

The gravity of Jonson's respect for historians is evident in the poems he addressed to them. For Camden he wrote that heartfelt and generous tribute: 'Camden, most reverend head, to whom I owe,/ All that I am in arts, all that I know...'.[16] Jonson's play *Cynthia's Revels*, a satire on the Elizabethan court published in 1601, the year of the conception of *Sejanus his Fall*, was dedicated to Camden by his '*Alumnus olim, aeternum Amicus*': his sometime pupil, his friend for ever. The dedication calls Camden '*musarum suarum parentem optimum*': (literally) the best parent of Jonson's muses.[17] In 1616, when Jonson proudly published his collected works, he dedicated the opening play of the volume, *Everyman in his Humour* (another work first published in 1601), to Camden.[18] Jonson relates that it was Camden who taught him to write his poems in prose first,[19] a significant moment, we must suppose, in Jonson's literary development. The masques and entertainments with which Jonson welcomed James I to England called the king's attention to Camden, 'the glory and light of our kingdom'.[20] (Selden in turn would hail Camden as the 'light of Britain', and as 'the English light of antiquity'.)[21] Elsewhere in his masques Jonson made frequent use of Camden's *Britannia*, which he would quote from memory.[22] We catch a poignant sight of the friendship of Jonson and Camden at the beginning of James I's reign, within months of the first performance of *Sejanus his Fall*. Driven from London by the plague, they stayed in the country house of Sir Robert Cotton in Huntingdonshire. At night Jonson had a fearful vision in which his eldest son, a child who had remained in London, appeared before him with a cross on his forehead. In the morning Jonson went, troubled, to Camden's chamber. The older man reassured him, dismissing the vision as 'but an apprehension of his fantasy'. Then came the news of the son's death, an event that prompted perhaps the most affecting of Jonson's poems.[23]

The poem addressed by Jonson to Selden was written in 1614 and affixed, in pride of place, to Selden's book *Titles of Honour*. Selden's preface repaid Jonson's compliment with a tribute which indicates the intimacy between the two men: he recalls having resolved a recondite point of scholarship 'in the well-furnished library of my beloved friend that singular poet M. Ben Jonson, whose special worth in literature, accurate judgement, and performance, known only to those few which are truly able to know him, hath had from me, ever since I began to learn, an increasing admiration.' On another occasion Jonson and Selden conferred about the Mosaic texts which were held to forbid male actors to impersonate females, an exchange in which Selden seems to have taken Jonson's knowledge of Greek and Roman commentaries for granted.[24] Selden himself – like Camden – made 'sallies into poetry'. He contributed historical notes to *Poly-Olbion*, the poem by Michael Drayton, another friend of Camden.[25] In later life Selden would 'brag' that it was Jonson who had 'taught' him to 'relish Horace'.[26]

In his poem to Selden, Jonson addressed a question that regularly exercised him. Where lies the dividing-line between praise and flattery? In Jonson's time, commendation of princes and courtiers was obligatory, detraction unthinkable. A poet who wished, as Jonson did, to educate his rulers in virtue and to deter them from vice had to operate within conventions of idealising commendation. Jonson might have preferred different conventions. In the alliance between royalty and poetry which he sought, poets, being of 'far rarer birth than kings',[27] would not be junior partners. They should be ready with the 'free and wholesome sharpness' which, in Jonson's account, Augustus had welcomed from Horace, Jonson's model.[28] But Jonson lived in a time when, he realised, flattery had reached a point of 'extreme folly, or rather madness'.[29] To his mind praise is healthy, for it brings out the best in people and, by pointing them to an ideal, encourages them to be better. Flattery, by contrast, debases both its author and its object. But can praise preserve its purity amidst the inflationary pressures of adulation in early seventeenth-century

England? Has Jonson not, asks his poem to Selden, 'too oft
preferred/ Men past their terms, and praised some names too
much'? Henceforth he will 'vex it many days/ Before men get a
verse, much less a praise.'[30]

Jonson's philosophy of praise is shared by Camden, perhaps
learned from him. Camden's *Britannia* supplies what its author
calls 'sparing commendations' of those noblemen of his time who
have preserved the antique virtue of their families, and reproach-
fully omits those 'who have least deserved of their country'. We
shall see that Jonson's poems about noblemen follow the same
principle. Camden, like Jonson, is anxious to avoid 'flattery'. His
praise, like Jonson's, exhorts its subjects towards fulfilment of
the virtues it describes. Through his 'commendations', hopes
Camden, 'such as are commended may be lessoned that their
deportments may be answerable, and that they preserve and daily
increase the same.'[31]

In a happy passage, Richard Peterson has noticed how in
Britannia Camden 'constructs a kind of Baedeker of English
virtue'. English virtue, for Camden and Jonson alike, is Roman
virtue too. Peterson gives Camden the credit for Jonson's 'lively
sense of England' as a classical setting: 'Perhaps no other poet of
the period shows such an uncontrived sense of the immediacy of
the Roman past, which was..., as his master demonstrated, directly
underfoot, an archaeological layer of England's history.'[32] Camden
and Jonson place their own time within a continuum of history,
where the torch of virtue is to be handed from generation to
generation. 'To praise good men', Camden tells us, 'is but to show
a light of direction as out of a watch tower to posterity.' Thus the
present Earl of Hertford is 'a singular favourer of virtue and good
learning, worthy in that behalf to be honoured and commended
to posterity'.[33] Camden follows the same principle in his *Annals*,
for 'I have learned of Tacitus that the principal business of Annals
is to preserve virtuous actions from being buried in oblivion, and
to deter men from either speaking or doing what is amiss, for fear
of after-infamy with posterity.'[34] Jonson, who praises to the same
end, invites Sir Henry Neville to 'doubt not what posterity,/ Now I
have sung thee thus, shall judge of thee.'[35]

The evils of flattery are a fitting theme for Jonson's poem to
Selden, for Selden, like Camden, holds flattery in contempt. The
dedicatory epistle of his *Titles of Honour*, addressed to his friend,
and Jonson's friend, the historian Edward Hayward, declares that
'my freedom of spirit... ever hated flattery'. Selden's prose is not

always light of touch, but in *Titles of Honour* it can acquire an exuberance reminiscent of Jonson's comedies – even if not quite as reminiscent as the high spirits that intermittently take over Camden's *Britannia*. An uncharacteristic momentum gathers as Selden derides the conventions which governed the kissing of Roman emperors by their subjects and suppliants: kissing of the forefinger, kissing of the hand, kissing of the feet, kissing of the mouth.[36] The mood recalls Jonson's annotation of his copy of an account of the conduct of Pope Alexander III, who, he read, had placed his foot on the prostrate neck of the Emperor Frederick Barbarossa at the altar of St Mark's in Venice, and had then granted a plenary indulgence to commemorate a victory over the emperor's son. '*O quam superbum, et quam absurdum!*', Jonson noted: oh how proud, and how absurd![37]

Selden traces the development not only of royal but of noble titles of honour. Here too he and Jonson are kindred spirits. Jonson always scorns 'titles' which derive merely from descent or power, not from merit or virtue. Though true nobility is likelier in ancient blood, ancient blood is no guarantee of it. Jonson and Selden alike turn to Juvenal in endorsing the conception of nobility dear to Renaissance Humanism: 'virtue alone is true nobility'.[38] In the same spirit Camden admired the prudence of Edward I, who had summoned to Parliament 'those of ancient families' who were 'the select men for wisdom and worth', but had 'omitted their sons after their death' if 'they were defective therein'.[39]

Selden acknowledges that his findings on the evolution of royal and noble titles owe a large debt to Camden, and to the passages in which Camden traced men's proneness – a sort of civic popery – to expand and inflate marks of honour. Though Camden, like Selden and Jonson, knows that what Bacon calls 'ceremonies and respects' have their point, his gentle scepticism mocks the growing pomp of power. He prefers the 'plain dealing, truth and simplicity' of earlier ages, like that fostered by Edward I. He admires the 'temperance' of Julius Caesar, whose willingness to be content with three personal servants was 'so short of the pomp of our age'.[40] On the day of James I's coronation, and of the royal pageant into which Jonson had inserted a puff for Camden, the historian noted drily that the royal party had proceeded '*magna cum pompa*', with great pomp.[41]

Camden viewed with thinly veiled distaste the modern proliferation of titles, 'which in ancient times were either none, or most simple'.[42] The term 'Lord' had been invented for Roman emperors, of whom Constantine was the first to be addressed as 'Our Lord'. 'Earls were created in old time without any compliment or ceremony at all', but now their installation requires a double ritual, for, thanks to 'a new ceremony come up of late days', they have first to be installed as barons.[43] The debasement of knighthood, which is mocked by Jonson in *Volpone* and in *The Alchemist*,[44] elicits from Camden the question 'whether these dignities of knighthood, in times past so glorious (as long as they were more rare, and bestowed only as the reward of virtue), may not be vilified, when it becometh common, and lieth prostitute (as it were) to the ambitious humour of everyone.'[45] Camden's refusal of a knighthood prompted Jonson's friend the historian Edmund Bolton to reflect that 'dubbing' and 'dignity', or 'the wearing of spurs and a sword', could not have made Camden 'wiser, or better, or healthier' than he already was.[46] In his relations with power, Camden adopted a stance of respectful independence that conformed to Jonson's ideal: 'I did never set sail after present preferments, or desired to soar higher by others. I never made suit to any man, no not to his majesty...'[47]

The inflation of royal titles disconcerts Camden no less than that of noble and gentle honours. 'As for Grace, it began about the time of Henry the Fourth. Excellent Grace under Henry the Sixth. High and Mighty Prince, under Edward the Fourth. And Majesty... came hither in the time of King Henry and Eighth, as Sacred Majesty lately in our memory.'[48] Selden, who takes over Camden's findings and probes further, can decide, in the mood of Jonsonian comedy, to 'laugh' at the 'ridiculous' excesses he locates among titles of honour.[49] Yet for Selden, as for Jonson, laughter has a serious purpose. Selden is disturbed by the 'increase of titulary majesty' and by the invention of titles 'too high for humanity'. He knows that 'the flattering language of lord and king', and the 'obsequious' deification of monarchy, can make men 'servile' and politically 'idolatrous' and can imperil their 'liberty'.[50]

Jonson's poems pay tribute to the historical writings of two other major intellectual figures: Sir Henry Savile, whose translation of Tacitus helped to shape the public preoccupation with the tyranny and corruption of imperial Rome, and Sir Walter Raleigh. In welcoming Raleigh's *History of the World*, Jonson reveres 'grave history' as 'the mistress of man's life'. 'Grave' is an adjective he bestows on Camden and on Savile too.[51] A word which Jonson more persistently associates with history, always gravely, is 'truth'. Selden is thanked for the 'truth' which his writing has 'redeemed'.

The poem to Raleigh commends the 'truth that searcheth the most hidden springs of history', and follows Cicero, as Camden's preface to his *Annals* does, in hailing history as 'the light of truth' (*lux veritatis*). Camden's *Annals* is dedicated upon 'the altar of truth' (and not, as convention might have urged, to a political master or patron). Its preface repeatedly insists on its author's 'love to the truth' and on the historian's duty to 'prize' and pursue it.

In Camden's England, historical truth was a risky commodity. Rulers expected history, as they expected poetry, to endorse the legitimacy and policy of their rule. Jonson pays tribute to the integrity of Sir Henry Savile's commitment to truth, a virtue which sets him apart from the norm. Savile 'dares not write things false, or hide things true.' His 'breast' is 'clear of present crimes', and he lives 'from hope, from fear, from faction free'.[52] Yet any historian of the age had to accommodate himself to the facts of power. Savile could be as deferential to his monarchs as anyone. Camden, Savile's friend, faced a still more delicate task, for his *Annals* related recent history, which contemporaries agreed to be the most sensitive kind of history. He overcame the problem by – as his preface to the *Annals* delicately put it – interpreting 'things doubtful' 'favourably', and by combining 'freedom of speech' with 'modesty'. Camden's history treads the dividing line between candour and misrepresentation: Jonson's poems, no less skilfully, navigate between frankness and flattery.

There were less tactful historians. Perhaps the least tactful was Sir John Hayward, whose *The Life and Reign of King Henry IV* caused a sensation on its appearance in 1599.[53] The government's response to its publication sent a chill of fear through the writing community. Hayward was lengthily interrogated, and imprisoned for the rest of Elizabeth's reign. The work was interpreted as a parallel with recent events, and was alleged to be an apology for the Earl of Essex and an incitement to Elizabeth's subjects to overthrow her, as Henry IV had overthrown Richard II. It is unlikely that Hayward had a seditious purpose, more likely that he wrote riskily in order to attract attention to himself. The government's alarm is nonetheless intelligible. Hayward cared little for the differences between one age and another, much more for the similarities. He was among the most self-conscious practitioners of the new 'politic history',[54] which invited men to probe beyond narratives of particular periods to the historical laws at work in all times. To the 'politic' historian it is the universality of causes and tendencies that gives history its relevance to the present. The past supplies parallels to the present and thus teaches us how to behave in it. Different periods of history – ancient Rome, medieval England, modern times – are readily interchangeable in Hayward's mind. The speeches he gives to his medieval characters are often lifted from Tacitus or from the modern historians Machiavelli and Bodin.[55] The characters are types, which have been present in all ages and which are present now.

Jonson's friends among historians had more respect than Hayward for historical evolution and relativity and, in the main, for historical evidence. Yet they shared Hayward's inclination towards historical parallels and historical types. When Sir Robert Cotton wished to attack the rule of favourites under the early Stuarts, he wrote a life of Henry III, replete with transparent modern parallels. His portrait of the overmighty subject Simon de Montford seems to have been modelled on Tacitus's portrait of Sejanus.[56] Camden, who called de Montford 'our Catiline', essayed a similar parallel between Richard III and the Roman Emperor Galba, both of whom emerge as representations of a recurrent historical type.[57] Jonson himself, seeking a subject for historical tragedy, attempted a play set in the reign of Edward II, *Mortimer his Fall*, a study of the supremacy and fall of an overmighty favourite in an effeminate court, only to drop it in favour of *Sejanus his Fall*, which sets the same theme in imperial Rome.[58]

The principal source for *Sejanus his Fall*, Tacitus, has spoken to no generation more compellingly than to Jonson's, a generation whose reading of him was prompted and coloured (and some-times distorted) by contemporary political experience. Jonson studied him in the standard edition by the modern Flemish scholar Justus Lipsius, whom, like Camden (and like Selden), he revered. Lipsius saw in Tacitus's account of imperial Rome a close and dark parallel to the tyrannies and persecutions of his own time, the time of late Renaissance monarchy and of the wars of religion. Just as the Roman Empire, while preserving the colour and the forms of republican liberty, had extinguished its substance, so the 'many' tyrants of the later sixteenth century were suppressing representative institutions and replacing the medieval politics of consent with arbitrary rule. 'There is almost no nation', remarked Lipsius's associate Antoine Muret, 'but hangs upon the beck and nod of one man, obeys one man, is ruled by one man: therefore in this respect at least the state of things in our time is... like that of Rome under the emperors. And the more like their history is to ours, the more things we may find to study in it that we can apply to our uses.'[59] Lipsius and his followers saw in the rise of Renaissance monarchy an argument for studying not only the substance of Tacitus but his style. Hitherto the sixteenth century had imitated the rhetorical prose of Cicero. But classical rhetoric and oratory had flourished in the times of Athenian and Roman liberty. Tacitean prose, the close, epigrammatic prose of the Empire, was better suited to modern times, when power was once more passing from the floors of representative assemblies to the secret consultations of courts and cabinets.[60]

In selecting the reign of Tiberius, and particularly the career of Sejanus, for his play, Jonson seized on the section of Tacitus's writings that made the deepest impression on readers of the late Renaissance. Jonson's generation became ever more troubled by the growing ostentation and corruption and duplicity of courts, and by the mounting influence and vaulting ambition of upstart favourites at the expense of ancient noblemen and ancient virtue: themes which are at the centre of *Sejanus his Fall*. Camden's portrait of the Elizabethan Earl of Leicester, that 'new upstart' whom the queen 'raised out of the dust', is as close to Jonson's Sejanus as is Sir Robert Cotton's Simon de Montford.[61] At the time of Jonson's play there was a Sejanus nearer to hand. In her last years Elizabeth endured widespread accusations that she had surrendered control of her regime to favourites, and especially to one favourite, Robert Cecil, who like his father was held to have risen at the expense of the ancient nobility. The hatred of him prompted scurrilous ballads and libels which named him 'Crookback', after Richard III, whose hunched body resembled Cecil's own.[62] In 1602, when *Sejanus his Fall* was maturing in his mind, Jonson accepted a large advance for 'a book called Richard Crookback' (though no such work survives).[63]

There was another modern figure of whom any watchers or readers of *Sejanus his Fall* would have been reminded. In 1601 the career of the Earl of Essex, the Icarus of Tudor politics, ended on the scaffold. Parallels with or allusions to Essex's career were widely drawn on the stage, by George Chapman, by Samuel Daniel, by Jonson himself in *Cynthia's Revels*, and arguably by other dramatists too. The fall and punishment of Essex elicited a wealth of classical parallels from contemporaries: with Pisistratus of Athens, with Coriolanus, with Catiline, with Pompey, with Sejanus's follower Brutidius.[64] Francis Bacon, in penning the declaration with which the government justified the condemnation of

Essex, observed another parallel. An interlinear allusion to Tacitus compares the earl's creation of a military party to Sejanus's challenge to Tiberius for mastery of the Empire.[65]

Essex's critics were free with charges against him of 'ambition' and 'dissimulation', qualities notorious in Sejanus. Yet in other respects Essex's character was very different from the imperial favourite's. Sejanus thrived by hiding his feelings: Essex, as Camden writes, 'could not cover his affections'. Jonson's Sejanus is the arch courtier: Camden's Essex 'seemed not to be made for the court'.[66] Camden's account of Essex's fall, which takes on a dark Tacitean colouring, alludes not to Sejanus but to Germanicus,[67] the lost leader whom the virtuous enemies of Sejanus in Jonson's play lament. The Germanicans, rather than Sejanus, are Jonson's equivalents to Essex. They resemble the earl in their adherence to antique values of martial prowess and of noble hospitality, in their swelling ranks of retainers, in their imprudent bursts of anger at the corruption of public life, in their conviction that the proper role of the nobility has been usurped by newly risen courtiers.[68]

One episode in the supremacy of Sejanus struck the writers of Jonson's generation more than any other. This was the trial of the historian Cremutius Cordus, merely for extolling the past virtues of the republican heroes Brutus and Cassius. The response of the Tiberian regime, at once barbarous and pointless, reminded Elizabethan and Jacobean writers all too vividly of their own government's capacity for misdirected interference. Cordus's books were burned, a fate shared by works of Jonson's fellow-writers. No writer of Jonson's time, admittedly, suffered a fate as severe as that which had confronted Cordus himself: he took his own life before Sejanus could take it for him. Yet the suppression of his work stood in the minds of Jonson's contemporaries for the extinction of that 'freedom of speech' which, as Camden's preface to his *Annals* insisted, 'becomes a historian'.

Writers of Jonson's time, by developing a code of allusion, learned to refer to Cordus's experience without naming him. Thus in Hayward's life of Henry IV, Sir Roger Clarendon, speaking at the scene of his own execution, is made to say: 'There is no man able with the force and felicity of his present time either to extinguish the memory of times past, or to stop the mouth of times succeeding.' The words are borrowed from Tacitus's statement on the futility of the proceedings against Cordus.[69] Camden – who half-expected his *Annals* of Queen Elizabeth's reign to be suppressed – repeats Hayward's tactic: in writing the work, Camden's preface tells us, 'I feared none, no not those who think the memory of succeeding ages may be extinguished by present power.' Cordus's trial occupies the central scene of *Sejanus his Fall*, where the virtuous Arruntius derides Cordus's persecutors, who 'think they can, with present power, extinguish/ The memory of all succeeding times!'[70]

No writer of his age expressed more resentment than Jonson towards literary interference, towards 'the red eyes of strained authority'.[71] When *Sejanus his Fall* was performed, Jonson's 'mortal enemy' the Earl of Northampton, who knew his Tacitus, had the author brought before the Privy Council, and charged him with treasonable intent.[72] In subsequently publishing the play, Jonson did what he could to protect himself. His marginal notes to the text, which are sometimes taken to be a parade of scholarship, have instead, or as well, the purpose of self-protection. The precaution was wise. Sir John Hayward, in defending himself under questioning, had been repeatedly asked to provide documentary evidence for statements in his life of Henry IV, and had been in trouble when unable to do so.[73] Two years later Jonson's *Poetaster*, which like *Sejanus his Fall* is set in imperial Rome and which has literary interference as its principal theme, explains that

> ...'tis a dangerous age:
> Wherein, who writes, had need present his scenes
> Forty-fold proof against the conjuring means
> Of base detractors...[74]

The marginal notes to *Sejanus his Fall* are Jonson's 'forty-fold proof': he provides them in order 'to show my integrity in the story, and save myself from those common torturers, that bring all wit to the rack: whose noses are ever like swine spoiling and rooting up the muses' gardens'.[75] Selden, in *Titles of Honour*, likewise relies for 'safety' – as its preface explains – on 'testimonies of times past', which he supplies as 'warrants' against the suspicions of a 'jealous age'.

The pernicious fears and indignities created by authority's 'red eyes' are incompatible, in the minds of Jonson and his friends, with a healthy or civilised form of life. So is authority's seemingly ubiquitous deployment of spies and informers.[76] Jonson's (undated) poem 'Inviting a Friend to Supper', which intimates the character of his friendships with historians (and perhaps of his celebratory banquet with them in 1605), also points to a shadow

over the urbanity of their gatherings. At the supper, friendship
will be warmed by openness: as the wine flows

> my man
> Shall read a piece of Virgil, Tacitus,
> Livy, or of some better book to us,
> Of which we'll speak our minds, amidst our meat.

Yet there is a spectre, if not at the feast, then too close to it for
comfort. In *Sejanus his Fall*, the favourite's enemies are provoked
into fatal indiscretions at their dinner-table, where his spies have
gained an entry.[77] At the 'supper' to which Jonson invites 'a friend'
there are no spies – or, in his words, there is 'no Pooly, or Parrot
by'. Robert Pooly, or Poley, was the legendary informer of his
time, who had lured the Babington conspirators to their cruel
deaths, and who had been present at the death of Marlowe. He
and Parrot may, it seems, have been the 'two damned villains' who
fiercely interrogated Jonson during his imprisonment of 1598.[78]
In their absence from the supper-table

> Nor shall our cups make any guilty men:
>   But, at our parting, we will be as when
> We innocently met. No simple word,
>   That shall be uttered at our mirthful board,
> Shall make us sad next morning: or affright
>   The liberty that we'll enjoy tonight.[79]

How often can Jonson and his friends be sure of such 'liberty'?

III

William Camden is often called a 'conservative' figure, and Jonson
is now noted for his 'conservatism' too.[80] In some ways the description fits both men. Both of them respect processes of gradual
evolution, and dislike sudden and violent change. Camden,
though a Protestant from his youth, has no fond memory for the
'giddy time' of Protestant radicalism under Edward VI. He prefers
moderation and institutional continuity and, like Jonson, admires
Erasmus and Richard Hooker. He dislikes Puritanism, which, like
Jonson, he represents as a hypocritical religion, a mask for self-
interest. Jonson's fun at the expense of Tribulation Wholesome

and Zeal-of-the-Land-Busy is anticipated by Camden's scorn of the 'singular and precise conceit', the 'vain absurdity', of 'the new names, Free-Gift, Reformation, Earth, Dust, Ashes, Delivery, Morefruit, Tribulation...'.[81] Jonson's dislike of the 'rapine' with which the laity plundered the monasteries at the Reformation[82] likewise has its counterpart in Camden, who, though no friend to monkish sloth or credulity, saw the end of the monasteries as a blow to learning and civility. To Camden, learning and 'orderly civility'[83] are among the natural products of a healthy religion. Another is loyalty to prince and country. Jonson agrees. He believes that 'the strength of empire is in religion', and that 'nothing more commends the sovereign to the subject' than it.[84]

Yet 'conservatism' can mean many things. Some literary critics cling to the habit, which historians have outgrown, of dividing early modern Englishmen into progressives and reactionaries. The complexities of Jonson's feelings will not submit to that classi-fication. Here is a writer grateful for the peace and moderation of the Elizabethan regime – for what Camden calls its 'most mild' rule[85] – which has contained fanaticism and preserved England from the bloody tyrannies of the Continent; but a writer, too, profoundly troubled by developments in his native land which could lead, perhaps are leading, to the evils that destroyed the virtue and liberty of ancient Rome. Had Jonson been merely con-cerned to endorse or congratulate Renaissance monarchy, he could have followed the historian William Fulbeck, who in his influential work of 1601 on Roman history, *An Historicall Collection*, praised the triumph of the Emperor Augustus as a deliverance from the chaos and corruption of the late Republic. Instead Jonson chose, in his first tragedy, to portray the tyranny of Tiberius.

Jonson, it is true, is not a man to question the institutions of his time and place, whatever he thinks of their exercise. Not to 'reverence' one's 'prince' is, he believes, to 'violate nature' and to 'put off man'.[86] He longs to be accepted by power, to belong. He wants to belong on his own strict terms, terms that will enable him to reform society by reforming its 'fountain of manners', the court – an aspiration that will run through his court masques under James I. As he tells us in *Cynthia's Revels*, which calls for a purge of the court, 'a virtuous court a world to virtue draws.'[87] Yet *Cynthia's Revels* is no challenge to the Elizabethan establishment. It is a bid for royal favour, albeit a clumsy and failed one. Its satire is contained within, perhaps blunted by, respectful conventions which absolve the queen from the defects of her entourage. In his next play, *Poetaster*, transferring the scene to Rome, he could afford to be less inhibited. In *Sejanus his Fall* he was less inhibited still. Yet it remained his aim to reform and so strengthen the court, not to undermine it. It was (apparently) at court that *Sejanus his Fall* was first performed.[88]

Admittedly *Sejanus his Fall* is not addressed to the court alone. It confronts the question, which so exercised Renaissance readers of Tacitus, how men should conduct themselves under tyranny. Yet Jonson's play also has the conventional purpose that guided Renaissance dramatisations of tyranny, which was to warn princes against it.[89] Just as, in 1603, the recently released Sir John Hayward urged James I to learn political lessons from Sallust,[90] so Jonson's play encouraged the new king to reflect on the lessons of Tacitus. Justus Lipsius had likewise been anxious that his translation of Tacitus should come into 'their hands, who have the steering of the commonwealth and government'.[91] Dedicating an edition of it to the Emperor Maximilian II, Lipsius warned him against evils which Tacitus portrays, and which Jonson's play would portray: informers, unscrupulous courtiers, the ruin of innocent men.[92]

What Jonson and Camden fear is not monarchical power but its ill administration: not absolute government, which is properly strong but can be healthy, but arbitrary rule. In both writers there is, admittedly, a nostalgia for some ill-defined liberty of more primitive times. Both men, conventionally enough, want England's monarchs to rule by – in Jonson's words – 'example more than sway',[93] and through the love and consent of their subjects. But the problem of good government, to Jonson and Camden, is one not of altering the constitution but of protecting it. It is a problem of counsel and of moral corruption. One evil to be feared is the rule of favourites, a theme explored in *Sejanus his Fall*. Another is oligarchy, a theme explored in *Catiline his Conspiracy*, where Jonson examines the fate of 'a commonwealth engrossed so by a few'.[94] Camden, for his part, deplored Simon de Montford's aim to 'change the state, and of a monarchy to bring in an oligarchy', while Sir Robert Cotton warned that monarchy can come to 'groan under the weight of an aristocracy'.[95]

In a monarchy, of course, we may be unlucky enough to live under an evil ruler. If so we must leave the punishment to God. Jonson's historical friends were contemptuous of theorists of resistance, like George Buchanan, whom Camden called a 'spite-king' and Selden a 'hater of monarchy'.[96] In the late 1590s Jonson commiserated with the Earl of Desmond, whose imprisonment in the Tower he blamed on 'the jealous errors/ Of politic pretext, that wries a state'. Yet he 'importuned' Desmond to bear with his provocations and to eschew 'revolt'.[97] Even amidst the ruthless proscriptions of *Sejanus his Fall*, the virtuous Sabinus knows that 'A good man should and must/ Sit rather down with loss than rise unjust.'[98]

Yet loyalty is one thing, contentment another. Camden, on the death in 1598 of his revered patron Lord Burghley, who had commissioned him to write the *Annals*, found – Camden's preface tells us – that 'my industry began to flag and wax cold', so that the project was laid aside well into James's reign. Burghley, thought Camden, had not lived long enough for his country's good.[99] Though Camden knew that flattery and deceit are perennial evils, his dislike of courtiers was sharpened in Elizabeth's last years, when too many of them ignored the declining queen and cultivated 'the sun rising' in Scotland (just as, in *Sejanus his Fall*, Macro, Sejanus's successor as favourite to the waning Tiberius, is careful to cultivate 'the rising sun', Caligula).[100] Camden shared the belief which was widespread in the late Elizabethan era – and which was held by the queen herself and by Burghley while he lived – that political morality was in sharp decline, public concern yielding to private interest. In *Sejanus his Fall* the onset of tyranny is recognised by the favourite's enemies as a just punishment, earned by a society that has yielded up its virtue. Their sense of malaise corresponds to the ubiquitous preoccupation with public corruption in Elizabeth's declining years. Its public virtue disintegrating, the nation seemed in no condition to confront the succession crisis that apparently awaited it. Would not England succumb to the fratricidal wars, the foreign invasions, the bloody tyrannies, to which her neighbours had become prey? When Elizabeth's death appeared to be approaching, Camden and Cotton were full of 'melancholy and pensive cogitations', 'terrified' of a future without 'her, upon whose health and safety we all depend.'[101]

For Burghley's son and political successor Robert Cecil, Camden has the decent minimum of praise and much interlinear criticism. Cecil's monopoly of favour was achieved through the fall of Essex in 1601. Though Camden unequivocally condemned Essex's rebellion, he had seen him as a 'magnanimous spirit'[102] who offered hope and promise to a stale and disordered commonwealth. To Camden, who had friends in common with Essex, the earl's fall was a dreadful waste – as it was to many others, and as it must have been to Sir Henry Savile, who was imprisoned on suspicion of complicity in the rising. Camden detested the 'subtle practices' of those 'envious adversaries' who had sought to 'entangle the heedless earl in their hidden nets', and who had set 'spies' upon him. 'To this day', wrote Camden under James I, 'but few there are, which have thought' Essex's crime deserving of the 'capital' sentence that Cecil had procured.[103] Jonson's feelings about Robert Cecil are as transparent as Camden's. He did publish three epigrams in praise of him under James I – a court poet could scarcely have done less – but beneath two of them he printed a sharp rebuke to the muse that had prompted them. His muse, whose duty it is to inspire 'Things manly, and not smelling parasite', instead 'hast betrayed me to a worthless lord' and 'Made me commit most fierce idolatry'.[104] Jonson's masque for Cecil at Theobald's draws attention to the favourite's 'vain desire,/ To frame new roofs' even as it ostensibly clears him of that defect.[105]

Jonson wrote no elegy on Elizabeth's death. 'Of her he seems to have no memory', remarked Francis Chettle tartly of 'our English Horace'.[106] In late Elizabethan England, as in Tiberian Rome, Jonson observed a grotesque extravagance of servility and flattery. In both settings he sensed an oppressive atmosphere, intensified by spies and informers, of suspicion and envy and mistrust. His views on the queen's reign were made plain in 1603–4, in the pageants with which he welcomed her successor – and which can be profitably read alongside *Sejanus his Fall*. Thus in the Roman play, to be 'too rich' is to become 'prey' to 'vile spies / That first transfix us with their murdering eyes'. In Jonson's entertainment for the king's coronation, we learn that under James

> No more shall rich men (for their little good)
> Suspect to be made guilty; or vile spies
> Enjoy the lust of their so murdering eyes.[107]

Perhaps a king who could be expected to welcome such criticism of his predecessor could equally well be expected to approve of the indictment of a corrupt regime in *Sejanus his Fall*.[108] James, says Jonson, will put an end to 'flattery' and to 'base and guilty' bribery; 'liberty restored' will tread on 'servitude'; 'Now innocence shall cease to be the spoil/ Of ravenous greatness'; and 'justice' will 'look as when/ She loved the earth, and feared not to be sold'.[109] Around 1598 Donne's fifth satire had complained that 'justice', or rather 'injustice', 'is sold', and lamented the queen's ignorance of the abuse. Jonson's *Cynthia's Revels*, as Howard Erskine-Hill observes, 'unmistakably echoes' Donne's previous satire, the fourth, that dark and trenchant indictment of the morality of late Elizabethan politics.[110]

Where the evils of Jonson's time corresponds to those portrayed in Tacitus, *Sejanus his Fall* follows Tacitus. Where they do not, Jonson adjusts Tacitus or adds to him. To Jonson's mind the late Elizabethan court was corrupted by pride and flattery, mesmerised by false values of outward display and extravagance. If Rome, or the evidence for Rome, provides no equivalent court, Jonson supplies one. He takes pains to inform us that *Poetaster*, his play about Augustus, is set in a court.[111] It is a court that looks more Tudor than Roman. Jonson expands Tacitus, even departs from him, in making *Sejanus his Fall* a play about the corruption and servility of courts, a theme announced in its opening speeches. To Jonson, Tiberius's court, like Elizabeth's court, is a sink of venality and bribery. The hunger for office and its ready sale, abuses so prominent in the complaints of Jonson's time, likewise achieve a larger prominence in Jonson's account of the Tiberian regime than in Tacitus's. The first time we meet Jonson's Sejanus he is arranging the sale of an office. The marketing of offices is a principal instrument of his tyranny, for in the recipients it destroys the independence on which the guarding of liberty depends. Venality has reduced the senate, which should be the principal guard of liberty, to craven submission. Towards the end of the play, when Sejanus's authority momentarily seems to have been restored, the senators sense his 'power/ More to reward than ever', and rush to vote for him as 'the way to have us hold our places' and to 'get more office and more titles'. Now only 'the bare empty shade' of senatorial 'liberty' survives. The senators are 'only called to keep the marble warm'. The party of virtue is an eloquent but impotent minority. 'Most' of the senators 'strive/ Who shall propound most abject things and base', and 'almost all' of them are Sejanus's 'creatures'.[112]

Was something similar happening to England's senate, its parliament? We should not expect parallels, here or anywhere in the play, to be exact or fair, for even in the gravity of tragedy Jonson remains a master of caricature. Yet parallels there may be. In *Discoveries* he complains that 'suffrages in parliament are numbered, not weighed'.[113] Does he see, in England as in Rome, a party of virtue being outnumbered? According to Sir John Neale,

the parliament of 1597 contained more placemen, and was subjected to more effective political management, than any before it.
Critics of the regime, spokesmen for what they called 'the liberty
of free speech', were in retreat. The crown made it plain that it
had had enough of 'vain and long orations',[114] just as in *Sejanus his
Fall* the doomed eloquence of Arruntius is swept aside. The crown
had had enough of Peter Wentworth, that veteran spokesman for
freedom of speech. Before the parliament of 1593 Wentworth and
his friends were imprisoned for holding a meeting to discuss
tactics. In the same parliament Roger Morice, in a bid for support
which achieved nothing except his own imprisonment, declared
that the nation's freedom from 'servitude and bondage', from 'will
and tyranny', had been 'dearly purchased... by our ancestors, yea,
even with the effusion of their blood.... And shall we, as a degenerate offspring, by negligence and security suffer the loss of a
precious patrimony?'[115] Was Morice consciously alluding to a similar passage at the opening of Tacitus's *Agricola*, of which Savile's
translation had appeared two years earlier? Hayward's life of
Henry IV, adapting Savile's translation, would place that passage in
the mouth of the Archbishop of Canterbury: 'Our ancestors lived
in the highest pitch and perfection of liberty, but we, of servility,
[are] in the nature not of subjects but of abjects and flat slaves.'[116]

In Elizabeth's last years, as Kevin Sharpe has shown, William
Camden and his associates in the Society of Antiquaries were
becoming 'increasingly interested in political questions'. Soon the
Society would be discussing 'the origin and nature of parliaments'.[117] Among the politicians in its membership was James
Whitelocke, who would be imprisoned for challenging the prerogative in 1613 and would be required in the following year to
destroy his rich collection of notes on medieval history. Selden, in
turn, would be twice imprisoned for his parliamentary activities
of the 1620s. The Society of Antiquaries would be abandoned
because of royal 'mislike' in 1614, and Sir Robert Cotton's library,
which had played so important a part in it, would be closed on
royal orders in 1629.[118]

IV

In *Sejanus his Fall*, tyranny prevails because the ruling class has
allowed itself to be corrupted. The English ruling class, thinks
Jonson, has likewise betrayed its responsibilities. He is dismayed

by the decay of antique and austere noble values. So is Camden. Both men are repelled by the vulgar ostentation to which honest simplicity has yielded. In his account of the Roman nobles in *Catiline his Conspiracy*, Jonson departs from his Latin source to glance at their modern counterparts: 'Their ancient habitations they neglect,/ And put up new.'[119] In England, Penshurst, 'that ancient pile', 'whose liberal board doth flow,/ With all, That hospitality doth know', defies the current of Jonson's age, but the future belongs to the 'prodigy-houses' of the new, upstart nobility, which lacks roots in the communities which bear it. Camden is no less troubled by what he calls 'the decay of the glory of hospitality' (which dismays Selden too).[120] Jonson associates its decline with the erection of houses 'built to envious show':[121] Camden connects it with the building of houses for 'beautiful show'.[122] Jonson and Camden alike condemn the excesses of fashionable apparel and the 'foolish pride'[123] of its wearers. Both writers, of course, are sophisticated enough to know what both of them, quoting Velleius Paterculus, point out: that all societies are susceptible to nostalgia, are prone to 'envy the present, and reverence the past'.[124] But they believe too (with many of their contemporaries) that surfeits of conspicuous consumption are, as Seneca had it, 'notes of a sick state'.[125]

The men most earnestly praised by Jonson are carefully chosen. He favours political failures or half-failures, whose antique virtue the court cannot accommodate: the Earl of Pembroke, Sir Robert Wroth, Sir Robert Sidney, Sir Henry Neville, and the Earl of Arundel (who is Camden's and Cotton's model too).[126] Jonson portrays such men in the same way that his tragedies depict the representatives of virtue in Rome: as the 'few', 'almost all the few/ Left', who preserve their integrity amidst the inducements of faction and corruption and venality.[127] Their virtues are set in contrast with prevailing vices. Thus Penshurst is '*not* built to envious show'; Arundel, showing 'true gentry', knows '*Not* to prize blood/ So much by the greatness as the good'; Wroth abstains from a series of courtly and metropolitan sins; Sir Henry Neville is '*not* one that wrestleth with dignities, or feignest a scope/ Of service to the public when the true end/ Is private gain.' (The italic is mine.) Neville, who had been imprisoned and heavily fined after the Essex rising, was thought by Camden to be 'a most noble knight'.[128] Like Jonson, he bemoaned the indifference of the Jacobean court to 'merit' among its would-be servants. As a member of parliament in 1606, remarking on the court's watch on

MPs and admitting to the congenital imprudence with which he responds to it, he says in prose what Arruntius, the most defiant (but also the most impotent) of Sejanus's enemies in Jonson's play, repeatedly says in verse. 'Not only speeches and actions,' complains Neville, 'but countenances and conversations with men misliked, have been observed. But... I cannot betray my own mind, speed as it will.'[129]

In representing the nobility of both ancient Rome and modern England, Jonson simplifies, ethically and politically. Tacitus has blackened Sejanus, but it is Jonson who whitens Sejanus's enemies. The party of virtue in Tiberian Rome is his invention.[130] The whiteness, it is true, is not unspotted. Weaknesses can be located among the favourite's opponents. Failings among the English nobles praised by Jonson can sometimes be discerned too, positioned where the conventions of the poetry of praise allow them to be placed: between the lines. Even so, Jonson creates in both Rome and England an unreal distance between court and country. One would not guess from his poems that his favoured nobles belong to parties or factions within the court, or that they are themselves office-holders or would-be office-holders, eager, even desperate, for further reward. The extremes portrayed by Jonson are in conflict not between individuals, but within them.

There are conflicting extremes within Jonson himself. The noblemen he admires, as he tells Pembroke, are those who 'though besieged with ill/ Of what ambition, faction, pride can raise', preserve their integrity 'in this strife/ Of vice, and virtue; wherein' – Jonson echoes Tacitus – 'all great life/ Almost is exercised' (that is, eliminated).[131] How should a writer conduct himself in an age 'wherein all great life/ Almost is exercised'? One model for Jonson is the genial Camden, whose philosophy, like that which he discerned in his patron Lord Burghley, is to 'yield unto the time':[132] to eschew gestures of protest, to acknowledge the limits of our capacity to affect events, to do what we can within them. But Jonson, 'passionately kind and angry',[133] is an altogether less equable man. Camden has lived through the formation of the Elizabethan regime, has known the precariousness of its survival, and has learned to count his country's blessings. Jonson counts them too, but has a sharper sense of their cost, especially while Elizabeth is alive and while the court will not acknowledge or employ his talents.

In 'yielding unto the time', Camden drew on the philosophy which won so many converts in the late Renaissance: the philosophy of Stoicism. It owed much of its impact to Justus Lipsius, the editor not only of Tacitus but of the Stoic Seneca, who is a powerful presence in Jonson's Roman plays. Amid the destruction and despair of Europe's wars of religion, Stoicism offered a system at once of consolation and of accommodation. The Stoic adheres, amidst external afflictions, to internal virtue and internal constancy. Virtue, explained Lipsius, 'is a sanctuary, since that she only is quiet, safe and assured, and under her own command, and all other things besides subject unto fortune'.[134] External circumstances of prosperity and affliction, war and peace, health and sickness, hope and fear, fall within the province of fortune rather than of virtue, and are therefore inherently neither good nor evil.[135] The relationship of fortune to virtue is repeatedly explored in *Sejanus his Fall*, as it is in Jonson's poems.

As the party of virtue in *Sejanus his Fall* shrinks, its two principal survivors, through friends, come to stand for alternative responses to the darkness of their age. One is the Stoical Lepidus, the aged survivor, who has 'the plain and passive fortitude/ To suffer and be silent'. Knowing 'never' to 'stretch' his 'arms against the torrent',[136] he contrives, as Camden does, to adapt to the system of power without surrendering his integrity to it. Though the political gain he secures for virtue in the play is a small one,[137] it is at least tangible. By contrast Arruntius, the other principal survivor, the choric figure whose anger is so eloquent, 'only talks'.

Arruntius knows his own failings. He admires the historian Cremutius Cordus because, like a good Stoic and unlike Arruntius, he 'is not moved with passion'.[138] Jonson is 'moved with passion', and one side of him repudiates it. Yet there is another side, the side that knows passion to be integral to his humanity. Jonson's dilemma finds reflection in the play *Poetaster*, where the Stoic philosophy is tested and found wanting. To hold out against grief, it there transpires, is to default on our debt to feeling. The character who asserts the point, the grieving Sextus Propertius, is praised as a 'Worthy Roman!', just as, in *Sejanus his Fall*, Arruntius commends Silius as an 'Excellent Roman!' for his bluntness, for the passionate fidelity of his tongue to his heart.[139] The conflict of philosophy between Lepidus and Arruntius is not resolved. It is a conflict, I suggest, within the mind of a writer who asks himself, in the desolate conclusion to the reign of Queen Elizabeth, how the political world around him can be endured.

4. Ben Jonson and the Limits of Courtly Panegyric

MARTIN BUTLER

I

One of the consequences of the revisionism which has swept through work by historians on the early Stuart court and its networks of patronage has been a transformation of attitudes towards the literature of compliment which circulated around Whitehall. At one time, the language and preoccupations of panegyric were a source of considerable discomfort to commentators. To literary scholars, the poetic idealisations which were lavished on king and courtiers seemed vastly out of proportion to the character of Whitehall as it was presumed to have been, and the inflated praises of panegyric appeared little better than poetic time-serving. Beneath this discomfort lay the intertwined assumptions that the patronage networks were riddled with venality, and that the court was already in decline, locked in a futile struggle with parliament that could only culminate in civil war. But now that this Whiggish teleology of progressive political collapse has been retired, and now that the patronage system is less damagingly understood as the system of reward and favour which a monarchy without a fully salaried bureaucracy needed in order to get its business done, we are much better placed to evaluate on their own terms the complex political transactions which poetic panegyric might have involved.

Once simplistically regarded as mere flattery or frivolity, masques and poems can now been seen as having had substantial functions to perform. Panegyrical poems represented patronage relations as mutually beneficial exchanges. Their language was orderly and ceremonious, and they depicted patron and client as interacting in a dignified climate of honour and largesse. Similarly,

91

the masques which were staged at the great Twelfth Night and Shrovetide festivals promulgated the values and agendas of Stuart kingship, and evoked admiration for a dynasty dedicated to peace, stability and prosperity. They represented the nation as happily unified under wise, rational and benign monarchs, and they validated Stuart rule by projecting stupendous images of all-competent sovereignty. The culture of masque and panegyrical poem had the real material functions of binding the court together in relationships of dependence and obligation, of representing the monarch to the political nation at large, and of stimulating confidence in the values with which he sought to have his government associated.[1]

So in our present perspective, the literature of compliment no longer seems to be shoring up a discredited monarchy but dignifying and facilitating the everyday business of Whitehall. Furthermore, it was widely assumed in early Stuart England that, as well as celebrating the prestige of the court, panegyric had the function of acting as a channel of counsel, a medium through which advice, exhortation and even criticism might tactfully be articulated. As Ben Jonson wrote in his preface to *Hymenaei*, it was thought that masques should be not only outwardly magnificent but inwardly weighty, and that their local celebrations should be heightened with some kind of ethical or political teaching: 'though their *voyce* be taught to sound to present occasions, their *sense*, or doth, or should always lay hold on more remou'd mysteries'.[2] Jonson's remark alludes to the old humanistic justifications for panegyric, that the role of the panegyrical poet was critical as well as complimental, and that his praises were legitimate because they could be made to seem educative. In praising king or patron, the poet was representing him not as he was but as it was hoped he would be, and the panegyric modelled an idea of responsible and virtuous behaviour against which its recipient was invited to measure himself. This way a distinction could be maintained between educative praise and improper flattery: compliment was permissable so long as it alluded to codes of duty or obligation of which the king or patron was invited to take notice.[3] Moreover a judicious poet might use his compliments, or the analogies and oblique allusions in which they traded, to smuggle in advice which might not be admissable in any less privileged context. By this means commentary on state affairs might be insinuated, and the panegyric used as a strategy whereby a critique of its recipient could be insinuated diplomatically. Fulsome praises were allowable if they were seen to be the only way by which the poet could address issues that were otherwise beyond his scope.

It clearly is the case that the old 'court holy-water' view of panegyric will no longer do, and that the opportunities which poems and masques offered for influencing politics and ideology at the centre have been discounted for too long. Indeed, in a recent study Kevin Sharpe has argued that this is precisely how the masque poets of Caroline Whitehall used their flattering fables, as a means of talking back to the king about the political ideals which they hoped his government could be persuaded to observe.[4] And yet if we wish to recover the more complex politics which the literature of compliment may have been enabling, it is needful to establish the limits to those persuasions as well as their possibilities. For all that panegyric offered strategies for advising king and courtiers, or for indirect commentary on matters of moment, it is by no means self-evident how effective such interventions were, or how easy it was for poets to reconcile such criticism with the equally significant functions of their panegyric as compliment. On the contrary, the environment in which panegyric was conducted was one in which the risks, frustrations and obstacles to the successful accomplishment of this educative ideal were likely to be many and substantial.

For example, in panegyrical poems the freedom of the poet's remarks would inevitably have been affected by considerations of tact, and his assertion of a strictly ethical viewpoint would have to be accommodated to the competition for power and place that was endemic to the life of Whitehall. Panegyric was subject to decorums of person and place, and exposed to the risks of misinterpretation and the dangers of overstepping the boundaries of the possible. A poet's exchange with his patron would always have been a negotiation conducted in code. As for the masques, the potential risks were even more considerable. As state events at which the glory of monarchy was proclaimed, masques were obliged to provide images and fables that broadly underwrote the priorities of Stuart power, and had to make the king admired before they could venture into the territory of advice. At the same time, the poet's ideas for the event would have been competing with the self-serving agendas of the other participants in the occasion, not least the courtiers who were dancing in it and the paymasters who footed the bill. If for the king masques were celebrations of his authority, for the dancers they were occasions on which to bathe in the reflected royal glory, to affirm their own sense of status at Whitehall, and to advance their claims to royal notice in particular. Inevitably, the poet's agenda would have to jostle for attention with the other social and political functions that the occasion served. Further, however much masques may have aspired to present an educational message, it is still hard to know how readily in practice that message could be disentangled from the tropes of praise. If a critique of the king had to be insinuated obliquely, the danger was that it might be defused by its very obliquity, or that the poet's contribution might be undermined if it were couched in language that was too servile. (Alternatively, by being too daring a poet risked provoking the opposite reaction, of outraged rejection.) Given these circumstances, the problem with the masques was that for all their educational or critical aspirations, they still might end up sounding rather like flattery.

Obviously these pressures would have varied from poem to poem and from masque to masque, and the poet could attempt to anticipate them in a variety of ways. But my point is that in all such productions there would always have been an interplay between text and event, and that their interpretation has always to take account of their inscription within the contingencies of court life. Plainly, a poet might turn the contingency of an event to his advantage and negotiate it successfully. Equally it might be possible for the contingency of things to obstruct the idealisations of panegyric, and present the poet with circumstances which he could not readily order or transform.

II

In the early Stuart period, it was perhaps Ben Jonson whose career was the outstanding instance of the successful interplay between cultural and political patronage.[5] By judicious deployment of his talent for poetic compliment, Jonson fashioned himself into the premier court poet of his day, and enjoyed a long and intimate relationship with Whitehall. He early on showed himself to be easily the most resourceful inventor of court entertainments, and masques from his pen dominated Whitehall's Christmas ceremonial under James. His adeptness with the strategies of panegyric brought him close ties with many of the most powerful figures at court, and clientage earned him substantial rewards. A former soldier, bricklayer and common player, he had by 1616 become poet laureate in all but name and was sufficiently secure financially to retire from writing for the professional stages. By 1621 he had gained the reversion of the office of Master of the Revels and was rumoured narrowly to have missed being knighted. His rivals in the cultural market proved far less adept than he at navigating the tidewaters of aristocratic favour. Samuel Daniel was bested by Jonson in the race for masque commissions at the outset of the period (and thereafter his career never really recovered), while George Chapman had the misfortune of attaching himself to two patrons, Prince Henry and the Earl of Somerset, who seemed to promise glittering prizes but who were fated to disappoint their dependents. Of all the Stuart panegyrical poets Jonson seems to have been virtually unequalled in his mastery of the arts of self-promotion, and he certainly achieved the most visible success in translating his talents into the rewards of cash and status.

It is important to stress that this traffic in favour was not merely one-way. While Jonson benefited from the prestige and rewards which association with Whitehall brought him, the court acquired an able servant skilled in devising the ostentatious pageantry that it needed, and one who excelled in his ability to combine praise of king and courtiers with ethical advice. Jonson particularly prided himself on his determination to sustain a pose of disinterestedness even within the arena of power itself. The poet who told his friend William Drummond that he wished he could be a churchman 'and so he might have favour to make one sermon before the King he careth not what thereafter should befall him, for he would not flatter though he saw death'[6] could hardly be accused of approaching the court in any spirit of obsequiousness. Jonson's career thus exemplifies the ability of cultural patronage to keep the crown in contact with a pool of talent that was diverse and plural, sustaining the ideological openness of the court by enabling it to accommodate the voices of men who did not always see eye to eye with the king. And yet for all that Jonson's progress at court was seemingly effortless and serene, and his masques a dazzling series of brilliant festivals, the partially visible underside of this career consists of traces of failure, frustration and upset which, even in his case, cast doubt on his power to turn panegyric to effective political use. Jonson may have been the most successful exponent of panegyric, but even his performances involved a complex and problematic negotiation with the material contingencies of power.

Consider, for example, Jonson's private discomfort about his inability to predict absolutely that what he says about his patrons in his poems will fit the person on whom the praise is bestowed. This is an issue that he confronted in his 65th epigram and in his 'Epistle to Master John Selden', both of which express regret about having written panegyrics to patrons who turned out to be disappointments. Though Jonson raises the issue as affecting only some poems, his perception is that, however well-intentioned a poet's eulogy of any patron, the fit between description and subject can never be guaranteed. The danger of eulogy is that praise can too easily be betrayed into flattery, or that compliments can be overtaken by subsequent events. Not all patrons would turn out to be as generous as the poet had anticipated, and it was far from unknown for the loss of favour to turn a courtier from an object of admiration into a focus for contempt. Jonson's response to the accusation of flattery is to say that he describes his patrons not as they are but as he hopes they will be:[7]

> ... I confess (as every Muse hath err'd,
> And mine not least) I have too oft preferr'd
> Men past their termes, and prais'd some names too much,
> But 'twas with purpose to have made them such.

Though this admits the problem it is difficult to feel that it actually solves it. Jonson's response creates a space for the poet's mental reservations and implies that eulogy turns into satire if the patron turns out to be unworthy of his praise. However, it skirts around the fact that the mistaken praise would already be in circulation, and that it would discredit not only the patron but the judgement of the poet as well. Jonson professes to feel untouched by the revelation that his poems sometimes praised men more than they deserved, but he was demonstrably disinclined to allow his own writings to testify against him in this way, since when he compiled the collected edition of his works he excluded at least two panegyrics lauding men who had fallen from favour since the poems were written, the Earl of Somerset and Sir Edward Coke.[8] By 1616 the discomfort generated by these pieces could not be alleviated even by the presumption that misplaced eulogy was a rebuke to undeserving patrons. Calculations such as these must have been all too common in the work of every courtly panegyrist.

So the tides of favour could unsettle the practice of panegyric even for someone as adept with the form as Jonson. And on his masques Jonson had a private perspective that was no less disenchanted. In the first decade of James's reign Jonson was building

his career as poet of courtly festival, but he was capable of per-
ceiving the idealisations of the masques in a more sceptical light,
as for example in his epistle 'To Sir Robert Wroth' (*c.*1606–12?)
which applauds his friend for not joining the throng at court

> (When masquing is) to haue a sight
> Of the short brauerie of the night;
> To view the iewells, stuffes, the paines, the wit
> There wasted, some not paid for yet ... (ll.9–12)

Subsequently, when towards the end of his career his working
relationship with the masque architect (Inigo Jones) broke down,
Jonson wrote not only scathingly about Jones the man but con-
temptuously of the masque spectacle itself as 'Showes! Showes!
Mighty Showes', the 'mere perspective of an Inch board'.[9] When
in his 'Epistle Answering to One that Asked to be Sealed of the
Tribe of Ben' (1623) he wanted a metaphor contrasting false
friendships with trusty ones, he used language that dwelt on the
gap between the masques' scenic illusions and the realities which
they purport (but fail) to represent:

> Not built with canvasse, paper, and false lights,
> As are the Glorious Scenes, at the great sights;
> And that there be no fev'ry heats, nor colds,
> Oylie Expansions, or shrunke durtie folds ...
> (ll.65–8)

Jonson's scorn for masque spectacle may have been motivated by
a fear of being excluded by Jones from future commissions, but
his own masques were not exempt from his censures, since in
deriding Jones here as the artificer who 'guides the Motions, and
directs the beares' (l.50) he was referring to the lumbering
animals that had danced in his own *Masque of Augurs* (1622).
Whatever his political investments in court festival, Jonson was not
devoid of a subversive sense of the crudity of their mechanics and
the wastefulness of their ostentation. And for the sake of sustaining the idealisations of the event, these were sentiments which,
on the whole, he would have to keep in check.

Throughout Jonson's career evasions of various kinds flicker
intermittently on the edges of his masques. His earliest major
masques, *Blackness* (1605) and *Beauty* (1608), *Hymenaei* (1606) and
The Haddington Masque (1608), focused on the issue of Union and

the political concord which James had brought to his two realms. On these occasions the magical name Britannia effected miraculous transformations, and courtiers from once opposing factions danced in a harmony expressive of James's peaceable rule. But for the sake of these political and aesthetic resolutions Jonson had had largely to de-emphasise the resistance which James's constitutional ambitions aroused in his English subjects, and to efface the mistrust between English and Scots which continued to prevail amongst courtiers. The disagreements which were effortlessly overcome in these fables were seen to be less amenable to persuasion outside the masques themselves. Indeed, Jonson was so sensitive to the gap between ideal and actuality in the case of *Hymenaei* (which had been written for the marriage of Frances Howard and the Earl of Essex) that when he included the text in his collected volume of 1616 he carefully suppressed all mention of the occasion from the text. His next body of commissions came from Prince Henry, for whom he wrote *Prince Henry's Barriers* (1610) and *Oberon* (1611). While these are amongst Jonson's most brilliant achievements, they are also two of his most uneasy masques. With his ideological preferences for stability, deference and discipline, Jonson's attitudes were not attuned to the more 'forward' policies associated with the young prince, and although his masques celebrate Henry they also hedge his militaristic iconography around awkwardly with advice about restraint, responsibility, and obedience to his father.[10] Not surprisingly, Jonson was not one of the masque poets to be found in 1613 enthusiastically hymning the alliance between Princess Elizabeth and the Elector Palatine.

Over the next ten years, Jonson's masques became an arena in which aristocratic competitors sought to promote their ambitions for inclusion in the royal affections. The fluid and unfocused politics of faction that occupied the middle decade of James's reign increasingly turned the masques into a showcase for the performances of aspiring favourites. For example, John Chamberlain reported in 1614 that the 'principal motiue' behind expenditure on *Mercury Vindicated* was thought to be 'the gracing of younge Villers and to bring him on the stage'.[11] These masques veer wildly between scurrilous demystification of the life of the court and transcendental eulogy of kingship, and at times it is hard to tell whether Jonson was celebrating the Stuarts or simply playing along with the political game (most notoriously in *The Gipsies Metamorphosed* (1621), in which his description of Buckingham as a gallant gipsy has led several critics to speculate that this eulogy must really have been a satire).[12] Finally, in James's last years, as the momentous events on the continent impacted onto domestic politics, Jonson's masques became increasingly defensive, insistently reiterating the mystique of sovereignty, and representing the monarch as having to crush challenges to his authority. They also became increasingly accident-prone. *Pan's Anniversary* (1621), with its ridicule of a puritanical prophet, provoked criticism that it was 'somewhat unseemly and unseasonable' to make jokes about matters of faith, given recent events in France and Germany,[13] and when Jonson included satire of George Wither and other dismal johnnies in *Time Vindicated* (1623) the king himself was angered that he should even have alluded to so tender a subject.[14] Finally, when Jonson wrote *Neptune's Triumph* (1624) for Charles and Buckingham after their return from Madrid, James intervened personally, first to cut out anti-Spanish passages which he found offensive, then to forbid the performance of the masque altogether. *Neptune's Triumph* is a masque which establishes that there *were* practical limits to the advice which could be smuggled into panegyric in this period. Whatever James might tolerate under the fictions of compliment, he was not going to allow a masque which urged him to send ships against Spain.[15]

Neptune's Triumph, it might be argued, was an exception. It was written at the moment of gravest crisis in policy-making of James's reign, and it foundered on a split in outlook between king and prince which nobody could have contained inside the masque form, with all its usual consensual emphases. But while the problems of *Neptune's Triumph* differed in degree from those which afflicted other masques, they were not essentially different in kind. In all of the masques Jonson's task was to find a way of negotiating between the parties involved in the event, accommodating their divergent perspectives on the occasion, and weaving a framework of praise around these potentially conflicting expectations. *Neptune's Triumph* was the only masque actually to be rendered unperformable by political circumstance, but given these conditions it would be far from surprising if all the masques, in one way or another, had not registered this recurrent dialectic between text and event, myth and contingency. What follow are more detailed analyses of three masques from the middle period of James's reign, in each of which Jonson's apparently integrated panegyric proves upon inspection to have been compromised and fractured. As a series they help to show that the politics of masquing must have been a matter not only of the poet's success-ful persuasions, but of the other, competing and contradictory transactions for which he was simultaneously having to find space.

III

The argument of *Love Restored* (performed at court on Twelfth Night 1612) can be summed up in a phrase: you don't need money to make a masque. This event opened with a single reveller apologising that the show was unable to start. The reason for delay became apparent when Cupid entered behind him, for instead of performing as Cupid should, the god railed against masquing, censuring its vanity, idleness, prodigality and unprofitableness. This startling conversation was then interrupted by the country spirit Robin Goodfellow who had his own lengthy complaints, that try as he might he could hardly get in to see the masque. Once arrived, though, Robin discovered the supposed Cupid as not the god of Love at all but Plutus, god of Money (often represented like Cupid, as a curly-headed boy), who had stolen Love's arrows and exiled him to the cold country. This enabled the real celebration to begin: Plutus was dismissed and the true Cupid restored by the warmth of royal favour. The ensuing dances, in which male masquers revel with court beauties, should have symbolically enacted the triumph of Love under King James. However, as we shall see, the masque did not in fact achieve quite so confident a culmination.

In mounting a revel about revelry that because of money problems was apparently failing to take place, Jonson was wittily responding to the court's financial difficulties of the previous twelve months. Not only had the parliament of 1610–11 failed to agree the fiscal package which Salisbury had put together as the 'Great Contract', it had voiced complaints about courtiers who 'waste the treasure of the State [and] take no pains to live of their own, but spend all in excess and riot, depending wholly upon the bounty of the Prince'.[16] The ensuing year had turned into an undignified scramble after hard cash, one element in which was cutbacks on revels such as Christmas masques. After the ruinously expensive spectacles that *Prince Henry's Barriers*, *Tethys' Festival* and *Oberon* had been, *Love Restored* was an ostentatiously economical masque that was danced by minor courtiers rather than great aristocrats[17] and which, using little or no scenery, cost a fraction of its predecessors.

Jonson's moral is that however much the revelry seems to be called into question by the lack of glorious display, the celebrations are all the truer for being frugal: they become revels done by Love rather than Money. On the one hand, Plutus's claim that without money masques fall short of their purpose is seen to be offensive: "Tis like to find most necessarie and fortunate euent, whatsoeuer is enterpris'd without my aides. Alas! how bitterly the spirit of Pouertie spouts it selfe against my weale, and felicitie' (ll.201–4). By proceeding to its revelry without the usual scenic splendours, the masque confutes Plutus; the majesty of the king alone can transform a bare court into a celebration. On the other hand, Robin's picturesque narrative about how he could not get into the court when disguised as a masque technician – a carpenter, an engineer, a musician, a feather-maker, a wireman, a chandler and so forth – scores an effective point against expensive celebrations: no amount of cost is valid if it excludes the very spirit of good-fellowship. And there is a lesson for a court discovered to be confused about which is Money and which is Love: Love has been frozen out because of the pursuit of cash which preoccupies everyone, within Whitehall and without. So although the king's revels are frugal, it is not because he is money-minded, but because his sovereign power arises above mere blandishments of cost, and nurtures inner fires of devotion:

> *Cupid*: Impostor Mammon, come, resigne
> This bow and quiuer; they are mine.
> Thou hast too long vsurp'd my rites,
> I now am Lord of mine owne nights.
> (ll.227–30)

The king's authority resides not in outward shows (that can be usurped by such as Plutus) but in the spirit manifested in the dancing of the masquers.

Love Restored is thus a striking example of Jonson's skill with matters contingent. Rather than the poverty of the occasion undercutting the court's magnificence, Jonson turns it to advantage by making a virtue out of necessity. However, though he capitalises on the central paradox of the event, in other respects his hold on contingencies seems less secure. For example, despite the argument's wit, there is a definite air of special pleading to it. Jonson may assert that Cupid flourishes in the absence of Money, but this flies in the face of the increasingly anxious manoeuvres in the treasury at this time. The crown had had a major loan from the city in 1610 and could raise no further credit from that quarter. In May 1611 honour was for the first time put up for auction with the creation of the order of baronets, a title invented solely in order to raise cash; in December this was already causing complaints from the barons over precedence.[18] Meanwhile, the ongoing negotia- tions for the bride for Prince Henry were becoming increasingly money-dominated. Throughout 1611 Florence and Savoy were competing intensely for the alliance, and while policy was officially the criterion by which the choice would be made, in practice it was evident that the state which offered the best dowry would be greatly advantaged.[19] And when the masque was performed, the crown was being kept temporarily afloat by a forced loan, the privy seals for which went out just before Christmas.

In offering his objections to Plutus's power, Robin alludes distinctly to some of these things:

> 'Tis that Impostor PLVTVS, the god of *money*, who ha's stolen LOVE'S ensignes; and in his belyed figure, raignes [i'] the world, making friendships, contracts, mariages, and almost religion; begetting breeding and holding the neerest respects of mankind; and usurping all those offices in this Age of gold, which LOVE himselfe perform'd in the golden age. 'Tis he, that pretends to tie kingdomes, maintaine commerce, dispose of honors, make all places and dignitarie arbitrarie from him
>
> (ll.172–82)

Though this passage is a generalised account of money's authority in the world at large, it makes specific reference to James's financial shifts. In complaining that money has too much say in disposing dignities, Robin was criticising the damage done to status by the sale of baronetcies, while the negotiations around Prince Henry are clearly glanced at in the observations that money makes marriages and ties kingdoms. Though James's power will exile Plutus and restore Cupid, Robin's remarks strongly imply that his rule is not a golden age, but is too possessed by monetary considerations. As for Cupid, his attitude is clearly coloured by the recent forced loan:

> The Maiestie, that here doth moue,
> Shall triumph, more secur'd by loue,
> Then all [Plutus's] earth; and neuer craue
> His aides, but force him as a slaue.
>
> (ll.247–50)

There is, to say the least, a significant slippage between the masque's avowal that Plutus is not wanted and Cupid's boast that James can force him if he needs to. The masque seems in two minds about Plutus: is he being simply dismissed, or knocked down in order to be more serviceable in future?

These tensions were entailed by the strategy that Jonson had adopted, and in the text they remain implicit rather than overt. In performance, on the other hand, the masque must have been more in the character of a negotiation between different court interests since (as far as we can tell from the scanty documentation)[20] it was staged not merely for the king but presented to him by the prince, as a joint production by gentlemen from the two royal households. At this time Prince Henry was actively building up his following at court. In December he was said to be adding to his servants every day, courting the king's gentlemen and favourites and looking so graciously on all that 'everyone is his most devoted servant and he can manage the king's most intimate and make them speak to the king just as he thinks best'.[21] Sponsorship of a masque was one obvious way of enhancing one's stature, and Robin's complaints about the financial constraints on Jacobean diplomacy very much echo what is known about Henry's anxieties towards his own wedding. Later that spring it was reported that he 'cares little for dowries' and 'had said that he did not desire either to be bought or sold'; he was also afraid that the money 'would not come into his hands nor be applied for the good of the Crown' but would be 'scattered by the king's profusion'.[22] If on one level the masque was reassuring the king that he could rule as effectively through love as through money, from the perspective of its sponsor the message was markedly more urgent.

How these differences may have impacted onto the masque in performance is suggested in the surviving eye-witness account, which indicates that at its climax it was disrupted in a unique and unprecedented way. Jonson planned the masque's 'revels' (the moment at which masquers and audience join in communal dancing) as his culminating manoeuvre, making them symbolic of the potency of Love at James's Whitehall. Whereas money 'quencheth all desire', the court's beauties 'reuiue / LOVES youth, and keep his heat aliue' (ll.212–5), their dancing in unity exemplifying the court's harmony and clinching the evening visually and thematically. But in the event, the ladies turned their backs on the masquers, forcing the men to dance unhandsomely with one another, and effectively subverting the masque at its climax. Why this happened we cannot be sure, but since the ladies who gave the lead were the Countesses of Essex and Cranbourne – and so the wives of two of Henry's closest associates – it is tempting to suppose that their refusal was related to the prince's part in the occasion. Jonson's text contains no hint of anything untoward, but Chamberlain's account makes it clear that the masquers and some spectators were seriously embarrassed. Whether it discredited Jonson's fable as well it is impossible to say, but given that this was the symbolic culmination of his argument, it is difficult to feel that it could have been unaffected by it. Certainly it would have blown a hole in the masque's pleasant fictions about the triumph of Love and Whitehall's '*harmonie*', '*honor*' and '*courtesie*' (ll.263–4). For all his ingenuity, Jonson's solution to the problem of praising a penurious king ran into the sand on the one area over which he had no control: the willingness of spectators and participants to conform to the roles of loving and obedient subjects which the masque had designed for them.

IV

With *The Golden Age Restored*, danced at Whitehall in January 1616, we have what is possibly the period's archetypal masque. In this grand and stupendous event, light-years away from the economy of *Love Restored*, the return of the Golden Age is announced by Pallas, goddess of Wisdom. Iron Age and his twelve attendant Evils attempt to prevent this epiphany, but their military dancing is confuted when Pallas reveals her shield. In their place Astraea (goddess of Justice), the Golden Age and the four English poets laureate descend and usher in the masquers in the roles of sleeping heroes dedicated to justice. With its magnificent images of heavenly wisdom banishing ill and creating courtly utopia, this masque testifies to the authority of Stuart monarchy; its values of peace, stability, prosperity and cultivation of the arts provide an idealised but still recognisable version of James's kingship. But since the masque's correct date was not established until recently,[23] it is only now apparent how immediately topical its fable was. It was in the autumn of 1615 that the scandal of the Overbury murder came out. The news broke in September, in October the favourite was placed under arrest, and in November the executions of his wife's agents in the poisoning began. The Somersets themselves would not be put on trial until May, but throughout Christmas the

court was in turmoil as a succession of notable figures fell under
suspicion: the Venetian ambassador wrote home describing the
emergence of a 'chain of accomplices'.[24] More crucially, the
scandal gave the necessary point of purchase to that group of anti-
Spanish, anti-Catholic courtiers who wished to unpick the
stranglehold on power held by Somerset and his wife's relatives,
the Howards. This faction had already introduced James to their
rival favourite, George Villiers, whose advance in the royal
affections was proceeding apace, but with Somerset destroyed the
political leader of their group, the Earl of Pembroke, became Lord
Chamberlain in his place and there was a radical redrawing of the
networks of patronage. Offices were shuffled, and there was talk of
an overhaul of royal expenses and even of a new parliament.[25]
While not dislodged, the Howards were seriously damaged, and the
scandal catalysed a remarkable revolution in the political identity
of Whitehall. The masquers were headed by Somerset's old rival,
the Earl of Essex, and at its performance Pembroke led in
diplomats from France, Venice and Savoy as guests of honour, an
action signalling the renewal of anti-Spanish alignments at court.[26]

The vindicated justice of *The Golden Age Restored*, its apocalyptic
disclosures and transforming of iron into gold could hardly have
been interpreted by contemporaries without reference to these
momentous events. Obviously Jonson could not directly represent
the Somersets on stage without breaching the dictates of tact, but
had to generalise and idealise, and find a myth within which events
could be shadowed diplomatically. But the family of Evils which
the Iron Age introduces is more than reminiscent of the dizzying
chain of conspirators so recently uncovered; the combination of
Fraud, Slander, Ambition, Pride and Scorn distinctly registers the
tangle of crimes of which Somerset stood exposed to accusation;
and there is an all but open reference to the murder when the
'babe last born, smooth Treachery' is summoned to appear (l.43).
At the same time, the representation of the masquers as a newly
recovered race of champions eager for justice seems chosen for its
topical pertinence. Of course such images were common stock,
but on this occasion the role of reawakened heroes was more than
usually plangent:

> Like lights about ASTRAEA's throne,
> You here must shine, and all be one,
>   In fervor and in flame.
> That by your union she may grow,

And you, sustaining her, may know
The age still by her name.
(ll.206–11)

Jonson's fable was intervening within the still developing events
and imposing onto them an ideological matrix of reform and
renewal. And as he did so, Jonson hinted at changes of a larger
kind which a myth of renewal might serve. In her opening address,
Pallas describes justice in socially coded terms – Joves's care, she
says, is not just to protect the weak from the strong but to rescue
the small subject from the depredations of the great (ll.5–8) – and
at the appearance of Astraea the chorus sings that under her the
great will have to learn to be good (l.103). Such remarks, to put it
mildly, cut wider than the Earl of Somerset. Further, the inclusion
of Astraea is itself provocative, since this goddess had been closely
associated with the iconography of Queen Elizabeth. In letting
Astraea preside, the masque might have been read as gesturing
towards a new agenda for the Jacobean state.

So Jonson was processing the events of the Overbury affair,
translating them into symbolic and ritual forms (the antimasquers
turning to stone as Pallas reveals her shield, the disclosure of the
masquers in a blaze of light) which legitimated political change
within an ethical agenda. And yet even as Jonson processes the
events he clearly has to manage them too, since there are difficulties in the conduct of this project, not the least of which was that of
making it acceptable to the king. Since the arrival of Villiers,
James's relations with Somerset had become rocky, and the loss of
an increasingly neurotic favourite did him no harm. But the exposure of fraud and betrayal at the highest level did the crown's
credit no good at all, and James was concerned to limit the damage as much as possible, in particular by avoiding the spectacle of
a former favourite going to the scaffold. On the other hand he
was understandably concerned that royal justice should be seen to
be vindicated, and at the various trials a great noise was made
about his justice being equal for all parties.[27]

In the masque this translates as a crux: Jonson has to find ways
of representing the new world order without seeming to cast aspersions on the conduct of sovereignty in the old. It was presumably
this difficulty that made him represent the old Evils not so much
as criminals but as political subversives. It is emphasised from the
start that, whatever their individual crimes, collectively the Evils
have committed rebellion. Pallas calls them 'insolent rebellion',

'prophaner eyes' who resist the heavens out of spite (ll.25–6), and Iron Age is characterised as a demagogue, inciting his followers to rebel in the hope of seizing Jove's thunder. For all that the masque celebrates the exposure of vice, the Evils are political entities, the enemies of hierarchy, order, Jove and (through him) of James himself. There is a curious contradiction here, one that skews the masque's topicality. The court was seeing corruption uncovered, yet Somerset was in no sense in revolt, nor were his crimes political. In representing the Evils as if they were opponents of kingship, Jonson's fable manipulated the issues in order to insulate James from blame by association. Far from having condoned crime, the king himself becomes the main target of the Evil's plots, and it is his peace which their violence disrupts. In this way, a disclosure of corruption which was potentially damaging to kingly authority is turned so that it reinforces James's stature, and the problem of corruptly behaving courtiers is displaced onto the altogether more neatly ideological issue of rebellion. The Evils become a generalised threat to order rather than a split within the symbology of order itself. Even so, the problem of insulating the king continues to press onto the masque in the handling of Astraea and the Golden Age, whose return is said to have been 'long wished and wanted' and who themselves seem scarcely able to believe that they might descend to earth (ll.79, 85–100). The inherent difficulty of a fable of renewal is what it risks implying about the age before the present renovation. As Pallas admits, virtue has been 'prest' and arts 'buried' (l.120), while the invitation to the masquers to emerge ('O wake, wake, wake, as you had neuer slept' (l.134)) is even more devastating, half-conceding as it does that the time before the present was one from which good men were absent. Plainly Jonson cannot imply that James's reign has hitherto been marked by corruption and self-interest. On the other hand, the danger of celebrating 'the ages quickning power' (l.157) is that it does invite awkward reflections about what the age is quickening from.

Of course Jonson handles these contradictions so that they remain submerged, rather than troubling the masque's texture. Nonetheless, their presence does indicate the difficulty of giving ethical coherence to a sequence of events in which the dignity of the king and the politics of faction were centrally interested. In order to make it a celebration of James, Jonson was forced to misrepresent the Somerset affair in crucial ways, and to avoid pressing home the perception that the gulf between iron and gold was less than absolute in practice. And at another level, what the masque was having to do was legitimate the displacement of one courtly faction by another. The champions of justice may discipline anarchic rebels, but in performance this would have been seen to be a recasting of courtly competition in moral terms. The private issue for the poet was that the favourite who had just fallen had until recently been the object of exactly such poetic praise.[28] In representing as evil the man who had been the hero of earlier panegyrics, and in praising the recovery of justice in a court whose justice had not apparently been in question in previous masques, Jonson was in the unenviable position of having to eat his own words in public. And even though the masque insists its praises are ethically determined, by the end it admits that its function has been to underwrite the redistributed royal largesse, and acknowledges the element of reward within the renewal. Although Corruption is said to be the Evil with 'golden hands' (1.39), by Pallas's closing speech to the masquers the material benefits of courtship have been reallowed: Astraea will ensure that 'want may touch you neuer', and they may serve Jove 'as his bountie giues you cause' (ll.203, 214). These are the rewards due to faithful rather than vicious service, but they are rewards nonetheless, and they threaten to contaminate the ethical scheme of the masque by acknowledging that the heroes' honour is as much a matter of James's favour as it is of abstract ideals of goodness. The all-too-concrete rewards of virtue undermine the iconography of the Golden Age by disclosing that even the reign of Astraea has links with more material forms of gold.

V

Considered from a purely formal perspective, *The Golden Age Restored* is one of Jonson's most successful masques, but once we attempt to recover the local transactions which it was serving it appears altogether more problematic, since its ethical agenda was so vexed by political and ideological considerations. Though Jonson celebrates the court's reform of itself, he cannot address the nature of that transformation too closely: James's justice has to be transcendent, and the element of competition between court rivals has to be effaced. Consequently the masque oscillates between the desire to praise ethically and the need to keep certain aspects of court life mystified, the price of which is a dysfunction

between what the masque says and what it does. And if we turn to
Pleasure Reconciled to Virtue, danced two years later in a Whitehall
increasingly dominated by the new favourite, we find an even
more overt dysfunction, one now so acute that in performance it
brought the rationale of the masque itself into serious question.

Pleasure Reconciled to Virtue was the first occasion on which the
future King Charles danced as chief masquer, and for the
seventeen-year-old prince Jonson's fable had a strongly educational thrust. It turned on the notion that even as the masquers
revelled, so they were tutored in the uses of pleasure. The hero of
the antimasques is Hercules, a prototype of the active warrior, one
episode of whose iconography involved him arriving at the crossroads between honour and virtue. In the first antimasque Hercules
chases away Bacchic revellers who live intemperately, perpetually
indulging in consumption and riot. As he observes, feasting bru-
talises them: 'these are sponges, and not men' (1.94). Having
defeated illicit pleasure Hercules rests from his labours, but relaxation must not mean unreadiness, since once asleep he is vulnerable to the otherwise inconsiderable pigmies. By chasing the
pigmies away the hero shows that even when off duty he is ready
to rouse himself, and this two-pronged moral lesson becomes a
gloss on the legitimate pleasure of Prince Charles. Though the
masquers sojourn with pleasure, it is stressed that they come from
the 'hill of knowledge' (1.204) and will return to it at the end.
Their evening of revelry has not involved losing sight of the life of
virtue, with which they are perpetually engaged. Indeed, even
their dances have an ethical twist, since they are made to symbolise
the masquers' inner intellectual confidence: their ability to negotiate the 'Laborinth' (1.262) of dance steps while retaining their
poise signals the inward self-possession which validates their relaxation. Like Hercules, they enjoy disciplined pleasures, which do
not involve indulgence or overconfidence. And while this fable was
apt for the young prince, it carried a lesson for the pleasures of
Whitehall more generally. In taking courtly pleasure as his topic
Jonson was thematising the occasion itself, and in demanding that
the masquers measure their revelry against the riot and triviality
of the antimasques, he was defining a dialectic of freedom and
restraint, indulgence and self-discipline which had the ethos of
court life itself as its larger target. The whole masque is an exercise in defining the values of courtly self-fashioning, and not
surprisingly it has evoked the admiration of generations of literary
critics. A festival which praised rightful pleasure and legislated

against improper sports, it seems to be the model panegyric yoking celebration with counsel.

By focusing on festivity, Jonson was returning to the economic territory of *Love Restored* but in an atmosphere of renewed crisis. Royal finances had been in disarray virtually since James's accession, not least because James was a spender rather than a saver, who had a large household, an entourage of Scots and a temperament inclining towards liberality. Of course his problems were not all his own. The system of office-holding which he inherited was riddled with slack procedures, waste, graft and peculation, yet he was expected to live high and reward service with bounty. As he told parliament in 1610, 'a Kings liberalitie must neuer be dried vp altogether: for then he can neuer maintaine nor oblige his seruants and well-deseruing Subiects'.[29] Yet James exacerbated his problems by being lavish with gifts when cash was short, by appointing James Hay as head of the Wardrobe despite his penchant for consuming vast sums of money in displays of courtly ostentation, and by taking the Earl of Suffolk as treasurer, who presided ineffectually over mounting debt and condoned peculation on an almost incredible scale. In 1610 the debt stood at the astonishing level of £500,000; by 1618 it had all but doubled. And not the least reason for insolvency was James's willingness to allow extravagant spending as a normal, indeed necessary dimension of court life. The year before the masque saw honours lavished on Buckingham, James Hay making feasts which (in one case) cost as much as £22,000, and a royal progress to Scotland for which James needed a loan of £100,000 from the city. 'The difficulty of raising money here augments daily', said the Venetian ambassador, but 'the natural prodigalities of his Majesty have in no way diminished'.[30]

Against this background, the pitting of moderation against riot in *Pleasure Reconciled to Virtue* seems more than merely accidental. The symbolic economy of courtly display for which the masque legislates was bound up with a material economy of consumption and waste that was impinging ever more nearly on the crown's freedom of manoeuvre. At the same time, the masque's support for waste management meshed with the attempts at household reform which just at that moment were getting under way. Late in 1617 James appointed Lionel Cranfield to lead a Privy Council committee with a brief to find sweeping economies. Over the next year, Cranfield slashed Household expenses by introducing competitive tenders, scrutinising fees and tightening up the accounts, and he went on to work wonders in the Navy, the Wardrobe, the Court of Wards and the Treasury. Understandably, he caused great alarm amongst the household officials, who were forced to submit their own plans for reform, only to have them torn up by the committee. When the masque was performed in January, the news causing howls of anguish was that remunerations through meals at the king's table were to be cut back, as they were inherently wasteful. The numbers entitled to such meals were grossly inflated and the diets they were supposed to consume every day had become gargantuan.[31] This harmonised with Cranfield's assurances to James that the financial problem lay not with royal generosity but with the wastefulness of uneconomic practices that allowed revenue to be frittered away,[32] but what looked like good management to a merchant seemed to many involved to be against the principle of courtly magnificence. As one courtier put it, 'in the king's honour, some prodigality is not so dishonourable as a little spending', or, as the officers fruitlessly complained at Christmas, it was in England's honour to have a court that was lavish with meat and drink.[33]

Performed at the outset of Cranfield's campaign, *Pleasure Reconciled to Virtue* sets out to promote the agenda of economy. The opening depiction of riotous pleasure creates a distinction between proper and improper festivity highly pertinent to a court where the diet was undergoing retrenchment. In rebuking the antimasquers for 'vitious hospitalitie' (l.92), Hercules was implicitly reflecting on the assumption that membership of the court was a licence for spending without let or hindrance. In place of conspicuous consumption, the masque offers a programme of consumer control, a symbolic economy in which reward is proportionate to effort. Hercules rests because his relaxation is earned, and the masquers' dancing is described in language which continually insists on the element of labour which it involves. In praising their grace, their leader Daedalus draws attention to the fact that it is not a natural quality but an illusion of poise which they constantly must construct. They 'enter-weaue' their knots, 'figure out' their steps, and continually choose between the correct and incorrect lines of pleasure (ll.254–7). Their grace is a product of effort, something engineered, and although they are men 'borne to know' (l.225), honour comes to them not because of their births but through their discipline. In other words, this masque constructs the ideal court society as a kind of meritocracy, and it asserts a necessary relation between the masquers' rewards

and their deserts. The king presides over the event, but what validates the masquers is less his favour than whether they are seen to
be worthy of their places. As the final lines provocatively insist,
the masquers must rely more on their virtue than on their courtly
status: "'tis only she, can make you great, / though place, here,
make you knowne' (ll.347–8).

This is, then, a remarkable masque, one which insisted that the
courtiers would have to earn their panegyric. And, as everyone
who reads any distance into the Stuart masque sooner or later
finds out, this was notoriously the occasion on which James nearly
fell asleep, and almost wrecked the masque by complaining that
the evening was not enjoyable enough. As the Venetian chaplain
Busino reported it:[34]

> the king, who is naturally choleric, got impatient and shouted
> out, 'Why don't they dance? What did they bring me here for?
> Devil take you all, dance.' Upon this the Marquis of Buckingham,
> his Majesty's favourite, immediately sprang forward, cutting a
> score of lofty and very minute capers, with so much grace and
> agility that he not only appeased the ire of his angry lord, but
> rendered himself the admiration and delight of everybody.

Generations of gleeful critics have seized on the irony here, pointing out that for all Jonson's densely articulated learning James was
more interested in the height of the capers, thus suggesting a
yawning gulf between what the masque promised and what it
achieved. Yet the real ironies go rather deeper than this. It was
not merely that James wanted better dancing, since the reports of
court correspondents were uniformly disparaging about the whole
design of the masque,[35] and when it was repeated a month later
Jonson had to devise alternative antimasques, which replaced his
strenuous ethical teaching with vulgar Welsh comedians and
fantastical dancing goats. Further, the *structural* contradiction in
Jonson's enterprise (as opposed to the bare issue of whether his
moral was persuasive or not) is that while the masque was attempting to promote a reforming agenda, its actual performance was
furthering the competition between reward-seeking courtiers
which its fable was, ostensibly, in the business of policing. The
critique of courtly consumption may have sought to tie reward to
labour, but James's response demonstrated that the investments
of the occasion were still very much in a system of favour and
freely electing royal will, while for Buckingham the event was a

forum in which he could dance himself into his master's heart without forfeiting the admiration of his competitors. Indeed, for Busino, this last point – that Buckingham recommended himself to the king *without* damaging his relations with his peers, many of whom, presumably, were competitors with him in the race for favour – represented the real miracle of his performance. His dancing exhibited a mastery of the arts of courtly self-promotion so absolute that it disarmed even those who had an interest in being his opponents or critics. And in doing so it spelled the failure of the poet to turn the masque from a vehicle of compliment into one of counsel. Jonson's masque may have been a uniquely ambitious attempt to bring the uncontrolled pursuit of courtly favour within an ethical agenda, but in the event it turned out at another level to have been peculiarly if inadvertently serviceable to it.

VI

Pleasure Reconciled to Virtue is the nearest we get to a limit case in reassessing the politics of the Jonsonian masque. No other masque makes such determined use of the tropes of compliment as a way of coercing its spectators, yet even here, as I have tried to show, it was compromised by its residual involvement in an encompassing politics of courtly competition. Of course, it is only by chance that we have the information about Buckingham's dancing, but even without it we still might feel that the masque was under strain. In seeking to promote an ideology of restraint within a form which was itself one of the customary aristocratic arenas of conspicuous consumption and display, Jonson was engaging in an enterprise which was fraught with contradictions of the Buckingham kind. But the larger point in the service of which I am offering these three analyses is that the conduct of court masquing could never presume to escape these kinds of necessary accommodations. It is perhaps not entirely surprising that *Pleasure Reconciled to Virtue* should have turned out to be residually implicated in a politics somewhat different from that with which it was ostensibly engaging, nor even that tensions scarcely less blatant should have been involved in the performances of *The Golden Age Restored* and *Love Restored*. However much Jonson might have wished to 'lay hold on more remou'd *mysteries*', the masques were always going to be mired in transactions between competing court factions, or marked by rival political agendas which could never entirely be sublimated into the realms of the purely aesthetic.

Jonson was himself well aware of these difficulties, and content to work within them. In a poem of 1624, he wrote that for twenty years he had

> ... eaten with the Beauties, and the wits,
> And braveries of Court, and felt their fits
> Of love, and hate: and [come] so nigh to know
> Whether their faces were their owne, or no[36]

A poet who knew this was unlikely to confuse his eulogies of the court with the character of the court itself, or to overestimate the likelihood of his panegyric actually changing those people whom, notwithstanding, it purported to be educating. A poet who the previous year had dismissed the court masques as 'the Glorious Scenes, at the great sights' was plainly less persuaded about the effectiveness of his panegyric than some of his subsequent enthusiasts have been.[37] And the double vision which such admissions involve helps to define the limits to revisionism within the study of court culture more generally. In recuperating the political functions which the masques served and in rewriting the old model that dismissed them as merely aesthetic events, there is a danger that in the interests of re-establishing the possibilities of persuasion we disregard the obstacles. It plainly is true that the masques could offer a point of contact between the crown and those with differing perspectives on the policies of the monarchy, and this (in its turn) helps us to understand the continuing openness of early Stuart Whitehall. Yet in looking at the breakdowns of communication, the failures, frustrations and difficulties experienced even by so adept a panegyrist as Jonson, it is evident that negotiation had its limits, that there were issues which the masques could not address head on, and contradictions which they were unable to discharge. Insofar as the masques performed political work, they were helping to bind the court to the nation, providing social glue which kept the courtly fabric together; but insofar as significant gaps existed between what they did and what they purported to do, they were testifying to difficulties within the politics of the time which were not amenable to easy solution. With their combination of criticism and compliment, their promotion of counsel within a framework of deference, the masques offered one potential model for a politics of accommodation, but the gap between the ideal communities presented in the masques' fables and the somewhat different transactions which the masques' performances were having to serve is one indication of the larger, structural dysfunctions on which the Stuart consensus was eventually to founder.

5. The King's Writ: Royal Authors and Royal Authority in Early Modern England

KEVIN SHARPE

In recent years literary and cultural critics have made us more aware of the inextricable interrelationship of discourse and power. Speaking, writing, discursive performances, they have shown, not only reflect social arrangements and structures of authority; they are themselves acts of authority. It is no coincidence that some of the most stimulating research in this field has been in the literature and politics of the Renaissance state.[1] For in Tudor England, the power of the crown and state depended largely upon its representation of authority. The monarch had no standing army or independent bureaucracy to enforce his will; both the co-operation of the political nation and the obedience of the lower orders rested more on a culture and ideology of order than on physical coercion. Images of royal power, palaces and pictures, coins and seals, festival and procession shaped that culture of authority and obedience which sustained the state. Most of all in the first century of printing, the royal word, through letters, proclamations and speeches, conveyed the king's power to the corners of the realm. During the sixteenth century in England, both the revival of interest in the classics and the growth of Protestantism emphasised the importance of the word – both as rhetoric and as signification. Words and names, Plato and Aristotle had argued, expressed the essential nature of animals and objects; language, theologians maintained, was the key to divine truths; to Protestant reformers such as John Bale, the word offered unmediated access to divinity.[2]

During the Tudor century, as we know, monarchs increasingly claimed that they ruled as God's lieutenants on earth, that is they

117

represented his divine justice, reason and will in the common-weal. Like God, the monarch through his word bestowed grace or anger and decreed life and death. In Shakespeare's *Richard II*, Bolingbroke, commenting on his sentence of banishment, compares the power of royal with divine discourse:

> How long a time lies in one little word!
> Four lagging winters and four wanton springs
> End in a word: such is the breath of kings[3]

As Richard II himself makes poignantly clear, the king's very power lay in the authority of his word.[4] And in the Tudor state as on the Tudor stage the monarch claimed authority over other voices and discourses: publication depended on royal licence; parliamentary debate was bounded by royal definition of 'free speech'; condemned traitors had, as their last act, to read what was almost an official script damning themselves and praising royal rule. The king spoke; good subjects, like good wives and children in early modern England's patriarchal society, listened but were not heard.[5]

Ironically, however, the very developments that led to the pre-dominance of the word in the exercise of political authority also sowed the seeds of challenge to a monopoly or control of dis-course, hence to power. First, rhetoric, ideally a device for the communication of truths, could become a mode of deception. Machiavelli counselled the prince to deploy language as a tool of self-interest, ambition and power untrammelled by moral norms; and others, as Shakespeare's Richard III reminds us, were to follow his advice.[6] Secondly the rise of Protestantism and religious division led to different interpretations of the Bible. Because the Holy Scripture was also a treatise for government such different interpretations fractured a common discourse of state into rival languages of power. By the end of the sixteenth century, radically in the Netherlands, France and Scotland, more quietly but no less significantly in England, the Calvinists turned God's word into a subversive political discourse.[7]

Faced with these threats to shared ideological vocabularies, monarchs endeavoured in the new circumstances they confronted to re-establish their authority by a reassertion of their interpretative power over rival voices. James I's patronage of a new authorized version of the Bible – the King James Bible – was as much an act of power as of piety: an official translation proscribed the Geneva Bible and sought to define the parameters of hermeneutic freedom opened by the translation of the Scriptures.[8] But monarchs did more: by the force of their own words they attempted to reclaim, appropriate and re-authorise the discourses and metaphors that had validated royal authority. Royal speeches and writings – exegeses of Scripture, translations of classics, epic poems – endeavouring to contest and contain challenges to order and sovereignty, were acts of government and power. Royal authorings, we might say, had become central to the sustenance of royal authority.

As a woman Elizabeth's allotted role was one of silence. Yet as a queen she is famous for her skilful oratory and familiar speech. Not least through her skill with words, Elizabeth turned the disadvantages of her sex into a powerful claim to sovereignty. Little attention, however, has been paid to the queen's writings – as self-presentation and as representation of monarchy. Yet from youth to old age Elizabeth wrote, translated and published a variety of works which invite analysis as texts of power. Elizabeth's volumes of devotions and prayers may be read as private and personal meditations, but their language and address is also directed to public and political concerns. Elizabeth's language is strongly gendered and erotic. The soul's deliverance from sin she compares to that of a birth of a child from the womb; she prays 'o most meek father...thou untie and loose me'. Such language places Elizabeth's prayers within the conventions of medieval Catholic female piety and, at a time when it was desirable to carve a path between religious extremes, there may be significance in that. More generally, the queen's metaphors and her language are often directly political. Having taken God as her husband, she will 'keep but one household with Him'; God's 'sovereignty sounds as a major note throughout the devotions'.[9] Elizabeth politicises the Christian struggle for faith. Sin she describes in her prayers as an internal insurrection needing to be quelled if she were to rule her own person: 'I would subdue all evil affections but they daily rebel and rise against me and will not be subject unto my spirit'.[10] Only when subject to God did she feel free, 'the prerogative of a free mind always minding heavenly things'.[11] Elizabeth's prayers echo with the language used of kings: God was a 'perfect physician', as the prince was to the commonweal; she prayed he would incline to her 'petitions', the medium of subjects' address to monarchs; she hoped her people might become 'heavenly citizens'.[12] As her subjects looked to her as queen, so she told God in her latin prayers of 1563, 'Tu es ipse Rex meus'.[13] Elizabeth's prayers were undoubtedly her personal plea for God's grace and counsel. But published in 1563, 1569 and 1571, as well as circulated in manuscript, they were also public texts.[14] Indeed the texts of the queen's personal subjection to God became a validation of her public claim (contentious in the eyes of Catholics) to be His chosen ruler. Her personal prayers enabled Elizabeth to appropriate the ideal of the good prince, one who made 'thy people my crown,...thy service my government,...thy gospel my kingdom'.[15] Moreover the prayers, more than self-guidance, became admonitions to all governors: 'This the Lord commandeth', she prayed, 'keep equity and righteousness, deliver the oppressed from the power of the violent... and shed no innocent blood in this place'.[16] Significantly Elizabeth's books of devotions reveal no narrow denominational preferences: they are Christian rather than obviously Protestant. Writing in Latin, French, Italian and Spanish as well as English, the queen established her own universality, her learning and her capacity to discern God's will.[17] God's words, she once wrote, 'are oftentimes mystical/And are not rightly understood by all'.[18] In her prayers Elizabeth interpreted and mediated God's word for her subjects. In the contentious decades of the 1560s, when many were vying to determine the nature of worship, the queen's interpretations were very much acts of authority too.[19]

As well as Scripture, the classics were validating texts in a Tudor society that looked to Greece and Rome as the pinnacle of civilisation. Interestingly, during the 1590s, Elizabeth took time from the business and cares of government to translate Boethius's *Consolation of Philosophy*, Plutarch's essay *On Curiosity* and Horace *On the Art of Poetry* – both in prose and in verse. The translations were done quickly, are by no means exact and may not have been completed.[20] Though they were not printed in the queen's lifetime it is not clear whether they were intended for publication: a copy is found in State Papers.[21] Nor is the motive for writing obvious: translation was a common pedagogic exercise in which Elizabeth had been well schooled, but her age dispels any such explanation and the dictation of the works to a clerk of the signet suggests more public import. If, as has been argued, Elizabeth 'chose to translate those things which were most central to her own thoughts', we need to ponder which contemporary concerns her 1590s translations addressed.[22]

Boethius's *Consolation* was a moral dialogue arguing the victory of philosophy over fate. Boethius, banished and awaiting death, laments his condition, having ruled wisely, protected the poor and followed his conscience. He fears all is governed by chance.

Philosophy (a female figure) reassures him that the world is 'ruled by divine reason' and urges him to adhere to 'conscience truth'.[23] It is difficult not to read Elizabeth's choice of subject and translation as a form of confession and search for reassurance. The 1590s were a difficult decade for the queen in which literally and politically the glamour faded from her regime. Through a reabsorption of Boethius in her own words perhaps Elizabeth (who in youth took 'Semper Eadem' as her motto) reassured herself of the continuance of reason and order in a volatile world. But the translation was more than just a personal document. The presentation of a female figure who triumphed over 'outward and mean matters' might itself have reinforced Elizabeth's authority.[24] More generally the *Consolation* proclaims the divine origin of all order and its necessity for human existence. All, Philosophy tells Boethius, partake of a unity framed by the creator; but it was a fragile unity: 'everything shall last while it is one, but when it leaves that order it perisheth'.[25] Men, she continues, consist of lust and appetite but also enjoyed reason. The virtuous, those in whom reason ruled, worked for 'the common end of all things'. Breaking God's order was not freedom; rather those that upset order 'are vexed with slaying affections which increasing...they heap that bondage to themselves...and are...captived by their own liberty'.[26] The thrust of the *Consolation*, we can see, was a re-inforcement of the organic concept of the state. 'Let persuasion of sweet rhetoric' Philosophy urged Boethius, 'assist thee' to reaffirm faith in divine reason.[27] Against rival discourses, Elizabeth too reasserted the ideology of order.

Perhaps we may also discern in the translation a more particu-lar address. One of the mounting threats to the idea of the com-monweal as a replication of divine order came from the puritans whose theology of predestination and an invisible church of the elect fractured the community of church and state.[28] Certainly Boethius is at odds with puritan and Calvinist tenets at several points. The argument that 'nature hath ingraft in men's mind desire of truest good' suggests a rejection of Calvinist emphasis on the condition of fallen man.[29] Predestination is specifically countered: 'there is no liberty in man's counsels nor acts which God's mind...constrains to one end'; 'there remains a sure liberty of will to mortal folkes' – a liberty to come to knowledge of God's reason.[30] If these sound rather like ideas that Hooker was to develop into a philosophy of church and state, therein may be the point. Boethius's *Consolation* offered a counter to the Calvinists' radical separation of grace and nature, as to other challenges to order. 'What place can there be left for rash men', Philosophy asks, 'where God in all order keepeth'.[31]

During the 1590s, Elizabeth also translated in her own hand Plutarch's *De Curiositate*, one of the essays in which he explored types of virtue and vice and the nature of a moral being. *De Curiositate* denounces those who seek to criticise the deficiencies of others, collect gossip and pry – even into courts. Such are directed to self-examination, self-regulation and real learning rather than idle tattle. Curiosity is categorised as one of the senses that dethrone reason in man. Elizabeth renders Plutarch's admonition that 'no man ought permit his sence abrode to range':

> And than againe in thy selfe with reasone make abodd
> and ther abide not strayinge out of office charg.[32]

That use of 'office' seems to politicise the moral counsel into advice for citizenship. Again, though it has been said that Elizabeth translated the piece for her private exercise, the tone suggests address to others as much as self address. During the 1590s, growing disenchantment with the regime was expressed in satires, newsletters and topical 'opposition' plays.[33] Plutarch's essay, not least in its specific injunction to shun the theatre, offers a reply.[34] More generally Plutarch, whose essays were held as a model for the 'heroically moral man', associated virtue with self-regulation, the ruler with reason. He also expounded the argument 'That the philosopher should converse especially with Princes'.[35] In her translation, Elizabeth, demonstrating her own learning and acquaintance with philosophy, reclaimed natural authority. And she reaffirmed what was increasingly becoming a polemical position whilst seeming to remain above the polemical exchange. A royal translation that could rebut the assault of Tacitean satire and 'classical republicanism' was an act of power indeed.

Elizabeth self-consciously took up the interrelationship of discourse and government in the last of her translations, her englishing of Horace's *De Arte Poetica*, which she wrote in 1598. In one of the most important works of classical and Renaissance critical theory, Horace, following Aristotle, expounded the relationship of good writing to wisdom and virtue. The purpose of poetry, he maintained, was moral: 'the giving of pleasure with some useful precepts for life'.[36] Because the poet possessed a didactic power to

direct men, so his deployment of language was a social responsibility that he must never forget:

> Nor eloquence shal he want nor ordar cleare
> For Grace and Vertu shall he place, or forbeare.[37]

Horace went so far as to associate the power of words with that of
armies, in determining victory or defeat:

> If speakars wordz unfit their fate,
> The army all with skorne will them deride.[38]

The right order of words could represent the natural order – 'let
all things be as sorteth best their place' – and, by representing,
reinforce it. It may be that at the time of factional strife, economic
hardship and disaffection, Elizabeth hoped that the *De Arte Poetica*
could revitalise a belief in natural order, that, as she translated
him, Horace could 'with new shewe the hiden yore expound'.[39]

Certainly the queen had an acute sense of the importance of
her own word in the exercise of her rule. In a letter to James VI,
she once reminded him of Isocrates' counsel to his emperor that
royal words were the 'ensigns' of royal authority – badges or banners around which a ruler might gather force to counter rival or
antagonistic ideologies and discourses.[40] Similarly in a speech to
Cambridge University in 1564 the queen recalled an axiom of
Demosthenes which she paraphrased: 'the words of superiors
have the weight of books with inferiors; and the sayings of princes
retain the authority of laws with their subjects'.[41] Elizabeth's
neglected writings, her devotional works and translations, no less
than her famous speeches, were themselves acts of command and
organs of government.

II

Elizabeth's successor, James VI and I, was probably the most
literate and learned king to have occupied the English throne: a
monarch who not only read all the classical texts of statecraft, but
one who believed the schoolmaster's life closest to that of kingship. Moreover, James possessed 'an indomitable faith in the
significance of the printed word'.[42] He commissioned a new
history of his mother's reign in Scotland because he knew the

ideological power of such representations; he dictated 'every word' of proclamations because he believed that control of their language was vital to their authority.[43] So great was his trust in words that, James himself jested, his chancellor had had to remind him that 'my house could not be kept upon epigrams; long discourses and fair tales will never repair my estate'.[44] James's verbosity was more than a vain desire to parade his learning, more too than an understanding of the force of rhetoric. 'One of the maynes for which God hath advanced me upon the lofty stage of the supreme throne', he wrote, 'is that my words uttered from so eminent a place...might with greater facility be conceived'.[45] If the King of Scotland spoke and wrote much it was because by doing so he fulfilled the first duty of a ruler: serving God.

Historians are familiar with what their editor C.H. McIlwain collected as James's *Political Works*: his speeches and addresses, *Apology for the Oath of Allegiance*, most of all his *Trew Law of Free Monarchies* and *Basilikon Doron*, his advice book to his son. The last, written originally in Middle Scots, was an attempt to counter the contractual theories of government advocated by Buchanan and John Knox, theories which had justified the deposition of his mother in 1567. But there is more to these works than polemical exchanges. In the *Trew Law*, James glossed the familiar metaphor of the king as head and the subjects as members to argue: 'As the *discourse and direction* flows from the head and the execution thereunto belongs to the rest of the members...so it is betwixt a wise prince and his people'.[46] It was because discourse and direction were so interdependent to him that James advised his son of the importance of his words which 'will remain as true pictures of your mind'.[47] The *Basilikon Doron*, written when James believed himself to be on his death bed, was the king's own last 'testament' and his (as the title means) 'royal gift' of word to his son.

While there is much to be said about the *Trew Law* and *Basilikon Doron*, it is more important to appreciate that all James's writings were penned as acts of government, not only in the sense of a polemical response to challenges, but in the broader didactic sense: as attempts to lead men to God's reason and goodness through royal representation of His divine truths. The preface to James's published *Workes* of 1616 makes the point clear. Bishop Montagu, James's editor, acknowledged that some might think it fitter for kings to wield a pike than a pen. But God, the King of Kings, became the word and his chosen Moses, David and Solomon wrote to lead men to understanding. Similarly, he claimed, 'we have seen with our own eyes the operation of his Majesty's works in the consciences of ... men so far as ... there have been [those] that have been converted by them'.[48] In the frontispiece to the volume James stands beside a table on which is placed a book bearing the title *Verbum Dei*; beneath the picture a caption announces: 'Knowledge makes the king most like his Maker'. 'God hath given us a Solomon', Montagu explained, and beneath the king's picture the Lord spoke as he did to Solomon: 'Ecce do tibi animum sapientem et intelligentem'. It was God's divine understanding that James was offering through his *Workes*.

The first of James's writings in the volume is his *Paraphrase Upon the Book of Revelations*. In what is essentially a commentary, James melds his own reading with the biblical text itself to turn exegesis into his own interpretation and world view. As he decodes the figurations he points out how 'the popedom is meant by the pale horse in the fourth seal', how Rome is the false monarchy.[49] There is admonition perhaps to puritans as well as Catholics in the passage the king rendered 'I have reserved the secret power of election and reprobation only to myself'.[50] In his closing remarks, James warned others against imposing their own opinion upon Scripture. For himself he presented not an interpretation of *Revelations* but a mediation of God's word; and so he joins his own words with St John's: 'and [God] said unto me write and leave in record what thou hast seen'.[51] Montagu drew attention to Revelations, the book of the last things, in his preface: 'Kings', he pointed out, 'have a kind of interest in that book beyond any other'; and James, he added, possessed an understanding beyond the measure of men. When we consider how Revelations had been (and was soon again to be) a primary text of revolution, we begin to grasp how great was that royal 'interest' and how important was an authorised royal reading of its ambiguities and opacities.

In his Meditation upon chapters of the first book of 'the Chronicles of the Kings' James was explicit about the politics of his reading. He desired that 'these meditations of mine may after my death remain to...posterity as a certain testament of my upright and honest meaning'.[52] The king reflected on King David's first act after victory, his moving the ark of the Covenant to his house, 'whereof' he observed and advertised, 'we may learn first that the chief virtue which should be in a Christian prince...is a fervency and constant zeal to promote the glory of God'.[53] James invites the reader into his private meditation on Scripture to witness that the realm was blessed with a godly ruler. More particularly he again explores the text to see 'how pertinently this...doth appertain to us and our present estate'.[54] James compares the biblical elders to the burgesses of parliament and notes in a description that is also prescription: 'that a godly king finds as his heart wisheth, godly estates concurring with him'.[55] In passing he is even able to find a passage describing the dancing of David to show his puritan subjects that 'dancing, playing and such like actions...are of themselves indifferent'.[56] Exegesis of Scripture once again becomes royal command. Indeed James's *Meditation upon the 27th Chapter of St Matthew* became a treatise on the office of kingship dedicated to Prince Charles. Interpreting the mock coronation of Christ with thorns, he reaffirms his sense of duty to God and his people, but also reminds his people as well as the prince that kings received their crowns from God only and were 'mixtae personnae', partaking of His divinity as well as humanity. A passing jibe at 'foolish superstitious puritans' who refused to kneel connects nonconformity to broader challenges to authority, in a work which transforms private meditation into a powerful revalidation of divine monarchy.[57]

James's *Meditation Upon the Lords Prayer* was written in 1619, the title page announces, 'for the benefit of all his subjects especially of such as follow the court'. The Lord's Prayer, of course, was a fundamental text for all Christians. James skilfully appropriates it to validate his vision of the Church of England and to exclude those, especially the puritans, who did not accept his vision. 'Trust not', he urges, 'to that private spirit or Holy Ghost which our Puritans glory in for then a little fiery zeal will make thee turn separatist'.[58] Against the threat of separatism, James reasserts the Hookerian axiom: 'everyone of us is a member of a body of a church that is compacted of many members'. As for puritans who rejected the visible church – 'to the woods and caves they must go like outlaws and rebels, to their sermons and divine exercises'.[59] The passage 'and lead us not into temptation' leads James to a theological ruling in what was becoming an increasingly contentious issue. Arminians, he observed, would not like the passage because it stressed God's will. But, he added, 'we are also to eschew the other extremity of some puritans who by consequent make God author of sin'. For, 'He doth force none to fall from Him'.[60] James turns the Lord's Prayer into a diatribe against the puritans and a defence of the true visible church as it then was, he claimed, in his kingdom.

That James's exegeses of biblical texts found no place in McIlwain's edition of his political works may be revealing. For though they are deeply politicised and partisan texts they claim a space above polemical exchange; they announce themselves as meditations on, rather than interpretations of, Scripture. James states it to be his duty 'to defend all those who profess the same faith'.[61] But it was also a necessary support to his rule, which is why he was led to intervene in the theological debate in the Netherlands sparked by the writings of Conrad Vorstius. Vorstius disputed 'the sacred and ineffable essence of God' and so, in the words of James's tract included in his English *Workes,* was a 'sworn enemy not only to divinity but even to all philosophy both human and natural denying God to be actus purus but having some kind of diversity or multiplicity in himself, yea even the beginnings of a mutability'. Diversity, multiplicity and mutability were in early modern Europe political as well as theological heresies. When James against Vorstius reasserted that 'God is unity and verity is one', he revalidated the premise on which all order and government was founded. Not surprisingly he also went to pains to denounce as an Anabaptist heresy Vorstius's argument that none could exercise authority over others in spiritual matters. For against his domestic 'precisians' who 'out of self will and fancy refuse to conform themselves to the orders of our church', no less than Vorstius, he declaimed it 'unlawful' to speak of the mysteries of God other than as the church prescribed.[62] The power and mystery of his lieutenant on earth depended upon it.

James VI and I's poetry has received no historical and little critical evaluation. Evidence of revision, however, suggests that the king may have intended a complementary volume of poetical works after his prose works of 1616. Certainly he returned actively to writing poetry which he had been famous for in Scotland, especially during the 1580s. Like his religious writings, James's poems, though often personal and meditative in tone, are permeated with the language and experience of power, difference and contest. Like them, too, they seek through discourse to shape the reader's moral vision to accord with the king's observation and will. One of James's earliest poetic enterprises was his verse translation of the Psalms. As with his other prose exegeses, James mediates Scripture through royal discourse and melds the king's words with those of King David and the King of Kings to whom he sang. The Psalms read as counsel to the self as well as other rulers, as James writes how 'cruel and bloodthirsty tyrants' are 'cursed' and how good kings are just, open to petition and 'serve the lord with fear'. But translating, as the title puts its, the 'Psalmes of His Majesty', James also presents himself as that good king who heeds God's counsel and speaks with Him:

> nou knou I godd preserves his oinctid king
> & from his holy Heavinns doth heare him well.[63]

The King 'does firmly put his trust in Jehovah' and becomes one with him. It is probably no coincidence that James began his Psalms during the 1580s when he sought to restore the prestige of Scottish kingship against the challenges of the Presbyterians and the contract theorists who forged, not least from Scripture, an ideology for rebellion.

Such circumstances also underlay James's major poetic enterprise of the decade, his verse translation of *The Furies*, which he rushed into print in 1591, describing its author – the 'divine' Du Bartas – as a mirror for the age.[64] *The Furies* tells the story of the fall of man and the collapse of natural order. When Adam sinned he not only cast the harmony of God's created universe into chaos and contest, he surrendered command over his own world.

> Man, in rebelling thus against
> The soveraigne great, I say,
> Doth feele his subjects all enarm'd
> Against him everie way.[65]

Even the animals formed 'rebellious bands' against man. Wolves, leopards and bears

> Most jealous of the right divine
> Against their head conspire.[66]

War ensued. And within the microcosm of man the Fall dethroned reason, leaving 'the king of beasts...of himselfe...not the maister now'. As passions rose against reason, so good government gave way to 'false contracts', 'unlawful measures' and 'oppressors'.[67] As with Elizabeth's *Boethius*, in his translation of the *Furies* (a text, he claimed, 'quite transformed by me'), James associates royal authority with divine order and the subject's constitutional health.[68] In a fallen world the only hope lay with those who were 'Dame Nature's counsellors and the Almighty's agents ay'.[69] Godly kings were the almighty's lieutenants and divine poets like Du Bartas were Nature's counsellors. Uniquely the poet/king might help reverse the Fall; meanwhile he associated with that first damnable rebellion of man all who contested with authority.

The subject of James's own original epic poem of the 1580s seems at first a surprising one. His *Lepanto* celebrates the famous Spanish victory over the Turk in 1571; and James himself acknowledged that some (especially the hotter sort of Protestants) might think it inappropriate for him to praise a 'foreign popish bastard'.[70] Throughout, however, in its references to election and the certainty of salvation, the poem is protestantised. But more interestingly in its representation of 'Christians' (James carefully avoids denominational tags) united against a common enemy, the poem gestures to an ecumenical hope for a reunified *respublica Christiana* which James cherished throughout his life. Not only perhaps a plea for ecumenism, the epic is also a cry for community. In passages reminiscent of Virgil (whom he invokes in his preface), in which the king vividly compares the preparations for the crusade with the labour of bees in the hive, there is a powerful, classical and Christian, evocation of and injunction to community. And in lines that are both polemical and admonitory, the devil's attempts to sow discord in the ranks are associated with all disobedience, indeed with individualism. At Lepanto such disaster was averted by strong and able leaders who formed 'voluntaires of conscience' – the pun is surely significant – into one co-operative force:

> Yet did the wisdomes of the Chiefes
> And of the generall most
> Compound all quarrels and debates
> That were into that Host
> Preferring wisely as they ought
> The honor of the Lord,
> Unto their owne, the publicke cause
> To private mens discord.[71]

James's *Lepanto* did not only celebrate a battle; it portrayed an ideal Christian commonwealth, in which virtuous rulers led all to subordinate their private conscience to the good of the community.

When James resumed writing poetry – in England after 1616 – his verse was more overtly partisan and polemical. When, in 1618, a comet raised fear of some impending doom, not least the possible success of the unpopular marriage negotiations with Spain, James sharply condemned the dangerous conjectures of gossips and puritans. 'To guess at God Almighty's mind', he snapped, was not the prerogative of subjects; the king might discern 'treason in him whose fancy overrules his Reason'.[72] In 1622, fascinatingly, James penned a mocking poem commanding nobles to leave London, in the hope that verse might disperse them whom 'scarce a Proclamation can expel'.[73] Most extraordinarily James replied in mock doggerel to the 'raylinge rhymes and vaunting verse' which lampooned the Spanish match. In their own language he reminds his critics:

> god above men kings inspires
> Hold you the publique beaten way
> Wonder at kings and them obey.[74]

The obvious question to which these outbursts give rise is why James responded to attacks in verse. While they reiterate the themes of the need for reason and order in the human and political constitution, these poems can scarcely claim to stand over the polemical fray like his earlier Scottish epics. Yet evidently James believed in the power of poetry to make his case – at the popular level as in more learned lines. In the case of his most famous political testament, the *Basilikon Doron*, the 'argument of the book' is distilled in a prefatory poem. With Sir Philip Sidney, James believed that poetry might 'lift up the mind' of fallen man to an understanding of God's natural order.[75] 'A breath divine', he wrote, 'in Poets brests does blowe':

> Wherethrough all things inferiour in degrie
> As vassalls unto them doe hommage showe.[76]

The political language associates poetry with government. Like kings, poets were God's lieutenants, trusted with raising men to virtue through representation of perfect nature. Poets were 'Nature's trunchmen, heavens interprets trewe'.[77] In other words verse, like James's exegeses of Scripture, mediated God's divine order and reason. And so in turn, the king became also a poet, in Ben Jonson's carefully chosen words of flattery, the 'best of Poets' as the 'best of kings'.[78] James himself conjoined royal and poetic authority in his *Urania*, through the familiar metaphor of the seal which authorised letters and documents:

For as into the wax the seals imprent
Is lyke a seal, right so the Poet gent
Doeth grave so vive in us his passions strange,
As makes the reader halfe in author change
For verses force is sic that softly slydes
Throw secret poris and in our sences bydes
As makes them have both good and eville imprented
Which by the learned works is represented.[79]

But if poetry were to fulfil its responsibility, like government it required – as Horace had appreciated – manuals, rules and law, so James therefore wrote, along with his political advice books, a *Short Treatise Containing some Reulis and Cauteles to be Observed and Eschewed in Scottis Poetrie*. 'If Nature be chief', he explained their purpose, 'reulis will be an help and staff to Nature'. Poets' words, he urged, should literally 'vividly represent', their epithets describe 'the natural of every thing'.[80]

In the *Basilikon Doron*, James had counselled his son to make his own example an exemplary text: 'let your own life be a law book'.[81] In his writings he hoped that text would wield authority. Like Elizabeth's, James's writings, through representation and self-presentation, attempt to reaffirm and reauthorise paradigms that sustained his divine right; and to control the arena of inter-pretation and discourse. Just as the Authorized King James Bible and his exegeses of Scripture claimed contested texts for the crown, so royal poetry, with its echoes of Virgil and Horace, Cicero and Sidney, appropriated an ambiguous classical tradition, which some deployed to defend republics, for the monarchy. There was more than flattery in the epistle dedicatory to James's *Essays of a Prentise in the Divine Art of Poesie*: 'Caesar's workes shall justly Caesar crowne'.[82]

III

After the death of Prince Henry in 1612, James bequeathed to Prince Charles his royal words: the *Basilikon Doron*, the 1616 *Workes* and the meditation on St Matthew's Gospel. In a painting of the late Jacobean period, Charles is depicted as the 'inheritor of the royal word'.[83] Charles, however, unlike his father, presented himself as a man of silence. It did not, the new king told his first parliament in 1625, 'stand with my nature to spend much time in

words'; he was often to repeat the statement.[84] Charles's silence is
traditionally attributed to a speech defect that caused him to
stutter. But there is plentiful evidence that he was capable of eloquence; moreover such an impediment does not explain his disin-
clination to *write*. Clearly, as I have argued elsewhere, Charles was
aesthetically more inclined to visual culture, but visual and verbal
were not necessarily antagonistic media and the Caroline court
continued to be a rich ambience for poetry and drama.[85] Charles
in fact was neither uninterested in words nor as silent as is sometimes believed. As prince and king he read widely – in Tasso and
Spenser and Donne, in Sandys, Bacon, Erasmus, Dallington,
Beaumont and Fletcher and Harington. Interestingly he read and
carefully annotated Aristotle's *On Rhetoric*, Bacon's *Advancement of
Learning* and Shakespeare's *Works*.[86] And he often painstakingly
corrected and amended drafts of letters that went out in his name,
spending hours alone with papers in his study.[87] Indeed Charles
began to edit his father's poetry and penned occasional verse of
his own, composed volumes of prayers, gathered all his papers for
the two-volume edition of his works which appeared in 1662, and
most probably substantially wrote the famous *Eikon Basilike*.[88] But
if Charles's reputation for taciturnity is in part a misconception, it
is one the king himself fostered. And the fact remains that the
bulk of his writing comes from later in his reign, especially the
period after 1640. What we need to understand is that in Charles's
case the chronology of both silence and speech/writing is significant in his discourse of power.

During the early part of his reign, Charles spoke and published
regularly whilst claiming his aversion to both. The business of war,
he told his parliament, 'needeth no narrative'. 'Three of the best
rhetoricians', he added, 'Honour, Opportunity and Safety plead
for expedition'. In 1628 he desperately urged, 'the times are now
for action, action I say not words'.[89] To Charles the obligation of
his people to support the monarch in war was not an argument
that needed to be made, but a truism that ought to be self-evident.
To accept the need to persuade men to do their duty would be to
acknowledge that there was no commonweal. The reluctance and
brevity of the royal word were themselves an ideological articulation: the reaffirmation of an ideal that was not sustained by his
political experience. We can sense Charles's uncomfortable negotiation with this problem in the declarations he issued after the
dissolutions of unsuccessful parliaments. The king, Charles
explained introducing the first of these in 1626, owed no account

to any but God. Yet he felt the need to justify himself to the world
and reply to criticism. Ideally, he continued, kings could remain
silent, their virtue and sense of duty being their best rhetoricians,
but some had doubted the monarch. Charles could not, however,
accept, and certainly not articulate, that this signalled fundamental divisions in the body politic. Sincerely therefore he concluded
that his parliament no less than himself had been 'abused by the
violent and ill-advised passions of a few members', that 'the
common incendiaries of Christendom have subtly...caused these
divisions'.[90] The explanation reinforced the ideal of an organic
Christian society challenged only by Satan, and so marginalised
dissent as disease or evil. The conceit was continued and developed in 1628 and 1629. Protesting again his freedom from the
need to give an account to his subjects, Charles presented himself
'in the truth and sincerity of our actions', that having 'laid down
the truth and clearness of our proceedings', all 'wise and discreet
men' could know their duty.[91] In these declarations, Charles
literally endeavoured to write away a political world of interest,
difference and contest and rescript a validating ideology of order.
When his last parliament in 1629 failed to act their part, the king
silenced their discordant discourse. In a lengthy declaration
explaining the dissolution, Charles presented a selective and personal narrative – of all that had been plotted since his succession
by 'envenomed spirits which troubled...the blessed harmony
between us and our subjects'.[92] It was literally the last word on the
matter, for the accompanying proclamation banned even discussion of future parliaments.[93] But it was, as we shall see, by no
means the last time that Charles deployed the partisan narrative
as a genre that claimed a space above political polemic.

It is the period of Charles's personal rule in which the king
most deserves his reputation for silence. The parliament doors
were closed; there were fewer proclamations; reforms of the court,
church and administration were enacted without long declarations or justifications; the decade was characterised more by the
visual representation of the king on Van Dyck's canvases than by
verbal exchange. Charles did write and publish volumes of prayers
in which he presented himself as the conscience of the nation,
praying that each of his subjects 'would be a magistrate unto
himself and his whole family'.[94] But in the court masques to which
he devoted so much attention, the king remained silent. The
debates of antimasque were eclipsed by his very appearance as the
embodiment of reason, love, harmony and order. Masques, like

Van Dyck's paintings, depicted royal authority as 'natural', needing no gloss or spokesman. Yet it is consummate artifice of technique and stage machinery that secures that 'naturalism', and
seeks to re-present it to the observer. The king's animated silence
is central to the ideology of that representation: a belief that a
natural ruler 'need not speak but simply be'.[95]

It is significant that Charles's most virulent critics, the radical
puritans, charged his government with censorship. For while
there was no effective control of literary production, there was a
larger truth to their claims: the king had triumphed over *debate*.
And it is revealing that when the king encountered opposition
from his Scottish subjects from 1637, the conflict that ensued was
as much a propaganda war as a military campaign. From the
beginning the Covenanters published and disseminated thousands of pamphlets denigrating the government. Charles was
forced to break his silence. And in his proclamation denouncing
their 'seditious practices', he listed the 'multitude of their printed
pamphlets' as the first of the Scots' 'traitorous' acts. A breach of
his control of discourse, he went on to explain, was a decisive
challenge to his authority:

> they have now assumed to themselves Regal power; for whereas
> the Print is the kings in all kingdoms these seditious men have
> taken upon them to print what they please though we forbid it,
> and to prohibit what they dislike, though we command it; and
> with the greater affront have forbid and dismissed the Printer
> whom we established.[96]

Proclamations ordered English subjects to read no pamphlets
sent from Scotland. But Charles could no longer rely on silence,
and he announced a 'large Declaration coming forth containing
all the particular passages which have occurred in this business'.
The *Large Declaration*, published in 1639, broke the royal silence
in a truly massive way. In its pages, Charles took up the narrative
on the grand scale as a device of polemical control.[97] The Prayer
Book rebellion ended the authority of silence in Caroline England
and instigated a new politics of discourse in which power depended upon the articulation of the royal voice.

For some time Charles sought to deny the new circumstances
and retreat from verbal engagement. In his Declaration to his
loving subjects published in 1641, he expressed himself 'sorry...
there should be such a necessity of publishing so many particulars'.[98] Even in his answer to parliament's message concerning

control of the militia, he held to the belief that 'it is below the high and royal dignity (wherein God hath placed us) ...to trouble ourself with answering those many scandalous seditious pamphlets and printed papers...' Now, however, circumstances necessitated he 'take more pains this way by our own pen than ever king hath done'.[99] In his declaration of 12 August 1642, Charles graphically linked the drift to arms with contested discourse. To sustain the truth and expose the pretences of his enemies, he was, he wrote, now 'enforced to use a dialect rougher and different from what we have used to treat in'.[100]

During the 1640s, with others now claiming divine support or natural right, Charles perforce became a rhetorician, a writer, in some ways a politician. He spoke frequently and issued a large number of declarations skilfully directed to their audience. His published volumes of prayers now cohered in communal worship a party rather than a nation. 'Deliver me', the king paraphrased the Psalms of David, 'from the hand of mine enemies'. Like Absalom and the conspirators of Korah, the Roundheads 'smite down thy people oh Lord'. After Edgehill Charles published a prayer of thanksgiving for the 'God of Hosts who goest forth with our armies'. Royal victories taught the enemies of the Lord 'that to take up arms against thy vice gerent is to fight against heaven'.[101]

Charles needed to appropriate the texts of Scripture and the law because even during civil war these remained validating vocabularies for any legitimate rule. But in the king's case his authority depended on their being not partisan but unifying ideologies, the 'common inheritance', as he put it to the freeholders of York, of king *and* people.[102] Charles therefore continued in his speeches and declarations to use the language of unity and community. The monarch was, he said, the father of the realm, the head of the body politic. Although there was 'a great misunderstanding betwixt the head and the body', 'these ruptures may yet in good time be made up'.[103] Once again the king attributed the troubles to 'an unquiet spirit' that infected the realm.[104] Charles used such language because he could not be seen to head only a party. But he used it also because (like many) he continued to believe in unitary principles and truths that were above politics and narrow interest – even his own. And he considered himself bound by conscience to uphold those principles whatever the short-term disadvantages. On occasions during the 1640s, most famously in sacrificing Strafford, the king was persuaded to put expediency first. Increasingly however, he came to believe that 'the obligation of mine oath' was a principal 'point of conscience' and that a

monarch could not, for any immediate political benefit, recede
from promises even when they had 'been obtained by force'.[105]
During the last years of his life, Charles carefully translated into
English and revised Bishop Sanderson's *De Juramento*, in which
promises were described as a 'bond' not only to men but 'of
divine natural law'.[106] If he were to reauthorise the divine laws that
were the foundation of the commonweal, the king's words had to
stand, uncompromised, above polemic and politics.

Accordingly after 1646 Charles again abandoned the war of
words and began to construct himself as a martyr to higher truths,
fulfilling the offices of a Christian and a king. At his trial, he
would not debate, speaking only of his trust from God. On the
scaffold, Christ-like, asking forgiveness for his enemies, he claimed
to eschew partisan rhetoric: 'I have delivered my conscience'.[107]

On 30th January 1649 Charles returned to silence. But from the
silence of the grave he bequeathed his most famous discourse and
most powerful act of authority: the *Eikon Basilike*, the '*portraiture* of
his Majesty', which went through thirty-five editions within a year
of the king's death. Surprisingly it has received little critical
analysis.[108] What I wish to argue is the genius of the text in fulfilling what Charles had struggled to attain throughout the 1640s
and even before: answering every charge or challenge whilst posi-
tioning the royal author above the polemical fray. That success
lay as much in its literary as its political strategy, in the authority
of its writing as much as its discourse on authority.

The *Eikon* opens with a narrative commencing with the calling
of the Long Parliament and continues through chapters on
Strafford's death, the Triennial Act, the king's departure from
Westminster and the raising of armies. It then goes back to the
Covenant and Irish rebellion. Like Charles's earlier accounts of
his 1620s parliaments, this was a narrative very much under the
king's control and written from his perspective. Throughout the
narrative is inscribed not with the third person 'his Majesty' but
the authorial I, its repetition underlining the personal control of
events and their representation. The *Eikon* presents the king, as
Charles always had, traditionally, as the head of an organic body
politic. Where his enemies acted from 'the partialities of private
wills and passions', he stood for 'Reason and public concern-
ments', a reason which mediated 'the divinest power'.[109] And that
reason, for the good of all, curbed the passions which threatened
the constitution both of a Christian commonweal and of man.
'Condemn us not', the king prayed for all his people, 'to our
passions which are destructive both of *ourselves* and others'.[110] Far

from being the interest of a party, royal authority was presented as the interest of each and all. Central to its organic conception was the reiterated argument for one church and law. Differences in religion, the *Eikon* argues, could not remove 'the community of relations, either to parents or princes'. Without mention of them by name, the saints' call for an invisible church of the godly is silenced. Threats to the law, Charles claimed, came not from him (in 'preserving laws...my interest lies more than any man's') but those who 'look more to present advantages than their consciences'.[111]

Such claims were made by many in the pamphlets of the 1640s. The power of the *Eikon Basilike* comes from its self-presentation as a text of conscience and its condemnation of rhetoric and politics. Where politicians 'wrap up their designs' in pretences, the king prayed, 'o never suffer me for any reason of state to go against my reason of conscience'. When others hid behind verbal artistry, 'I am content...my heart...should be discovered to the world without any of those dresses or popular captations which some men use in their speeches'.[112] In the pages of the *Eikon*, the king becomes what Elizabeth in her devotions and James in his exegeses of Scripture had claimed to be: not the rhetorician but the direct mediator of God's word and will.

Indeed, like James's paraphrases of Revelations or St Matthew's Gospel, the *Eikon Basilike* is a meditation on Scripture in which skilfully the king's own words meld with Holy Writ, and his conscience blends with God's will. At the end of each section, the king turns, as if in one of his earlier books of devotions, from his earthly reader to prayer to his God, as though through the king's words, like a priest's mediation, the subject came closer to the Lord. When we review the structure of the text we begin to read the narrative passages, framed by the prayers, as sermons in a text for a service conducted by a king who in the *Eikon* expressed his belief that 'both offices regal and sacerdotal might well become the same person'.[113] The frontispiece, almost like the proscenium arch to the masque, frames the reading: looking to a heavenly crown, Charles kneels with a crown of thorns in his hand before an altar on which an open book bears the text 'in verbo tuo spes mea'. In the king's words too, it would claim, lay the hope and salvation of all men.

The responses to the *Eikon Basilike* offer eloquent testimony to its political/rhetorical power. The questioning of Charles's authorship (which began as soon as the *Eikon* was published) and royalist counter arguments for its 'authenticity' underline the mutual

associations of text and authority. Milton took up his pen immediately, sensing the *Eikon*'s polemical capacity to 'catch the worthless approbation of an inconstant, irrational and image-doting
rabble'.[114] Writing at far greater length than the *Eikon Basilike*,
Milton painstakingly contests all its claims, replacing them into
the arena of verbal contest above which its author had succeeded
in elevating them. Most interestingly he also recognised that to
challenge the arguments or assertions of the text were not enough;
in *Eikonoklastes*, Milton was forced to critique the *Eikon Basilike* as
text: as a work of literature and authorial performance. 'I began',
he wrote in his preface, 'to think that the whole book might be
intended [as] a peece of poetry' and it was the aesthetic power of
the text, its aestheticisation of the king's (to him) contentious
claims, that Milton felt most need to undermine. Accordingly he
derided its verbosity and metaphor, mocked its form and genre,
and questioned the originality of its composition – pointing to
prayers stolen from Sir Philip Sidney and Shakespeare.[115] Making
the aesthetic into an accusation led Milton, as Steven Zwicker has
recently argued, into some uncomfortable positions.[116] Yet he had
no choice. The power of the *Eikon Basilike* lay in its literary proper-
ties as much as its politics: the two were one. To challenge its
authority Milton had to undermine it as authorship – both as the
king's words and as a piece of mere poetry. For all his skill he
failed. With more editions over the next decade, the *Eikon* ensured
that the king's writ ran current throughout the realm. It was
Charles I's most authoritative performance.

About the time of the publication of the *Eikon Basilike*, in exile in
Paris, Thomas Hobbes was attempting to devise a philosophical
justification for the state and defence of sovereign power in
circumstances in which the naturalness of the commonwealth and
authority could no longer be assumed. Language Hobbes saw as
central to his problem and purpose. For in the state of war each
man called 'good' or 'bad' what attracted him or served his interest. Society, however, required a shared public language: 'The
power of Hobbes's sovereign was thus above all an *epistemic* power,
to determine the meanings of words...', to impose a common
language.[117] Before civil war had thrown them irrecoverably into
contest, Elizabeth, James and Charles had spoken and written to
reinforce, authorise and control the common languages on which
their power was founded. Their authorings were as vital to their
exercise of authority as the authority of Hobbes's sovereign was
necessary for a common discourse of state.

6. Politics and Pastoral: Writing the Court on the Countryside

LEAH S. MARCUS*

Since classical times, pastoral as a literary form has characteristically used distance in terms of social class and geography as a way of offering political critique. The word *pastoral* will be used here in a very broad sense to refer to literature in any genre that employs rural landscape and/or rural people to comment on non-rural subjects: simple shepherds or goatherds poetise, in a language that may bear little resemblance to actual rural speech, of matters far beyond their ken, but of interest to a city or court élite. In the May Eclogue of Spenser's *Shepherds Calendar* (published 1579), for example, two shepherds, Piers and Palinode, represent, according to the Argument of the poem, a Protestant and a Catholic priest who debate issues of ecclesiastical governance through their contrasting attitudes towards country May-day revelry; while appearing on the surface to be a mere disagreement about the value of traditional pastimes, the eclogue engages some of the most hotly contested issues within Elizabethan church and state, taking Archbishop Grindal's side against both the Catholics and the less stringently anti-ceremonial Anglicans, including, at least implicitly, Queen Elizabeth herself.

In the early Stuart period, pastoral was much more closely associated as a device for political argument with the monarch's own policy initiatives. James I wrote pastoral verses designed to promote key programmes; both James and Charles I attempted in various ways to 'repastoralise' England by advocating a return to rural merriment of the kind commended by Spenser's shepherd

The Politics of Mirth: Jonson, Herrick, Marvell, Milton and the Defense of Old Holiday Pastimes (Chicago and London, 1986), p. 221. © The University of Chicago. All rights reserved.

Palinode. Unlike earlier versions of the form, Stuart pastoral was designed to reduce the distance between the urban and the rural. By remaking the court in the image of an idealised countryside, or by imaginatively recasting the countryside itself in terms of an idealised pastoral image, early Stuart monarchs sought to promulgate a vision of the nation untroubled by evils of modernisation – by the movement of population to London that crowded the city while leaving at least some rural areas in decay, and by a new commercialisation of rural life that threatened a time-honoured post-feudal agrarian image of 'Merry England'.

That is not to say that all pastoral literature produced during the early Stuart period needs to be read as a reflection of royal policy: writers felt free to rearrange the standard elements of the form to create their own commentary on the state of the nation. Nevertheless, the Stuart image of an idealised countryside, dotted with the prosperous seats of a loyal gentry and aristocracy and with happy villages whose loyal inhabitants cultivate the land and their holiday pastimes with equal energy, was an image that increasingly had to be contended with as the seventeenth century progressed, and that exerted a decided ideological pull upon pastoral as a whole.

In *The Art of Describing*, Svetlana Alpers has noted a key difference between two ways of constructing landscape. Seventeenth-century Dutch landscape painting was cartographic in impulse: as in Rembrandt's *The Goldweigher's Field* (Figure 6.1), it 'mapped' and pictured fields, towns, churches, country villas, in a way that paid evenhanded tribute to all the elements there to be described, without turning any one feature into a focal point that controlled the way other elements could be perceived. In Rubens's *Landscape with Het Steen* (Figure 6.2), by contrast, landscape has become seigneurial: the painting is subtly dominated by a country house that had been purchased by Rubens himself and that provides the 'perspective' from which the rest of the landscape is viewed.[1] English literary pastoral makes use of a similar set of discriminations that point to differing patterns of political engagement. The Stuart genre of country house poem (as represented by Ben Jonson's 'To Penshurst') is a pastoral form[2] derived from the classical epigram but also closely tied to a set of Jacobean and Caroline initiatives for reversing the growth of London and increasing the prosperity of the countryside. Seventeenth-century country house poems commonly express harsh criticism of the court, but they are

Figure 6.1   Rembrandt: The Goldweigher's Field

Figure 6.2   Rubens: Landscape with Het Steen

nevertheless a form closely tied to the court. Insofar as they link the rural landscape both with the domination of a 'great house' and with the more distant authority of the king, country house poems may be regarded as seigneurial in Alpers's sense. They present an idealised landscape dominated by a single controlling perspective: the interests of the monarch, the landowner, and the poet himself are aligned. But there are other depictions of rural life during the period that correspond more to Alpers's character- isation of standard Dutch landscape painting. In Drayton's *Poly- Olbion* and other quasi-Elizabethan works by poets usually cate- gorised as seventeenth-century Spenserians, the rural landscape is not dominated by a single reference point, but presented in a broader, cartographic perspective dotted by villages, towns, rivers, rural estates, and nymph-crowned mounts, all of them competing equally for the reader's attention. In these poems, which may usefully be considered under the rubric of pastoral, royal authority is conspicuous by its absence: the landscape, through its decen- tralised configuration, subtly undermines the Stuart vision of an England repastoralised from the court through the promulgation of Stuart policies towards the countryside.[3]

Along with its praise of the country house, early seventeenth- century pastoral frequently also advocates rural holiday pastimes and superstitions – Maying, wakes, wassails, a wide array of folk beliefs about fairies, magic, and the like. Here again, a seemingly neutral set of literary motifs often carries a strong political charge, for the eruption of poems in praise of the simple festivities of a 'Merry England' past can be closely correlated with James and Charles I's promulgation of the *Book of Sports* – a royal declaration designed to preserve and reintroduce the old holiday customs in a benign and 'harmless' form as a bulwark against rural unrest and rioting, against the growing commercialisation of the countryside, and (not least) against puritan and judicial condemnation of the old pastimes as 'disorders'. In Spenser's May Eclogue, May-day customs are condemned as a symbol of ecclesiastical custom, but in Stuart pastoral, they are regularly idealised and promoted as a sign of affection for the king and the Anglican Church. That does not mean that every pastoral featuring peasants on holiday can be read as a defence of James or Charles I. As with country house poetry, pastoral of the 'Merry England' type can take on a variety of political colourations, depending on the way the old sports are portrayed, the larger forces with which they are aligned, and their ultimate influence as a force for good or evil within the pastoral world in which they appear. Stuart pastoral is rarely ideologically simple, despite its heavy ideological freight: by evoking the Stuart motifs, poets and playwrights could support royal policy, display its contradictions and limitations, or even reject the court as a source of revitalisation for the countryside.

The primary artistic medium by which Stuart policy was promulgated to the court and nation was the court masque, an extravaganza of music, dancing, lights, allegorical personages, and elaborate scenic tableaux frequently centring on important royal initiatives of the preceding year. Stuart masques from about 1614 onward frequently culminate in pastoral landscape, a vision of the countryside viewed through the frame of the proscenium arch, and from the perspective of the king and court. Such landscapes sometimes strive for the appearance of topographic verisimilitude, but they are charged with energies from elsewhere. As Stephen Orgel has suggested, idealised visions of a rural world restored become increasingly prominent in the masque as efforts to extend royal power into the countryside become more central to government policy.[4] During the early Stuart period, particularly from 1614 onward, there were no fewer than nine royal proclamations ordering the gentry and aristocracy (who tended to gravitate towards London and the court) to 'get them to the country', return to their rural estates to 'keep hospitality', suppress insurrections and riots against enclosure, and generally keep the king's peace. Several Stuart masques recapitulate the pattern advocated in the proclamations. In *The Golden Age Restored* (performed January 1615) Pallas shows English nobles the idealised countryside which is their proper realm and admonishes them:

> Behold you here
> What Jove hath built to be your sphere;
> You hither must retire.
> And as his bounty gives you cause,
> Be ready still without your pause
> To show the world your fire.[5]

By leaving the corruptions of London and the court, the nobles will cause the virtues associated with James I (Jove)'s Golden Age to take root and grow 'forever' in the countryside. They will serve as conduits for royal authority, their 'fire' inspired by Jove, but spread out to energise the surrounding territory with devotion for the king. *The Vision of Delight* (performed January 1617) follows a similar pattern – English courtiers are shown the hollow futility of their frantic search for 'novelties' in London and at court, and transported out to the rural landscape, where their civilised arts merge inseparably with nature so that the seeming opposites of court and country become a new synthesis inspired by the power of the king. An allegorical personage named Wonder asks, 'Grows / The wealth of nature here, or art?' The court is grafted upon the countryside.

Not content to leave the task of persuasion to his proclamations and masques at court, James I, who liked to think of himself as a 'bard' unto his people, wrote a Horatian Elegy of his own to further his programme for renewing the countryside. In one manuscript version, this poem is entitled 'An Elegy written by the King concerning his counsel for Ladies & Gentlemen to Depart the City of London according to his Majesty's Proclamation'. The poem's probable date of composition is in the early 1620s; it may have been written to accompany James's 1622 renewal of earlier proclamations to the same effect. Like the masques, James I's 'Elegy' sets the court against the court: Whitehall's 'visors, masks and plays', its 'debauched' hazards to virtue, are disparaged; more wholesome country arts are offered as substitutes for the vice-ridden practices of the court. Even good household economics was part of the king's incentive to get the upper classes back to rural life. He admonishes the nobles, 'The country is your orb and proper sphere. / There your revenues rise; bestow them there.'[6]

We do not know the date of James I's poem and it did not appear in print. Nevertheless, it circulated widely in manuscript and had imitators. Richard Fanshawe, the translator of Guarini's *Il Pastor Fido*, renewed James's anti-court rhetoric in his Caroline 'Ode upon Occasion of His Majesty's Proclamation in the Year 1630, Commanding the Gentry to Reside upon Their Estates in the Country'. The poem praises English peace, chides the upper classes for enclosing themselves in the 'walled town' of London as though under siege, and orders them to spread their 'quickening power' back through the countryside, where they will find (in what by now was a common rhetoric strategy) all the necessities of court life inscribed upon the wholesome natural landscape:

all
The commonwealth of flowers in its pride

Behold you shall.
The lily (queen), the (royal) rose,
The gillyflower (prince of the blood),
The (courtier) tulip (gay in clothes),
    The (regal) bud,
The violet (purple senator) –
How they do mock the pomp of state,
And all that at the surly door
    Of great ones wait.[7]

Fanshawe's ode sounds remarkably like a poem of hostility to the court. It is, instead, a poem openly designed to further Stuart policy. Annabel Patterson has suggested that there may be an element of irony in its depiction of rural peace at a time when many in England were anxious to go to war in defence of Protestant interests abroad,[8] but if so, the irony is muted: the extent to which it was read as ironic by Fanshawe's contemporaries would depend on the degree to which they sympathised with Charles I's determined isolationism during the Thirty Years' War.

Even Thomas Randolph's rakish 'Ode to Mr Anthony Stafford to Hasten Him into the Country' fits the Stuart pastoral pattern of the court against the court. Randolph, who also wrote the court pastoral *Amyntas*, urges his friend to abandon the City (in obedience to the royal proclamations) and return with him to country 'liberties' – the two will watch the country lasses make hay, steal a few kisses, listen to choirs of birds, and go fowling: 'For to my Muse, if not to me, / I'm sure all game is free; / Heaven, earth, are all but parts of her great royalty'.[9] Randolph's Muse is 'free'. At least implicitly, there is an element of competition between the royalty of his rakish muse and the chaster royalty of King Charles: except in verse, the poet could not claim the same freedom as the king to hunt wherever he liked, nor were the poem's fashionable elements of sexual libertinism officially countenanced by the king. But what Randolph expects to discover out in the countryside is a liberty modelled on courtly pleasures and pastimes. Yet once more in seventeenth-century pastoral, the court is inscribed on the countryside.

The same rhetorical inversions shape country house poetry of the period. The form goes back to Horace and Martial, but the first seventeenth-century English country house poem was, in all likelihood, written by a woman, Aemilia Lanier, whose *Salve Deus*

Rex Judaeorum (published in 1611) includes 'The Description of Cookham', honouring the Dowager Countess of Cumberland and her estate.[10] However, it was not Lanier's poem, but Ben Jonson's 'To Penshurst' (written in or before 1612) that set the form for Stuart country house poetry, which is often closely tied to royal policy as promulgated through entertainments at court. In Jonson's masque *The Golden Age Restored,* aristocrats object to returning to the countryside in accordance with the royal proclamation because there they will not be able to live in the same 'state' and glorious visibility that they have at court. They are promised that a 'train' of poets will be enlisted to praise their country virtues. What Jonson seems to be doing in this masque is calling for the creation of the genre of the country house poem: 'To Penshurst' and his related verse epistle 'To Sir Robert Wroth' had in all likelihood been written only shortly before. Father Ben's country house poems were imitated by his poetic 'Sons', who followed but also altered the Jonsonian pattern. What we discover in moving from Jonson's poems to those of succeeding generations is an increasing 'colonisation' of the country house by the court. From its beginnings, the country house poem redeemed courtly arts by planting them in a more wholesome soil: the court became its own best self by fusing imperceptibly with its opposite. But over time, the genre's careful balance between court art and country 'nature' tipped more and more towards the court; the rural estate was increasingly remade in the image of arts at Whitehall. Simultaneously, the country house itself came unmoored from surrounding landscape, from its rootedness in a larger rural topography. It is perhaps worth noting that, despite their advocacy of traditional rural life, the Stuart monarchs were deeply involved in the enclosure movement: as we pass from the work of Jonson to that of his 'Sons', we find that country house poetry more and more 'enclosed' the estates it celebrated, rather than making them the centre for interactions with the surrounding countryside. The rural estate became less a site for the fusion of court and country than an island of courtliness cut off from the very structures on which, at least in James I's interpretation, its economic wellbeing depended.

As Don Wayne has shown, Jonson's 'To Penshurst' is a poem that mediates in complex ways between Nature and Culture with the 'walls' of the estate 'marking an ideological boundary which the poem is attempting to establish and yet to hide.'[11] The landscape outside the walls – the Mount, the copse, the pastures, and the river – is a 'cultured Nature' shaped by the history and achievements of the Sidney family; the house and gardens within the walls are the locus of a 'natural Culture' – a form of culture that is itself the bountiful provision of nature and by which other great houses ('proud, ambitious heaps' built to 'envious show') are defined as deviant.[12] This set of negotiations is very close to the amalgamation of court and country worked out in Jonson's masques in celebration of the royal proclamations: the Sidney estate is a place where the opposites encounter one another and achieve some kind of fusion. King James, the poet assures us, had visited the estate, as had the poet himself, and found it to func-tion, even in its owners' absence, just as royal policy towards the countryside specified that such great houses should:

> There's nothing I can wish, for which I stay.
>   That found King James, when hunting late this way
> With his brave son, the Prince, they saw thy fires
>   Shine bright on every hearth as the desires
> Of thy Penates had been set on flame
>   To entertain them; or the country came,
> With all their zeal, to warm their welcome here.
>   What (great, I will not say, but) sudden cheer
> Didst thou then make them!

Jonson's 'or' is characteristically ambiguous: his lines suggest at least two contradictory interpretations of the warm fires of Penshurst. If 'or' is taken as offering alternative possibilities, Jonson's lines mean *either* that the household gods burned with zeal to entertain the king *or* that country folk had assembled to welcome him. But the lines can be read instead as a temporal sequence: the fires blazed first, 'or [ere]' the country folks could assemble to add their 'zeal'. Is the welcome offered by the estate, then, a substitution for the devotion of the countryside, or a prelude to it? The relationship between court and country that these lines refuse to specify is precisely the nexus that Stuart policy left ambiguous. Nevertheless, Jonson's poem celebrates the mode of life that royal policy aimed to restore. 'To Penshurst' is anti-court in its deliberate avoidance of excess and ostentation, but *of* the court in its praise for an upper-class family devoted to the virtues of rural life. Penshurst can serve as a fit dwelling for the king; it is also at least potentially – depending, we may suppose, on the king's capacity and willingness to make use of it –

a place where new 'warmth' is generated between the monarch and the 'country'. The alacrity for service fostered by nearby farmers, who bring fruit, cheese and marriageable daughters as offerings to the lord and lady of Penshurst, is just the type of country devotion that James and his advisers found wanting in many rural parts, and hoped to increase by restoring the upper classes to their places of origin. Contemporaries commented that a gentleman's hospitality towards all comers increased his reputation and authority in the neighbourhood. Great 'hospitality' was a sign of great power. The Stuart hope was that such 'honour' for the local magnate could be channelled into devotion for the king. The estate at Penshurst provides the necessary link.

'To Sir Robert Wroth,' which immediately follows 'To Penshurst' in Jonson's *The Forest* and was composed sometime between 1606 and Wroth's death in 1614, offers a far sterner attack upon the city, the court and the 'short bravery' of its wastrel pastimes. But the poem follows the 'court' strategy of planting aristocratic pastimes in the countryside, so that they can be cured of vice and the country rendered less inhospitable towards royal power. Wroth absents himself from masques of 'state', but Comus, the god of revelry, 'puts in' at Wroth's hall to offer 'new delights'. The 'rout of rural folk come thronging in' and, as at Penshurst, James I himself is also a visitor. Jonson addresses Wroth,

> if thou list the night in watch to break,
> Abed canst hear the loud stag speak
> In spring oft roused for thy master's sport,
> Who, for it, makes thy house his court.

David Norbrook has pointed out that Wroth had close connections with the royal forests; Wroth's 'master' James was in fact a frequent guest.[13] Even more obviously than in the case of Penshurst, the anti-court sentiment surrounding Wroth in his simple country 'retirement' is recast as the expression of a courtly ideal. Out amidst Wroth's meadows and 'copses green' is James I's Golden Age 'Restored'.

Thomas Carew wrote two country house poems, 'To Saxham' (probably dating from the late 1620s), and 'To My Friend G.N. from Wrest' (probably written in 1639), both consciously and obviously modelled upon 'To Penshurst'. Although the two poems were written years apart and under very different circumstances, both depart from the Jonsonian paradigm (and its parallel in

James I's own verse) in that the estate is sharply separated from a surrounding landscape. Saxham belonged to the courtier Sir John Crofts; it was a favourite stopping place for Charles I and his court on their way to the races at Newmarket. The poem was very likely written well before Carew himself finally gained an official place in the royal household in 1630. In Carew's poem, Saxham is an island of warmth and hospitality amidst winter weather so severe that the grounds are 'locked' from the poet's eyes. While the neighbouring estates suffer extreme want, Saxham is miraculously favoured. It has within its doors a microcosmic round of seasons that is impervious to extremes outside:

> Yet, Saxham, thou within thy gate
> Art of thyself so delicate,
> So full of native sweets that bless
> Thy roof with inward happiness,
> As neither from nor to thy store
> Winter takes aught, or spring adds more.[14]

The house is directly supplied by nature and the heavens, without the intervening presence of humankind and the negotiation of country loyalties that was such an interesting feature of 'To Penshurst'. Saxham is its own countryside; the world without the walls matters only insofar as it is magnetically drawn to the estate to become part of it. All else is undifferentiated dearth.

In 'To My Friend G.N. from Wrest', the estate (owned by Henry de Grey, Earl of Kent)[15] is more literally an island than Saxham, in that it is surrounded by an elaborate moat whose 'double crystal heaven' marks out, once again, a magical self-enclosed space of peace and plenty whose economic underpinnings are mystified. Outside the estate there is winter, but in this case the 'bad weather' is political rather than meteorological. The poet has retreated to Wrest after the 'raging storms' of the First Bishops' War in 1639, perhaps with others who had fought, like Carew, on the king's side: the first person pronoun in the poem is always plural. As Michael Parker has shown, Carew's celebration of the estate is shaped like Carew's own court masque, *Coelum Britannicum* (performed Shrovetide, 1634),[16] but in its depiction of sharp contrast between a Stuart dream of pastoral life and the ravagement of war it is even closer to William Davenant's *Salmacida Spolia* (performed January 1640), the last of the Stuart 'spectacles of state'. Carew's country house translates the court masque from a temporal sequence into a set of spatial relationships. The political and military discord of the antimasque is banished to the world outside the charmed enclosure of Wrest; within it we find the usual transmutation of court arts into country virtue and the 'flowery birth' of a perfected nature; the boundary moat is Wrest's empyrean, equivalent to the final vision in the court masque that characteristically links the worlds of the main masque with the heavens. Jonson's poem to Wroth alluded to the performance of a masque at Wroth's estate; in 'To My Friend G.N. from Wrest', the rural estate has *become* a masque whose natural elements are sometimes 'written' upon its grounds by the assembled company in much the way that a masque-writer or designer would order the landscape of a masque. Carew asserts, 'with various trees we fringe the water's brink'; and (with obvious reference to the masque, in which courtiers often played the roles of emblematic figures), 'We offer not in emblems to the eyes, / But to the taste'. Wrest is not art and nature fused, but nature transformed into a conscious artistic overlay to achieve something equivalent to the masque's striking visual effects. In Carew's country house poems, we are considerably further from the mapping impulse than we were in Jonson's. The country estate becomes an outpost of the court, a microcosm of the 'magic' of arts at Whitehall. And yet, in Carew's poems, the ordering of space can only with difficulty be termed seigneurial in that the actual owners are all but effaced, not even so much as named. The hidden perspective from which Saxham and Wrest are interpreted is that of King Charles himself and his royal arts at court.

Lovelace's 'Amyntor's Grove' takes the isolating consolidation we have noted in Carew to its logical endpoint: the country house in Lovelace's poem is not only a mirror of the court, it is, amidst the ravages of the Civil War, the only court left. Amyntor's is the most 'natural' house of all in that it is figured forth as a grove; yet it is also the most artificial, in that the grove turns out to be a series of walls hung with paintings. Outside and inside are indistinguishable. The poem was probably written in 1648 – that perilous year for Charles I. The 'Amyntor' of the poem was almost certainly Endymion Porter, friend of poets, who had been responsible for the acquisition of much of Charles I's celebrated collection of art. Porter's country house was like a miniature Whitehall in that it displayed his own smaller art collection put together in the course of his purchases for the king. In Lovelace's poem, Endymion Porter's paintings, displayed on the walls of his country house, define the precincts of a sacred grove which serves as a setting for a Royalist ritual of Bacchanalian transcendence. Although the king's art collection at Whitehall was already threatened with dispersal, Porter's 'grove' is intact, graced with a noble 'stand / Of Titian, Raphael, Giorgione' which recall the splendid canvasses displayed at court. Within the 'embroidered' walls of Porter's house metamorphosed to landscape, the company deck themselves with 'vine, / The poppy, and the eglantine,' drink the 'oriental bowl', kindle a 'sacrifice' of tobacco, amber and thyme which 'through our earthen conduits soar / Higher than altars fumed before'.[17] The ritual before the 'sacred flame' removes its participants from the harsh realities of the Royalist situation in 1648 and takes them back to a solemn-festive paganism like that cultivated in court entertainments and in pre-war Caroline poetry. By retreating to the countryside, they recapture vestiges of the lost court.

Endymion Porter's country house is its own landscape within the walls. What might look from outside like the political and economic 'evil' of enclosure – a severing of the estate from its matrix of communal obligations – is, viewed from within, the achievement of a new, more intimate mode of aristocratic life. In the enclosed aestheticism of this poem we are not far from Joseph Addison's later comment that 'A man might make a pretty landscape of his own possessions', except that Porter's 'private' estate has not quite yet become private. Lovelace's poem gains a measure of poignancy from its recapitulative preservation of an almost vanished 'public' pattern. Now, in wartime, the court is found only in the country.

Not all seventeenth-century country house poetry can be so closely identified with the court: Andrew Marvell's 'Upon Appleton House: To My Lord Fairfax' is addressed to a former parliamentary general during the Interregnum, and playfully adapts the Stuart motifs to an estate that proves markedly inhospitable to their courtly connotations. In Marvell's poem, the house and its surrounding gardens behave in proper seigneurial fashion, obediently shaping themselves in accordance with the presence of their lord. But Nun Appleton's more distant holdings are less tractable: the meadows become the scene for a bloody 'masque' of violence; the pastoral grove is not (as in Lovelace's 'Amyntor's Grove') a viable retreat from the perils of the Civil War, but a place in which to view the decay and fall of the noble 'oak' of kingship. Marvell places Fairfax's estate within a vast, various topography of hostile, neutral and friendly forces. The poem itself, in marked contrast to its predecessors in the genre, is also rambling and vast, much closer to the cartographic model for landscape as represented in neo-Spenserian poems like Drayton's *Poly-Olbion* than to the seigneurial model we have traced in Jonson and his 'Sons'. In 'Upon Appleton House', the aestheticised enclosure of the Stuart country house poem is imitated, mocked, and broken open.[18]

Just as they encouraged the deurbanisation of England, the Stuart monarchs also encouraged the revival of rural holiday pastimes. Through the *Book of Sports*, promulgated in 1618 and reissued in 1633, they specified 'for our good people's lawful recreation, our pleasure likewise is, that after the end of divine service, our good people be not disturbed, letted, or discouraged from any lawful recreation; such as dancing, either men or women, archery for men, leaping, vaulting, or any other such harmless recreations, nor from having of May-games, Whitson Ales, and morrisdances, and the setting up of maypoles and other sports therewith used, so as the same be had in due and convenient time, without impediment or neglect of divine service.[19] *The Book of Sports* was designed to buttress another rural institution which, like the country estate, was declining in some areas of the country – the traditional Anglican parish, still (ideally at least) marked as it had been in late medieval times by a round of seasonal pastimes that cemented community and loyalty to the church. As we have seen, in Spenser's May Eclogue, the advocacy of a religion permitting May-games and merriment was strongly associated with the 'corruptions' of Catholicism; during the Stuart period, such advocacy became instead a mark of loyalty to the monarch and the *Book of Sports*. An evocation through pastoral of the benignity of 'honest pleasures and recreations, which have ever been peculiar to this nation' is a regular feature of court masques, along with a banishment of more irregular forms of mirth; as with the motif of return to the countryside, defence of the *Book of Sports* began at court and spread outward through tracts and poems to the nations.

The anonymous *Pasquil's Palinodia* (printed London 1619) is perhaps the earliest of these: it associates the preservation of traditional pastimes with an idyllic past in which England was blessedly at peace, free of the communal discord created (in Pasquil's view) by City commercialism and by legal and religious opposition to the games:

> Then reigned plain honest meaning and good will.
> And neighbors took up points of difference,

In common law the Commons had no skill,
And public feasts were courts of conscience.

  . . . .

The lords of castles, manors, towns, and towers
Rejoiced when they beheld the farmers flourish,
And would come down unto the summer-bowers
To see the country gallants dance the morris,

  . . . .

But since the summer-poles were overthrown,
And all good sports and merriments decayed,
How times and men are changed, so well is known
It were but labour lost if more were said.

(Sig. B3)

Such sentiments about the 'good old days of Merry England' are so commonplace that it is hard for us to think of them as specifically Stuart and Anglican. But during the early seventeenth century they were promulgated with particular zeal by traditionalist Anglican churchmen. Bishop Richard Corbett's 'Proper New Ballad, Intitled The Fairies' Farewell, or God a Mercy Will' (probably written during the early 1620s) laments the decline of the late medieval fairies, country mirth, and pastoral 'rings and roundelays' as a result of the economic inroads of puritanism.[20] Robert Herrick's *Hesperides* (published London 1648), similarly, defends the *Book of Sports* by evoking an England of pastoral innocence, in which lads and lasses play at their rural pastimes. Herrick himself held a good ecclesiastical living in Devon; his volume is dedicated to Prince Charles (the future Charles II) and promises the reader in its 'Argument',

> I sing of brooks, of blossoms, birds, and bowers,
> Of April, May, of June and July-flowers.
> I sing of May-poles, hock-carts, wassails, wakes,
> Of bridegrooms, brides, and of their bridal cakes.[21]

Numerous poems in the collection celebrate the traditional customs enumerated in the 'Argument'. Most notably, 'Corinna's Going a Maying' contains a probable reference to the *Book of Sports*: the poet invites Corinna to join in a traditional maying celebration – to go out to the woods to gather boughs of whitethorn and transform the village streets into an extension of the forest and fields:

> Can such delights be in the street
> And open fields, and we not see't?
> Come, we'll abroad, and let's obey
> The Proclamation made for May;
> And sin no more, as we have done, by staying;
> But my Corinna, come, let's go a maying.

The 'Proclamation made for May' would readily have been identified by Herrick's contemporaries as the Stuart *Book of Sports*. While puritan opponents of the old communal pastimes branded participation in them as 'sin' (especially on Sundays or religious holidays), for Herrick the 'sin' would instead be to omit the rites of May in the face of royal and ecclesiastical encouragement. The final stanza of the poem, with its bitter-sweet message of *carpe diem* in the face of eventual decay and 'endless night', does not cancel out the poem's Stuart and Anglican resonances, but intensifies them by echoing the *carpe diem* motif of the Anglican May-day liturgy itself.[22]

Particularly during the 1630s and early 40s, Laudian priests sometimes went out of their way to revive the traditional customs. Thomas Laurence, George Herbert's successor at Bemerton, 'caused a May pole to be set up at his door and also in the same place a bowling green and kitling alley, it being adjoining to the churchyard, wherein every Sabbath day here was dancing, bowling, and kitling, and himself to countenance it'. Laurence himself paid the fiddlers and commended parish dancing as 'very fit for recreation'.[23] In much the same way, Herrick's poems of country festivity invite the reader's participation in the embattled pastimes. The 'Argument' invites us to think of the whole collection as an enchanted image of England repastoralised, a *Hesperides* derived from the Garden of Hesperus, a mythological place of retreat Herrick associates with Prince Charles and with other members of the royal family in his dedicatory epistle to the volume.

That is not to say that Herrick or any of the other literary defenders of the *Book of Sports* was simple-minded in his loyalty. Like the court masques that it in some ways resembles, *Hesperides* is simultaneously celebration and critique of royal policy. Although some of its individual poems were written decades earlier, the collection as a whole was published under Herrick's close supervision in 1648, by which time the Stuart and Anglican 'Merry England' ideal had been extinguished by parliamentary ordinances banning the old customs, by which time the Stuart cause was close to final defeat. Part of the fascination of *Hesperides* comes from its simultaneous invitation to the old pastimes and undercutting of the vision of England they were designed to promote. Some of the poems of country festivity, like 'The Wassail' and 'To Meadows', are more lament for the rupture of traditional patterns of festivity than advocacy of such forms in the present. Still other poems demystify the old customs even while arguing for their continuance. In 'The Hock-cart or Harvest Home: To the Right Honourable Mildmay, Earl of Westmoreland', Herrick calls upon the lord and his rural labourers to join in the celebration of a traditional harvest home, with decorated hock-cart, general feasting and much merriment. But the final lines of the poem admonish the rustics that the primary function of their revelry today is to fit them for renewed labour on the morrow:

> And, you must know, your Lord's word's true:
> Feed him you must, whose food fills you.
> And that this pleasure is like rain,
> Not sent ye for to drown your pain,
> But for to make it spring again.

As Raymond Williams has noted, Stuart pastoral generally over-looks or mystifies the harsh realities of rural labour. In Herrick's poem, by contrast, the 'pain' of farm work is allowed to enter the poem directly, made part of an equivocal system of reciprocity: does the pain-drowning pleasure make the pain 'spring' again, or bring on 'spring' the season and its renewal through new growth?[24] Herrick's verses invite both readings simultaneously. Other poems of *Hesperides* offer similar 'reality checks' to the 'Merry England' ideal by recording the progress of the Civil War, at least obliquely critiquing the king's leadership through a series of epigrams on proper royal leadership, and even in one or two cases celebrating relatives of Herrick who participated in city and parliamentary initiatives against Charles I.[25] The visual image of England left by the collection as a whole is of a golden Stuart landscape of pastoral mirth, but a landscape overshadowed by dark, implacable clouds.

Some of the seventeenth-century advocates of the *Book of Sports*, as well as more recent historians who have described the contro-versy surrounding it, saw its effect on the nation as profoundly polarising: the Stuart kings became associated in the public mind with a conservative agenda for the reimposition of immediately post-feudal communal patterns of work, play and worship, while those who opposed the old pastimes on religious or economic grounds became, perforce, increasingly alienated from the court. This bipolar model may accurately describe two extreme ends of a seventeenth-century spectrum of opinion, but it fails to capture a vast intermediate range. Some of the most interesting pastoral of the early Stuart period cuts across the polarities in highly creative ways. Milton's *Comus*, for example, can easily be regarded as a strongly pro-sport document if one considers the occasion of its performance (the installation of John, Earl of Bridgewater, as Lord President of the Council of Wales [a royal prerogative court] on the eve of Michaelmas 1634) and its many interpretive links with court masques like Ben Jonson's *Pleasure Reconciled to Virtue*, which was performed in January 1618 to celebrate James I's initial promulgation of the *Book of Sports*, and Thomas Carew's *Coelum Britannicum*, which, among other things, took note of Charles I's renewal of the *Book of Sports* in 1633.[26] But it is not precisely the standard Stuart landscape of rural jollity that Milton's Lady encounters as she traverses the Forest of Dean on her way to Ludlow Castle. Rather, she is accosted by the enchanter Comus, whose call to revelry hauntingly echoes Stuart motifs like the call for holiday merriment, the May-day *carpe diem* as we have seen it articulated in Herrick's 'Corinna's Going a Maying', and even perhaps the most recent masque performed at court. In Carew's *Coelum Britannicum*, danced only a few months before *Comus* by (among others) the same sons of the Earl of Bridgewater who were to perform in *Comus*, Jove (Charles I) is said to be 'tempering purer fire' to brighten and refine the heavens; in Milton's masque, the enchanter Comus associates himself with just such 'purer fire' shortly before his attempted seduction of the Lady. The 'wandering morris' and 'merry wakes and pastimes' to which he invites his retinue eerily echo the pastimes encouraged by the royal *Book of Sports*, which had been reissued the previous year. If Milton's masque is to be regarded as a defence of the *Book of Sports*, then it is a defence hedged by circumspection. Before the Earl of Bridgewater's children can safely join in the wholesome holiday revelry at Ludlow, they must demonstrate their ability to escape its sinister double at Comus's court in the forest. In Milton's Ludlow masque, as in the tainted grove of Marvell's 'Upon Appleton House', motifs suggesting the court and its pastimes are negativised and thrust out of alignment with the poet's praise of a lord, his family and his noble seat. Milton's masque may celebrate traditional pastimes, but only insofar as they are divorced from their close association with the Stuart court.

In public drama of the period, similarly, the Stuart idealisation of the countryside is both invoked and interrogated. Because of space limitations, one play will have to stand in the present discussion for many. *The Witch of Edmonton*, attributed on its 1658 title page to 'William Rowley, Thomas Dekker, John Ford, Etc.', is a particularly interesting example of the numerous early seventeenth-century devil plays that probe into a hypothetical connection between old holiday customs and demonism. Just such a connection was repeatedly asserted by puritan and judicial opponents of the *Book of Sports*, some of whom viewed the old customs as the work of the devil. Like Milton's *Comus*, *The Witch of Edmonton*, despite its composite authorship, is clearly designed to speak to the controversy surrounding traditional pastimes, but cannot be read as either advocacy or condemnation of the Stuart position. The play was performed at court in December 1621, shortly before James I issued the 1622 version of his oft-repeated proclamation ordering nobles and gentry about London to return to their country estates. The Stuart kings advocated this retreat at least in part (as James I articulated it), to save chaste wives and daughters from the rapacious sexual licence of the court; James's 'Elegy', which may have been written at about the same time as the play, made a special point of urging women back into the country to preserve both their chastity and their husbands' fortunes. But in *The Witch of Edmonton*, James's sharp distinction between court vice and country virtue is erased. A country estate near Edmonton is made the scene for Sir Arthur Clarington's debauchery of his serving-maid Winnifride, who then enters into an ill-fated marriage with the bigamist Frank Thorney. The play seems to go out of its way to assert that the vices of the court and city are equally to be encountered in the countryside. Bucolic Edmonton has its 'roaring boys' and predatory upper-class rakes, just like London and the court, and the court, conversely, has its share of witches, just like the country. In some of its plot elements *The Witch of Edmonton* seems to support the Stuart contention that the breakdown of old communal patterns of hospitality had contributed to rural decay. Mother Sawyer, the title character, was based on a notorious witch of the same name executed in April 1621; in the play she is a curiously sympathetic figure, attributing her fall into witchcraft to the alienating miserliness of the townsfolk, who refuse her even a few sticks for fuel and systematically exclude her from the tight-knit village community. But the play does not support either the Stuart contention that traditional rural pastimes could become a conduit for fertility and restored community or the puritan contention that they were instruments of the devil. Old Carter, a rich and hospitable yeoman, is highly valued for his beneficence, but it brings him more harm than good: his daughter is murdered at least in part as a result of his old-fashioned generosity towards Frank Thorney and the community. Cuddy, the clown figure, plans a morris dance at which he is to perform the coveted role of hobby-horse. He unwittingly enlists the aid of Dog, Mother Sawyer's familiar, thus bringing to life contemporary puritan assertions that May games and morris dancing were vehicles of the devil. But the morris as played by Dog brings neither good nor evil; certainly it fails to cement community according to the Stuart formula, since as it comes to a close two of its onlookers are falsely arrested for murder and Cuddy is left commenting, 'This news of murder has slain the morris.'[27] At the end of the play Mother Sawyer is hanged, and her familiar, Dog, has resolved to ply his demonic wares in the city. To the extent that the court is written on the countryside in *The Witch of Edmonton*, it is the source of cultivated vices like Sir Arthur Clarington's debauchery. Instead of an idealised court being written on the countryside, at the end of this interesting play the countryside (in the person of Dog) will write itself on the court, and not to the benefit of the latter. *The Witch of Edmonton* repeatedly employs Stuart themes to undo the Stuart idealisation of the countryside and to expose the oversimplicity of the standard Stuart dichotomy between urban vice and pastoral virtue.

A generation ago, reading early seventeenth-century pastoral in terms of its political implications would have been anathema to most literary critics: to attach literature to history was somehow, inevitably, to subject it to history. As the present essay has suggested, however, to examine pastoral motifs in terms of Stuart policy initiatives is not so much to chart the subservience of the former to the latter as to recognise the intertwined complexity of both. Even as they replicated the broad outlines of significant Stuart initiatives towards the countryside, poets and dramatists of the period recast and realigned the issues in nearly as many ways as there were writers. Pastoral as a literary form may have been more closely tied to royal policy than it had been under Elizabeth or would be later in the century, but what it offered writers was less a fixed ideological position than a supple language of exploration, analysis and contestation.

7. Chivalry and Political Culture in Caroline England

J.S.A. ADAMSON

Amid the controversies surrounding the culture of the early Stuart court there has, at least, been general agreement that the accession of Charles I marked a major change in the cultural forms by which monarchy was represented. A new, classicising, and cosmopolitan aesthetic profoundly affected painting, architecture, and literary forms from the verse lyric to the masque.[1] In few spheres was the change more marked than in the culture of chivalry in Caroline England. The tournament, which had been under Elizabeth and James among the principal and costliest occasions of courtly display, came to an end on Charles's accession.[2] Triumphal entries into the city – occasions when the monarch presented himself in heroic guise as Renaissance *triumphator* – were rarely staged by the new king.[3] In contrast to the chivalric epics of the Elizabethan age, the poets of the Caroline court favoured short (and essentially classical) lyric forms; there was no 'epic poetry' of the Caroline court; and the already moribund Spenserian tradition of the chivalric epic was abandoned.

Few juxtapositions epitomise the contrast between the mid-Jacobean and mid-Caroline court cultures more clearly than that between Robert Peake's equestrian portrait of Henry, Prince of Wales (*circa* 1610) and Van Dyck's great equestrian portrait of Charles I (*c.*1638) (Figures 7.1 and 7.2.) The one represents Prince Henry as the hero of the tilt and tournament, the other depicts his brother King Charles as classical *imperator*. Both pictures have been taken to be 'chivalric' images: they ennoble the martial qualities and prowess of their subjects. But they do so by utilising very different points of reference. Peake defines the martial virtue of his subject by means of a repertory of allusion to the chivalric tournament: the accoutrements of the knight on his way to the

161

Figure 7.1   Robert Peake: Henry, Prince of Wales on horseback,
c. 1610–12

jousts of the tiltyard. Van Dyck, painting less than thirty years later,
defines the martial virtue of Charles I in contrast by reference to
the classical images of command: the tournament lance is replaced
by the *imperator*'s baton of command, the background of the tiltyard
by an open landscape suggesting the field of campaign. At one level
the contrast between these two pictures may be taken simply to
witness to changes in artistic fashion which had taken place
between the 1610s and the 1630s: from the relative insularity of
Jacobean painting to the cosmopolitan, Flemish-influenced artistic
tastes of the Caroline court – so much so that Peake's Prince Henry
was later over-painted, obliterating all references to the trappings of
the tournament and depicting the prince in a landscape derived

from Van Dyck's exemplar. This retrospective recasting of Prince
Henry in King Charles's image epitomises a broader change in the
political culture of Caroline England: a 'painting out' of a series of
iconographic points of reference which had been the stock-in-trade
of the Jacobean past.

Figure 7.2   Sir Anthony Van Dyck: Charles I on horseback,
               c. 1638

The chivalric 'tradition' was, of course, in no sense monolithic. It encompassed a spectrum of sensibilities from the earnest idealisation of the godly knight to the 'mock-heroic' parodies of armour-clad Don Quixotes. But while Caroline courtly chivalry worked within the inherited language of the past, it simultaneously imposed new priorities on, and new standards for the reassessment of, that tradition's divergent elements and forms. Throughout the reign of Charles I a divergence subsisted within the culture of politics (that is to say, the iconographic, literary and ceremonial forms in which political values were expressed), as to what were the elements within this chivalric tradition which it was appropriate to emphasise. Moreover, these rival affirmations of what were the chivalric values proper or appropriate to the age could come, through a process of association, to express tensions within the conduct of politics itself: not as a simple polarity between mutually exclusive modes of chivalry, but more often as differences of emphasis within a common, though multi-faceted, culture.

In early Stuart England, chivalry was a rhetoric of ideals and values, not a precise political or moral code. The Order of the Garter might enjoin upon its members unswerving knightly loyalty to the person of the king, but were there no circumstances in which that loyalty might be qualified? Dramatic works like the anonymous play, *The Wasp, or the Subject's Precedent* (*c.*1636–40), might enjoin a chivalric obligation upon the nobility, *in extremis*, to resist evil counsellors of the king – but who was to decide when such an extreme point had been reached?[4] Insofar as there was a 'political' dimension to the values represented by these role models, it did not inhere in the values themselves, but in the circumstances in which it might be thought appropriate to act upon them. Whether chivalry was deployed to stress loyalty to the crown (the chivalry of the Garter) or loyalty to the commonwealth (the chivalry of the rebellious Hotspur in Shakespeare's *Henry IV*), its political implications remained, in general, unspecific. There were occasions, of course, when attempts were made to invest chivalric rhetoric with political meaning, and (as we shall see) there were regular attempts to identify chivalry with a given political stance. But here the political significance of chivalry lay in the circumstances in which the rhetoric of chivalry was employed, rather than in any specific 'ideology' inhering in the rhetoric itself. Thus the culture of Caroline chivalry glorified a series of almost universally agreed moral values – the dignity of loyalty and military service to the crown, to the commonwealth, and to the Protestant religion – while papering over the fact that those who shared these values might come to very different conclusions as to how they should inform an individual's conduct in affairs of state.[5] This essay is an attempt to begin to map out this part of the intellectual topography of Charles I's England, to explore connections between chivalry and the language and symbolism of politics, and to examine the role of chivalry in defining individuals' sense of identity in political life – as it did never more emphatically than during the conflicts of the English Civil War.

I

The most obvious change in English chivalric culture at Charles I's accession was the discontinuance of the tournament. Between the 1580s and the death of Prince Henry in 1612 the annual tilts celebrating the monarch's accession day had been at the centre of English chivalric culture.[6] Spenser and Sidney wrote about it; Oliver, Segar and Peake painted its heroes; and the elaborately decorated tilting armour worn by tournament knights was itself an art form. More money was lavished upon the tournament than upon any other form of public ceremonial. By the late 1620s, however, the tournament was coming to be seen as a costly anachronism. Prince Charles's first tournament was in 1620 and jousts were held for accession day in 1621; but the jousts for 1622 were postponed and eventually cancelled; none was held in 1623 and it is doubtful whether the jousts planned to celebrate accession day in 1624 and the marriage of Charles and Henrietta Maria in 1625 (both of which were postponed) ever took place. No further accession-day tilts were held after the accession of Charles I.[7] The tournament knight had had his day.

The demise of the accession-day tilts witnessed to a change in attitudes towards chivalry. Something of the nature of this change during the 1620s can be discerned in the way knighthood and the orders of chivalry themselves came to be objects of satire. This satirical tradition went back at least to the middle of James's reign: to the English translation of Cervantes's *Don Quixote* (first published in 1612, the year of Prince Henry's death)[8] and Francis Beaumont's *Knight of the Burning Pestle* (printed in 1613) – with their images of the knight as armour-clad buffoon, unable to discern the difference between windmills and giants.[9] But from the early 1620s there were signs of a new mock-chivalric subculture associated with the retinue of the Duke of Buckingham and the pro-Spanish party at court.

This anti-chivalric subculture took a variety of novel and colourful forms. From 1623 there were reports of the formation of mock-chivalric 'orders' on the fringes of the court, and in the Inns of Court, composed of young men in their twenties. This was the generation who, like Prince Charles, had been born at the beginning of the century and who could remember neither the reality of the Spanish threat before the Treaty of London in 1604 nor the chivalric heyday of the tournament from the 1580s to the death of Prince Henry in 1612.[10] Disquieted by reports of the formation of 'secret societies', the Privy Council ordered an investigation.[11] This revealed the existence of at least three such societies of knights and gentry, meeting in alehouses in the verge of the court, as burlesques of the chivalric orders of knighthood. They took mock oaths, 'mixed with a number of other ridiculous toys, ... as having a Prince whom they call Ottoman, wearing of blue or yellow ribands ... [and] having certain nicknames (as Titere-tu and such like) for their several fraternities'.[12] Another investigation disclosed the 'Order of the Bugle', rivals of the Titere-tu, who sported ribbons of 'Orange Tawny' in mockery of the ribbons worn as favours and as badges of political allegiance by tournament knights.[13] The nicknames taken by members of the 'Order of the Blue' (some of whom were shortly to be members of the king's household) were parodies of the gargantuan bogey-figures of contemporary chivalric literature – 'Giant Asdriasdust, ... Giant Drunkzadoge, Giant Drunassaratt, Giant Neversober, Giant Neverbegood'.[14] Their robustly anti-puritan character seems also to have had a political edge. The Titere-tu had its origins in 1623 in the English regiment fighting on the Spanish Hapsburg side in Flanders under the command of the Catholic fourth Lord Vaux of Harrowden.[15] The Order of the Bugle – with its livery parodying the 'favours' of tournament knights – had similarly pro-Spanish origins. Its founders, Ralphe Marshe, Robert Knaplocke and Thomas Manners, had been part of Buckingham's entourage accompanying the duke and prince on their journey to Spain to woo the Infanta.[16] The Order of the Bugle was formed on their return.

The facetious anti-puritanism of these mock orders of chivalry parodied another contemporary chivalric stereotype: the image of the godly knight as the champion of the 'Protestant Cause'. This image had figured prominently in the polemical writings of the opponents of the Spanish Match, and was to become a cliché of anti-Spanish and anti-popish polemic during the 1630s and 1640s. In John Reynolds's vehemently anti-Spanish pamphlet, *Vox Coeli* (written in 1621 and published in 1624), the pantheon of English princes – from Henry VIII to Henry Prince of Wales – confer in the 'Star Chamber' of heaven to bemoan the collapse of chivalry, warning that appeasement with Spain is a betrayal of England's divinely appointed mission as an Elect Nation against the Catholic Powers.[17] Parliament was urged in characteristically chivalric language to act as 'great *Britain's* greatest Palladins and Champions'.[18] Appropriately, the figure of the Elizabethan Earl of Essex – the hero of the 1596 expedition against Cadiz and the 'rebel' of 1601 – figured prominently within this anti-Spanish chivalric pantheon. 'Essex's ghost' was recalled from the 'Elizian' fields in the early 1620s by the Puritan pamphleteer, Thomas Scott of Norwich, and appears as the ghostly interlocutor in his anti-Spanish pamphlet, published in 1624, *Essex his Ghost, Sent from Elizian*.[19] Scott's Essex recalls the glories of 1588 and exhorts the contemporary English nobility and gentry to unite against Spanish tyranny. Indeed, Essex became a byword for chivalrous opposition to Spain, and ballads commemorating him as the scourge of the Spaniard and the 'Valiant Knight of Chivalry' were republished at intervals throughout the 1620s and 1630s. In *The Dignitie of Chivalry*, a sermon issued in 1626, the godly divine and protégé of the second Earl of Warwick, William Gouge, expounded a similar theme to the City of London Artillery Company, invoking the hallowed memory of the 'valorous Earl of Essex': the Elizabethan Essex became, in effect, the Protestant patron saint of the anti-papist cause.[20]

In this polemical context the symbols of the tournament could come to acquire a retrospective significance as the emblems of this romanticised, and supposedly godly, martial past. The title page drawn by Samuel Ward, the town preacher of Ipswich and another vehement opponent of the Spanish Match, for his much-reprinted sermon of 1622, *Woe to Drunkards* (Figure 7.3), employs the chivalric iconography of the tournament to contrast an idealised warlike (and, by implication, moral) past with a foppish and degenerate present.[21] The gauntleted fist grasping the tournament lance is contrasted with the emblems of the contemporary vices of gambling, tobacco and the cockatrice-cup of the literally demon drink; the soldier's boot with the effeminate courtier's shoe (of a piece with those depicted by Inigo Jones in

168

Figure 7.3   Samuel Ward: *Woe to Drunkards* – a Sermon, 1622

his costume designs for the Caroline masques).[22] What the likes of Gouge, Scott and Ward meant by the 'dignity of chivalry' was, of course, a romantic myth. From their perspective, to be chivalric was to be generally anti-Hapsburg, anti-Spanish, and of course anti-Catholic. In the specific context of English political debate during the first decade of the Thirty Years War, to be 'chivalric' was to be associated with support for English military intervention against the Catholic forces of the Empire.

Yet it is important to stress that this outlook was by no means confined to the 'godly' critics of the crown. Once Charles and the Duke of Buckingham had opted for a policy of war against Spain after 1624, the myth of Elizabethan chivalry was one which they too deliberately sought to exploit. In the Reynolds's *Vox Coeli* of 1624, the ghost of Prince Henry is made to applaud 'brave *Buckingham*' as an admiral who had strengthened the English fleet.[23] There was an element in the 1625 expedition against Cadiz, for example, which was a conscious emulation of the Elizabethan Essex's famous 'Cadiz raid' of 1596 (a raid which had produced spoils of 'twelve millions of ducats', Fulke Greville had claimed in his biography of another Elizabethan chivalric hero, Sir Philip Sidney).[24] This evocation of Elizabethan triumphs was also evident in Buckingham's choice of the scions of two of Elizabeth's most famous councillors as commanders of the expedition: Burghley's grandson (Sir Edward Cecil) and Essex's son (the third Earl of Essex).[25]

For Charles I, the problem was that such emulation invited comparison. The Elizabethan Cadiz expedition was a glorious (and lucrative) Protestant triumph; the Caroline expedition a costly fiasco. Others followed, at the Isle de Rhé and at La Rochelle. Even when Charles and Buckingham had adopted an overtly anti-Spanish policy after 1624, the legend of the Elizabethan chivalric 'golden age' remained an embarrassing point of comparison beside which the martial enterprises of 1624–8 looked, in Dr Cogswell's words, 'a pathetic failure'.[26] Buckingham was never completely dissociated from his image as the hispanophile stooge of 1621–3, and for Charles I, 'Elizabethanism' remained an awkward reminder of the military successes he had so conspicuously failed to attain. By the beginning of the 1630s, the myth of Elizabethan chivalry had become something of a political embarrassment. No comparisons were more odious than those between the Elizabethan Cadiz expedition of 1596 and Charles's of 1625, or between the Elizabethan victory over the Armada and the Caroline débâcle at

La Rochelle. One of the principal achievements of the court culture of the 1630s was the creation of a new chivalric ideology, one deliberately distanced from the constricting (and, to Charles, politically awkward) mythology of a 'golden age' of military triumph against Spain.

II

Among the most effective accomplishments of the Caroline court was a redefining of the ideal of the knight, during the 1630s, no longer principally as a prosecutor of war, but now as the guardian of the Caroline peace. The chief means towards this redefinition was the masque. While the historical relationship between the tournament and the masque is highly complicated, what is clear is that by 1630 Charles had repudiated what Bacon (who liked neither) had termed the mere 'toys' of the tournament[27] and transferred expenditure which had hitherto been lavished on the accession-day tilts to a new style of masque which finally usurped the tournament's long declining status in the calendar of courtly display.[28] The survival of elements of tournament ceremonial into the Caroline masque of the 1630s is perhaps most clearly seen in the opening of the Inns of Court masque, James Shirley's *The Triumph of Peace*, presented in February 1634. The most expensive of the Caroline masques, it began like a tournament, with an elaborate triumphal procession of chariots 'made after the fashion of the Roman Triumphant Chariots' – a chariot procession perhaps also inspired by the recently acquired showpiece of the royal collection, Mantegna's *Triumph of Caesar*.[29] On the procession's arrival at Whitehall, the company was instructed to 'fetch a turn about the *Tilt-yard*, that their Majesties might have a double view of them'.[30] Knights had yielded place to masquers. The procession around the tiltyard, that ritual of the military sport of the tournament, now served to celebrate the Caroline Peace.

This change represented more, however, than the transference of resources from one form of courtly display to another. The masque had a didactic purpose – albeit in the intellectual formation of a small and highly privileged section of the political élite. It was utilised, as Dr Sharpe has persuasively argued, to show in idealised microcosm the vision of order and equipoise which the king hoped to realise within the kingdom at large.[31] Part of that didactic purpose was to reappraise and redefine the chivalric tradition. During the 1630s one of the central themes of the masques of Shirley, Carew and Davenant is that the simplistic knightly codes of the past were now obsolete, and had been replaced by a new, purified, chivalric ethos. The achievement of the diverse court culture of the 1630s was not in rejecting the culture of chivalry, but in salvaging an image of the king which remained emphatically chivalric while deriding as outmoded and absurd the image of the belligerent knight-errant: a figure who could not discriminate between a just and a risibly mistaken cause. In Shirley's *Triumph of Peace* (1634), the final antimasque depicts the arrival of the questing knight-errant: 'Enter a Windmill, a fantastic knight and his Squire armed'. There follows a burlesque of the famous tilting-at-windmills passage in Cervantes's *Don-Quixote* in which the fantastic knight is incapable of distinguishing between real and imaginary enemies.[32] 'The Fantastic Adventurer with his lance', runs Shirley's stage direction, 'makes many attempts upon the Windmill, which his squire imitates'. When an innocent 'Country Gentleman and his Servant' enter, they too are assaulted by the Knight and his Squire, who are duly sent off lame for their folly.[33] This Cervantean comic stereotype is replicated in the parodic image of the knight-errant in the anti-masque of Davenant's *Britannia Triumphans* of 1637: a doggerel-speaking buffoon, spouting paraphrases of the popular chivalric romance, *Amadis the Gaul.*[34]

This is a comic image of the knight which is of a piece with the mock-chivalric burlesques of the 1620s, of the Titere-Tu and the Order of the Bugle. The continuity between these 1630s burlesques of knighthood and the roistering, anti-puritan clubs of the Spanish Match crisis is explicit in the figure of Thomas Carew: the author of the spectacular court masque of 1634, *Coelum Britannicum.* Indeed, during the 1620s, Carew had actually belonged to the mock-chivalric 'Order of the Blue'.[35] Of all the poets of the Caroline court, Carew was the figure most intimately acquainted with the king – a gentleman of the Privy Chamber from 1630, Sewer in Ordinary to the king and a member of the royal household singled out to attend personally upon the monarch.[36] Carew's treatment of the theme of chivalry in *Coelum Britannicum* not only illuminates the attitudes of one of the principal literary figures at the court, but also sheds light on the chivalric values which Carew's master, Charles I, thought appropriate to the Caroline peace.

Carew's *Coelum Britannicum* operates at one level as an allegory of the king's repudiation of the outmoded culture of the old-fashioned knight, and its replacement by a new, purified, order of the 'moderne Heroes', men distinguished by moral virtues rather than any specific commitment to a martial, much less an anti-Spanish, Protestant cause. Insofar as martial prowess survives as an element of those virtues, it is in a refined and etiolated form, as Inigo Jones's costume designs suggest. Much of Carew's text for the masque is a free translation of a work dedicated to Sir Philip Sidney: Giordano Bruno's philosophical dialogue, *Lo Spaccio de la Bestia Trionfante* (1584),[37] and throughout Carew's masque there is a subtle dialectic between a new, Caroline image of the knightly hero and a contrasted chivalric stereotype: that represented by the dedicatee of Bruno's dialogue, Sidney, the figure who had come to be seen as the epitome of Elizabethan chivalry, the perfect Protestant knight, who had met his death campaigning against the Spanish in the Netherlands in 1586.[38] When Momus (the central character of antimasque) enters, he appears grotesquely attired – 'upon his head a wreath stuck with feathers and a porcupine in the forepart'.[39] A heraldically literate audience would not fail to recognise this visual pun: Momus is wearing Sir Philip Sidney's crest, a wreath surmounted by a porcupine. This recognition shades with irony the fact that it is Momus, becrested with the Sidney porcupine, who reads the major speech of the antimasque: Jupiter's decree proclaiming the end of the old martial order and the 'disfurnishing' of Olympus's star chamber of all its symbols of triumph in war. Equally a source of irony is the setting for Momus's reading of Jupiter's decree. This is the Olympian 'star chamber', the setting which had also served as the scene for the anti-Spanish orations in Scott's and Reynolds's notorious polemics of the 1620s; Essex's ghost had spoken in 'the most High Star Chamber Court of Heaven' in 1624, just as Reynolds's Protestant princes had gathered in the 'star chamber' of heaven to counsel war against Spain.[40] In the 1620's, the Olympian star chamber had been the place where Protestant heroes rehearsed the catalogue of victories; in Carew's masque, it was the place where the reminders of those victories were about to be banished. The chivalric tradition was being turned on its head. In fact, Jupiter's star chamber decree proclaims an attitude to the chivalric tradition diametrically opposed to the glorification of the military triumphs of the past.[41] Reading from Jove's proclamation, Momus announces the banishment from the heavenly court of all the trophies and mementoes of past wars. The proclamation warrants quotation at length:

We having observed a very commendable practice taken into frequent use by the princes of these latter Ages of perpetuating the memory of their famous enterprises, sieges, battles, victories, in picture, sculpture, tapestry, embroideries and other manufactures, wherewith they have embellished their public palaces; and [having] taken into Our more distinct and serious consideration the particular Christmas hangings of the Guard-Chamber of this court, wherein the Naval Victory of [15]88 is to the eternal glory of this nation exactly delineated; and whereas We likewise out of a prophetical imitation of this so laudable custom, did for many thousand years before, adorn and beautify the eighth room of Our celestial mansion, commonly called the Star-Chamber, with the military adventures, stratagems, achievements, feats and defeats, ... It hath notwithstanding ... seemed meet to Our Omnipotency, for causes to Our self best known, to unfurnish and dis-array Our foresaid Star-Chamber of all those ancient constellations ... and to admit into their vacant places such persons only as shall be qualified with exemplar virtue and eminent desert.[42]

This Olympian banishment of the mementoes of the martial past had its contemporary parallel in Charles I's court. The one object specifically singled out in Momus's catalogue of the now ostracised mementoes of war is the great series of 'hangings of the Guard-Chamber of this court wherein the Naval Victory of [15]88 is ... exactly delineated'.[43] The fictional Momus was referring to a factual work of art. Indeed, this was one of the major works of art in the royal collection; the great series of Cornelius Vroom tapestries commemorating Elizabeth I's victory over the Spanish Armada, which had been purchased by James I for the prodigious sum of £1628 in 1616.[44] Just as in the masque's Olympian court these trophies of 'military adventures' are to be 'unfurnish[ed] and dis-array[ed]', so at Whitehall Charles gave orders for these Armada tapestries to be removed from the palace and stored in the relative obscurity of Oatlands.[45] Like Jupiter on Olympus, Charles I had decreed the court's banishment of the now outmoded anti-Spanish military tradition of 1588.

Yet the image of Charles I represented during the 1630s, in Carew's *Coelum Britannicum* as much as in the iconography of Van Dyck, is not as the outright rejecter of the traditions of chivalry, but as the one who would purify and perfect them. The 'toys' of the tournament, the knights-errant, the tapestries commemorating an Elizabethan martial tradition, are gone. But in their place is a purer and supposedly more ancient chivalric tradition, represented in Carew's masque by the fourteen masquer-peers who are presented to Charles dressed as 'heroes' in 'antique helms'.[46] In Carew's masque, these new constellations (the fourteen masquers) now appear 'stellified' with the king in the final apotheosis of *Coelum Britannicum*, over the 'prospect of *Windsor* Castle'.[47] In the firmament of heaven, the 'ancient constellations' had yielded place to the Bright Young Things. The king, who took his place among the masquers, is presented to the queen as '*St George* him-selfe', accompanied by 'A *Guy*, a *Beavis*, or some true/Round-Table Knight'.[48]

The apotheosis scene in Carew's masque highlights another central element of the chivalric culture of the Caroline court, the Order of the Garter – an element in the chivalric culture which had undergone during Charles's reign a similar process of redefinition. From the late 1620s, the Garter became the cynosure of the Caroline reformation of chivalry. At its simplest, the emblems which proclaimed membership of the order became far more visible at court. From April 1626, all Knights of the Garter were ordered to wear the escutcheon of the cross of St George embroidered on their cloaks, coats and riding habits 'at all times ... and in all places and assemblies' when not wearing the order's full regalia.[49] As Sharpe and Strong have demonstrated, the Order of the Garter was reformed by Charles I to provide the model for a new and purified chivalric ethic.[50] The religious rituals of the order – in particular the liturgy for the celebration of the feast of St George – were endowed with a new importance in the life of the court. The Garter's knightly ceremonial reemphasised not merely martial valour, but sacred loyalty and idealised moral virtue. What dominated the ceremonial was no longer (as in the tournament or in Tudor Garter ceremonial) the individual display of knights and their retinues, but the sacral figure of the king, attended by knights companion uniformly attired and unaccompanied by private retinues.[51] The canopy over the king became the most prominent element of the procession. In Elizabeth's day, Ashmole noted, 'there were not above six appointed' to carry the canopy over the monarch; from the Caroline reforms of 1632 they were 'increased to double that number'.[52] The 'holiness' of knighthood was reemphasised, the historicity of St George reaffirmed.[53] And this sacralised aspect of the order was further stressed when Charles ordered that the escutcheon of St George be surrounded with an aureole of silver rays in imitation of the insignia of the French order of the Knights of the Holy Spirit.[54] Of course, Charles I was by no means unique in seeing true 'godliness' as a central element in chivalric virtue. Religious piety had been no less strong an imperative for chivalric action in the writings of such 'puritans' as Scott, Reynolds and Gouge. The difference between the two positions lay in what each held knightly religious duty to entail. To men such as Reynolds and Gouge, 'the dignity of chivalry' lay explicitly in the military advancement of European Protestantism; to Charles I it lay primarily in the religious bonds of loyalty between the sovereign and his knights: a sacralised loyalty within his order of chivalry that was to serve, in microcosm, as the highest example of the loyal service which was every subject's obligation. To this extent, the public rituals of courtly chivalry were no less didactic in intention than was the masque.

This dual process of reordering the priorities of chivalry and redefining the image of the knight can also be traced in contemporary portraiture; nowhere more clearly than in those most famous images of Caroline monarchy, Van Dyck's great equestrian portraits of the king. Despite the classicism of their imagery – defining Charles I as Roman *imperator* – there remains a clearly defined chivalric dimension to these portraits. In the earliest of the heroic equestrian portraits of Charles I – completed by Van Dyck in 1633 (Figure 7.4), less than a year before Carew's *Coelum Britannicum* – the topos of knight and squire, so much a convention of English chivalric portraiture, is both accepted and radically redefined. The armour the king is wearing is English tournament armour made at Greenwich c.1610–20;[55] and the identification of the king as one who has once proved himself in the lists is made explicitly by the lance-rest fixed conspicuously to the right side of the breast-plate. Similarly, in Van Dyck's second great equestrian portrait of the king (Figure 7.2), dated to around 1638 (when the king was on the verge of war against the Scots), the king is again wearing Greenwich tilting armour, with lance-rest again fixed on the breastplate. Yet for all these oblique references to the now anachronistic tournament, the image of the chivalric knight has here been classicised. The oak tree bearing the royal style ('Rex Magnae Britanniae') as a motto painted on a suspended cartouche alludes to a repertory of imagery in which the oak was sacred to Jove; the symbol of 'one who had done famous deeds', and of the warrior whose 'fame endures by his name alone',[56] rather than to the topos, common in late Elizabethan iconography, of the 'tree of chivalry', in which the subject was identified by a shield or *impresa* cartouche suspended from a tree.[57] Such, too, was the knightly

Figure 7.4   Van Dyck: Charles I and the Seigneur de St Antoine,
            1633

image the king wished to project to this court and to the world.
Van Dyck's *modello* (or preliminary study) for the large-scale
version of the picture hung in the 'chair room' (or throne room)
of the privy gallery of Whitehall Palace.[58] In Van Dyck's portraits of
the king in armour the context of iconographical reference is
classical; yet it remains one which is nevertheless emphatically
chivalric: an image of the king as *former* tournament-knight, as
'St George himself', the champion of the Caroline peace.

  The chivalric culture of the court was thus redefined during the
1630s: by the religious rituals of the Garter; by the masques of

Shirley, Davenant and Carew; and by the classicised chivalric iconography of van Dyck. Knighthood was almost wholly emancipated from associations with the Elizabethan and Jacobean culture of the tournament; it was distanced from any necessary association with a mythologised Protestant cause against Spain; and, in the Order of the Garter, Caroline chivalry was renovated by reference to supposedly purer and more ancient traditions. But to what extent did this redefinition of chivalry succeed in imposing its values on the political culture of the court, and on the world beyond?

III

Distinctive and influential though this courtly image of the knight undoubtedly was, it would be misleading to see Caroline chivalry as marking a clean break with the models and traditions of the immediate past: as yet another instance of the triumph of Caroline 'classicism' over the 'gothic'. The culture of the Caroline court was syncretistic: Elizabethan and Jacobean images of the knight – both visual and literary – survived into the 1630s and were no less part of the chivalric culture of Caroline England than were the 'classical' conventions of the Van Dyck portrait. Representations of a leading courtier such as the Earl of Northumberland could thus employ a diverse repertory of points of chivalric reference. In Van Dyck's painting of Northumberland as a knight in armour (c.1636), the martial element in the portrait is subordinate, as Professor Smuts has argued of Van Dyck's portraiture generally, to the stress upon 'civility enlivened by wit and grace' (Figure 7.5); indeed, this portrait has been taken to be a characteristic image of the courtly Caroline knight.[59] But this stress on knightly elegance and refinement coexisted with older conventions of chivalric iconography. The great seal engraved for Northumberland within a few years of this Van Dyck portrait defines its image of the earl by reference to a distinctly gothic visual language (Figure 7.6). Here the earl is depicted as an armour-clad, broadsword-wielding warrior-knight, charging into battle on his war-horse: an iconographic tradition which derived from the great seals of medieval peers.[60] This gothicised image of Northumberland is further reinforced by the chivalric emblems on either side of the equestrian figure. To the left, Northumberland bears as his device the royal emblem of that most chivalric of kings, the founder of the Order of the Garter,

Figure 7.5   Van Dyck: The 10th Earl of Northumberland, *c.*1637

Edward III, who 'bore for his devise' – as Thomas Blount noted in his iconographic handbook of 1646 – 'the rays of the sun streaming from a cloud without any motto'.[61] Balancing this image, to the right, is another badge of Edward III: the circular badge of Edward III's order of chivalry, the Garter.[62] There is also a complementary emphasis on antiquity of lineage: Northumberland's shield bears his arms quartered with those of the dukes of Brabant, thus attesting to the descent he claimed from Charlemagne – a point which was not lost on the future member of the Long Parliament, Edward Bysshe.[63] Courtly 'civility and grace' are here supplanted by images of knightly prowess and lineage and baronial power. The insouciant elegance of the Van Dyck courtier-knight coexisted in a culture which also accommodated a sharply contrasting repertory of chivalric allusion.

Literature offered a similar pluralism. Beside the classical Horatian lyrics of court poets such as Thomas Carew, Sir John Suckling and Aurelian Townshend, there was also a taste for distinctly gothic forms of chivalric literature throughout the reign of Charles I, both within and outside the court. Court patrons continued to sponsor the production of those traditional genres of chivalric literature, the prose romance and the extended verse narrative, even while these genres were being parodied by Davenant, Carew and other authors of the literary *avant garde*. Thus the future royalist, Francis Quarles, completed his chivalric poem, *Argulus and Parthenia*, in 1629, an extended narrative

Figure 7.6   Seal of Algernon, 10th Earl of Northumberland,
              c. 1637

poem, drawing heavily on Sidney's *Arcadia*, that was amongst the
most influential and widely-read poems of the reign. Its dedicatee
was no less a figure than the Groom of the Stole, the Earl of
Holland, that 'great example of true honour and chivalry' – a
Knight of the Garter and, perhaps significantly, an erstwhile
tournament knight.[64] Another veteran of the tiltyard, the fourth
Earl of Pembroke (the Lord Chamberlain of the household and
nephew of Sir Philip Sidney), was a patron of that distinctively
conservative genre of chivalric literature, the prose romance. In
1619, Pembroke had been the dedicatee of the English edition of
one of the most celebrated works in the chivalric canon, the
medieval romance *The History of Amadis de Gaule*.[65] And while

playwrights of the 1630s – Davenant and Jonson among them – poured scorn on the romantic tradition of Amadis of Gaul, Pembroke did not lose his taste for the genre. In 1640 he paid for the translation of two large volumes of Gilbert Saulnier's chivalric romance, *The Love and Armes of the Greeke Princes*, issued with his crest and cypher prominently displayed on the title page.[66] Arthurian chivalric tales also enjoyed a new-found vogue. The *locus classicus* of Arthurian romance, Malory's *Morte d'Arthur*, was published in a new edition in 1634 (the year of Carew's *Coelum Britannicum*) – the first edition of the work since 1582.[67] All these works were replete with accounts of knightly challenges to combat, of jousts and tournaments and of the glories of the pursuit of arms. In the intellectual world of the political élite there was no clear-cut divide between classical and medieval images of the knight. The mental horizons of a would-be courtier like the third Earl of Essex encompassed the sacralised chivalry of the Garter ceremonies at Windsor in 1638 (where he served as cupbearer to the king), *and* the fantasy-world chivalry of the knightly romance: when he returned from the ceremonies at Windsor, Quarles's *Argulus and Parthenia*, *The History of Amadis the Gaul* and *The Love and Armes of the Greek Princes* awaited him among the books he kept in his study at Essex House in the Strand.[68] Nor were such tastes confined to the culture of the élite. Abbreviated and simplified in chapbooks, these chivalric tales also formed an important part of the cultural diet and mental world of the semi-literate and the middling sort.[69]

So, too, with the London stage. Here, beyond the fantastic gothic heroes of the romance, a more concrete (though scarcely less romanticised), point of chivalric reference was provided by the reign of Elizabeth. For Charles I, the legacy of Elizabethan chivalry was, as we have seen, an awkward one – particularly after the 1630s rapprochement with Spain. The Cornelius Vroom tapestries commemorating the victory of 1588 could be easily banished from court; but eradicating that myth of the golden age of Elizabethan chivalry which these tapestries had symbolised was not so easily accomplished. As Dr Butler has argued, a concern for the 'Elizabethan values' – in particular for opposition to Spain and support for international Protestantism – was one of the pervasive themes of works written for the popular stage in the 1630s: 'the values of the old national myth of England's greatness which Elizabeth was supposed to have been furthering and which Charles certainly was not'.[70] The theme is equally evident in the

Caroline plays of Ben Jonson (and in particular his late play, *The New Inn*, printed in 1631); and it appears still more forcefully in the plays written during the 1630s by Jonson's patron, the Earl of Newcastle.[71] In *The Variety*, Newcastle's hero, Manly, is a plain-speaking critic of the fopperies of the court who dresses as an Elizabethan: he recalls the days when 'men of honor flourish'd, that tam'd the wealth of Spain' and 'set up the States [of the United Provinces]'.[72] Manly contrasts nostalgically the way Garter Knights once made their way to Windsor attended by magnificent retinues, and the fashion-conscious courtiers who were now the knights, travelling to the Garter ceremonies privately, for reasons of economy, with only a page and a barber as their foppish entourage.

Manly: To have seen but a St George's Feast then!
Sir William: Why what difference, Sir?
Manly: When [the Knights of the Garter] were installed, to see the twenty mile[s] to Windsor strewed with blue-coats, feathers and cognizances, as they do country towns with boughs and flowers for Princes' Entries, and not to go privately in a coach, with a page and a barber, to cut off charges,... then you should have the best knight of the Country, with the ragged staff on [the retinue's] sleeves .... Every knight had his hundreds, and these would take up all the Taverns in the town, [and] be drunk to the honour of their Lords...[73]

The ragged staff with a white bear was, of course, the badge of the Elizabethan Knight of the Garter, the Earl of Leicester[74] – a figure who, in one posthumous tradition (of which Newcastle's play is an example), came to be regarded as a symbol of Elizabethan military daring and aristocratic magnificence.[75] The element of nostalgic 'Elizabethanism' in Newcastle's attitude to the chivalry of the Garter was a world apart from that of Carew's *Coelum Britannicum* – with its Olympus swept clean of the 'mementoes' of the Elizabethan past, and its knights dancing – quite literally – their attendance upon the king.

There were clearly tensions within the culture of Caroline chivalry, and the language of historical allusion could be used to encode hostility towards the prevailing ethos of the court. But this is not, however, to discern in the 1630s an incipient 'opposition' whose hostility to the policies of the crown would lead inevitably to parliamentarianism in the conflicts of the Civil War. Newcastle, for all his nostalgic Elizabethanism, was to be a leading royalist-in-arms during the 1640s. Similarly, there was no polarity in literary or artistic reference during the 1630s which can be taken as an indicator of an unbridgeable political divide between two cultures, or between two opposed and incompatible views of chivalry – much less as anticipations of a 'royalist' or 'parliamentarian' cultural divide before the civil war. The diversity of Caroline chivalry bears witness not to a political culture neatly divided, but to an eclectic tradition which offered a variety of role-models and a plurality of values. There was no single stereotype of ideal chivalric virtues and values, no single package of iconographic reference which can be neatly equated with a given political stance. Van Dyck's 'royalist' portrait of Charles I in armour (now in the Hermitage), for example, could be adapted during the Interregnum as the pose for the parliamentarian general and regicide, Cromwell's son-in-law, Henry Ireton.[76] Likewise, what has been seen as the quintessential Caroline 'courtly' image, Van Dyck's portrait of Northumberland as Lord Admiral,[77] could serve a decade later as the prototype for the portrait of another regicide: Robert Walker's portrait of the Commonwealth's general-at-sea, Richard Deane. Knights of the Garter might pledge their loyalty to the crown, but confronted with the choice of allegiance in the civil wars of the 1640s senior Garter knights – Pembroke, Salisbury, Northumberland, Holland among them – were to opt for allegiance to the parliamentarian cause, not for an unquestioning loyalty to the king. There clearly were tensions implicit within the chivalric culture of the 1620s and 1630s; yet we should nevertheless be sceptical of any attempt to discern a neat dichotomy between 'royalist' or incipient 'parliamentarian' images of chivalric values, rhetoric or iconography in the years before the Civil War.

IV

When war broke out in England in 1642, it was because chivalry was a common currency within the political élite that it could be adapted, by both sides, to serve diametrically opposed political ends. Nor, in the early 1640s, had the reality of war yet been wholly divorced from the formal rituals of the High Court of Chivalry. It was not yet an antiquarian curiosity that wars, like tournaments, were begun by the heralds, the officers of that high court; and that heralds initiated hostilities with challenges and proclamations in the Anglo-Scottish war of 1640, at the battle of Edgehill in 1642 (the first great battle between royalists and parliamentarians), and before besieged towns in the early stages of the Civil War.[78] Challenges to personal combat or trial by battle issued by such principal commanders on both sides as the parliamentarians Lord Brooke and the Earl of Essex, or by the royalist Earls of Lindsey and Newcastle, purported to substitute the conventions of chivalric combat between the 'champions' of rival causes for the realities of war.[79] During the royalist and parliamentarian mobilisation in Warwickshire, Lord Brooke offered (to 'avoid the profusion of blood') that he and his royalist opponent, the Earl of Northampton, 'might try the quarrel by the sword in single combat'.[80] The royalist Earl of Newcastle issued a similar challenge to the parliamentarian commander in Yorkshire (Ferdinando, Lord Fairfax) in 1643, seeking trial by battle 'conformable to the Examples of our Heroic Ancestors, who used not to spend their time in scratching one another out of holes, but in pitched fields determined their doubts'.[81] In such grandiloquent gestures one is never very far from the heroic bravura of the knights of chivalric fiction, from the world of Malory and *Argulus* and *Amadis of Gaul*. In the behaviour of such men as Brooke and Newcastle, chivalric culture can be discerned as informing their sense of what was fitting in the conduct of war, and shaping their sense of identity within the conflict.

Gestures towards the chivalric conventions of the tournament were also evident in those formal emblems of identity, the standards of officers in military command. Like the shields of tournament knights, the standards of officers down to the rank of captain had their own *impresa* or device: a motto or inscription, usually accompanied by some form of symbolic or allegorical representation. The *impresa* of the tournament became, in time of war, the device by which one company distinguished itself from another. The Leicestershire knight, Sir Edward Hartham, for example, adopted the rock-amid-the-waves *impresa*,[82] familiar from Elizabethan and Jacobean emblem books, which had been used by the Earl of Sussex in a tournament of *c.*1559–60.[83] Captain Copley adopted the *impresa* of a sword-bearing hand appearing amid the clouds;[84] while the Earl of Essex, predictably, adapted the famous 'nulla figura' *impresa* his father had used in the accession-day tilt of 1590:[85] a blank shield 'without any figure' but now inscribed with the punning motto, 'Virtutis Comes Invidia' ('Envy is the companion of Virtue').[86] Popular interest in the production of such *imprese* or 'devices' was met by the translation of the continental handbooks on the rules governing their construction and display. Henri Estienne's popular treatise on *imprese* was translated from the French by the Inner Temple lawyer, Thomas Blount, in 1646, as *The Art of Making Devises*. War had created a renewed interest in chivalric iconography; and as Blount observed, 'as these Jousting or jesting wars are disused, so have we now an earnest though much to be lamented war which renders [emblems] more useful then ever'.[87] In this respect, it may perhaps be significant that many of the senior commanders of 1642–3 had first acquired their martial experience not in the field of battle but in the tiltyard: parliamentarians such as Essex (parliamentarian Lord General), Pembroke, Warwick (parliamentarian Lord Admiral) and his brother, the Earl of Holland. Royalists such as the Earl of Lindsey (the royalist commander at Edgehill) and the Earl of Dorset represented this generation on the opposing side. Indeed, the 'martial' character of the Jacobean tournament was so etiolated that it was more a training in the manners than in the methods of war.

Chivalric culture also impinged, inevitably, at a psychological level: contemporaries filtered their perceptions of contemporary politics, and of their own identity within the political process, through the prism of literary and historical reference. Poetry had a direct effect on 'leaders of armies', the poet and playwright Sir William Davenant later observed, 'since Nature hath made us prone to imitation (by which we equal the best or the worst), how much those images of action prevail upon our minds, which are delightfully drawn by poets'.[88] It was natural, then, that on crossing the River Tweed during the campaign against the Scots in 1639, the poet Sir John Suckling, then an officer in the king's army, should recall *Henry IV, Part I* and 'that River, about the uneven running of which my Friend Mr William Shakespeare makes Henry Hotspur quarrel so highly with his Fellow Rebels'. He feared that negotiation might cheat him of the chance of winning honour through military exploits – that 'Men of Peace will draw all this to a dumb show [a theatrical mime]', and so foreclose the opportunity 'of producing glorious matter for future chronicle'.[89] Once again, the repertory of reference employed by Suckling is self-consciously literary. Nor were such perspectives confined to poets. Hotspur – the chivalrous rebel against the usurping Henry

IV referred to by Suckling – was also in the thoughts of the Earl of Essex, soon to be the parliamentarian commander-in-chief. Writing to the Marquess of Hamilton in August 1641, Essex recalled Hotspur's sense of pessimism at his fellow nobles' indifference to the fate of the commonweal. 'We may say well, as Hotspur said, our members love the commonwealth well; but their own barns better': Parliament's future Lord General was quoting from Hotspur's soliloquy in *Henry IV: Part I* – the point at which Hotspur ponders his decision to rebel against the king.[90] Essex's wartime rival on the parliamentarian side, Sir William Waller, also defined his identity in self-consciously literary terms. 'We are both upon the stage', he wrote to his friend and royalist adversary, Sir Ralph Hopton in 1643, 'and must act those parts that are assigned us in this tragedy: let us do it in a way of honour…'[91] His impresa figured a 'tree of chivalry' hung with a shield depicting *fleurs-de-lys* (Figure 7.7), recalling the moment when an earlier knightly Waller, fighting beside Henry V, had captured the duc d'Orléans at the battle of Agincourt – and perhaps also suggesting an identification with the popular hero of chivalric romance, the 'Knight of the Flower *De-Luce*', whose deeds were celebrated in such works as the *Love and Armes of the Greeke Princes*, published in 1640.[92] Conversely, Lord Fairfax's reply to Newcastle's chivalric challenge to 'trial by battle' in 1643 was couched in terms of a disdain for the empty gestures of the knights of chivalric romance: he chose to fight a war 'without following the rules of *Amadis de Gaule*, or the Knight of the Sun, which the language of [Newcastle's] declaration seems to affect in appointing pitch'd battles'.[93] Fairfax's riposte to Newcastle asserts a direct relationship between the 'affected' chivalric gesture and its literary exemplar. His reply is almost a direct quotation of Lovel's comment on the virtuous Lord Beaumont's studies in Ben Jonson's *The New Inn* (1631): that Beaumont had no regard for '*Knights o'the Sun*, nor *Amadis de Gauls*'. If – as seems plausible – Fairfax was citing Jonson, his rejoinder had an added sting when addressed to Newcastle who, during the 1630s, had been Jonson's loyal friend and patron.[94] The literature of chivalry provided a common language within which both men could articulate their contradictory attitudes to the conduct of the war.

It was precisely because chivalric rhetoric provided this common repertory of allusion that the contrivers of civil war propaganda sought, by repetition and association, to appropriate particular elements within this common chivalric tradition to

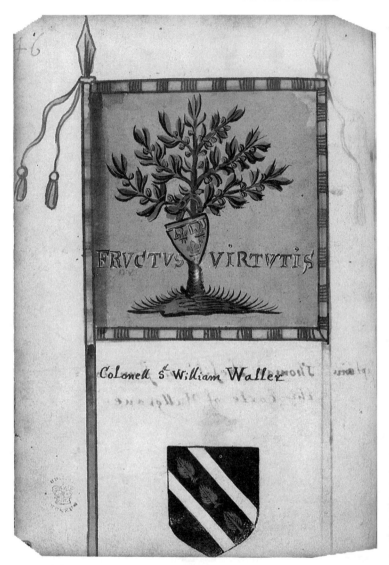

Figure 7.7   Banners of the Parliamentary Armies

serve the ends of a specific political cause. Perhaps the clearest example of this 'denominationalising' of elements within the chivalric tradition was the attempt by parliament to exploit the popular nostalgia for the reign of Elizabeth, and to portray its cause as the continuation of a Protestant Elizabethan chivalric tradition – one of the several strands within the parliamentary propaganda of the 1640s. The trait is most clearly discerned in the propaganda associated with parliament's commander-in-chief for most of the war, the Earl of Essex (Lord General for Parliament, 1642–5). Essex, the product of the union between the second earl (Spenser's 'flower of Chivalry') and Sir Philip Sidney's widow, was easily cast as the heir of that Elizabethan tradition: the chivalric champion of the revived Protestant cause against a popish plot. 'The Earl of Essex', a remonstrance of the London apprentices enthusiastically declared in August 1642, was 'that renowned piece of chivalry ... impoverishing [London] with the lustre of his presence'.[95] Parliamentarian propaganda syncretised the fame of the rebel earl of 1601 – widely regarded as a popular martyr for the commonweal – with the name and public image of his son, the parliamentarian 'rebel' of 1642. 'I need not to commemorate here the noble actions of your worthy father', the parliamentarian Lord Robartes declared in a public speech in September 1642, 'whom the Commons doe still remember with a reverend adoration, thinking all the praises and prayers that they can accumulate on the name of *Essex* ... is now with the same fervour and heat of applause, by general vote of the people, cast upon your Honourable Excellence.[96] The identification of Essex as a champion of the commonweal out of this Elizabethan mould is a recurrent theme in the propaganda and commemorative verses issued by the earl and his partisans during the civil war. Reminders of the third Earl of Essex's role as continuator of his father's chivalric crusade against evil counsel culminated in a spate of epicedian verses commemorating Essex, at his death in 1646, as the son of the Elizabethan Essex who had been alike the hero of the tiltyard and of the commonweal:

> He was the wonder of his time,
> For virtue, Martial Discipline,
> *Eliza* great full oft did view
> How fast her Knights he overthrew:
> When he, like *Mars*, in armour bright,
> Did Shine, none durst be opposite.[97]

Such references were not merely intended to represent the contemporary Essex as the continuator of the 'name and fame' of his Elizabethan father; they located the parliamentarian cause itself in a romanticised Elizabethan past of knightly heroes and of godly campaigns against the Antichrist. The fate of the Cornelius Vroom tapestries depicting the victory over the Spanish Armada in 1588 (which we have seen alluded to in Jupiter's proclamation in *Coelum Britannicum*) is characteristic of this attempt to identify the parliamentarian cause with this Elizabethan past. The 'disfurnishing' of the court of mementoes of England's martial past had been the central theme in the new order proclaimed in Carew's court masque of 1634. In a gesture laden with symbolism, a decade after Carew's masque of 1634, in the midst of civil war in May 1644, these tapestries were taken out of the mothballs to which they had been consigned by Charles I and rehung in the parliamentarian House of Lords. The peers were making a point: just as their Elizabethan forebears had led the crusade against the Armada's threat of popery and arbitrary government, so the parliamentarians of the 1640s were the latter-day continuators of that struggle. In Hollar's engraving of the House of Lords in 1644, the tapestries depicting the victory of 1588 – which cover the walls of the House of Lords on all sides – provide a historical backdrop to the action of the present (depicted in the foreground): the parliamentarian peers sitting in judgement on the new agent of popish conspiracy, Archbishop Laud (Figure 7.8).[98]

Portraiture was adapted to fulfil a similar role, relocating contemporary military heroes in an archaic and idealised martial past. The widely circulated broadsheet portrait of Fairfax as a 'champion of England', issued in 1646, is one of the most self-consciously anachronistic portraits issued during the civil war[99] (Figure 7.9). 'Champion of England' had been a traditional designation for St George, and, before Fairfax's appointment to the Lord Generalship, had been appropriated in encomiums of Essex during the Civil War: in this respect parliamentary propaganda was mining the same vein of national mythology which was so central to the cult of the Order of the Garter.[100] This 1646 portrait of Fairfax, published to celebrate the general's victories, depicts him as the perfect Elizabethan tournament knight: there is elaborately chased and decorated tilting armour of a kind which had not been current in England for twenty years[101] and his warhorse is adorned with an elaborate ostrich-feather plume and shaffron, a sumptuous tasselled caparison and a saddlecloth of damask or cloth of gold. A rival general wearing a helmet *à l'antique* dominates the centre of the background. Only the musketeers in the far distance provide any suggestion of modernity in this otherwise archaising image. It is the classic image of the 'champion' – the triumphant hero of the lists. It was, moreover, an image with which the new lord general seems to have

Figure 7.8   Wenceslas Hollar: The Trial of Archbishop Laud in the House of Lords: frontispiece to William Prynne, *Canterburies Doome* (1646)

Sir Thomas Fairfax
Knight, Captain-Generall
of the Parliaments Forces.

Figure 7.9   Anon. Sir Thomas Fairfax as Champion of England,
1646

identified. In 1646 he had a cockade made bearing the same
legend which had appeared on the woodcut portrait of that year:
'EN/GLANDS/CHAMPION'.[102] The visual allusions to the world
of the tournament and of what might be termed the age of Prince

Henry are not coincidental: the model for the pose of the horse, for its plume, and for the elaboration of its caparison was François Clouet's equestrian portrait of Henri II of France – the same model which had provided the pattern for Peake's portrait of the Prince of Wales more than thirty years before.[103] The iconography of this highly sophisticated 1646 woodcut casts Fairfax as a hero out of the world of the tournament, a survivor of a chivalric golden age, returned as 'champion of England'.

Appropriately, the occasion which most explicitly linked the now victorious parliamentarian cause with the chivalric past was the spectacular state funeral accorded the Earl of Essex in 1646. Like the portrait of Fairfax, this too was a calculated exercise in anachronism: a chivalric funeral, presided over by the heralds, the officers of arms, on the most extravagant scale. By the 1640s such ostentatious funeral ceremony was almost as passé as the tournament itself. Apart from James I's funeral (which, under-financed and ill-organised, had turned into a rain-sodden fiasco), the last time such chivalric funeral ceremonial had been witnessed on this regal scale had been at the obsequies of Prince Henry in 1612.[104] In 1646, marshalled by the heralds with the full panoply of chivalric pomp, Essex's accoutrements of knighthood – his helm, crest, armour, spurs and target – were carried beside the earl's hearse and effigy, accompanied through the streets of Westminster by a vast concourse of mourners (including the members of the two Houses of Parliament) to the funeral ceremonies at Westminster Abbey.[105] The heralds' notes surviving in the state papers and in the College of Arms attest to the fact that it was royal precedents which formed the model for Essex's funeral ceremonial, and for the procession from Essex House to the interment in the Abbey. Like Henry in 1612, Essex was represented as a dead prince,[106] and almost all the details of the composition of the cortège seem to have been copied directly from accounts of Prince Henry's funeral: the design of the funeral chariot; the effigy of the dead general – armour-clad, in coronet and creation robes of scarlet and ermine; and the hearse, the focus of the ceremonial in the Abbey, with its great baldachin of six Tuscan columns supporting a canopy of escutcheons and pennants surrounded by the alternating cross-and-*fleur-de-lys* pattern of a prince's coronet, appears in William Hole's engraving to be modelled on Prince Henry's catafalque of 1612 (Figure 7.10). Such archaic chivalric ritual was also an appeal to the imagination: to order and rationalise the traumatic and dislocated

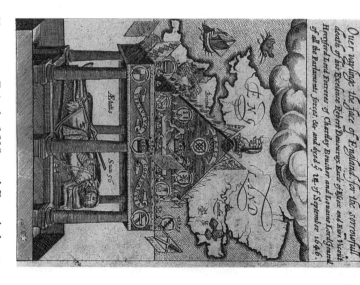

Figure 7.10   Prince Henry's hearse: frontispiece to George Chapman, *Epicede*, 1612; and Essex's hearse: A *Mournefull Cloude ouer vayling the Face of England*, 1646

politics of 1646 by an act of relocation in the past; in the romanticised heroic age of Prince Henry and in the values for which that episode was held to stand. By referring to the iconographic and ceremonial usages of Prince Henry's age – to the world of Peake's equestrian portrait of the prince – contemporaries were seeking to represent the parliamentarian cause in general, and Essex's career in particular, as the proper continuation of this godly, martial, chivalric tradition. Where Charles I had sought during the 1630s to redefine chivalry in such a way as to distance himself from its Elizabethan and Jacobean inheritance, Parliament sought to portray its dead lord general as its rightful heir. In the 'revolutions' of civil war, Caroline chivalry had come full circle.

V

Thus at least until the late 1640s, the language and imagery of chivalry remained a central element of the political culture of Caroline England. In no small measure this was because Charles I had deliberately made it so. From his accession, he had sought both to reinvigorate and to impose new priorities upon the chivalric culture of the court. The obsolete culture of the tournament was repudiated. Loyal service to the crown once again became the central element affirmed in the Caroline rituals of knighthood – most notably in reformed ceremonies of the Garter. And in the idealised portraiture of Van Dyck, as in the didacticism of the masque, a rich variety of chivalric imagery – from the cult of St George to the classical imagery of the Roman *imperator* – was synthesised to define a 'modern' image of the knightly prince. Yet this Caroline redefinition of the values and imagery of chivalry was never monopolistic, nor the court the only source of chivalric ideas. Indeed, what gave the Caroline redefinition of chivalry point and resonance was the fact that it was itself part of a diverse and pluralistic chivalric culture; one informed by the gothic heroes of Malory's *Morte d'Arthur*, by the knightly adventures of Quarles's *Argulus*, by Shakespeare's Hotspur and Jonson's Beaumont, and by the role-models provided by the pantheon of Elizabethan heroes from Sir Philip Sidney to the rebel Earl of Essex. The exploits of these Elizabethan champions of Protestantism served as a point of reference and comparison: for Buckingham and Charles I in 1625 as they sought to emulate the success of Essex's Cadiz raid of 1596, as well as for the parliamentarian generals of 1642. And chivalric iconography could serve, with equal elasticity, to glamorise Garter knights and regicides alike. Despite the efforts of parliamentary propagandists to appropriate elements within the chivalric tradition for its own ends, chivalry remained sufficiently diffuse a congeries of ideals and values to resist exclusive appropriation by any particular political cause.

Such conclusions prompt a further question: how were attitudes to chivalry – whose ideas and values were so much concerned with the culture of the knight – affected by the experience of almost a decade in which contemporary knights were engaged in the conduct of civil war? A full consideration of this question lies beyond the scope of this essay, but some preliminary suggestions may be made. The end of the civil wars in England seems to have brought in its wake a reaction against chivalric culture. Part of the explanation for this is to be found in the fact that the military failure of royalist arms could not be disassociated from the moral failure of royalist chivalry: membership of the Order of the Garter had proved no guarantee of loyalty in 1642; by 1645, the supposed 'flower of royalist chivalry' had been decisively vanquished in the field; and in the aftermath of the king's defeat, Charles's knights had failed to redeem him from the captivity of a regicide parliament. Yet even before the public execution of the king, in a letter written in July 1645, a few weeks after the collapse of the royalist cause at Naseby, Sir Kenelme Digby came close to implying that 'King Arthur' – Charles I as chivalric king – had died on the battlefield of Naseby. When the king's ministers reconvened in exile in Paris, he argued, it would be like that meeting 'at Glastonbury of all King Arthur's knights to celebrate the exequies of their founder'.[107] No less important, however, to the waning of this chivalric culture was the fact that from the late-1640s, those who viewed war as a millenarian conflict, as a struggle with the Antichrist, came increasingly to dominate the conduct of England's wars. Cromwell found his models not in the chivalric tales of Argulus and Amadis – the romantic fictions which had informed the mental world of, and perhaps even provided role-models for, men such as Essex and Newcastle – but in the zeal of Phineas and in the struggle of Israel against the Midianite.

Ironically, during the 1650s and 1660s it is the fortunes of the epic, that most characteristic genre of chivalric literature, which attest most clearly to the redundancy of both the values and cultural forms of Caroline chivalry. Digby was not the only one to think that King Arthur was now defunct. Milton abandoned work on the great Arthurian epic poem he had projected on the eve of the Long Parliament: 'Arthur as the pattern of chivalry, who, with his Knights of the Round Table, fought to defend Britain against the Saxon invaders'.[108] And by the 1650s Milton had repudiated the epic quaintnesses of King Arthur for the millenarian struggles of St Michael and the angelic host. Indeed, the post-civil-war verse epic – at the hands of its other principal masters, Sir William Davenant and Samuel Butler (1612–80) – was characterised by a rejection of that union between the worlds of politics and of the imagination which had been so central a feature of the intellectual culture of Caroline England. Sir William Davenant's *Gondibert: an Heroick Poem*, published in the first years of the Commonwealth, rejects the prescriptive authority of fictive conceits and didactic allegory as models for political action – ideas which had been among the central axioms of Elizabethan and early Stuart chivalric culture. Spenser's use of allegory is peremptorily dismissed by Davenant as resembling 'a continuance of extraordinary dreams'.[109] The heroism of the dedicatee of Davenant's 'heroic poem' is not a protagonist of the world of martial action, but of the world of philosophical contemplation: Thomas Hobbes. Hobbes responded in kind, praising the author's attempt to write a new, rational form of epic; one which stayed within the bounds of nature while jettisoning the imaginative paraphernalia of chivalric epic: 'Impenetrable Armors, Enchanted Castles, Invulnerable Bodies, Iron Men, Flying Horses, and a thousand other things' which exceed the possibility of nature.[110] Likewise, Samuel Butler's mock-epic of the civil wars, *Hudibras*, published in three parts between 1663 and 1678, strove to redeem 'Virtue ... and Honour' from the 'Enchanted Castles' of chivalric fiction.[111]

This literary reaction was, perhaps, symptomatic of a more fundamental change in sensibilities between the political and intellectual world of Caroline England and the post-Restoration world of Charles II; a change which may be characterised in terms of the role of the imagination in the political culture. In its diverse manifestations – in masques, in ballads, in the iconography of seals and portraits – Caroline chivalry had sought to inform contemporary perceptions of men and affairs through the constructs of the imagination, in which politics was naturally likened to stagecraft, 'virtue' defined in the terms of the romance, and in which the 'imagining' of the adversary had never been more imperative than during what that cultivated and perceptive soldier, Sir William Waller, had termed 'this war without an Enemy'.[112] In Restoration satire, however, the attempt to use chivalry to glamorise war was emphatically repudiated. 'Truth and Reason', as Butler put it, had to be rescued 'out of the captivity of Giants and Magicians'.[113] War and the profession of arms were brusquely demythologised. Butler's sneer that 'that noble trade/That *Demigods* and *Heroes* made' was nothing but 'slaughter and knocking on the head',[114] voiced a long-standing objection of the anti-chivalric moralist; in the aftermath of *civil* war, the fictive conceits of the tournament and the once glamorous stereotypes of chivalric literature had lost their potency. And in the chivalric burlesques of those conceits in *Hudibras*, Butler's Sir Knight is at once the pious hypocrite and the dupe of chivalry's empty bombast. Of course the mock chivalric burlesque was, in itself, nothing new: it was a strand in the chivalric tradition which went back to the 1620s parodies of orders of knighthood, to the English translations of Cervantes, to *The Knight of the Burning Pestle*, and beyond. What marks out the chivalric culture of the Restoration is that satire and irony have become, overwhelmingly, the dominant element.

Posthumous satire, however, should not blind us to how vigorous that chivalric culture had been in the reign of Charles I, nor to how recent had been its demise. Far from indicating the wholesale repudiation of chivalric culture, the discontinuance, at the king's accession, of the accession-day tilts signalled a reappraisal of the inheritance of Elizabethan and Jacobean chivalry, and its redirection into new forms of expression. In various guises – in the masque, in literature, in portraiture, and on the popular stage – the language and imagery of chivalry had continued to occupy a central place in the intellectual world of the Caroline court: to underpin loyalty and allegiance to the crown through the re-formed practices of the Order of the Garter; to dignify present-day military enterprises by representing them as parallels to glorious enterprises of the past; even to assert, as did that most literary of soldiers, the Earl of Newcastle, that chivalric culture defined the conventions appropriate to the honourable conduct of war. Yet in the sense that chivalry had played a central role in informing the language and even the values of politics, that was a role which did not survive the civil war. As the 'revolutions' of the 1640s swept away first the court, then royal government, and

finally even *Coelum Britannicum*'s Arthurian king, so too it seems
to have induced a sense – most articulately voiced by Davenant,
Butler and Hobbes – of the redundancy of the chivalric culture
which had served to inform the world of the broken *ancien régime*.
In retrospect, what Cromwell had termed the 'absolute victory' of
Naseby was as much a cultural as a political point of no return.

8. The Politics of Portraiture

JOHN PEACOCK

I Introduction

Exactly a month after the death of Queen Elizabeth I, Giovan Carlo Scaramelli, the Secretary of the Venetian Embassy in London, reported to the Doge and senate on the arrangements for her funeral. The new king, he wrote, had ordered it to proceed before his arrival; the disgraceful memory of his mother's execution would make the sight even of the queen's dead body repugnant. Everywhere, Scaramelli added, portraits of Elizabeth were being put away, and those of Mary Queen of Scots displayed instead, with unanimous assurances that the only reason for her death had been her Catholicism.[1] It seems clear enough that the people who had the motives and resources to switch their portraits – courtiers, government servants, substantial citizens – were signifying their readiness to co-operate with the new regime. The portraits of Mary were in themselves powerful signs of political docility; the extenuating explanation added a further dimension, a narrative about *Realpolitik* and martyrdom which undertook, through a swift revision of recent history, to make sense of the collective volte-face.

It is unlikely that these portraits of the beautiful and (as might now be said) wronged Mary Stuart had an aesthetic quality to match the suggestive legend that was coming to be attached to them. They would have been copies, and copies of copies, many incalculably distant from any putative original, and done by painters of modest ability. Some would have been brand new, produced to meet the sudden demand. They were not exactly, to use our kind of language, 'works of art'. But our kind of language, or more specifically the language of conventional art criticism, which uses the concept of 'the aesthetic', distinguishes 'originals' from 'copies', and may deplore 'art as a commodity', will not be

199

much help in starting to look at early seventeenth-century portraits and trying to understand their political meanings. The first thing we need to know about is their function – how were they used?

II   The politics of representation: (1) Reformation and figuration

In answering this question some more fundamental problems must be considered. The very practice of representing the human figure had been made by the Reformation a controversial religious, and therefore political, issue. In their return to a pristine Christianity which swept away the proliferating abuses of the Church, the Reformers were especially mindful of the second commandment:

> Thou shalt make thee no graven image, nether anie similitude *of things* that are in heaven above, nether that are in the earth beneth, nor that are in the waters under the earth. Thou shalt not bow downe to them, nether serve them: for I am the Lord thy God, a jelouse God, visiting the iniquitie of the fathers upon the children, upon the third *generacion* and upon the fourth of them that hate me...[2]

It was in this particular prohibition, against idolatry, that God had chosen to expatiate on his fearful power and exacting justice. To say that the second commandment made visual representation an issue is to put the matter mildly.

The result, in the earliest years of the Reformation, was great unease. Iconoclasm attacked only religious images in churches, leaving other kinds of imagery and setting untouched, but the radical force of the attack could have effects beyond its defined limits. The ban on public religious art closed down one of the largest areas of painting in Protestant Europe of the sixteenth century, greatly enlarging the scope of secular genres such as the portrait – or so the logic of the situation seemed to be. In 1550 Christopher Hales wrote to his friend Rodolph Gualter, asking him to commission six portraits, of himself, Zwingli, Bullinger, and others associated with the Reformed Church in Zurich. Gualter, abetted by Bullinger, delayed, was finally persuaded, had the portraits painted, then refused to send them all, for fear that they became occasions of idolatry. Hales had to argue strenuously on Biblical grounds against the view that 'portraits can nowise be

painted with a safe conscience and a due regard to godliness...'
and defend their circulation and display. What he says, in effect, is
that God's commandment does not forbid the production of
likenesses, but their abuse; it depends where they are displayed
and how they are treated: 'Who is so senseless, as to worship a
painting or picture deposited in a library?'[3]

Although Hales, from the context of the Edwardian Reformation, is rejecting this radical distrust of figurative art, it was also
present in English Protestantism, or at least was thought to be. It
is usually heard about from its opponents. Sir John Harington
attacks it in his translation of Ariosto's *Orlando Furioso*, published
in 1591. In the thirty-third canto Merlin shows Bradamante a
series of paintings which prophetically depict the invasions of
Italy by French kings; Harington's commentary gives a potted
history of ancient and modern painting, which he justifies in
these terms:

> my selfe (I must confesse) take great pleasure in such workes
> (as pleasing ornaments of a house and good remembraunces of
> our frends) as also to show in what great reckning that science
> hath been with Emperours and great Princes and with Prelates
> and Religious persons howsoever some austere or rather uncivil
> persons will seeme either to condemn it or contemn it.[4]

When he describes pictures as 'good remembraunces of our
frends' he implicitly recognises that, because of the disappearance
of public religious art, most English painting is now portraiture;
and he sees its enemies prepared to 'condemn' as well as
'contemn': not just disparaging but radically opposed. They pre-
tend to be more 'austere' than the 'Prelates and Religious persons'
who esteemed painting, and are at 'uncivil' variance with 'Emper-
ours and great Princes'. Who exactly these religious precisians and
political dissidents are is not clear. They cannot be puritans like
William Perkins, whose position was to allow various uses of secular
imagery in civil and religious life, and even paintings of Biblical
narratives in private places.[5] The point however is not whether
Harington could identify these people but how he characterises
them: what sort of people are they who would condemn painting
and portraiture? The threat he sees is a political one: the enemies
of portraiture are the enemies of church and state.

This threat continues to be felt into the seventeenth century,
until the attitudes which give it substance emerge plainly in the
iconoclasm of the 1640s. When English writings about painting

begin to be produced in the Jacobean period, their tone is initially defensive, since they assume they must prove the godliness of pictorial art. Henry Peacham begins his *Art of Drawing* (1606), half treatise and half manual, with both a definition and an apologia:

> Picture, or painting in generall, is an art which either by draught of bare lines, lively colours, cutting out or embossing, expresseth any thing the like by the same: which we may find in the holy Scriptures both allowed, and highly commended by the mouth of God himselfe; where he called *Bezaleel* and *Aholiab, Men whom he hath filled with the spirit of God in wisedom and understanding, and in knowledge, and in all workmanship, to find out curious works, to worke in gold, and in silver, and in brasse, also in the art to set stones, and to carve in timber, &c.* [margin: Exod 31] There plainly shewing, as all other good arts, so carving or drawing to be an especiall gift of Gods spirit.[6]

The italicised passage is quoted from Exodus 31, where God tells Moses of the two Israelites He has chosen to construct the tabernacle and the ark of the covenant, which, as we learn from Exodus 36, was surmounted by the figures of two cherubim. Bezaleel and Aholiab were a godsend to the apologist for figurative art in a Protestant culture. Peacham enthusiastically recommends the acquisition of graphic skills to the Jacobean gentry, and readers who aspired to gentry status. At the same time he warns that 'there be some things that ought to be free from the pencill' [i.e. the painter's brush]; and he instances 'the picture of God the father: or (as I have seen) the whole Trinitie painted in a glasse window'.[7] In the second edition of his book, six years later, this discussion is both longer and more relaxed. On representing the godhead and the Trinity he now quotes Catholic controversialists, especially Bellarmine, against Calvin and others, obviously to emphasise the Protestant position. He excludes the idolatrous display of pictures of 'our Saviour, the Apostles and Martyrs of the Church', but then makes a qualification:

> That pictures of these kindes may be drawne, and set up to draw the beholder *ad Historicum usum,* and not *ad cultum* [i.e. for record, not for worship] I hold them very lawfull and tolerable in the windowes of Churches and the private houses, and deserving not to be beaten doune with that violence and furie as they have beene by our Puritanes in many places.[8]

'Our Puritanes' sound not unlike Harington's 'austere or rather uncivil persons'. Peacham's stance has become less defensive.

Between the two editions of his book (1606 and 1612), Peacham had made contact with the court of Prince Henry. The second edition is dedicated to Henry, to whom, Peacham writes, he had recently presented a book of emblems painted by himself, based on 'his fathers *Basilicon Doron,* which I had turned a little before throughout into Latine verse'.[9] We can see how *The Art of Drawing* has become a more courtier-like book. The added citations from Bellarmine and Calvin would fit with the king's taste for theological controversy. In general, the continued assertion of a strict Protestant position on idolatrous images accompanied by a more nuanced view of religious art corresponds to the cultural tone of Henry's court, where reformed religion and continental art were both esteemed. One of Peacham's new allowances is for pictures 'of Christ according to his humanity'. He accords this subject the highest value, 'neither of the lawfulness thereof I thinke any wise man will make question'.[10] Henry had acquired a painting by Hans Vredeman de Vries of *Christ in the House of Martha and Mary.*[11] In Peacham's revisions, and in Henry's circle, we can see the anti-figurative bias in Reformation Christianity coming to terms with the new cultural policies of the Stuart court, where figurative art and especially portraiture were to be used for political purposes on an unprecedented scale.

The most conscious attempt to justify figurative art, and specifically portraiture, in the context of Protestant culture was made by Nicholas Hilliard. He is famous as a portrait miniaturist or 'limner' – the term indicates the derivation of the practice from manuscript illumination. Hilliard was limner to both Elizabeth and James I, although his greatest celebrity belongs to the Elizabethan period, when contemporaries uniquely recognised him as the equal of any European painter. In family terms Hilliard was a child of the Reformation. His father, an Exeter goldsmith who encouraged his precocious talent, was also a committed Protestant, and sent him at the age of about nine to live in the household of the Calvinist John Bodley, a Marian exile who spent time in Germany, finally settling in Geneva between 1557 and 1559. One of Hilliard's first surviving miniatures, produced in 1560 when he was only thirteen, was a posthumous portrait of Edward Seymour, Duke of Somerset, the protagonist of Edwardian reform.[12] Over the next forty years, the practice of his art immersed him in a world of sensuous aesthetic experience; but when, around the beginning of the next

century, he wrote a treatise on that art, it was articulated through
the key religious concepts of his early education.

In the first, properly theoretical, part of his *Treatise*, Hilliard
concentrates obsessively on the social status of his own art. This
obsession with the status of the artist was common in such treatises, nearly all of which had so far been produced in Italy;[13] but
Hilliard gives the theme an ingeniously unItalian, that is to say
non-Catholic, inflection. He wants to insist that limning is 'a kind
of gentle painting': only gentlemen are fit to practise it. But he
also wants to redefine, or at least shift, the concept of gentility. It
does not necessarily come from birth or education: it is the gift
of God, who does not work according to established social
norms:

> He giveth gentility to divers persons, and raiseth man to repu-
> tation by divers means: we read that he called Bezaleel and
> Aholiab by name, and filled them with wisdom, skill and
> understanding, without any teaching, but only of His own gift
> and grace received.[14]

As usual, Bezaleel and Aholiab are enlisted into the argument, but
this time with a twist, as cases of social advancement through an
infusion of artistic talent by divine grace. The point is pressed
home:

> Here is a kind of true gentility, when God calleth: and doubtless
> though gentlemen be the meetest for this gentle calling or
> practice, yet not all; but natural aptness is to be chosen and
> preferred, for not every gentleman is so gentle spirited as some
> others are. Let us therefore honour and prefer the election of
> God in all vocations and degrees...[15]

Hilliard's awkwardness in sliding between different meanings of
'gentle', as he tries to distinguish and not distinguish between
social rank and innate ability, is resolved by a stroke of ideological
audacity, as he appropriates for his purpose the Calvinist doctrine
of election. Artists belong to a social élite because they are elect of
God. They have a divine entitlement to gentility.

An equally urgent matter on Hilliard's theoretical agenda is his
own style of limning, and its justification. Around the time when
he composed the *Treatise*, his commanding position was being
challenged by his pupil Isaac Oliver, whose style was closely related

to contemporary continental painting, and was to find favour in the progressive cultural milieu of the Jacobean court. Oliver modelled his figures with a greater plasticity, using marked contrasts of light and shadow. Hilliard's style was essentially linear, with shadow eschewed or minimised. In his discussion he insists on the rightness of line and the wrongness of shadow:

> Forget not therefore that the principal part of painting or drawing after the life consisteth in the truth of the line... For beauty and good favour is like clear truth, which is not shamed with the light, nor needs to be obscured; so a picture a little shadowed may be borne withal for the rounding of it; but so greatly smutted or darkened as some use, disgraceth it, and is like truth ill told.[16]

Line is identified with truth, shadow with visual prevarication. These are more than moral concepts, as Hilliard emphasises when he goes on to give an instance of a theme where shadow logically belongs, the betrayal of Christ by Judas, 'the traitorous act done by night'.[17] The idea of a 'clear truth' which can only be obscured or defiled by mediation is one of the fundamental motifs of Protestantism; by using it Hilliard's argument acquires an exceptionally powerful resource.

III   The politics of representation: (2) Theories of portraiture

Although Hilliard's treatise was never finished, remaining in draft form, and never published (until parts were pirated by later writers), it circulated in manuscript during the seventeenth century.[18] The interest of many readers may have centered on its technical passages, but it is the combination of theoretical and technical discourses which makes it historically important. By the very activity of theorising about his art Hilliard was validating the claim that it was a vocation proper to the educated and leisured élite. The established members of that élite, the patrons who commissioned portraits from Hilliard and many other painters – Harington would be a good example – took for granted the privilege of entertaining and expressing general ideas about such matters as portraiture. These ideas, unlike Hilliard's, were not usually the result of practical experience and determined reflection, but their prevalence in the dealings between patrons and painters gave them an obvious authority, and for that reason they need to be examined.

Early Stuart patrons picked up ideas about art from two over-lapping traditions, one more available and one more specialised. Those who had received a conventional education based on classi-cal texts would have access to the history of ancient painting and sculpture in Pliny's *Natural History* (which was in any case trans-lated into English in 1601); the evocative descriptions of works of art in the *Imagines* of Philostratus; the influential discussions of visual representation by Plato, Aristotle and Xenophon; the mate-rial about painting used for analogy and illustration in treatises on oratory by Cicero and Quintilian, and in Horace's *Ars Poetica*; and anecdotal information about portraits in biographical and histori-cal writers such as Plutarch. All this material, and more, was sifted and commented on by Franciscus Junius, Lord Arundel's librar-ian, when he published his treatise *De Pictura Veterum* in 1637; it appeared in English as *The Painting of the Ancients* in 1638.[19] No courtier or member of the gentry could possibly approach Junius's vast learning; his book was partly aimed at their instruction. But many would have known some of the texts he quoted, and be able to adduce ideas or instances from them, even if only in support of favourite truisms or prejudices.

A minority of patrons, principally courtiers, would have been familiar with the modern ideas about art disseminated from Renaissance Italy since the later fifteenth century. On the subject of figurative art the key texts were Alberti's *De Pictura* (1435, first printed 1540), Vasari's *Lives* (1550, 2nd edn 1568), and the com-pendious *Trattato dell'arte della pittura, scoltura ed architettura* (1584) by G.P. Lomazzo; the last of these, which contains the most extensive body of theoretical ideas and practical instruction, was translated into English by the Oxford scholar Richard Haydocke (1598).[20] Although he did not include the last two of Lomazzo's seven books, he communicated his thinking effectively, as well as the general thinking about the arts of late Renaissance Italian culture. This culture was to become established at the Stuart court, through the efforts of Anne of Denmark, Prince Henry, his younger brother Charles, and an increasingly influential circle of supporters, led by the Earl of Arundel. Their efforts were focused and publicised by the painter, architect and stage-designer Inigo Jones, whose knowledge of the Renaissance tradition, unmatched by any English contemporary, eventually made him the dominant court artist. The accession of Charles gave this Italianate culture the sanction of kingly authority. Its art was an intellectualised and consciously theorised art; and the full range of ideas which informed it was only familiar to artists formed in its traditions, like Jones, or connoisseurs of an intellectual bent, like Arundel. But since these ideas were in part based on antique texts, their diffusion at the court was aided by the classical culture already taken for granted.

The most fundamental ideas about portraiture in European culture were to be read in Aristotle's *Poetics*. After its rediscovery in the Renaissance, this became the most powerful text of literary theory throughout the sixteenth and seventeenth centuries. Although Aristotle is writing about poetry and drama, he continually supports his argument with analogies from painting, and the type of painting he always appeals to is portraiture. Central to his discussion is the concept of *mimesis*, which has usually been translated as 'imitation', and which these days we might translate as 'representation'. For Aristotle, the first cause of the development of poetry is the mimetic instinct – which he sees as basic to humanity – and the pleasure associated with it, what Franciscus Junius calls 'the inbred delight men take in the imitation of the workes of Nature'.[21] Even distressing things can please us if they are skilfully represented, 'such as the forms of the most ignoble animals and of dead bodies.'[22] The point is taken up by Rubens in his painting of *St George and the Princess*, where the principal figures are idealised versions of Charles I and Henrietta Maria; he represents the dead body of the dragon and the corpses of its victims with all the resources of his remarkable technique.[23] Our pleasure in seeing a likeness, Aristotle continues, is the pleasure of acquiring knowledge: so when seeing a picture of somebody we are delighted to recognise who it is. This puts him to explaining how a likeness can please us if we are not familiar with the original: it does so not through the representation as such but through the means of representation, 'the execution, the colouring, or some such other cause'.[24]

Aristotle's argument makes painting the paradigm of representation, and portraiture the paradigm of painting. He distinguishes (at first, awkwardly) two pleasurable qualities in portraits: recognisable likeness, and aesthetic skill. Later, as his discussion of poetry turns specifically to tragedy, he produces an idea of portraiture which brings these qualities back together: since tragedy represents people of exalted status, the example of good portrait-painters should be followed. They, while reproducing the distinctive form of the original, make a likeness which is true to life and yet more beautiful.[25]

Aristotle's analogy expresses both a philosophical doctrine and an assumption about society. Understood philosophically, *mimesis*, whether in a tragic character or the subject of a portrait, is not the mere replication of natural appearances along with their possible defects, but a representation which, while paying due regard to nature, aims at the ideal, the universal. But the analogy also suggests that the privilege of being portrayed by the best artists, like the privilege of being represented in the highest poetic genre, belongs only to eminent people; and their eminence entails the further privilege of idealisation. Their portraits will be both like and beautiful, both mimetically accurate and aesthetically accomplished.

The immense prestige of Aristotle's theory of representation, which remained basic for early modern European cultures, ensured that the social exclusiveness and tendentiousness of portraiture could be understood as an expression of philosophical truth. Renaissance writers on painting, who dedicated their works to rulers and magnates, often reiterated or elaborated an Aristotelian position. Alberti and Vasari, for example, rehearse a concern for the problematic relationship between likeness and beauty. Alberti repeats material from Plutarch about Pericles, who, because of his awkwardly long head, was always painted or sculpted wearing his helmet; and about the practice of antique painters in minimising physical defects in portraits of kings.[26] Vasari debates the relative merits of portraits which are successful likenesses, but unflattering, and those which are perfect works of art, but unlike; he concludes: 'When portraits are like and beautiful, then they may be called rare works, and the artists exceptional'.[27] Here the easy resort to an Aristotelian formula suggests how this kind of thinking may be philosophically limited; but its social sway was more potent. Vasari's contemporary Michelangelo refused out of philosophical abhorrence to make portraits from life, since the representation of nature could never result in ideal beauty. In his sculptures of Lorenzo and Giuliano de' Medici he notoriously took no account of their actual appearance, and replied to a critic that in a thousand years' time the matter would have become irrelevant.[28] This intransigent idealism simply carries to an extreme the assumption of the Aristotelian tradition which Michelangelo is rejecting, that it is philosophically right for the best people to be represented in the most beautiful way. When Nicholas Stone imitated Michelangelo's Giuliano de' Medici in his tomb sculpture of Francis Holles, son of the recently created Earl of Clare, he followed the idealising example of his model, which he used to enhance the ambivalent prestige of new nobility.[29]

By the end of the sixteenth century, idealism such as Michelangelo's had become predominant in Italian writing about art. In theory this idealism gave no countenance to portraiture as usually understood. Michelangelo's disciple, Vincenzio Danti, made a crucial distinction between two kinds of representation: *ritrarre* (to portray), a representation based on natural appearances, and *imitare* (to imitate), one based on a conception of the perfect form which the natural data could take.[30] Since the Italian word for portrait is *ritratto*, Danti is doing the opposite of Aristotle: instead of making portraiture the paradigm of imitation he uses the concept to express inferior or degenerate imitation. This kind of position finds a voice in England in Sir Philip Sidney's *Apology for Poetry* (1595), which critically contrasts

> the meaner sort of painters, who counterfeit only such faces as are set before them, and the more excellent, who having no law but wit, bestow that in colours upon you which is fittest for the eye to see...[31]

Scorn for the 'mean' empiricism of portraiture is reinforced by the social eminence and cosmopolitan culture of the writer, who would anyway have seen the incompetence of much Elizabethan portraiture by continental standards. At the same time, this was exactly the sort of person who would expect to (and did) have his portrait painted repeatedly. It was all very well for Michelangelo, who was a law and a culture unto himself, to eschew portraiture in practice as well as theory. For a late Renaissance courtier, especially one aiming to exercise political power, the representation of his status and power in portraits was a necessity. Idealist philosophies of art could not be allowed to challenge this practice, but had to be enlisted in its support. And so they were.

The task was performed by academic art theorists of the late sixteenth century. One of these especially, as we have seen, would have been known to the more informed members of the early Stuart court, Giovanni Paolo Lomazzo. His *Trattato* contains an entire chapter on portraiture;[32] and, although this was in the later part of the treatise not translated by Haydocke, it was known to court artists such as Hilliard and Jones, and to those courtiers knowledgeable in Italian culture. Lomazzo's account is divided into two parts: a history of portraiture, and a set of precepts or conventions to be followed by portrait painters. Historically, he gives portraiture a pre-eminent position, and identifies it with political pre-eminence. He sees it as the origin of all painting, the primordial and exclusive function of which was to make commemorative images of great rulers, which would stimulate posterity to 'imitate' them.[33] By using this familiar term, which (all his readers would know) denotes artistic representation as well as moral emulation, Lomazzo sees portraiture as reproducing political power. He couples with this explanation a passage from Pliny, which relates that in Greece only free-born boys were allowed to be taught painting. By translating free-born as 'nobili' (nobles) and painting as 'ritrarre dal naturale' (portraying from life) he wrenches the text of his classical authority to suggest that in antiquity portrait painters had a social status proportionate to their sitters. In modern times, he complains, undistinguished people succeed in being painted, and unworthy artists in painting them.[34] Lomazzo invokes the authority of antiquity to restrict portraiture to élites (of both sitters and artists), and defines it as a privileged space where the sitter's political power and the artist's social status reinforce each other. The model of a symbiosis between portraiture and power had already been substantiated by certain famous relationships, between Raphael and Julius II, Titian and Charles V; that between Charles I and Van Dyck would follow the same pattern.

Lomazzo's historical analysis, which identifies representation with action, and puts power first, is supplemented by his precepts for the modern portraitist, which deal with methods of idealisation. Firstly, he instructs, every sitter must bear the sign of his social identity, his rank. So an emperor must wear a laurel crown, just like the Twelve Caesars of Titian painted for the Duke of Mantua, who also carry batons as a sign of their authority.[35] Such examples could come to seem very pertinent for Stuart courtiers, since Titian's Caesars were bought by Charles I and displayed in St James's Palace with his own equestrian portrait by Van Dyck. Secondly, says Lomazzo, monarchs must be shown as majestic, whether they are so in fact or not. Personal defects must be glossed over or concealed, as was done by the artists of antiquity; and here he repeats the story from Plutarch about Pericles's misshapen head and the helmet worn to mask it, with similar anecdotes. The tail-end of his advice concerns sitters of lesser status: soldiers and ecclesiastics must wear the dress of their profession, as must men of business, who should not masquerade in military costume; women must be made to look beautiful.[36] That is, portraits must reproduce professional roles and gender stereotypes; by methods of generalisation and abstraction they must reinforce social distinctions. Idealisation becomes a means to represent power and subordination.

IV   Uses and functions

Lomazzo's precepts affirm familiar doctrine. In early seventeenth-century England their underlying principle would have been taken for granted – that portraiture, in Roy Strong's words, 'is concerned with recording and defining in visual terms the position of a sitter in society'.[37] Even the existence of a special type of portrait, the miniature, which seems to be personal rather than social in its meaning, reinforces this principle. Miniatures often took their meaning from the context of an intimate relationship, being designed to evoke the presence of a loved one. They were exchanged between husbands and wives, parents and children, siblings, lovers, or close friends. But at the same time they could be treated as objects of adornment, worn on the person in special cases or jewelled settings. There are large-scale portraits showing miniatures worn in this way. There are also miniatures of people wearing miniatures: Charles I had a 'limned piece' by Isaac Oliver of his mother, Anne of Denmark, 'a picture box at her left breast'.[38] So even these exquisitely wrought private portraits can be used for manifest display, and assume a function in the public sphere.

Portraits 'in large' or 'in great' (as distinct from those 'in little' or 'in small') were similarly exchanged, circulated and displayed, but on a larger and more complex scale. They were used to record the likenesses of members or friends of a family, both living and dead; to show loyalty to the sovereign and members of the royal family, or to powerful superiors; and to affirm bonds to patrons, clients, political allies and others who figured in those relationships where the personal and the public intertwined. The two poles of reference were the family and the state, and they remained so when the domestic scene shifted to the international one. European ruling houses habitually intermarried, and family affinity accompanied political negotiation, either in harmony or in counterpoint. Portraits were extensively used in diplomacy, as documents to provide information and as gifts to strengthen bonds: they would be exchanged when princely marriages were discussed, or presented by friendly sovereigns to each other. Once received, they might take on different functions, so that the portrait of a rejected suitor or an estranged ally might continue to be displayed as a sign of one's weight in the world of international politics, a part of a prestigious art collection, or a valuable historical record.

One ensemble of portraits from the Jacobean court illustrates this interrelationship of family and politics on the international level. It was arranged in the Queen's Gallery at Greenwich Palace by Anne of Denmark, and apparently left intact by Henrietta Maria. The inventory by Abraham van der Doort begins: '1. In primis the King of Denmark in armour at length', thereafter listing Charles I when a child as Duke of York, and 'the old Queen of Denmark'.[39] His reading of the group, which gives primacy to Christian IV, Anne of Denmark's brother, is clear: the main theme is the queen's family and its connections. So there are portraits (two) of her sister Hedevig, Duchess of Saxony, and her nephew Christian the electoral prince; of her nephews Friedrich Ulrik and Christian, sons of the Duke of Brunswick, and their sister the Countess of Nassau; and of her cousin the Duke of Mecklenburg. Along with these are portraits of her Scots relations: Lord Darnley, the Earl of Lennox, Lady Arabella Stuart, the Duke of Richmond. There are portraits of a Grand Duke and Duchess of Tuscany, probably Ferdinand I and Christine of Lorraine, who would have become family connections if Prince Henry had married Ferdinand's daughter. Mixed in are notables inherited from the previous reign, including Leicester and Alençon (who *might* have become family); and various figures who, in the twenty years since the queen's death, have become unidentifiable. But the inventory is rounded off with a significant picture: 'item in the Queen's bedchamber above the chimney the piece of a family with a father and mother playing with their daughter.'[40] The mention of this here seems gratuitous, since it is not part of the group in the gallery, and is not said to have belonged to Queen Anne. But its position, as if summing up what goes before, shows how van der Doort is reading the gallery group, as essentially a representation of a family, however politically momentous its members. In this typical assemblage of princely portraits, family and politics intersect.

Queen Anne's closest ties, with the court of Denmark, can be illustrated from the other side. Christian IV's relationship to the King of Great Britain became vital to his foreign policy, and he visited England twice, in 1606 and 1614. At home he received portraits of James I by John de Critz, and of Anne by Marcus Gheeraerts the younger. Most of these were destroyed in the fire of 1859 at Frederiksborg Castle, but one painting of Anne survives, which originally belonged to a uniform group of family portraits. Also displayed at Frederiksborg were two full-length portraits of Charles I as Prince of Wales by Daniel Mytens. The earlier is a dynastic image of the prince enthroned, wearing robes of state and the Garter, with an elaborate architectural perspective background, the later a more informal study in an interior setting; the two images, one more 'political' and one more 'familial', complement each other.[41]

Portraits do not always make simple statements of relationship and alliance. We might return to the Jacobean court and examine one complex case in detail. This is an unusual painting of Prince Henry, produced by Robert Peake around 1610 (Figure 8.1). It shows Henry in a landscape setting, with buildings in the background and a bridge over water. He is standing in a posture of defiance, about to draw his sword, with one foot planted on a decorated shield bearing the Prince of Wales's badge of three feathers with the motto *Ich dien* (I serve). The pose is directly imitated from an engraving by Hendrik Goltzius, in his series of *Roman Heroes*, showing Titus Manlius Torquatus.[42] Livy tells two famous stories about Manlius, in youth and in manhood. Goltzius's print shows him in maturity, and refers to the second episode, when he defeated a Gaul in single combat in the sight of the Roman and Gaulish armies, who were contesting the possession of a bridge.[43] But Peake shows Henry as a youth, and is evidently conflating the second episode with the first, which concerns Manlius's upbringing. His father, who was notorious for his domineering nature, repressed his son's talents and refused to accord him his proper position in society. Charged with this, and other offences, he was brought to trial by a tribune of the plebeians. Manlius was determined to affirm his filial piety, and not to be used by his father's critics. He threatened the tribune with a knife, and made him swear to stop the trial.[44] Peake's image of Henry as a Roman hero out of Livy, according to a programme for

214

Figure 8.1 Robert Peake: Henry, Prince of Wales, *c.*1604–10

which the prince himself must have been responsible, subsumes two clashing motifs in the prince's notoriously difficult relationship with the king. His military bent, and ambition to fight for the Protestant cause, were deeply unsympathetic to his peace-loving father. But his sense of duty and obedience was equally strong. The posture of defiance in the portrait, read in the light of Livy, expresses both attitudes: Henry prepares to draw his sword equally against the enemies of his country and religion, and the critics of his father. His foot braced against the shield is just as ambivalent: the motto 'I serve' seems to be proudly indicated, with an uneasy impression of being simultaneously spurned. The picture makes a statement which is complex but not reticent: the forceful nature of the image challenges the spectator to engage with its meanings.

Those meanings became simplified when it was later taken out of its original context. Today the portrait is to be found in Turin, where it must have been sent as a present to the Duke of Savoy. This was presumably during the negotiations for a marriage between Henry and a Savoy princess, which entered their most serious phase during the summer of 1612. Although the picture showed the prince as younger than he then was, and may have been sent as a stopgap until a more recent likeness could be provided, it could be thought suitable for two reasons. Firstly, it shows him almost in full face, and with his features precisely delineated. Secondly, since from the English point of view the Savoy match was meant to promote the Protestant cause in northern Italy, the image of the youthful English prince in fighting posture (and he stands under an oak tree, symbolic of fortitude[45]) signifies that the Duke is being offered a sturdy political and military ally, whatever their religious differences. In the international context, as in its original domestic setting, the picture could make a statement which, while less complex, was equally pointed.

V   Contexts and ensembles

While specific portraits had specific meanings, which might be changed or shifted by a change of context, the usual way in which portraits acquired meaning was by being displayed in groups or series. Few inventories or descriptions of these arrangements have survived, and those usually refer only to the grandest establishments; but there is enough evidence to give some idea of how Stuart aristocrats, and the royal collector Charles I, organised

their portraits. Many would have accepted arrangements made by
their forebears, simply adding portraits from their own generation or other new acquisitions without substantially altering an
existing scheme. At Theobalds, Robert Cecil seems to have inherited a scheme devised by his father Lord Burghley. This was
recorded on a visit by the Moravian Baron Waldstein.[46] In the
principal gallery were both sculptured busts and painted portraits
of the twelve Caesars, with pictures of English kings from Henry IV
to Henry VII. On the opposite wall were portraits of such famous
Europeans as Don John of Austria, the Duke of Parma, Count
Egmont and the Prince de Condé. The historical importance of
these figures was emphasised by the presence of a large terrestrial
globe, and a series of views of major cities. The point of the
scheme was suggested by another visitor, Sir Roger Wilbraham,
who tersely recorded 'a large gallery, one side all the emperors
beginning with Caesar; th' other the pictures of the chief in
Europe ...'[47] In other words, here was a careful attempt to represent the historical and political milieu in which Burghley the
statesman had pursued his grand designs, with reference not only
to the pressures of contemporary European events but also to the
legacy of statecraft left by antiquity. Robert Cecil, deliberately
trained as his father's political heir, would have every reason to
preserve this arrangement intact. Waldstein also described a lower
gallery displaying portraits of the Cecil family, 'with an account of
the notable acts of each under different reigns'.[48] For the average
great family this would have been the main focus of attention; but
he mentions it as an afterthought, showing much more interest,
as a visitor was clearly meant to, in the greater ensemble which
places William and Robert Cecil in a world-historical perspective.

An equally calculated and tendentious arrangement of portraits
was installed in Hardwick Hall by the Countess of Shrewsbury,
where she willed it should 'remain and continue', to be passed on
to her seventeenth-century descendants.[49] The object was to
glorify herself and her family. As a woman, however socially powerful, she is constrained to celebrate her own position through her
relations to others. The problem can be read from the decoration
of the Withdrawing Chamber, a room properly for her own use,
which was hung with tapestries representing famous women of
antiquity and the virtues they exemplified. The main emphasis is
on wifely virtues, shown by the pious widow Artemisia and the
patient Penelope; a rare mythological painting in the room, of
Ulysses and Penelope, reinforces this theme. The portraits

indicate the spectrum of her family connections. They range from her deceased husband Sir Charles Cavendish to the Scots royal family, who became related by the marriage of her daughter Elizabeth Cavendish to Charles Stuart, Earl of Lennox, Lord Darnley's brother. So this mere nucleus of family portraits includes Darnley, Mary Queen of Scots, and her parents James V and Mary of Guise. The full story is spelt out in the Long Gallery. Pictures of English sovereigns from Edward II onwards lead on to Darnley, James VI, her son-in-law Lennox, and her granddaughter Lady Arabella Stuart, cousin to the King of Scots and the Queen of England. At different stages in this momentous procession come foreign monarchs such as Henri III and Philip II or assorted Cavendishes.[50] Even from the breathless summary of the inventory it is clear that attention has been paid to order and placement: no Christian or Catholic majesty is demeaned by the nearness of an obscure member of the Derbyshire gentry. Even so the countess, a powerful woman forced to represent her sense of importance only through relationships, has triumphantly worked this fix to its logical conclusion. On the strength of her connection to the Scots and English royal families, she has conjured away the boundaries that normally mark differences in even the grandest portrait collections. The Cecils had put their sovereigns in the upper gallery and themselves in the lower; she refuses to subordinate kinship to sovereignty.

Both arrangements, at Theobalds and Hardwick, are traditional in form. They use portraits almost entirely to the exclusion of other types of painting; and it is the sitter who gives the portrait its meaning, the question of the painter being irrelevant. As interest in modern European art grew at the early Stuart court, more and more courtiers came to regard portraits not just as likenesses of specific persons but also as what we might call works of art. The collecting of European paintings and the arrival of accomplished foreign artists intensified this new consciousness. One result of regarding portraits in new ways was that they came to be displayed in new ways, and could produce new meanings. The most informative document about these new methods of display is the inventory of Charles I's collection compiled by Abraham van der Doort. It concentrates especially on Whitehall Palace, revealing in great detail how portraits were grouped, how far they were mixed with other paintings, and how they were displayed in both the more public and more private areas of the palace.

In the Bear Gallery at Whitehall van der Doort lists thirty-five pictures, most of them portraits, many falling into traditional categories.[51] There are immediate family: James I and Anne of Denmark; the king's deceased cousin, the Duke of Richmond; his mother-in-law, Marie de Médicis. There are continental relatives: Prince Rupert, and the Duke of Brunswick. There are portraits of royal forebears, modern versions of older paintings produced as part of his duties by the king's painter Daniel Mytens: James IV of Scotland, his wife Queen Margaret, Mary Queen of Scots. There are European monarchs of previous generations: Charles V, Philip II, Henri II, Henri IV. There are deceased courtiers: Buckingham, the Earl of Nottingham, the third Earl of Pembroke. The traditional concept of family, both in itself and as a model for political relationships domestic and foreign, seems as always the basis of the arrangement. But there are also new elements to be seen. Paintings other than portraits have been introduced at intervals. Several of these are overdoors, oblong paintings placed above doorways, which seem to be a kind of decorative punctuation to the lengthy expanse of portraits: they are Italian works of the sixteenth century, of which the king was exceptionally fond. One is an anonymous portrait, attributed to Parmigianino; there is a note that the king purchased it himself. The emphasis here, by the king's own choice, is on the work of the painter rather than the identity of the sitter. Alongside the regular portraits themselves are two large subject pictures by Rubens. One is the allegory of Peace and War which he presented to the king after his diplomatic mission to London in 1629.[52] It is next to a portrait of Charles V by Titian, and close to another of Philip II by Anthonis Mor. Rubens's allegory seems placed so as to make a commentary on the portraits, on the chequered relations between England and the Hapsburg powers; and the virtuosity of the three painters also brings the pictures together. The conventional configuration of portraits is animated in new ways, by bringing aesthetic considerations more into the foreground, so as to set off or dramatise political themes.

Elsewhere in the palace, spaces which in the Tudor period would have been seen as suitable for displaying portraits are put to other uses. The Long Gallery is given over to a display of sixteenth-century Italian paintings, with some more modern works[53] – groups of rulers and notables are replaced by families of paintings. The few portraits here do not figure for the usual reasons. There is an early self-portrait of Rembrandt, suggesting an interest in the young artist's work, and akin to the self-portraits of Rubens, Van Dyck and Mytens kept in the Privy Lodgings. The head of an anonymous old man is there because it is a Van Dyck, and a portrait of Lady Denny because it is ascribed to Francesco Salviati. The only portrait with an overtly political meaning is the 'great piece' which Van Dyck painted of the royal family on his arrival in England in 1632, showing the king, the queen, Prince Charles and Princess Mary[54] – the king appears solemnly in his interchangeable roles of father and sovereign, monarch of his family and father of his people. Its presence among the works of the Italian masters affirms the eminence of the artist, whose comparable mastery enhances his representation of the king's authority.

This new emphasis on the representational power of the artist is most clearly seen in the hanging of paintings throughout the king's private apartments, the Privy Lodgings. A portrait of the Doge Andrea Gritti figures because it is a Titian, and is accompanied not by other rulers but by other great artists, such as Raphael, Giorgione and Correggio.[55] The king's bedchamber contained portraits of those closest to him, but all by the best available painters; and this relationship between family ties, with their political implications, and the power of artists to represent their importance is carried through consistently in the decoration of the room.[56] Henrietta Maria is portrayed by Van Dyck, and Charles's sister the Queen of Bohemia by her favourite painter Honthorst; there are also portraits of her husband and children. Specially placed over the chimney is the family of the assassinated favourite Buckingham, also by Honthorst: the king had promised to be a father to his children. The dead Prince Henry is painted by Mytens after a miniature by Isaac Oliver; clearly there was no surviving large-scale portrait of his brother that Charles would have found aesthetically tolerable. In two religious paintings of the Virgin, Christ and St John, earthly affinity is transposed into the theme of the Holy Family. The king no doubt used these pictures to aid his devotions; that they were painted by Parmigianino and Raphael will have added greatly to their spiritual effect. The one painting which directly expresses his love of the arts, a small piece of the Muses by Perino del Vaga, persists with the overall theme, since the Muses were all sisters, and figure the arts as a family. The whole carefully constructed setting places the king at the centre of various interconnected systems of kinship – personal, political, religious and cultural – which are represented with an unprecedented attention to the quality of

representation itself. The aesthetic interests of the royal paterfamilias, head of church and state, are enlisted to intensify the
demonstration of his authority, and bring it continually to his own
attention.

VI   The politics of style

Between the proudly regimented portrait schemes of Hardwick
and the aestheticised genealogies of Whitehall only a few decades
elapsed; but during that time the art of painting, as practised and
patronised at the court, made rapid advances. Elizabethan portraiture had been backward-looking, partly through incapacity
and partly through choice. From his long service as court artist to
Henry VIII, Holbein had left behind an impressive body of work
which showed the strongly developed representational possibilities of Italian High Renaissance painting as taken up in Northern
Europe. His English followers tended to revise his style,
attenuating its realism and over-stressing its linearity. Their
figurative designs tended to be decorative, schematised and two-
dimensional, declining the means which the Renaissance
tradition had worked out for producing the illusion of solid
figures in a real space.[57] In the hands of Hilliard (the only
Elizabethan painter who really understood Holbein's work) this
style was skilfully adapted to portraits in miniature; but for lesser
artists, and on a large scale, it was more uncertain in effect. It
became established, however, by royal sanction. The queen's
policy of controlling as far as possible the production and
dissemination of her own image, which had always to be mystified
and mythologised, adopted the prevailing non-realist style of
English painting and turned it to advantage. 'Semper eadem' was
the queen's motto, and a representational style which turned away
from naturalism towards abstraction was obviously suited to figure
that enduring majesty which was beyond the vicissitudes of
nature.[58] Cultural regression is established by royal authority.

   At the Stuart court the situation was reversed. Anne of
Denmark's passion for the visual arts, which she passed on to her
sons Henry and Charles, meant that royal power now promoted
cultural modernity. James I's Serjeant Painters, John de Critz and
Robert Peake, had both been formed in the conservative
Elizabethan tradition, and their portraits showed it.[59] But the
miniaturist Isaac Oliver, who was Queen Anne's 'painter for the
Art of Limning', had travelled in Italy and was familiar with recent

movements in Italian painting. This made him a prized artist, and he was eventually taken up by Prince Henry. When Henry was created Prince of Wales in 1610, and granted his own establishment at St James's and Richmond Palaces, he began to invite continental artists into his service. One of these was the Florentine Costantino de' Servi, who was, among other things, a portrait painter; he produced several portraits for the queen soon after his arrival in 1611 which pleased her very much.[60] Henry also tried, but failed, to secure the leading Dutch portraitist Mierevelt. Although his household was dissolved on his death in 1612, he had set down the main lines of early Stuart cultural policy. With regard to portrait painting, this was to encourage native painters who were in touch with developments on the continent, and to persuade capable, or if possible distinguished, continental painters to settle in London. The prestige of the Stuart monarchy and its aspirations to play a part in the wider scene of European politics (whether conciliatory, as favoured by James I, or interventionist, as favoured by Henry) were to be represented through the medium of modern European art.

Two talented foreign portrait painters eventually settled at the Stuart court. The first was the Dutchman Daniel Mytens, who came to London around 1618 under the patronage of the Earls of Arundel and Southampton, and was later taken into the royal service. Soon after his arrival he painted companion portraits of the Earl and Countess of Arundel (Figures 8.2 and 8.3).[61] These follow a carefully devised programme which comments on the new cultural policies of the court, of which Arundel was one of the leading promoters, and on the new portraiture which Mytens had been chosen to expound. The countess is shown seated in front of the lower range of the new gallery wing recently added to Arundel House. It contains a meticulously placed series of family portraits. Only two, which face the spectator directly, are shown as identifiable: they could represent the countess's parents or her husband's, but what is quite obvious is the self-conscious note they strike, as twin portraits within one of a pair of twin portraits. The other portraits in the gallery, all full-lengths, are seen in side view, placed between large windows. This arrangement, where the splendour of noble ancestors is enhanced by a measured excess of light, belongs to the previous century. The fact that the sitters are indistinguishable focuses attention on the layout itself, and its historical associations with an obsolescent culture. The earl is seated before the upper gallery, which contains the best pieces – all life-size figures – from his new collection of antique sculpture;

222

Figures 8.2 and 8.3   Thomas Howard, Earl of Arundel and Aletheia Talbot, Countess of Arundel, c.1618

they are arranged on uniformly designed classical plinths in a setting of classical architecture. The whole conception announces the belated but deliberate introduction into England, by those patrons and collectors whose leader Arundel took himself to be, of Italian Renaissance culture. Each figure is distinguishable, and an informed spectator would know that they include Venus, Minerva, Homer, Marius, and so on.[62] The precious antique statues, to which their noble owner points meaningfully with his staff, become a symbol of antiquity of lineage, superseding the literal narrative of a glorious ancestry made by the merely old-fashioned portraits in the lower gallery.

Arundel's gesture with his staff (and the object itself, caught by the light, is painted with the most skilful verisimilitude) points the lesson of the two portraits. The aesthetic and cultural power of the Renaissance tradition, with its representational language intelligible on the European scale, is to be enlisted to represent the social and political power of the Stuart court. Mytens's pictures do not themselves realise this aim, being too caught up in the intricate labour of articulating it: the backgrounds required the collaboration of a perspective artist, and are composed awkwardly with the figures. But the aim was to be achieved by the second, more cosmopolitan master recruited from abroad, Anthony van Dyck.

When Van Dyck first came to London in 1620–1 he was the most talented pupil of the greatest living painter, Rubens. When he returned in 1632 to become 'Principal Painter in Ordinary to their Majesties' he was a famous master in his own right.[63] Talent had been supported by privilege. He came from a wealthy Antwerp family; and in the successful years of his early maturity grew accustomed to moving in the highest society. He learned his special skills as a portraitist by painting the aristocracy of Genoa in the 1620s; and his own aristocratic style of life became the outward sign of his achievements as an artist. When Charles I knighted him soon after his appointment, following a tradition which went back to Charles V's knighting of Titian, the king was simply acknowledging that he had secured the perfect type of court artist, one whose ability to portray his sitters with commanding conviction was a kind of power comparable to the power they themselves exercised in the world.

The idea that ability of such a high order as Van Dyck's was a kind of power was intrinsic to the Italian Renaissance tradition which had been chosen by the artist as the context of his ambitions, and by the King as the medium of his cultural policy.

That tradition had been constructed in the definitive account of Vasari, the *Lives*; and the idea of artistic power which he put into currency can be briefly summarised. At the centre of Vasari's account is the Preface to the Third part of the *Lives*, where he analyses what he sees as the climactic achievements of modern art.[64] To explain them he resorts to the language of warfare: Raphael, for example, in his use of colour is said to have 'conquered' nature. This language is most insistent when Vasari tries to express the supremacy of Michelangelo, who is for him the greatest of all artists. So Michelangelo has 'conquered' all those predecessors who have already 'conquered' nature; he 'triumphs' over all others. There are several criteria on which Vasari makes these judgements. As far as painting goes, the important criteria are representational competence (*disegno*) and style (*maniera*). Although he distinguishes these concepts, in the course of his argument Vasari tends to assimilate the first to the second, and make *maniera* the more inclusive category and the test of effect: the real power of a painting lies in its style.

Van Dyck's sophisticated, post-Renaissance style, which associated a masterfully realistic portrayal of the visible world with a self-conscious display of the process of painting itself, certainly made an impact on the courtiers of Charles I; and the more knowledgeable would have seen how Van Dyck took over the styles of past masters, especially Titian, and made them his own. His conquests in the field of representation were such as had not been seen in England before. The idealised images of Elizabethan portraiture were preternatural fantasies, not based on a tradition of naturalistic painting – Van Dyck's were. He could create the appearance of material substance, bodily presence and real space. In the painting now known as *Le Roi à la chasse* (Figure 8.4) the king is seen from the side, left hand on hip, his elbow sticking out at the spectator.[65] The bold nonchalance of the asymmetrical pose presents a challenge to the artist, who must paint the protruding arm in foreshortening. He meets the self-imposed challenge triumphantly, thus empowering the king's convincingly realised figure to keep the spectator at bay. The jutting elbow is in fact an allusion to Titian, and the notion it creates of an inviolable ambience around the royal person is complemented by another Titianesque motif, the king's other hand placed on his walking stick, both seen, together with his extended arm, against the distant landscape.[66] The representation of this distance through its constituent parts – countryside, sea, sky and atmosphere – is

Figure 8.4 Sir Anthony Van Dyck: Charles I ('Le roi à la chasse'),
         c. 1635

entirely convincing, as is the superimposition on it of the king's
right arm, hand strongly clasping his stick. The artist's command
of space becomes a metaphor for the ruler's territorial authority.

The effect of Van Dyck's portraits was enhanced by their setting,
about which Charles took great care. His concern was often to

bring out the powers of the painter by stressing his kinship to other painters, rather than consign his works to some conventional gathering of royal relations. So the 'great piece' of the royal family in 1632 was hung appropriately near one entrance to the Privy Lodgings at Whitehall, in the Long Gallery, but it was accompanied not by ancestors, cousins and potentates but by a long series of Italian sixteenth-century paintings which made up a kind of stylistic ancestry for Van Dyck. His picture of the king in armour riding a white horse through a triumphal arch (Figure 8.5)[67] was similarly placed. This highly theatrical piece closed the vista at one end of the Gallery in St James's Palace. Leading up to it was an exceptionally choice collection of sixteenth-century Venetian, and modern Roman and Bolognese, paintings – including works by Titian, Tintoretto, Caravaggio and Guido Reni. In this spectacular series was one specifically set episode: Titian's portraits of the twelve Caesars, with Giulio Romano's smaller portraits of them on horseback. The dominating image of the king, which to contemporaries was so realistic that he seemed to be about to ride down the gallery, summed up both the aesthetic and political implications of the whole display. The spectator was impelled to see Charles as the imperial heir of the Caesars, and Van Dyck as the heir of the great Italian masters. This was the king, and this the painter, that history had been waiting for.

VII   Conclusion

The substance of such claims can be gathered from the hostility they eventually aroused during the civil war. In June 1644, *Mercurius Aulicus* reported on the iconoclasm of the committee for the destruction of monuments of superstition and idolatry, led by Sir Robert Harley. After destroying the statues of saints in Westminster, he

> betook himself to the reforming of his Majesty's palace of Whitehall...his first care was to get a ladder (though commonly a ladder is the end of such reformations) which having pro-cured, he caused it to be set up against the east window in the chapel, which he reformed of all the glass, because all was painted...Thence he proceeded in his visitation to his Majesty's gallery, which he reformed of all such pictures as displeased

Figure 8.5 Sir Anthony Van Dyck: Charles I and M. de St Antoine,
        *c.*1633

his eye, under pretence that they did favour too much of
superstitious vanities (for Kings and Queens, as well as apostles,
fathers, martyrs, confessors, are counted monuments of vanity
and superstition) and so went on, according to the principles of
reformation, till there was nothing left which was rich or
glorious.[68]

The report may be fully accurate or not; the point is rather its
emotional force and rhetorical design. In projecting his own
perfervid fears onto Harley, to suggest that these outrages are
the work of a single crank, the newswriter represents him as an

archetypal figure, and composes a portrait of the puritan icono-clast. His forebears are Harington's 'austere or rather uncivil persons', the anonymous extremists who push the spirit of Reformation to its limits, and regard all figurative art as an affront to 'a jealous God'. For them the images of royalty are on a par with the images of the saints, and both must be swept away. The writer depicts this belief as a comic obsession, putting the word 'reform' through all its grammatical paces with remorseless joviality, and clearly enjoying the irony inherent in producing a caricature, in figuring the enemies of figuration. The text reveals two powerful forces informing the overt conflict: the pleasure of representation, which Aristotle confidently claimed as a basic human instinct, and the prohibition of idolatry, which God handed down to His chosen people. The politics of portraiture appear to reach even beyond matters of law, custom, government and social utility.

9. Inigo Jones and the Politics of Architecture

J. NEWMAN

'Architecture has its political use, public buildings being the ornament of a country; it establishes a nation, draws people and commerce, makes a people love their native country, which passion is the original of all great actions in a commonwealth'. So wrote Sir Christopher Wren at the end of the seventeenth century, and he mentioned by way of illustration an ancient example, Pericles's construction of magnificent marble buildings on the Athenian Acropolis during the war against Sparta, and a modern one, the sense of nationhood felt by the Jews, though scattered, because of their 'love of their temple' in Jerusalem.[1] Wren, who served as royal architect through four reigns and designed and supervised the construction of that great symbol of revival, St Paul's Cathedral, was writing from personal experience as well as expressing a traditional evaluation of magnificent building.

Inigo Jones, Wren's predecessor as Surveyor of the King's Works for a quarter of a century through the second half of James I's reign and the whole of Charles I's up to the outbreak of civil war, had good cause to hold a similar view. He was not only an architect but a man of culture, well read in ancient authors, and perfectly capable of devising the text of a court masque as well as its visual setting. And he worked for two monarchs who were passionately addicted to building, even if much remained in the realm of daydream. The most interesting issue, however, in discussing the political force of Inigo Jones's architecture in particular is its self-conscious classicism, the deliberate use as models of the structures of the ancient Romans, which he not only knew from books but had seen with his own eyes, in Rome itself, elsewhere in Italy and at Nîmes and Arles in Provence. Jones's innovations as an architect have been evaluated primarily as revolutionary in an artistic sense; but it is worth exploring the possibility that Jones deliberately used this artistic language, quite unfamiliar in early

230 INIGO JONES AND THE POLITICS OF ARCHITECTURE

Stuart England, in order to express royal power by distinguishing visually new royal buildings and buildings erected under royal patronage and influence from the traditional structures around them.

Two concepts found in ancient texts were taken to justify princely building: 'magnificence' and 'decorum'. Aristotle had brought the two ideas together in his *Ethics*, when he wrote that 'the expenditures of the magnificent man are both great and appropriate'.[2] Jones came across this idea of 'magnificence' when he read and noted Aristotle's *Ethics* and in other ancient authors too. The Greek historian Thucydides for example had pointed out that sumptuous buildings demonstrate our grandeur to posterity, an observation which Jones noted when he found it referred to by Alberti, with the words 'Thucydides commends sumptuous buildings and why'; and Jones translated the remarks of Giorgio Vasari, the biographer of Italian Renaissance artists, 'Rich princes should leave behind them a fame of building richly'. He made detailed notes on Herodotus's description of the Labyrinth: 'the 12 Kings make a building for memory ... 12 huge courts [and] covered porticos ... one would not think it a work of mortals ... the covering of marble and carved. The walls of marble figured', and so on. And finally, from Vitruvius, the only treatise specifically on architecture to have survived from antiquity, he translated the particularly pointed comment, 'Cost gives magnificence and authority to Buildings'.[3]

The notion of decorum or propriety dictates that buildings should reflect and demonstrate the status of their builders. Decorum is a key concept for classical architecture, since it justifies the different 'orders' or forms of the essential structural elements, the vertical post (column) and the horizontal binder and roof-eaves (entablature). Vitruvius identifies three 'orders': Doric, the stockiest and plainest; Corinthian, the slenderest and most richly decorated; and Ionic, a mean between the other two. Thus proportion and decoration are the two distinguishing characteristics. (Renaissance writers who developed Vitruvius's ideas added two more orders: Tuscan, stockier than Doric; and Composite, more elegant than Corinthian.) Vitruvius also explains how the orders are to be used with decorum, so that for instance the order of a temple must be appropriate to the god to which it is dedicated. What applies to the orders applies to buildings as a whole, so decorum dictates that the magnificence of princes should be expressed in magnificent buildings.

The most coherent expression of Jones's ideas on the relationship between architecture and society is to be found in his
account of Stonehenge, published posthumously in an edited
form by his pupil John Webb.[4] He interpreted Stonehenge not as
a Druidical place of sacrifice but as a Tuscan temple built by the
occupying Romans and dedicated to Coelus, the god of the sky.
What lay behind this surprising conclusion was his observation
that Stonehenge was laid out on a sophisticated mathematical
basis and constructed of stones of awe-inspiring grandeur. And he
fastened on a passage in Tacitus which relates how the Roman
governor Agricola civilised the Britons by encouraging them to
build 'Temples, Houses and places of publick resort'.[5] So the
scale and sophistication of Stonehenge was, as Jones saw it, a permanent witness to the civilising force of Roman rule.

In James I, Jones, as Surveyor of the Royal Works from 1615,
had a receptive patron, for the king had a lively sense of the role
which buildings could play in the projection of a royal aura and
the embodiment of royal policy. The two personae which James
wanted to project were the wise Solomon, benevolent judge of his
people, and the peacemaker, reconciling hostile nations with one
another. Inigo Jones's Banqueting House at Whitehall Palace
provided, it can be argued, a setting which actively promoted the
appreciation of the king in both these roles.

James's expenditure on palaces soared above the essentially
care-and-maintenance level at which Queen Elizabeth I had kept
it. Of the seven palaces which he improved, all of them first built
during the period c.1480–1550, two (Greenwich Palace, and
Somerset House in the Strand) were assigned to the queen, Anne
of Denmark, and a further two (Richmond Palace, and St James's,
close to Whitehall and Westminster) were required for the heir to
the throne, Prince Henry (who died in 1612) and subsequently
Prince Charles. Hampton Court and Eltham received only a
moderate amount of attention, and two new hunting houses,
Theobalds and Newmarket, were acquired; but on the king's own
London palace, Whitehall, the seat of his power, he lavished
nearly £50,000 by 1615.

Whitehall Palace, first built by Cardinal Wolsey as the London
palace of the archbishops of York, was taken over in 1529 by
Henry VIII and thereafter replaced Westminster as the principal
seat of the monarch. Today Whitehall is the name of a road, but
in the Tudor and Stuart period the road was King Street and the
palace of Whitehall stood on its east side stretching to the river.

To the west side of the street lay ancillary parts of the palace, mainly for sporting purposes, cockpit, tennis courts, tiltyard, etc., with St James's Park stretching away beyond. The street was spanned by two splendid gateways, built by Henry VIII, and immediately north of the northern one, the so-called Holbein Gate, it expanded into a broad roadway, forming in effect a forecourt in front of the entrance which led to the hall and royal apartments. Here, beside the entrance archway to the palace, stood the Banqueting House.

The first Banqueting House in this position had been put up for Queen Elizabeth, and had not been considered a permanency, being constructed of canvas on a framework of timber masts 40 ft high. Its immediate purpose was to provide a setting for the reception of the Duke of Alençon in 1582, but it was so stoutly constructed and handsomely decorated that it was kept in use; in fact with its ten tiers of staging for people to stand on and its probable dimensions of over 100 ft by nearly 50 ft, it was by far the most capacious structure for crowds within the palace.

In 1606 James I decided to replace it with a permanent building. This too was rectangular, measuring internally 120 ft by 53 ft, built of brick with full-height window bays of stone, four towards the west facing the street but only three on the opposite side. Internally it had side galleries supported on Doric columns, nine per side, and above them Ionic columns carrying the roof. These inconsistencies in design suggest the lack of a controlling architect, and, as Sir John Summerson has pointed out, as many as five officials in the Office of Works were paid for making drawings for the building. When the king saw it in September 1607, the structure then being largely complete, it was reported that he 'could scarce see by reason of certain pillars which are set up before the windows and he is nothing pleased with his Lord Architect for that device'. (The significance of 'Lord Architect' is not clear, and may be meant ironically.) At that stage about £5,000 had been spent on the new building; decoration continued for a further eighteen months and may have cost about as much again. Much painting, gilding and carving are mentioned in the accounts, and the roof was decorated with fretwork and pendants.[6]

Both these banqueting houses, the Elizabethan and the first Jacobean, were arranged with the royal dais and throne at the short southern end, which communicated directly with the king's private apartments in the palace. Everyone else entered from the north; thus there was the traditional arrangement typical of any ceremonial hall, with an upper and a lower end. The building had become indispensable for certain public events, at which the king could show himself to a representative group of his subjects and to significant foreign visitors: 'for', as Per Palme has listed them,

> the sumptuous entertainment of foreign princes and ambas-
> sadors, for the ratification of diplomatic treaties and agree-
> ments, for the gracious reception of the Houses of Parliament,
> for public audiences, for ceremonies connected with the cre-
> ation of new peerages, for the pomp of St George's Feast, and
> for the solemn rite of touching for the "King's evil". In short, it
> was built as a stage for the display of royal might and glory.[7]

In practical terms this meant that the Banqueting House had to present externally an effective backdrop to processions which might approach either from within the palace (as the St George's Day procession there moved from the palace chapel) or from Westminster (as in the case of the reception of the Houses of Parliament). This the 1606 building did with its projecting stone window bays front and back. And internally a processional route was also required, up to the dais, where the king could be seated flanked by favoured personages, and in view of a select but numerous assembly. Perhaps James disliked the free-standing columns because they threatened to encroach on the processional space and supported galleries from which a too panoramic view of proceedings would be possible.

In January 1619 the Banqueting House burnt down. Its significance for the king is vividly demonstrated by the immediate decision to rebuild, the speed with which rebuilding took place, and the cost, over £15,000 at a time when royal expenditure on building was in general declining. As Per Palme has pointed out, the spring of 1619 was a time when James's long-cherished project, the heart of his claim to be the peacemaker of Europe, was reaching a critical stage.[8] This was the marriage of Prince Charles to the daughter of Philip III of Spain. Just as his daughter Elizabeth had in 1613 married one of the foremost Protestant princes in Europe, the Elector Palatine, so now he hoped to achieve the counterbalancing half of his strategy, by betrothing his son and heir to the first Catholic Hapsburg princess. Through-out the three years during which the new Banqueting House was under construction, marriage negotiations continued, and it was only in 1623, with the madcap journey of the prince and the

Marquis of Buckingham to Spain to claim the bride, that they concluded in failure.

The king therefore had a powerful political reason for pressing ahead, even when the state's coffers were low, with a new building which would provide a setting more splendid and impressive than ever for the reception of foreign ambassadors. And the fact that it was brought into use while clearly in an incomplete state may reflect his disillusionment at the collapse of his policy.

We must now turn to examine the design of the new building, for royal determination and the allocation of adequate funds could not of themselves guarantee a building equal to the role envisaged for it.

Inigo Jones had succeeded to the Surveyorship of the King's Works a year after his formative visit to Italy of 1613–14 during which he self-consciously studied the ruins of antique temples and basilicas in Rome and Naples and admired in Vicenza and Venice the works of the sixteenth-century architect, Andrea Palladio. He had previously made a systematic study of books on antique and modern Italian architecture and theory, studying in particular Daniele Barbaro's edition of Vitruvius (1567) and Andrea Palladio's *I Quattro Libri dell'Architettura* (1570). Vitruvius was the only ancient Roman writer on architecture the text of whose treatise had survived, and Barbaro's illustrated edition provided copious commentary on it. In Palladio's four books on architecture, by contrast, the illustrations are primary, illustrating model forms of the five orders, a wide range of reconstructions of antique temples and a rich selection of Palladio's own architectural designs for palaces and villas. Together they formed the best introduction to the architectural vocabulary of the Italian Renaissance and its foundations in the theory and practice of ancient Roman architects. The visit in 1613–14 to Rome, Naples and northern Italy consolidated his understanding by enabling him to examine relevant buildings for himself.

Jones's designs for the Queen's House at Greenwich, made in 1616, already showed that he proposed a total revolution in British architectural expression, turning his back firmly on the picturesque and flamboyant style of his contemporaries, embodied no doubt in the Banqueting House of 1606 and familiar to us still from great courtier houses such as Knole, Hatfield and Audley End. But the Queen's House was abandoned less than half built in 1618 (to be completed only in the 1630s) and was anyway obscurely situated between the garden and deer-park of the queen's out-of-London palace. The new Banqueting House presented a much more exciting challenge, an opportunity to demonstrate his concept, totally new in England, of a monumental and ordered architecture based on antiquity and the Italian Renaissance, in the most sensitive context, and harness them to the expression of the grandeur of his monarch.

A few obvious points leap out. The new Banqueting House was much loftier than its predecessor can have been, and towered over the rest of the palace, as numerous contemporary engravings show. It was also more grandly scaled, only seven bays wide instead of nine outside, and provided an unimpeded internal space of double cube form, dramatically different from the room it replaced, with its maze of columns and galleries. Externally the materials of the new Banqueting House showed a new sophistication: instead of the vertical bands of brick walling and stone window bays there were three types of stone, buff Oxfordshire for the basement and honey-coloured Northamptonshire for the walling above, against which the Portland stone of the projecting columns and entablatures stood out white. This colour contrast drew attention to the strongly sculptural treatment of the façades, something else quite unfamiliar in Jacobean London. All these

Figure 9.1 Inigo Jones: Banqueting House, Whitehall exterior, 1619–22

characteristics will have combined to give the new Banqueting House an unprecedented presence, singling it out as a building of special prestige and significance.

However, the Banqueting House has a further characteristic, less obvious than any of these but more fundamental, which may be summed up as coherence. Its overall internal dimensions were intended to form a double cube, in the simple ratio of 2:1:1. As built, the Banqueting House does not quite conform to these proportions, but replicates those of the former building, 120 ft long and 53 ft wide, but in the estimate the dimensions are given as 110 ft long, 55 ft wide and 55 ft high, and they recur in the building accounts, clearly demonstrating Jones's intention.[9] Easier to observe was the coherent relationship between exterior and interior. Instead of the awkward lack of alignment between columns and window bays which had so offended the king in the previous building, there were now no free-standing columns at all, and the Ionic pilasters inside corresponded in level and size with the Ionic order on the exterior. The correspondence between the upper orders was not so straightforward, but none the less coherent. Jones was following the sequence of orders given in Vincenzo Scamozzi's newly published architectural treatise, *L'Idea Universale dell'Architettura* (1615), where the Composite order is treated, not as an elaboration of the Corinthian but as literally a composite between Ionic and Corinthian, having features of both and logically placed between them. Thus the external Ionic order has Composite placed above it, but Jones stressed the greater significance of the interior by here substituting Corinthian for the upper order, so that we experience a leap up from Ionic to the order which crowns the sequence. (By contrast, as noted above, the previous building had used Doric and Ionic orders only.)

All these characteristics impart to the building the special qualities of good architecture which had been identified by Vitruvius, in particular 'decorum' or appropriateness and 'eurithmia', the use of mathematical relationships to produce visual harmony and so a pleasurable impression on the viewer. For such an ideologically significant building as the Banqueting House where the king could both appear in regal splendour and act out his chosen role as mediator and healer, architecture that embodied both hierarchy and harmony was doubly valuable.[10]

The interior of the Banqueting House was conceived by Jones as a suitable setting for the enthroned monarch in a much more precise sense. In Palladio's *Quattro Libri*, the book which he had studied so carefully, there are reconstructed plans and elevations of various types of antique room, attempts to visualise the descriptions in Vitruvius. First there was the basilica,[11] the place, as Palladio says, where judges delivered judgment under cover or transacted other important business. For this purpose the judge sat in a broad niche at the further end of the colonnaded room. The Banqueting House was originally built with such a niche at the dais end, but for some reason it was demolished after only a few years and the end wall built up straight. For the superimposed orders of the room Jones was guided by another model, the Egyptian hall,[12] which Palladio describes as suitable for feasts and entertainments; in fact he copied the elevational treatment very closely, but with one important exception. The Egyptian hall, like the Basilica, had aisles and free-standing colonnades. But these, as we have seen, were not to the king's liking. So Jones was forced to treat the lower order as half columns embedded in the side walls and to run a narrow gallery round on brackets above them, a drastic reduction in internal gallery space compared with the previous Banqueting House (in future, audiences would have to be accommodated on temporary staging). In concept and in detail the interior of the Banqueting House is an antique/Palladian judgment hall and 'salle des fêtes' combined; here we see Jones's first deliberate attempt to reinterpret antique architecture for modern purposes, to enhance the splendour of the court by scale, fine materials, the sense of order which comes from proportion and by specific correlations with the architecture of antiquity.

How far James I was aware of these overtones in the new room is impossible to know, and it must be admitted that they were lost on the only contemporary commentator whose opinion has survived: John Chamberlain remarked sourly that the new Banqueting House was 'too fair, and nothing suitable to the rest of the palace'. Such monumental classicism may well have been incomprehensible to a generation which still felt gothic to be the national style.[13] Jones himself had acknowledged this as recently as 1610, when in a masque backdrop he depicted 'St. George's Portico' with gothic gables and crockets.[14] His theories about the architectural productions of the Romans in Britain only began to be formulated after 1620 when James I ordered him to examine Stonehenge. It was in the 1630s rather than earlier that a series of masques on nationalistic themes, 'Albion's Triumph', 'Coelum Britannicum', 'Britannia Triumphans', were enacted in front of scenery depicting magnificent classical buildings.[15]

To give the Banqueting House a more specific eloquence the services were required of what Sir Henry Wotton called 'two arts attending on architecture, like two of her principal gentlewomen, to dress and trim their mistress; Picture and Sculpture'.[16] For painting and sculpture can not only embellish, they are 'representational' arts. With their aid a building can convey much more specific messages.

The building accounts for the Banqueting House which were closed at the end of March 1622 show that at that time the interior was painted entirely white.[17] This is such a drastic contrast to the rich colouring and gilding of normal Jacobean interiors that it is probably a further sign that the building was being left incomplete. Furthermore we know that the celebrated Flemish decorative painter, Peter Paul Rubens, had in 1621 been approached by the English agent in Brussels, William Trumbull, to provide decorative paintings for it. He had responded enthusiastically, stressing that a large-scale work like this was something for which he felt himself naturally suited;[18] but nothing more was heard of the idea until 1629, when James I was dead and Rubens was on a diplomatic mission in London to the court of the new king, Charles I. This must have been the occasion when the programme of the ceiling decoration was worked out, though the paintings were not completed and delivered for a further six years (partly because the artist was not sure that he was going to be paid for them). Finally in October 1635 they were delivered, and the following June Rubens received his payment of £3,000. After they had been set into position in the massively beamed ceiling, the interior was repainted, now with generous gilding.

So James and Charles had gone to the most celebrated decorative painter of their time; his canvases were clearly considered to form the crowning element of the room, without which it was not complete. But Rubens was a Catholic, his ambassadorial activities being conducted on behalf of the King of Spain; so he must have been advised and guided by a member of the English court in the particulars of the subject-matter of the Banqueting House ceiling paintings and its presentation.

Sir Roy Strong has argued persuasively that it was Inigo Jones who devised the programme of the Whitehall ceiling.[19] Jones had, after all, a great deal of relevant experience, having since 1605 devised the scenery and costumes of most of the court masques, the semi-dramatic court entertainments for which he had developed very advanced stage settings. A fundamental purpose of the masques was to represent the court to itself in an idealised form. In particular during the 1630s, when Charles and his court were increasingly isolated and embattled, the masques took on a strong colouration of political propaganda. It was during these years, after Ben Jonson, the poet of the Jacobean masques, had refused to continue to collaborate with Jones, that the latter had taken on more and more of the devising of the programmes. Rubens's ceiling paintings can be seen as, in a sense, masque tableaux made permanent. In them, as in the Caroline masques, the king appears in person, surrounded by personifications of virtues and vices and engaged in heroic political gestures which relate to the goals of his policies as much as to their actuality.

The rectangular canvas at the lower end of the room, orientated so that the king, but not those facing him, could see it the right way up, brilliantly unites James I's fundamental achievement, the unification of the crowns of Scotland and England, with his own idealisation of himself as the British Solomon. A crowned James is shown seated on a high throne and gesturing towards a group of figures which consists of a young male child supported by two female figures and crowned by a helmeted Minerva. The female figures must represent Scotland and England and the child between them is the infant Great Britain; but the way they stand before the king, as if they are suppliants, unmistakably refers to the Judgment of Solomon. But unlike the biblical Solomon, who ruled that the child should be cut in two in order to discover who was its rightful mother, the British Solomon creates a new child by his unification of the two kingdoms. The interpretation was not a new one: a court preacher had made it already as early as 1604.[20]

The other main ceiling canvases face towards the entrance door and are thus directed towards a general audience rather than the king himself. At the upper end of the room James I is seen again as Solomon, for he sits in a semi-domed niche like a judge and flanked by twisted columns of the sort specifically associated with Solomon's Temple. Here too the king makes a sweeping gesture with his arm, towards two embracing women who clearly represent Peace and Plenty. Below him Minerva and Mercury drive away aggressors who would assail the throne. In the great oval canvas which forms the centrepiece of the ceiling, James I is shown raised to heaven by a figure representing Justice and accompanied by Faith and Religion. The Protestant overtones of the manner of depicting these figures, pointed out by Strong, illustrate how

Figure 9.2 S. Gribelin: James I as Solomon, Engraving after
         Rubens's ceiling painting, 1635, in the Banqueting
         House, Whitehall

Rubens's composition is based on a programme which, given a
free hand, he would not have devised. Strong also relates the
painting to the text of James's own book, *Basilikon Doron*, in which

he set out for the benefit of his son and heir his concept of kingly duty.

The elaborate, even arcane, symbolism of the Whitehall ceiling contrasts with Rubens's normally more direct iconographical manner; though the painter has breathed his robust and vigorous spirit through the most abstracted of these personifications. Inigo Jones in his masques, particularly in the figured borders with which he decorated the proscenium arch for each stage setting, alluding to the theme to be unfolded by the action of the masque, pursued an allegorical strategy comparable with that in the Whitehall ceiling.

The policy and achievements of James I, celebrated in the painted ceiling, were therefore intended to inform all the activities which took place in the room itself, so many of them themselves loaded with symbolic meanings which transformed the mere actions. As for the masques, the closest allies to the ceiling paintings, their continued performance in the Banqueting House was intended to ensure for Charles and his court that present actions were in harmony with the achievements and aims of his father; but even this symbolism was not in the event powerful enough to outweigh a practical consideration. The flaming and smoky torches which illuminated the production of the masques were immediately recognised as a threat to the brilliance of Rubens's painting, so in 1637 a timber masquing house was erected, a room as big as the Banqueting House itself and set behind it at right angles. This is where Jones's last three masques were performed.

So James's self-identification with Solomon outlived him, to provide the *leitmotif* of Rubens's potent scheme of decoration. Not surprisingly, the theme was at the heart of the oration preached at his funeral, on 7 May 1625, and subsequently published under the title *Great Britain's Salomon*. This sermon was delivered by John Williams, Bishop of Lincoln, in front of the hearse or catafalque within which the king's body lay in Westminster Abbey. Inigo Jones's design for this catafalque survives, noted approvingly by an observer as 'the fairest and best fashioned that hath been'.[21] In this instance the evidence for Jones's involvement in formulating the programme of the *mise en scène* is particularly strong, for the Bishop in his sermon refers to features visible on the catafalque, and draws on texts, Serlio's *Architectura* and Xiphilin's epitome of Dio Cassius, which Jones is known to have read.

Earlier royal catafalques, such as those of James's heir (1612) and queen (1617), had been little more than semi-pyramidal

Figure 9.3 Inigo Jones: design for James I's catafalque, 1625

canopies supported on columns over the body lying in state on the bier. The catafalque which Inigo Jones devised for James I was completely different in scale and concept, nothing less than an octagonal domed tempietto set on a high podium. The tempietto idea was obviously antique in inspiration, but it has recently been shown that Jones did not derive his design from the most obvious book of antiquities, Palladio's fourth book, but, surprisingly, from the catafalques of two Counter-Reformation popes. This is where the steep egg-shaped dome decorated with scrolls and cartouches comes from, and the colonnaded enclosure, not to mention the four standing statues that surround it, identified by Bishop Williams as War, Peace, Justice and Religion, which are virtually copied from the engraving of Pope Sixtus V's catafalque. But Jones drastically purified his source material, subduing the Mannerist decoration and of course removing all indications of the papal source. One feature does suggest that Jones consulted his Palladio while making the design: the plain rectangular podium cut through by a steep and narrow flight of steps derived from Palladio's plate of the temple of Vesta at Tivoli. This is also a feature which directs attention to a significant parallel, that with the funerals of Roman emperors. Williams in his sermon asks his hearers 'to remember in Herodian and Xiphilin what costly beds the Emperors lay in when in their *apotheosis* they were to be burnt and changed to Gods'. Xiphilin's epitome of Dio Cassius includes a description of the funeral ceremonies of the Emperor Pertinax and the high timber podium on which his bier was placed, surrounded by a great number of columns. Jones's design can then be seen as an evocation of this passage.[22] The preacher's reference to apotheosis is made more significant by the appearance of the catafalque imitating the funeral practices of Roman emperors. Such a reference would have seemed natural at the funeral of a king who claimed to rule by Divine Right, and, as we have already seen, Rubens would ten years later paint the apotheosis of the king for the centre of the Banqueting House ceiling.

So far we have been considering the way in which Jones's architectural design enhanced James I's kingly image, during his lifetime and after his death. But the imperial analogy, implicit in the form of his catafalque, was not merely courtly rhetoric, for it impelled the king himself to practical action. In the architectural context his ambition to control and systematise the growth of London was fuelled by a desire to be compared with the Emperor Augustus, as he expressed it in one of his series of proclamations on the subject:

As it was said by the first emperor of Rome, that he had found the city of Rome of brick, and left it of marble, so We, whom God hath honoured to be the first King of Great Britain, might be able to say in some proportion, that we had found our city and suburbs of London of sticks, and left them of bricks.[23]

Controls on building in London had first been imposed by Queen Elizabeth I. Her concern had been to curb the growth of the city by banning building on new foundations. James I had continued and developed the policy, though it was already clear by 1605, the year of his first proclamation on this subject, that the pressures for growth were well nigh irresistible. But the king widened the scope of the policy by requiring the fronts of reconstructed buildings to be of brick or stone and no longer of timber, which was still the universal structural material for all but the grandest houses. Reasons given were to conserve scarce timber and to reduce fires; but there was an aesthetic dimension too, in that the fronts of houses were ordered to be made 'uniform'.

The proclamation in which the king compared himself with the Emperor Augustus came ten years later, in 1615. So by the middle of the second decade of the century aesthetics had become a significant concern. The raising of revenue, however, was also a consideration; the fining of transgressors was authorised from the start, though in 1608 it was emphasised that only a few exemplary fines had been imposed, to show 'that it was not his majesty's profit that was sought'. But later a system developed, of advance fines paid by developers who were permitted to contravene the regulations against building on new foundations, until in the 1630s this system burgeoned into one of Charles I's more notorious means of supplying his finances without the aid of parliament.

Supervision of the working of these proclamations was at first put in the hands of the city magistrates; but in 1618 a court-dominated commission was appointed, under the chairmanship of the Earl of Arundel, Inigo Jones's friend and patron, and with Jones as its professional member.[24] From this time the tone of James I's proclamations changes. Jones's drafting is evident in the provisions of the proclamation of 12 March 1619 which outlaws overhangs and bay windows, lays down minimum storey heights and wall thicknesses, and states the preferred shapes of windows in each 'whole storey' and 'half storey', so that it would almost be possible to draw a complete model house elevation on the basis of the clauses in the proclamation. However, in 1620, a further proclamation, prohibiting the building of thatched hovels and patching up of worthless old buildings, noted that earlier proclamations were beginning to have an effect, in that rebuildings were being carried out in brick and stone, 'tending to the general good'. The screw was further tightened in 1622, when the making and sizing of bricks was regulated, since 'for this small time of proceeding with Brick is greatly applauded and approved as well by Ambassadors of foreign nations as others'.[25] This was as far as royal policy was ever spelt out, as James's last proclamation in 1624, and those of his son in 1625 and 1630, merely repeated the clauses formulated in 1619–22; but these quotations suggest the broader political context in which the policy on new buildings was being seen in the last years of James I's reign as contributing to national pride and impressing influential foreigners.

In the early Stuart period London still consisted of two physically distinct urban centres. First there was the City of London, densely packed within the Roman and medieval walls which enclosed it on the north bank of the river Thames, but also beginning to spill out into *faubourgs* on Tower Hill, along Bishopsgate, Aldersgate and Holborn, and elsewhere. And two miles further upstream, the City of Westminster, a much more straggling agglomeration clustering round the Abbey and Palace, the latter now the seat of government, and the royal palace of Whitehall, extended northwards to Charing Cross. The two were linked by the Strand, along which were strung many of the grandest mansions of the nobility, with the legal quarter – The Temple and Lincoln's and Gray's Inns – further east adjoining the boundary of the City of London.

One means of checking the growth of the metropolis was to lay out public open spaces on its margins. Among the recent improvements which the king was able to praise in the preamble to his proclamation of 1615 were the paving of Smithfield and the planting of trees on Moorfields, the major recreation space on the northern edge of the City of London. In 1617 the privy council took notice of the threat to another important inner open space, Lincoln's Inn Fields, and ordered that it be laid out in formal walks.

The following spring a commission was set up for this purpose, and Inigo Jones was ordered to draw up a 'map or ground plot' of the proposed layout, which it was claimed would be a 'great ornament to the City, pleasure and freshness for the health and recreation of the Inhabitants thereabouts, and for the sight and delight of ambassadors and strangers coming to our court and city, and a memorable work of our time to all posterity'.[26] This statement of the political value of an aesthetically attractive urban environment was soon incorporated, as has been noted above, into the building proclamations.

However, it proved impractical to seek such improvements to London without allowing landowners and would-be developers to profit by building. A decade or more later the ideal solution was found. This was the development of Covent Garden, just north of the Strand.[27] The Earl of Bedford, who wanted to develop the land immediately north of the garden of his Strand mansion, was in 1631 allowed to do so on condition that he pay two successive fines of £2,000 each. He was also required or thought it prudent to consult Inigo Jones, who was able to ensure that the earl's new houses were erected as formal terraces on two sides of a rectangular open space laid out immediately north of the garden. Bedford was also obliged to provide a church for the benefit of the new residents, and this was erected to Jones's design in the centre of the west side of the square, flanked by handsome gateways into the churchyard. Jones must also have advised on the design of the houses, which were not only of a nobly austere classicism but scrupulously conformed to the dimensions and materials laid down in the building proclamations. The arcaded walks at ground level, their most memorable feature, however, could only have been designed by someone familiar with up-to-date urban developments in France and Italy. The effect of the new development on foreign opinion, in particular ambassadors, the most important of whom were normally lodged in the Strand area, may once more have been a conscious influence on the design of the terraces, dictating the inclusion of the arcades.

The whole scheme was dominated by the monumental but even more austere Tuscan portico of the church. Here then was the first of London's formal squares, the equal in impressiveness if not in size of such modern continental layouts as the Place des Vosges in Paris, or the Piazza delle Arme in front of the cathedral at Leghorn (a parallel drawn at the time). The square also formed the nodal point of a layout of streets leading west, north and east, and so helped to bring order into a wider area. The Earl of Bedford certainly saw his development as a unified whole centred on the church, for he campaigned to have it designated as a new parish (a campaign which did not succeed during his lifetime).

Covent Garden was the prototype of the squares which are such a typical and handsome feature of London's West End. But these are a post-Restoration development. Before the outbreak of war the influence of Covent Garden was perceptible but patchy. When the Earl of Leicester in the early 1630s obtained permission to build himself a new house in the northern suburbs of Westminster it was on condition that he lay out a formal open space in front of it for public use. At the end of the decade a developer called

William Newton was finally permitted to build on Lincoln's Inn Fields. His development, which took the form of two long terraces at right angles to one another, on the western and northern edges of the Fields, was Jonesian in style and consistency, with a particularly handsome house in the centre of the west range, which has been persistently attributed to Jones himself. This is the only house in the scheme that still survives today.

The route regularly taken by the king when he left London for sporting recreation at Theobalds in Hertfordshire and Newmarket in Cambridgeshire skirted round the northern edge of these developments, and formed a natural boundary to growth in this area. Part of this route, Long Acre, had been developed during James I's time, but its eastward extension, Great Queen Street, was another development of the 1630s, and here too brick terraces were erected the appearance of which proclaimed the influence of the King's Surveyor, Inigo Jones.

It was undoubtedly the area centred on Covent Garden which developed fastest during the Caroline period, and it must have been the interest of the building commission and the active involvement of Jones which gave it its architectural distinction. It is surely significant that when the engraver Wenceslas Hollar began in the mid-1640s to prepare a bird's-eye perspective map prospect of London the trial sheet should have covered this area, with Covent Garden prominently at its centre.

But this was not the only part of London with which Jones concerned himself: in the 1630s he intervened in the City of London too. Here, however, court influence was harder to impose. While a handful of City monopolists and financiers ardently supported the king, the city as a whole was hostile to his policies and suspicious of his agents, among whom the King's Surveyor should undoubtedly be counted. Significantly, Jones's greatest success was in connection with the rebuilding of their hall by the Goldsmiths' Company, a dominant force in the financial activity of the city.[28] In 1634 the company resolved to enlarge its hall in Foster Lane to the design of one of its members. When Jones got to hear of this he suggested that instead the company should rebuild their hall in its entirety on an enlarged site and recommended as architect a close associate of his, Nicholas Stone. Jones's continued involvement in the project is attested by Stone's admission to the court of the Goldsmiths' Company on submitting his final designs, that Jones 'did advise and direct before the perfecting and finishing of each piece'. The handsome new build-

Figure 9.4 Wenceslas Hollar: engraved bird's-eye view of newly developed areas of London around Covent Garden and Lincoln's Inn fields, mid-1640s

ing, which survived the fire of 1666 with relatively minor damage, thanks to the strength of its construction, became a model for the numerous rebuilt city company halls in the 1670s.

Not much more than a hundred yards from Goldsmiths' Hall, in a prominent position at the western extremity of Cheapside and close to the east end of St Paul's Cathedral, was the little church of St Michael le Querne.[29] In 1637 a rebuilding scheme was under discussion and here too Jones, this time with the backing of the privy council, stepped in. In fact he himself provided a design for a new church. But the parishioners, inspired in part no doubt by hostility to court interference, proved less tractable than the liverymen, and insisted on their right to choose their own design, turning to the city master bricklayer, Peter Mills.

Jones's interest in the west end of Cheapside must have been bound up with the repair and modernisation of St Paul's Cathedral in which he was engaged at this time. The sorry state of this great medieval structure, which rode high above the city, stood, after the collapse of the crossing spire in 1561, as a reproach rather than as a symbol of London's religious and secular power. In 1608 Jones had made a design for crowning the crossing tower with a semi-classical domed lantern. But nothing came of this initiative. A decade later the attempts of a private citizen, Henry Farley, to promote repairs, again led to nothing. Only when the dynamic William Laud became bishop of London was the requisite commitment generated to get work started. Jones was put in charge of the campaign which, between 1634 and the outbreak of war in 1642, succeeded in repairing the external stonework of the choir, and recasing the transepts and nave. For the latter, Jones made no attempt to recreate the medieval forms but converted them into his own architectural vocabulary, with powerful use of rusticated walling. Architecturally the most impressive element of Jones's reshaping of the exterior of the cathedral was the great portico of ten 40-foot high Corinthian columns which he erected before the west front of the cathedral. He took enormous pains over this portico, having full-size mock-ups hauled into place to test how the upper parts of the portico would look before authorising the permanent stonework. Jones saw the portico of the cathedral as his major realisation of what he called 'the Roman greatness'. His model was the original portico of the great vaulted building on the edge of the Forum in Rome which we today call the Basilica of Maxentius, but which during the Renaissance was identified as a temple dedicated to Peace. The portico of the temple of Peace

Figure 9.5 Wenceslas Hollar: St Paul's Cathedral from the west,
engraving, 1658, showing Inigo Jones's portico

had been destroyed in antiquity, but Jones believed he knew what
it looked like from the evidence of Roman coins. It is impossible
to know whether Jones selected this appropriate model for political reasons or essentially for aesthetic ones; but the king's commitment to the project was demonstrated by his personally paying
for the portico, and by the statues of himself and his father that
crowned its balustrade.

The reconstruction of the cathedral, which, had not war intervened, would no doubt have progressed to include the remodel-
ling of the interior and the rebuilding of the crossing tower, was a
tremendously important gesture by Laud on behalf of the
Anglican Church in asserting both its links with the pre-
Reformation church in England and its determination to renew
itself. St Paul's Cathedral was, in the words of Charles I himself, in
appointing the repair commission in 1631: 'the goodliest monument and most eminent church of his whole dominions; as also ...

the principal ornament of the City of London, the imperial seat of this his realm'.[30] The renewal of its fabric accompanied a campaign by Laud to renew its ecclesiastical life, by means of an archiepiscopal visitation in 1633 which led to what was in effect a new set of statutes in 1639. The two concerns, for religious and architectural order, came together in the portico, which was to serve as a covered meeting place for those who had hitherto desecrated the nave of the cathedral and disturbed the services in the choir by their secular activities.[31]

However, the renewed cathedral, and in particular its portico, also formed part of a secular dream, a dream to link the city to a rebuilt Whitehall Palace by means of an architecturally enhanced Strand. There is contemporary evidence that around 1638 the king seriously entertained the idea of rebuilding Whitehall Palace in its entirety.[32] Large numbers of design drawings, in the hands of Jones's assistant, John Webb, allow us to evaluate the vision in detail, and its is probable that the most elaborate of the many schemes dates from c.1638. This, which is planned round a total of eleven courtyards, the entrance courtyard being circular, and which has as its central feature a grand domed chapel, has many similarities with the great palace of El Escorial, built for Philip II of Spain. Charles had himself seen the Escorial in 1623 on his trip to Spain to win the hand of the Infanta. If it was the king who now, a decade and a half later, suggested this model for Jones's palace designs, they demonstrate his continuing naivety in presuming that in the political climate of England in the later 1630s such connotations of royal autocracy would have been acceptable to his subjects.

Also in 1638 Jones made a design for rebuilding the range of Somerset House which faced the Strand. Three hundred yards along the Strand east of Somerset House stood Temple Bar, marking the boundary between the Cities of London and Westminster. In 1636 the Privy Council had ordered Jones to discuss with some Aldermen and the Recorder of the City the erection of a gate here. Drawings by Jones show that he envisaged this 'gate' in the form of a magnificent triumphal arch, strongly reminiscent of the imperial arches in Rome dedicated to Constantine and Septimius Severus. Two drawings, one by Webb dated 1636, the other by Jones himself dated 1638, show that the project was seriously considered for some time; and the rich programme of sculpture sketched out by Jones shows that the imperial theme would have been strongly reinforced. The arch was to be surmounted by an

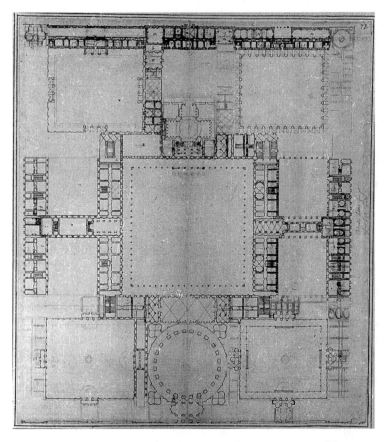

Figure 9.6 Inigo Jones: plan for rebuilding Whitehall Palace,
*c.*1638, drawing by John Webb

equestrian figure of Charles I reminiscent of the famous antique
statue of Marcus Aurelius on horseback which stood on the
Campidoglio in Rome; and flanking figures represented marine
divinities. At Temple Bar, then, entrance to the City of London,
where the king in procession would be greeted by the loyal
citizens of the capital, the sculpture on top of the triumphal arch
would denote his domination over land and sea.[33] Similarly, at the
end of the processional route, the statues of James I and Charles I
in the portico of the cathedral signified the position of the king as
head of the Church. No money was ever put up for either

Figure 9.7 Inigo Jones: design for Temple Bar, 1636, drawing by
          John Webb

Somerset House or Temple Bar; but the conjunction in these
years of building schemes for two palaces and a triumphal arch
with the executed west front and portico of the cathedral suggests
that links between the king's court and his church and city were

intended to be strengthened both physically and visually by the creation of a grand processional way from Westminster to London.

Urbanistically, such a long, straight processional way is not related to the layout of ancient Rome, but rather suggests recent papal ambitions, and indeed achievements, in creating a rational and impressive modern Rome by cutting long, straight routes through the historic fabric of the city. Jones had seen the Via Giulia and the Via Sistina, and owned Bordinus's *De Rebus Praeclare Gestis a Sixto V Pontifex Maximus* (1588), a treasured item in his library, given to him at the outset of his career, in 1606, and flatteringly inscribed.

In architecture the distance between the wish and its fulfilment is greater than in any other art. To achieve such grandiose schemes as these would have required vast sums of money and many years of commitment. It was completely unrealistic to hope for either as the period of Charles's personal rule drew to a close.

So far, Jones's buildings and architectural visions have been discussed as if they were primarily political in nature. But Jones was an artist, determined to express himself artistically. For him commissions to design buildings were first and foremost artistic opportunities. He designed with equal conviction a chapel for Roman Catholic worship (St James's Palace Chapel, 1623–7), a church for a Puritan patron which was recognised as 'godly' when first built (St Paul Covent Garden, 1631–3),[34] and the reconstruction of St Paul's Cathedral (1634–42) for the established church. For all three, antique temples provided creative inspiration. What Jones's own religious loyalties were is unknown and beside the point; it has often been suggested that he was a crypto-Catholic, like other Italianised Englishmen of his generation, but a papal agent in 1636 described him as 'puritanissimo', and it may be that he had no strong religious convictions at all.[35]

Jones had a high concept of the role of the architect, and the skills required of him. This is apparent from many marginal notes in his books, as for example where he sides with the ancient Greek architect Pythias against Vitruvius in asserting that an architect ought to be able to accomplish more in each art and science than a man who is merely an expert in any one such art,[36] conceiving of the architect as a polymath.

His own personality, we know, tended towards the dictatorial: 'Dominus Do-all' was how Ben Jonson once described him; the parishioners of St Gregory by St Paul's complained that he demanded to be 'sole monarch' in rebuilding their church; and

Bishop Williams, his collaborator at James I's funeral, had his own word for people in control of a situation – he called them 'Inigos'.[37] Such attributes in the climate of the late 1630s were in no doubt themselves counter-productive and added to the hostility with which the building enterprises of king and archbishop were viewed by the public.

After Jones's death in 1652 John Webb erected a monument in his memory in the little city church, St Benet Thames Street, where Jones had been baptised nearly eighty years before. It consisted of a tomb chest on which stood a portrait bust of the architect between two obelisks, symbols of eternity. On the ends of the chest were carved reliefs, one depicting the Banqueting House, the other the portico of St Paul's Cathedral, the masterpieces which would perpetuate the memory of the architect.[38]

Jones himself, however, also expressed the view that monumental architecture preserves and glorifies the memory of nations. As he wrote on the closing pages of his book on Stonehenge:

> The magnificence of that stately [Roman] Empire, is at this day clearly visible in … the ruins of their Temples, Palaces, Arches Triumphal, Aqueducts, Thermae, Theatres, Amphitheatres, Cirques, and other secular, and sacred structures.
>
> History affords only contemplation, whereby their great actions are made conceivable alone to reasoning, but the ruins of their buildings demonstration, which obvious to sense, are even yet as so many eye-witnesses of their admired achievements.[39]

By the same token, the Banqueting House and the portico of St Paul's Cathedral, Jones must have believed, would stand as witnesses to the admired achievements of the early Stuart monarchs.

Yet by the time *Stone-Heng Restored* was published in 1655 both Laud and Charles I had been put to death by parliament. Jones's portico was the sort of triumphalist gesture which had contributed to the unpopularity of archbishop and king. Posterity however, once the political significance of his buildings was forgotten, valued their purely architectural qualities. His classicism formed the foundation of Wren's achievements, and at the end of the century Roger North believed that his 'grand manner' was still unmatched.

10. Deeds against Nature: Cheap Print, Protestantism and Murder in Early Seventeenth-Century England

PETER LAKE

In much of the recent literature on the English reformation the relationship between Protestant ideology and 'the people' has been presented as essentially negative, indeed adversarial. Protestantism was a religion of the word, its basic means of communication the Bible, the sermon and the improving book. Not only were the forms of Protestant expression ill suited to a largely non- or semi-literate audience but, so the argument goes, the content of Protestant literature was unlikely to strike a chord with 'the people'. The central doctrines of Protestantism – justification by faith alone and its concomitant predestination – scarcely fitted in with what has been termed 'popular pelagianism'. Attached to the old religion – a religion of priestly and saintly intercession, of ritual performance and practice – the bulk of the population responded to Protestantism with a mixture of sullen disinterest and hostility, or so at least Professor Scarisbrick and Dr Haigh have argued.[1]

Moreover, as the English Reformation entered its second phase and Protestantism made gains among scattered groups of literate lay people, this interpretation has it that the values of 'perfect Protestantism' came to be allied with the cause of social order and moral discipline. Acting alongside various processes of social and economic differentiation – which during the period were dividing many English villages between substantial householders, farmers and the poor – the spread of Protestant or puritan values served to effect a division between the literate, prosperous middling sort and their humbler, poorer neighbours. Zealously Protestant or puritan religion thus, according to this view, became a means of defining the self-consciously respectable ruling élites in town and country and of controlling the behaviour of the social groups at or near the bottom of the social order. There resulted a cultural clash between, on the one hand, the culture of the godly – sober, pious, word and sermon based – and on the other, a residual popular culture, centred on the alehouse and village green, where the traditional forms of popular recreation and affirmations of social unity and solidarity acted out. Zealous Protestantism, on this view, was an instrument of social differentiation and control, a source of legitimation for new and austere concepts of social order and discipline, concepts rendered necessary by demographic growth and intermittent economic crisis. In short, there was a clean break effected between the Protestant and the popular; 'perfect Protestantism' was an external entity, unpopular even 'unnatural', which had to be imposed on an unwilling populace from above.[2]

In the present essay, I want to suggest that this view is both too neat and too extreme. In order to do so I want to examine a fairly common literary genre or sub-genre of the period 1580–1640 – the murder pamphlet. These were short, cheap pamphlets written for profit and therefore for a popular audience. Examples are extant from the 1570s and 1580s, and they have a continuous existence through to the civil war years and beyond. The pamphlets were certainly not an explicitly Protestant, still less a puritan, genre. So ambiguous was their relationship to the cheap godlies of the period that Tessa Watt omits them altogether from her seminal study of cheap print and religion in the period down to 1640. Some were written by clergymen (for instance Henry Goodcole, the Ordinary of Newgate Prison, wrote several), but many were not. Thomas Kyd the dramatist, John Taylor, the pot poet and notorious anti-puritan, and Anthony Munday the pamphleteer and playwright, all wrote murder pamphlets, and it is to their milieu that the pamphlets most obviously belong, to 'grub street', the bottom end of the market where publication was for profit and the consequent aim was to pander to popular taste.[3]

I Titillation

The appeal of the pamphlets to that market seems clear enough – it stemmed, most obviously, from their capacity to shock and titillate. Nearly all the pamphlets concentrate on particularly bizarre, bloody and grotesque killings. The quotient of both sex and violence to be found in them is very high. Thus one pamphlet features the stabbing of a pregnant woman in the stomach and the cutting out of a young girl's tongue. Both events are lovingly described, complete with dialogue and diverting circumstantial detail. In the first instance, a group of thieves, about to kill their two victims, are brought to a temporary halt by the husband's plea that they kill him but spare his wife and children. At this point the female member of the gang steps forward

> with these words 'talkest thou of pity', quoth she, 'if thy eyes have yet left so much sight to be witness how I'll be pitiful? Behold how I'll perform thy petition.' So drawing out her knife (O act too terrible to report, but the most damnablest that ever was heard of, executed by a woman) she ripped her up the belly, making herself a tragical midwife, or truly a murderess, that brought an abortive babe to the world and murdered the mother.

Later in the pamphlet, having killed one of the two surviving children of these hapless parents, the same female robber (referred to throughout as 'the whore', the 'bloody tigress', 'the she-wolf', this 'more than monstrous woman') beguiled the remaining child, a little girl, by asking her questions 'as what she walked upon, what she saw withal, and what she spake withal'. The child 'answered to every one directly, pointing to her foot, her eye and to her tongue, that with those and by the help of those, she saw, went and spoke. Whereupon this bloody tigress, to make herself more monstrous, bade her put out her tongue that she might feel it.' The child 'doing what she bade her, she presently caught it by the end, and with her thumb wresting open the child's jaws to the widest she could stretch them, she cut it out even by the root.'[4] All this circumstantial detail is, almost certainly, pure invention, designed to dramatise the picture of pure, helpless innocence at the mercy of sheer unadulterated cruelty and evil. Both passages draw out the agony, so that the reader, no matter how certain he or she is that something unpleasant is coming, feels a jolt of shock and disgust as the peculiarly nasty blow is struck. Here, surely, is the literary equivalent of a John Carpenter film.

In other cases the presentation of the violence was rather less sophisticated. One pamphlet simply recorded, in sickening detail, the blows and injuries suffered by a Lincolnshire clergyman, assaulted by an irate parishioner.[5] Other pamphlets featured gory descriptions of corpses in various stages of mutilation and decay. One noted how 'worms crawled in his mouth, nose, ears and his whole body was puttressed' and another described in vivid detail the mutilations visited on an unidentified corpse found in Finchley.[6]

Other pamphlets dwelt similarly lovingly on the details of the crimes they describe. There are several quite spectacular accounts of aristocratic young men drinking, fornicating and finally murdering their way into an early grave. One of these, Sir John Fitz, having murdered one man and secured a pardon, then proceeded to whore and drink his way through life until finally he went berserk. Mistaking an innkeeper and his family for a posse led by his estranged father-in-law who, he was convinced, was coming to kill him, Fitz murdered both the husband and wife before finally turning his sword upon himself. He fell on it three times and then took two full days to die, continually tortured by the thought of Sir William Courtenay's men coming to blow him up with gunpowder.[7]

Such shocking scenes from the lives of the gentry were echoed and balanced by some equally lurid and sensational slices of low life. One pamphlet of 1614, called graphically *Deeds against Nature and Monsters by Kind*, told two stories from 'the by places and suburbs of the city [London] which is ever more the receit of such begging vagabonds and disordered livers, instruments of the devil prepared still for deeds of mischief.' In one story, a crippled beggar who lived off the proceeds of charity, a life of depravity and sexual licence, strangled to death his female companion, a prostitute, who was pressing him to marry her. Throughout, great stress was put on the cripple's physical disabilities. In the second, a prostitute killed her baby by throwing it down a privy, where it was only discovered by the barking of a dog, similarly dispatched down the privy as a prank by 'an untoward lad' living next door. Much play was made with the sight of the 'sweet babe lying all besmeared with filth of that loathsome place'.[8]

Henry Goodcole the ordinary of Newgate made something of a speciality of these notes from the London underground. His pamphlets, like *Deeds against Nature*, dealt with the prostitutes and thieves of the London backstreets. Ostensibly heavily moralised diatribes against sin and dire warnings to the unsuspecting visitor to the great wen, Goodcole's pamphlets nevertheless luxuriated in the details of the crimes they described. One of them, the story of

Country Tom and Canberry Bess, a prostitute and her accomplice who lured unsuspecting gentlemen and merchants into the fields around London, before murdering and robbing them, actually ended with a list of 'places in and about London that harlots watch their opportunities to surprise men'. Another, *The Adulteress's Funeral Day*, involved the murder of an old and cruel husband who used not only to beat his wife 'with the next cudgel that came accidentally unto his hand but often tying her to his bed post to strip her and whip her'.[9]

Nor were the pamphlets limited to the spectacular crimes of gentry rakes or the excesses of London low life. Many of them were located in more commonplace social settings – the households of farmers, merchants, artisans. Here wives and their lovers killed husbands, husbands killed wives, parents killed children and children or servants killed parents or masters. Usually these crimes were prompted by the most commonplace and obvious of motives – lust, greed, adultery, envy, revenge. The pamphlets, of course, concentrated on the most spectacular and bloody of these crimes. In one, a fairly commonplace dispute over ecclesiastical patronage became the occasion for a bizarre murder involving the dismembering and pickling of the victim's body and the discovery, a fortnight later, of bits of it in a series of pots and tubs both in the victim's house and the house of the alleged murderers. In another pamphlet three servants conspired together to kill and rob their miserly master. There was nothing noteworthy in that, save that they chose to do the deed with a pickaxe, each man taking a turn to strike a blow and then swearing a bloody oath never to reveal the identity of his partners in crime. This allowed the author to focus on the sight of the master lying 'embrued in his own gore with his brains most brutishly dashed out'. Another pamphlet described the murder in Rye of a fisherman's wife by her husband. This was another commonplace crime, save that the method chosen was the sprinkling of a mixture of ratsbane and powdered glass on the woman's genitals.[10]

The point to be made here is that the relationship between the pamphlets and the acts they describe was not straightforwardly condemnatory, although that claim was certainly advanced for them. One pamphlet claimed as its aim that 'God in his power might be known, satan in his meaning no doubt overthrown and the world's idle fabling by a contrary meaning known'. Another author claimed that he had written his pamphlet that 'God's holy name might be glorified … the justice of the realm cleared and magnified ... and disordered people terrified from running the like course'. Henry Goodcole cited the 'common good and the preservation of my country's welfare' as the justification for his warnings to the unwary about the dangers of the London back-streets. One author in 1577 actually bit the bullet and denied the obvious; his pamphlet was not intended 'to feed the fond humour of such curious appetites as are more inquisitive of other folks offences than hasty to redress their own'.[11]

However, as the various examples cited above are intended to show, the relationship of the pamphlets to their subject-matter was not merely edificational or admonitory, it was rather exploitative, indeed, in some sense, pornographic. Examples of extreme violence, sexual licence, outlandish and disgusting acts were presented to the reader, ostensibly for his or her moral instruction but, in fact, in order not merely to edify but also to shock, titillate and engender that *frisson* of horror laced with disapproval which allows both pleasure and excitement at the enormities described to be combined with a reconfirmed sense of the reader's own moral superiority. This was true even of some of the most heavily moralised pamphlets – like Goodcole's – as well as of the more straightforward narratives of enormity, like those written by Kyd or Taylor.

II   Inversion

The inherently mixed and morally ambiguous nature of these pamphlets is further reflected in their use of the technique of inversion. In recent writing, inversion has been depicted most frequently as a festive mode, operating both in the literature and popular culture of the period as a source of humour and release, whereby the unity and fecundity of the social body could be both celebrated and sustained. In certain popular customs, rituals of inversion could be invoked to turn the world the right way up. For instance, as Martin Ingram and David Underdown have shown, Skymingtons or Charivaris guyed supposed offences against the gender hierarchy and, at least at the symbolic level, righted them through shaming rituals which themselves embodied and played out the deviant and inverted behaviours they were in fact designed to censure.

Such popular rituals were, thus, inherently mixed affairs; festive, satiric, unruly, they were attacked by some contemporaries as disorderly, and yet were themselves designed to embody and sustain certain popular notions of order.[12] The murder pamphlets partook of that same ambiguity. For murder constituted (and was certainly represented in the pamphlets as) perhaps the ultimate rent or rupture in the social body. As such, the violent events described in such loving detail functioned as apertures or peepholes through which could be glimpsed a nightmare world turned upside-down in which basic human impulses – lust, greed, revenge – having broken free from the normal social and religious moorings which otherwise contained their destructive potential, threatened to plunge the world into chaos and disorder.

One author sketched just such a vision of the world turned upside-down in the introduction to a pamphlet of 1595.

> The son desiring his fathers living and to be great before his time, murdereth him; the friend, his dearest friend; the wife, the husband and the husband, the wife; brother against sister and sister the brother; whereby the world is grown to such a pass that no friend dare commit any secret to his most nearest and dearest friend without some jealousy of his truth and faithfulness. If he have money, he feareth to reveal it to his wife, his servants, his children, his friends or any, doubting lest the knowledge thereof shall abridge his days. If he have a wife, which as himself he loveth, although he see with his own eyes her chaste life given over to the lecher and another enjoy that only proper to himself yet with hearts grief is he fain to smother so vile and most odious abuse doubting the revealing thereof should work his shame in the world and his life thereby dangered. If his children neglect their duties he is forced to bear with their enormities lest it happen to them as to many fathers who have lost their lives in seeking to correct such headstrong youth. Is there not the like in servants whose credit with their masters hath been admirable, that in the end have enriched themselves and beggared their masters.[13]

Order, on this view, was fragile; the least infraction of social discipline, the most commonplace corrupt impulse could end in disaster. In the passage I have just quoted, of course, a whole series of corrupt impulses, economic as well as fleshly, are hinted at as likely causes of disorder. But in the murder pamphlets perhaps the most common source of disorder, violence and murder was a human, and in particular a female, sexuality that had escaped from patriarchal control and was now free to wreak havoc on the social order.

The most powerful image or model of this nightmare world of untrammelled impulse, lust and greed is to be found in the pamphlets (mostly by Henry Goodcole) which dealt with the low life of the London backstreets. Within this milieu, where all the inhabitants could be presented as having been simply brutalised by sin, the representative figure was the prostitute, and her representative sin, infanticide. In the person of the whore, readers were confronted with the ultimate example of a sexuality freed from any of the constraining limits of familial or patriarchal power. In the infanticides committed by prostitutes to rid themselves of the unwanted consequences of their trade, the pamphlets provided a symmetrically perfect inversion of the normal ties, feelings and obligations of human society. Infanticides were presented, as the title of one pamphlet had it, as 'natures cruel stepdames or matchless monsters of the female'. These were in many ways the ultimate 'deeds against nature', as the title of another infanticide pamphlet termed them. The paradoxical image of the 'pitiless mother' (to quote yet another pamphlet title) seemed to sum up the inverted moral order of the London backstreets as Goodcole depicted them. The most symmetrically inverted personification of this vision of London low life was to be found in the almost laughably wicked and anti-social figure of Margaret Ferneseed. An utterly shameless prostitute and bawd, and, after her marriage to a respectable craftsman, an habitual adulterer, Ferneseed humiliated, ignored, cuckolded and finally murdered her husband. In Ferneseed we are confronted by the apotheosis of the whore as a figure for human sexuality escaped from patriarchal authority, a symbol for a fallen human nature untrammelled by social or familial control.[14]

In this moral universe the term 'whore' becomes almost a free-floating signifier whose origins in certain forms of sexual conduct can at times be all but forgotten. Hence, in the Annis Dell pamphlets described above, the female robber, in the act of tearing out the young girl's tongue and stabbing the pregnant mother, was transformed into a whore, an appellation which had no basis in anything the pamphlet had to say about her sexual behaviour, but was grounded instead in the unnatural cruelty and perverse pleasure inscribed in her peculiarly bloody assault on family values.

To this extent, the image of the world turned upside-down, of depravity and evil, depicted in the pamphlets was gendered. In many pamphlets women were portrayed as leading men into sin. In *News from Perrin* it was the wicked stepmother who persuaded the rather unworldly and generous paterfamilias to kill the stranger who turned out to be his son. In a ballad based on the Canberry Bess and Country Tom narrative it was Bess who led the man on. Indeed, the theme of the young man led into sin, robbery and murder by the blandishments and demands of a prostitute anxious for payment recurred more than once in the pamphlets. Not that the woman had to be a prostitute. In a pamphlet of 1583 a woman conducting an affair with a servant became so overcome with 'lust' that she beguiled the young man into murdering her husband, badgering him to do the deed and even supplying him with a forest bill specially sharpened for the purpose. She was, editorialised the author, 'a most horrible and wicked woman, a woman, nay, a devil'.[15]

It may not be going too far to see in all this a certain tendency to project onto women the negative, sinful, fleshly aspects of human nature; a tendency if anything confirmed by the elements of sado-masochistic misogyny in the more pornographic sections of the pamphlets. And yet there were male analogues and equivalents for Margaret Ferneseed and the prostitutes and infanticides of the London backstreets. These were the patriarchs run amok described in a number of pamphlets concerned with the doings of gentry rakes, young men who, having started on a slippery slope of debauchery, drunkenness and whoredom, ended up as murderers paying the wages of their sins on the gallows.

In the story of John Rous, the descent into murder and death started with an act of adultery with a maidservant. The upset following that affair sent his first wife to an early grave. Rous married again, all the time continuing his liaison with the maid. Next he left his second wife to live a life of debauchery in London with his mistress. Defrauded of his property, he went abroad for a time. At last, ruined, he returned home to his wife and children where Satan tempted him to 'mischief and despair', reminding him that he had squandered friends, lands, money, apparel and credit and 'that now he had nothing left him but poverty and beggary and that his two children were like to be left to go from door to door for their living'. In this devil-induced mental state he killed both his children, to save them, as he thought, from a life of beggary and shame. His story parallels the similar descent into debauchery, debt, despair and child murder described by Mr Caverly of Caverly.

But perhaps the most developed example of these rakes' progresses through sin and murder to damnation was that of Sir John Fitz. As a young man Fitz fell into a dissolute life. This youthful wildness culminated in his killing a man for an imagined slight. Fitz secured a pardon which, far from serving as an occasion for repentance and amendment, merely drove him further into sin. By now, the author commented, 'he was naturally hardened in ill'. He deserted his marriage bed, giving himself over to 'lawless desires'. He began to drink, swear and blaspheme. His retainers terrorised and vandalised the locality. Fitz himself took to coming home at night with various prostitutes. Finally he turned his wife out of the house altogether and erected instead 'a little commonwealth of many iniquities'. Now his former crime together with the public fame of his present debauchery and the complaints of his estranged father-in-law seemed set fair to ruin him. And it was on a trip to London to head off the plots of his enemies at court that Fitz went berserk and committed the murder of the Surrey innkeeper and his wife and the particularly messy and protracted suicide outlined above.[16]

The parallels between the likes of Margaret Ferneseed and these gentry rakes are considerable. Both rakes and whores had the sin of infanticide in common and the corruption and ruin of the gentry patriarchs was often marked and accelerated by contact with prostitutes. In both the Ferneseed narrative and the rake pamphlets the actions of the protagonists transcend what one might term the rational pursuit of sinful self-interest, as the sinner becomes utterly depraved by his or her sins. Here is sinful humanity at the end of its tether utterly corrupted and enslaved by sin.

In the figures of these patriarchs gone berserk and the whores of Goodcole's narratives we have the two limiting examples of the lurid consequences of the breakdown of patriarchal control over the social order. On the one hand, we see the awful consequences of female independence in a female sexuality untrammelled and uncontained by the normal structures of familial stability and male authority. On the other, we have the equally dreadful sight of that same authority run amok, breaking through the constraints of divine and natural law, obedience to which alone could render the authority of prince or patriarch genuinely legitimate.[17]

On the most obvious level the appeal of the pamphlets lay in rubbing the noses of the reader in the details of the resulting depravity. But titillation also contained and implied its morally improving opposite. For the message of the pamphlets was that any breakdown of control, any abuse of authority by those on top or dereliction of duty by those underneath threatened to loose the peccant tendencies of fallen human nature with disastrous results.

Many of the pamphlets can be read as containing an implicit critique of a whole variety of behaviour patterns and abuses which in the wrong circumstances could lead to disaster. In the ballad, Canberry Bess may well have been depicted as enticing Country Tom into a life of crime but in the original pamphlet by Goodcole it was made clear that Bess was initially led 'into folly' by a young man and then cast off without a penny by the family where she was in service. Blame for her subsequent descent into prostitution and crime was laid clearly at their door. Even in one of the infanticide pamphlets Goodcole pointed out that Elizabeth Barnes's crime had been caused by a man, a man who had promised her marriage, taken her money, made her pregnant and then run off. Perhaps most interesting of all, in several pamphlets the murders of husbands by wives and their lovers were attributed, at least in part, to the tragic legacy of marriages arranged contrary to the woman's wishes by her parents. In one of these pamphlets the marriage was styled 'the work of satan'.[18]

In these instances, for all the gendered language of many of the pamphlets, women were not the prime origin or locus of evil; the real origin of these sins lay in abuses of patriarchal or familial power, derelictions of duty by those in authority which in turn set up cracks and fissures in the delicate skein of social obligations, rights and duties which alone protected the human world from the potentially devastating depredations of sin and the devil. Here lay the moral message of the pamphlets. If sin were to be controlled and disaster averted, all elements in society, masters and servants, husbands and wives, parents and children, must play their part in maintaining the delicate balance of the social order. The author of 1595 juxtaposed his nightmare vision of a world turned upside-down by human sin, quoted above, with an equally idealised vision of what a social order purged of the sins that led to murder would look like.

Ah would every estate would but look into himself, and everyone in himself seek a reformation. Then should the usurer's stock decrease, when charity doth abound. The covetous grazier and farmer should take such reasonable prices for their corn and cattle, that their poor brethren handicraftsmen might

live by them without oppression. Lawyers should not then be so
followed neither of poor or rich.[19]

Thus, the inverted, perverted world turned upside-down of the
pamphlets implied and contained its opposite. As ever, festive
inversion had its moralising, repressive aspect. Without it, the
pamphlets warned, fallen human nature and the depredations of
Satan would together plunge the world into chaos and disorder.

III   The devil

The devil was ubiquitous in the murder pamphlets. Virtually every
one contained (as indeed did indictments for murder themselves)
a phrase along the lines of 'by the fury and assistance of the devil',
'by the inspiration and instigation of the devil'. Murder, as the
greatest of sins, had a peculiar affinity with the devil. As the
instigator of the first murder of Abel by Cain the devil was 'the
murderer's master'.[20]

Always ready to take hold of the 'least advantage that may be to
increase his kingdom' the devil seized every opportunity offered
to his malice by the sins and foibles of humanity. Any opening
would do; any element of discord between man and wife, any
covetous impulse, any envious or lustful glance, any corrupt desire
offered Satan a chance. Moreover, to entice a sinner into one sin
was never enough for Satan 'that loves to have his bond-slaves
sooted all over with the coal of damnation'. Having started,
therefore, with one sin, the devil almost always moved on to
another. He operated, in fact, through chains of sins, as one
infraction led to the next and the sinner moved ever closer to
eternal death and damnation. 'As a chain consists of divers links,'
observed John Taylor,

> and every link depends and is yoked upon one another, even so
> our sins, being the chain wherewith Satan doth bind and
> manacle us, are so knit, twisted and sodered together that with-
> out our firm faith ascending and God's grace descending we can
> never be freed from those infernal fetters. For sloth is linked
> with drunkenness, drunkenness with fornication and adultery,
> and adultery with murder and so of all the rest of the tempta-
> tions, suggestions, and actions, wherewith miserable men and
> women are ensnared and led captive into perpetual perdition,

except the mercy of our gracious God be our defence and safeguard.

Sin was cumulative: 'evils go not alone unaccompanied, but as in a chain one link draws on another, so one sin begets another till with the plurality thereof the sinner be fettered'. All this allowed considerable advantage to 'the malice of the devil, whose will and endeavour is that none should be saved'. One author spoke of the 'tempter with alluring baits' enticing 'those chosen of his to such horrible sins' and another observed that once 'Lucifer had found a means how to accomplish his will he never left him, till by his devilish practises he had brought him [his victim] to the gallows'.[21]

It was this vision of the all-pervasive malice and presence of Satan, combined with the human propensity to sin, which provided a central narrative thread for many, if not most, of the pamphlets. For they nearly all shared an attempt to locate what one pamphlet called the 'very original cause and first ground of this ungodly deed'.[22] In many cases the original sin involved was obvious: lust and adultery when husbands killed wives or wives and their lovers killed husbands; envy or covetousness when, for instance, servants killed masters for gain, or one neighbour killed another over property. In most cases the sins lay festering for some time; in some the crime was a result of sudden temptation. In many instances the motives or sins were mixed. Lust and greed compounded one another in the stories of, say, apprentices who killed their masters at the prompting of prostitutes whose services they had to finance. Envy, lust and covetousness all lay behind the crime of the curate who killed his ministerial employer in order to inherit both his living and his wife. In most cases the pamphlets make the chain of sins leading up to the murder explicit. The initial incision was made by one sin, in the curate's case envy; this led to others, here lust and adultery, which culminated in murder. The pattern was repeated over and over again: an initial corrupt impulse or desire, a concatenation of sins, and then murder.[23]

IV   Providence and divine justice

In the world of the pamphlets, therefore, order could become disorder, the world could be turned upside-down with frightening rapidity. How, then, could it be set to rights? Just as the devil lay behind the lurid crimes and enormities described in the pamphlets, so an even more powerful supernatural force was depicted righting these wrongs, turning the world the right way up. For over against the forces of sin and the devil was ranged the awesome power of divine providence. As it was described in the pamphlets, the resulting struggle amounted to a species of pseudo-Manichaeanism – a view of the world stretched tight between God and the devil, with the room for human agency left between them constricted and confined at times almost to nothing.

But even here, at their most moralistic, when the presence of God in the world was most manifest, the pamphlets retained their peculiar mixture of the titillating and the admonitory. For the bizarre and outlandish aspects of the pamphlets were not limited to the crimes themselves. As well as outstandingly brutal or disgusting murders, what attracted many authors to the crimes in question were the spectacular or unlikely ways in which the criminals were discovered and brought to book. Thus in the pamphlet in which the pregnant woman had been stabbed and the little girl's tongue cut out, the malefactors were only discovered four years later by frankly miraculous means. Having had her tongue removed, the little girl was left by her tormentors in a tree stump to die. Rescued by a passing stranger, she spent the next four years wandering the roads of Essex, Hertfordshire and London as a dumb beggar. Then, chance (or rather divine providence) brought her back to the village in which her brother had been killed and she mutilated. Confronted by the very house in which the foul deeds had been done she was able to alert the attention of the neighbourhood, but not, of course, to explain what had happened. The owners of the house, who were indeed implicated in the crime, seemed about to brazen it out when the little girl, playing with some local children, was heard first to crow like a cock and then to speak. Thus restored to speech she was able to testify against the culprits and they met their deserved fate. At the assizes the girl's mouth was examined by the jury, but despite her restored capacity to speak they 'could see not so much as the stump of a tongue therein'. This event the authors of both the pamphlets about the murder described as a 'miracle'. God, said one, had 'lent her a speech by miracle'. 'If we look,' said the other, 'into [the case] but with the eyes of natural reason and human sense it will be thought incredible and impossible. But with God nothing is impossible.' Indeed, the whole affair had been a direct product of the 'providence and appointment of God'. He had 'decreed to bring this cruel, barbarous and bloody massacre to light'. He had preserved the girl and guided her back to the scene of the crime and given her speech all in order to bring the murder to light and the perpetrators to justice. 'Such is the just judgement of God, to the plague of murderers and terror of them that delight in bad, the dumb shall speak ere they shall escape undiscovered.'[24]

In other pamphlets equally miraculous or pseudo-miraculous events served to unmask the culprits. In one case a father who had suborned a servant to kill his three children was confronted with the three corpses. At once the children's wounds began to 'bleed afresh':

> which when the coroner saw he commanded the party appre-hended to look upon the children, which he did, and called them by their names whereupon, behold the wonderful works of God, for the fact being still denied, the bodies of the children, which seemed white like unto soaked flesh laid in water, suddenly received their former colour of blood ... which wonderful miracle caused the murderer there present not only to confess ... but also to accuse the father of the children as principal procurer of their untimely deaths.

On another occasion a murderer returning to view the corpse of his victim suffered a severe nose bleed and had to run away home, lest he be discovered.[25]

In still other pamphlets the elements and the natural world took a hand. Several murders were attended by omens. In the case of the old man who unwittingly killed his long-lost son, a drop of blood fell from the father's nose onto the son's sleeping body, and an owl screeched just as the blow was struck. In another instance, the murder took place to the accompaniment of wild rain, thunder and lightning, or, as the pamphleteer put it, 'the heavens threatened vengeance in thunder ... and dart forth flashes of lightening to make him see his sin and put him in mind of those eternal fires in hell ... the compassionate clouds burst into tears to put his hard heart in mind of remorse'. The pamphlet *Page of Plymouth*, which dealt with the murder of an old husband by his young wife and her lover, described, at its close, three omens seen on the nights immediately following the crime. A bear appeared with eyes of fire, carrying the murder weapon (a linen cloth); a raven hanged itself on a length of rope and a wreck was seen to turn itself completely in the water.[26]

The line between these miraculous and semi-supernatural happenings and the more conventionally providential is often very hard to draw. The elements and, behind them, God, were deemed to have taken a direct hand in the apprehension of various murderers. For instance, two murderers, having fled to Chester, spent days trying to take ship for Ireland but were constantly frustrated by contrary winds. No sooner had they been caught than the wind changed 'fitting transportation or sailing into Ireland'. According to the author of the pamphlet, this was the operation of 'digitus domini, the lord's doing, marvellous in their eyes'. On another occasion a murderer having despatched his victim leapt upon his horse – 'a lusty, strong gelding as any is in England' – in order to make good his escape, only to find that it 'presently fell lame and was not able to carry' him, thus ensuring his capture. 'Such is the just judgement of God that abhorreth murderers and will not their villainy be concealed.' Coincidence or even the astute detective work of the investigating magistrates was often directly attributed to the workings of God's providence. The decision of a judge to place a suspect under surveillance and to interrogate some of his visitors in prison was described as God 'wonderfully' disclosing 'the secret of his [the murderer's] heart and 'laughing to scorn' his intention to cover up his crime.[27]

Thus far, providence has been seen operating almost entirely through external agencies, but very often it was presented in the pamphlets as working internally through the bad conscience of the murderer. God, claimed one author, often allowed murderers an element of impunity so 'that the guilt of the conscience is hereby so increased and at length enraged, that though all other means fail, yet their own tongues shall be forced to betray them, to ease the inward pangs and to justify the lord even out of their own mouths'. Thus murderers often blurted out incriminating remarks when in fact their guilt was as yet unsuspected. One suspect condemned himself by his 'usual crying and calling out in his sleep "let us fly Mr Peter, let us away or else we shall all be undone and hanged"'. Another murderer against whom no case could be made was compelled to confess by a 'heavenly sermon made to terrify murderers' by the local minister.[28]

What we have here are a number of distinct but related beliefs about murder, being gradually incorporated into an austere vision of the power of divine providence over all second order causes in the world and of the inexorability of divine justice. These beliefs ranged from what amounted to a species of sympathetic magic, in which the blood of the victim cried out against the murderer, through belief in omens and natural signs, triggered off by human crimes and unnatural acts. The sorts of events through which the providence of God was deemed to work ranged from the frankly miraculous (the tongueless girl restored to speech, the freshly bleeding corpse) through the merely coincidental concurrence of entirely natural phenomena (a lame horse, contrary winds, accidental meetings and disclosures) to the purely internal workings of the murderer's conscience. In short, these pamphlets contained attitudes and beliefs which were certainly not explicitly Protestant, which pre-dated the Reformation and which could be found in both Protestant and Catholic countries. For instance, as Dr Maddern points out, the view that 'murder will come out' and that God will not allow any murderer successfully to conceal his or her crime was proverbial in the fifteenth century. In the murder pamphlets, such attitudes were being appropriated by, grafted onto what, in the context of early seventeenth-century England, Keith Thomas and others have identified as a Protestant, even rather a puritan, providentialism.[29]

Either way the view of the world in question was dominated by the providence of God working usually with and through, but sometimes cutting across, second order causes to bring about God's secret purposes; purposes which in the case of the murder pamphlets involve the disclosure, punishment, sometimes the repentance and, it is often implied, the ultimate salvation of hardened sinners and murderers. The pamphlets were certainly drenched in the language of divine providence and justice. According to one author, 'God seldom or never leaveth murder unpunished.' 'God ... hath iron hands' claimed another pamphlet, and 'will at last strike heavily'. One writer praised 'the goodness of this omnipotent God, that sees sin, hates sin and will punish sin', and acted through such unlikely agents as stray dogs and dumb women to reveal hidden murders.[30] In the course of vindicating these claims the pamphlets presented a world that was, in Thomas Beard's famous phrase, 'a theatre of God's judgements'. At every point, God's judgment was seen actively intervening in human affairs, frustrating the intentions of the men and women involved in the crimes, bending their puny efforts to his own higher purposes. On the one hand, he was shown turning what was intended to be a mere beating into a murder in order to punish the previous sinful life of the murderer. On the other, he appears frustrating attempts at escape, forcing murderers through the power of conscience to confess or, alternatively, preserving desperate malefactors from death at their own hands in order to give them time and opportunity for subsequent repentance and hence salvation. In short, human beings appeared throughout the pamphlets as mere playthings of the divine will. The room for creative human agency left in these pamphlets, either for the murderers or for their pursuers, is often very small indeed.

V   Inversion again; the festive and moralised alternatives

The pamphlets thus pictured, on the one hand, a vision of an inverted and perverted social order, and over against that vision an equally idealised view of a perfectly integrated, stable and harmonious society. The doorway between those two worlds was provided by the dreadful deeds perpetrated by the murderers. These were the most overt eruptions of Satan into the social world, and, as such, they pointed the way into the inverted moral order implied by the pamphlets. The only way the door between those two worlds could be closed, the only way in which the world could be turned the right way up, was through the, often providential, apprehension and punishment of the murderer. And here punishment meant death. The pamphlets were quite clear that pardons were not a good idea, not even for the most repentant murderer. For it was the 'law of God' that the 'murderer, without any admittance of privilege or psalm of mercy, must die the death, that so blood might be recompensed with blood and the land may be cleansed from the guilt thereof'.[31] But, in many pamphlets, the murderer's death alone was not enough to set the world to rights; for that to happen a public confession of guilt and expression of repentance was required as well.

As many of the pamphlets make clear, considerable efforts were often made to bring such a repentance about. Sometimes executions were delayed to allow those condemned to prepare themselves for repentance and death. Ministers attended murderers in prison, endeavouring, where necessary, to instruct them in the basic points of religion and bring them to a proper sense of sin and repentance. The ministers involved were sometimes rather exalted figures; in one pamphlet Alexander Nowell, the dean of St Paul's, was shown ministering in gaol to certain murderers; in another Bishop Fletcher of Bristol, the queen's almoner, performed the same role. The willingness of the secular magistrates to arrange such visits was praised in several pamphlets. Their ostensible aim was the salvation of the prisoners' souls, but they had other motives too. Many of the crimes described in the pamphlets were the objects of considerable public interest and attention, and the executions of notorious criminals often drew large crowds. These were public events, of considerable propaganda value, and they needed to be stage-managed in order to bolster the cause of order and obedience in church and state. Thus a central feature of the 'theatre' of public executions appears to have been (where it could be extracted) a public confession and expression of repentance by the criminal. The supposed texts of some of these statements, which often turned into little sermons of warning and moral exhortation, were sometimes printed at the end of the more moralised pamphlets. According to one author, in London convicted felons being drawn on a cart towards execution were always 'stayed before St Sepulchres church ... to move prayer and compassion in men's hearts'. However, the edifying and admonitory impact of such spectacles was entirely ruined if the condemned man or woman displayed the symptoms, not of sorrow and repentance, but of a desperate or light-hearted defiance or unconcern. In the narrative in question the murderer, who was a papist, 'stopped his ears' at the sound of the crowd's prayers, desiring only the invocations of devout Catholics for his soul's health.[32]

But, as Tom Lacqueur has recently pointed out, the subversion of the 'official' messages – encoded in the public executions by the victim's refusal to keep to the script provided by the authorities – was not limited to the ideologically charged example of papists. In many instances felons met their maker drunk, defiant or playing the fool. The point of Lacqueur's argument is to undermine the now modish view of the public execution as a theatre of punishment, in which the power of the centralising state was ritually inscribed in the flesh of the victim, a public demonstration of the power of the prince and the awful majesty of the law. On the contrary, for Lacqueur, public executions and the junkettings that accompanied them, were genuinely popular and festive occasions, carnivalesque displays of popular energy and inversion, which very often entirely escaped from the meanings and messages which the official script for the event attempted (often rather half-heartedly) to impose on them. According to Lacqueur the main difference between this and other sorts of popular festivity was that in this instance, by the end, the carnival king or lord of misrule really was dead. On this view, the executions themselves and the popular festivities which accompanied them, were structured by precisely the same principles of inversion, followed by the reaffirmation of social unity and stability, as were the pamphlets themselves. However, the vision of the social order being upheld in the pamphlets was rather different from that figured in the festive crowds that attended the executions. What we have here, therefore, are a set of genuinely popular, yet morally contested forms and assumptions. There can be no doubting the symbolic power generated by the cycles of infraction, inversion and reaffirmation of order, which both the executions and the pamphlets were trying to bring to a satisfactory close. What were in doubt were the moral or polemical purposes to which that power might be put. The majority of the pamphlets were designed to efface that doubt or ambiguity. With their concern either to emphasise the murderer's repentance or to register his or her damnation, they were seeking not merely to close the circle of infraction, inversion and reaffirmation by recording the death of the murderer, but also to close off other, subversive or festive readings of the event, by imposing their own moralised interpretation upon it. Repentance was thus the moral hinge, whereby a world turned upside-down by the crimes recounted in the pamphlets could be righted and the moral and religious values which underlay the social order reaffirmed. In these narratives considerable symbolic power was generated by the repentant murderers' quiescent, even welcoming, acceptance of death, as at least deserved and, in some of the more religiously exalted of the pamphlets, even liberating. This power was then enlisted in order to close down the Rabelaisian, festive vision of the executions outlined by Lacqueur. In some cases, it was also mobilised to serve more particular ideological or polemical purposes.[33]

It would be tempting, therefore, to see in the pamphlets a classic, controlling imposition of an 'élite', 'official' meaning, on a 'popular' or festive form. There would certainly be some truth in that view. However, it needs to be remembered here that the genre itself was in part structured by precisely the same sort of carnivalesque inversions which Lacqueur has discerned in the swaying, surging social body of the crowds that attended the executions. The pamphlet narratives themselves were a mixture of the edifying and the titillatory, the admonitory and voyeuristic. This, then, was a decidedly and inherently mixed genre, trapped by its very nature between the controlling and the festive, the

moralising and the pornographic. As such it offered to some
Protestant authors a potential entry point into the mental world
of 'the people' and in conclusion I want to examine some of the
ways in which those authors exploited it.

VI   A Popular Medium and a Protestant Message?

As we have seen, in the pamphlets the world was pictured as the
locus of a struggle between the forces of good and evil, God and
the devil, Christ and the Antichrist. The pamphlets offered two
opposed visions of the social order – one, an idealised image of a
stable, hierarchical society, the other an equally idealised image
of sin, chaos and disorder. The real world existed somewhere
between those two ideal types, pushed one way and then the other
by the struggle that was raging between the wiles of Satan and
human sin, on the one hand, and the forces of divine providence,
justice and mercy on the other. On neither side of that struggle
was there much room left for positive human agency. To describe
the view of the world portrayed here in terms taken from early
heresies we should perhaps do better to talk of popular
Manichaeanism rather than of Dr Haigh's popular Pelagianism.
This is not to suggest that the constellations of values evoked by
those two catchphrases were mutually exclusive. Elements of both
systems could be found in the murder pamphlets, and no doubt
in the wider society as well. What is being suggested here is that
there were elements in the murder pamphlets and the attitudes
they reflected that lent themselves to a Protestant reading and
thus offered Protestants an opening or series of openings which
they could use to bring the Protestant message to a wider audience. Moreover, many of the central motifs in the pamphlets
analysed above lent themselves to interpretation in terms of those
predestinarian elements in the Protestant view of the world which
are often assumed to have been peculiarly repellent or unintelligi-
ble to popular audiences.

At one level the stories told in the pamphlets were extraordinary, notable precisely because they were utterly untypical,
marked off from everyday experience by some episode of extreme
violence, some miraculous conclusion, some dramatic twist or
turn of fate. Therein lay their peculiar capacity to shock, titillate
and terrify; that was what made them both safe and saleable.
However, as we have seen, the root sins which lay behind most of

the crimes recounted in the pamphlets were anything but extra-ordinary. Drunkenness, covetousness, lust, adultery, these are scarcely exceptional sins. Idle, gossiping, shrewish wives; drunken, brutal husbands; mean and unkind masters; greedy, disloyal or dissolute servants; aspiring would-be gentlemen; wild young men about town – these were all common enough social types, and they all figure prominently in the chains of sin that, in the pamphlets, led with seeming inevitability to murder and death.

This enabled the dreadful crimes and summary judgments recorded in the pamphlets to be presented by some authors as paradigms for the condition of all sinners and Christians. Every-one, after all, was a sinner; all sinners were potential prey for the devil. Not everyone who fell prey to the devil and sinned would end up a murderer, but all sin was potentially mortal, and all sin-ners were subject to the chains of sin which in the pamphlets led to murder and execution. Other Christian sinners, guilty of less spectacular sins, might not end up on the gallows, but they would surely languish in hell.[34]

Given the all-pervading human propensity to sin and the ubi-quity of the devil, it was only the protection of God which stood between sinful humanity and perdition. 'That we stand it is the benefit of God's grace and not the goodness of our nature nor the strength of our own will,' concluded Arthur Golding.[35] The authors of various pamphlets were thus able to cite the irreligion and ignorance of various felons as an awful example of what happened to you if you ignored God, his word and his ministers. Thus one murderer, Mistress Sanders, was found by the minister who visited her in prison to be utterly 'unprovided to die'. Indeed, she only came to repent at the sound of the hammers erecting the gallows outside her cell window. The reason was not far to seek. She was 'very raw and ignorant in all things pertaining to God … yea and even in the very principles of the Christian religion'. Sanders's accomplice later admitted that he had 'not heretofore frequented sermons, nor received the holy sacrament nor used any calling upon God, private or public, nor given himself to reading of holy scripture or any books of godliness'.[36] In a similar vein, John Taylor (who was no puritan) attributed the decline of John Rous into debauchery and desperation to the absence of a preaching minister from his home parish, 'for where God is least known and called upon, there satan hath most power and domination'. In another pamphlet, which proclaimed itself a narration of the 'diabolical seducing of Elizabeth Barnes', Henry Goodcole attributed Satan's success to his capacity to stop Barnes from consulting either God or one of his ministers during the month she was pondering and plotting her crime. According to Goodcole, prayer and fasting were sure antidotes against Satan's wiles, God's spiritual aid being attached to them. He ended the pamphlet with an admonition to all Christians to confess their inmost thoughts and secret sins to the ministers of God.[37]

An inducement to Christian reformation still more powerful than the mere contemplation of the bodies of various murderers twisting on the gallows, came from the power of their often very tardy speeches of repentance to bring them to salvation. Three aristocratic rakes who had been quick to respond in prison to the promptings of the attendant clergy spent their last days leading their fellow prisoners in prayer. This resulted in the apparent conversion of even that notorious and hardened sinner, Margaret Ferneseed. They were described as dying as 'true servants of their captain Jesus Christ'. Elizabeth Caldwell, the attempted murderer of her husband, repented with similar spectacular effects. She spent her time in prison 'serving of God and seeking pardon for her sins with great zeal and industry, continually meditating on the bible, excluding herself from all company, saving such as might yield her spiritual comforts, as learned divines, and such the faithful servants of God'. Caldwell 'all the time of her imprison-ment' 'used all possible means, both of herself, and by those good members that did visit her, to convert all the rest of the prisoners'. Her evangelism even encompassed her husband (the intended victim), to whom she sent a long letter (reprinted at the end of the pamphlet) exhorting him to repent. Caldwell's end was all that could be wished for; she went to her death repentant, singing psalms, praying for herself and for the repentance of her husband. The result was that Dugdale was sure of Caldwell's ultimate salvation;[38] a confidence shared by Henry Goodcole in his account of Francis Robinson, an erstwhile papist executed for forging the Great Seal, who, Goodcole assured his readers, 'is received into the fold of that most blessed heavenly flock whereof Jesus Christ ... is the keeper and defender.' One woman steadfastly refused to repent and resisted all the blandishments of her clerical prison-visitors. She only broke down at the stake, when the minister refused her communion, but she was still described as 'surrendering her soul into the hands of the Lord Jesu'.[39]

Repentance, in many of the pamphlets, was presented as the ultimate triumph of the justice and mercy of God over sin and the devil. In these narratives the murderer's repentance was as often as not attributed entirely to his or her providential and sometimes miraculous discovery and conviction. It was, in short, a direct product of the workings of God's providence rather than of any exercise of human free will. In one pamphlet, two malefactors proved impervious to all attempts to bring them to repentance. Neither the lure of salvation, nor the threat of perdition, indeed, not even the sight of the house in which the deed had been done had any effect. It was only at the very end that one Wilson, 'the softer of the two', broke down, an event the pamphleteer attributed entirely to the workings of God's will. 'Neither time nor place wrought any alteration in them at all, till he that turned the hard rock into a standing water and the flint stone into a springing well, did break and bruise their stoney hearts.'[40]

Gilbert Dugdale described Elizabeth Caldwell as having been 'picked out by the hand of God' 'as an example to the rest to keep thousands in fear of God's wrath, and the world's terror'. That choice could, of course, have led to her ruin and damnation, but in the light of her repentance Dugdale felt able to conclude that it had in fact worked 'to her comfort, though in our eyes terrible'. The fact of her sin need not worry us, he argued, since 'the deceitful devil' sometimes received 'permission from God to attempt the very righteous (as Job)'. Caldwell was comparable to Job because her temptation by the devil had led merely to an increase in her faith. As she herself said, her soul might have had to sink 'to the very gates of hell' but the result of her trial was the divine gift of repentance and the eternal salvation that went with it. Thus in the confession Margaret Sanders supposedly read out at the place of execution, she actually thanked God that

> he hath not suffered me to have the rein and bridle of sinning given me at my will to the danger of my eternal damnation, but that he hath found out my sin and brought me to punishment in this world, by his fatherly correction, to amend, to spare and save me in the world to come.[41]

Of course, not every malefactor confessed and repented. Some went defiant to the grave, protesting their innocence or justifying their fault. Sometimes, of two accomplices, one repented and the other did not. Given that the stakes involved here were very high indeed, nothing short of eternal life or death, how was this to be explained? It was at this point that several authors had recourse to God's double decree and in particular to his decree of reprobation.

God in his justice gives many over to a reprobate sense, that they have no remorse or feeling of the breach or violating of the sacred laws of their immortal creator and so ... as they live dissolutely, they die desperately and after all ... they live a dying life eternally, and die a living death everlastingly.

Another writer spoke of the 'savage natured people in this land ... whom God hath marked with his secret brand of secret purpose' and who 'impiously attempt things against nature'. A third author talked of 'satan's bondslaves' who 'commit sin' and 'boast and brag of the same'. This, he concluded, was 'the full height of a reprobate soul'. Thomas Cooper, telling the story of two partners in crime, one of whom repented and one of whom did not, was put in mind of the two thieves crucified with Christ.

Have we not examples of the like in the book of God, one thief being penitent on the cross and the other continuing obstinate to the death. And may not the eternal decree of God ... electing the one, and rejecting the other, justify the execution thereof, in the very last breath, the one justifying his sin on the gallows, and so condemning himself, the other acknowledging his fault and so interesting himself in the mercy of God.[42]

In fact, it was Cooper who, in his tract of 1620, *The Cry and Revenge of Blood*, produced what amounted to a coherently predestinarian reading of the entire genre. Cooper's represents the most clear-cut example of a Calvinist, indeed, a puritan appropriation of the genre for religious purposes. In this he looks forward to several fascinating examples from the 1650s and 1660s[43] when full-scale puritan conversion narratives were grafted onto the basic murder pamphlet format.

It would be going too far to claim that all Cooper and these later authors were doing here was drawing out the providentialist, predestinarian meanings latent in the genre. Cooper was not simply laying bare the assumptions that structured all the other pamphlets, rather he was glossing or interpreting them. Of course, his was not the only theological reading that those narratives allowed. A genre in which such emphasis was often placed on the necessity, at the hour of death, of a full and sincere repentance could not but invite an Arminian as well as a Calvinist reading, and in 1634 Peter Studley provided just such an interpretation in his anti-puritan pamphlet *The Looking Glass of Schism*.[44]

This was clearly a theologically contestable genre. However, the point to be made here is that Cooper's reading of the genre was not some Calvinist excrescence, stuck awkwardly and anachronistically on a 'popular' literary form, but rather that many central features of the pamphlets lent themselves to precisely such a providentialist, predestinarian and anti-popish reading. The claim is being advanced here that the semi-Manichaean, determinist, inversion-ridden world revealed by the pamphlets, while not in itself explicitly puritan, Calvinist, or even Protestant, nevertheless provided zealously Protestant authors like Cooper, Golding and others with a series of openings or opportunities, openings which they could exploit for their own proselytising purposes. There was, in short, a certain fit between the attitudes revealed in the pamphlets and Protestant ideology, a fit or congruence which we can see in some, at least, of the pamphlets being self-consciously exploited by the author.

The task undertaken by the most overtly Protestant of the writers analysed here was to take those elements in the genre that were most conducive to a Protestant reading and rearrange and codify them into a coherently edifying whole. Let us assume, for example, that certain central tenets which structure a good number of the pamphlets did indeed command the assent of many readers and let us take as examples the following three propositions or images: first, the notion that the perpetrators of some of these crimes, particularly those who committed suicide or died defiant or unrepentant, were so evil, so mired in sin, so much under the devil's thrall, as to be beyond all hope, to all intents and purposes, reprobate; second, the idea of an implacable divine justice tracking down, unmasking and visiting justice upon even the most secret and well hidden murders; third, the image of the repentant murderer, saved on the very steps of the gallows from the claws of Satan and the jaws of hell by a merciful God. Taken on their own as discrete propositions all these might be acceptable enough. They were certainly compatible with a number of theological positions (Catholic and Protestant). But it was surely possible for the reader to enjoy the pamphlets for the *frisson* of horror or disapproval, the warm glow of sentimental satisfaction, which such images might induce, without extracting from them any very abstract notions of divine omnipotence or predestination and still less without applying such notions to his or her own life and experience. It was, in short, one thing to believe that somewhere there were desperate sinners so evil as to have been abandoned even by God himself; it was quite another to wake up at night wondering whether you were such a sinner. The very extremity of the events retold in the pamphlets militated against such an internalisation or personal application of the pamphlet's message. The fact that these things happened at all was shocking, dreadful, titillating, but if Professor Cockburn's and Dr Sharpe's conclusions[45] about the incidence of murder and interpersonal violence in early modern England are anything like right, it had very little to do with the readers' everyday lives. It was, therefore, perfectly possible for readers to enter the mental world of the pamphlets and, for all the narrative's implicit Manichaean determinism, still to be one of Professor Collinson's popular Pelagians; still, that is, placing their hopes of salvation in the avoidance of extraordinary sin, taking pleasure and relief from the contrast between the enormities described in the pamphlets and their own trivial misdemeanours, extracting solace from the power of last minute repentance to save even the worst of sinners, and hoping themselves to earn salvation through regular church attendance and the discharge of everyday social duty.

The more Protestant of the authors discussed here were trying to subvert this easy coexistence in the popular mind of both Pelagian and Manichaean assumptions. To do so, they were using certain central themes in the pamphlets in order to raise some very sharp questions about salvation, damnation, sin, the power of the devil and the need for repentance. The situations portrayed in the pamphlets thus became extreme *exempla* of spiritual truths, truths which applied to all those who wanted to be saved. Thus these authors were not merely transplanting alien doctrines of justification by faith, election and reprobation into popular contexts in which they were quite out of place. On the contrary, they were seeking to gloss, exploit, codify certain pre-existing and free-floating notions about the world, God, sin and the devil and to enlist them for their own vision of true religion. The point, therefore, is not that certain 'popular' attitudes or genres were naturally protestant or puritan, but that it is a mistake to see the relationship between 'the popular' and the puritan or zealously Protestant as simply adversarial or anti-pathetic. This may be of some significance as we come to evaluate claims about the necessary failure of Protestant evangelism based on the essential foreignness or strangeness of Protestant assumptions to popular ways of thinking.

11. 'Raylinge Rymes and Vaunting Verse': Libellous Politics in Early Stuart England, 1603–1628

ALASTAIR BELLANY

> Though some make slight of *Libels*, yet
> you may see by them how the Wind sits:
> as take a Straw and throw it up into
> the Air, you shall see by that which
> way the Wind is, which you shall not
> do by casting up a Stone. More solid
> Things do not show the Complexion of
> the times so well, as Ballads and Libels.
>
> John Selden, *Table Talk*

It was clearly a case of mistaken identity. The poem in praise of the assassin of the Duke of Buckingham was certainly Jonsonian in style. Ben Jonson had even seen the verses before, at dinner in the house of Sir Robert Cotton. But, as he had told the dinner guests at the time, he had not written them. Zouch Townley, an Oxford cleric, had written the verses, or so Jonson had heard. Jonson knew Townley – had recently given him a knife as a gift – but when they last met Jonson did not know that Townley had penned such seditious lines. Jonson was free to go. Some days later, Townley, summoned to Star Chamber, fled to the Hague.[1]

The works of Ben Jonson have proved rich sources for studying the marriage of politics and high culture in early Stuart England.[2] I want to suggest that comparably rich benefits may reward attention to the works of Zouch Townley and of the countless other writers, mostly anonymous, whose political verses, too daring to be printed, circulated by word of mouth or in manuscript copies. These poems and ballads – which were sung, read and heard at least as extensively as the works of Jonson – were commonly classified by contemporaries as 'libels'.

'Libel' is clearly a pejorative term. As an epithet, 'libel' evoked multiple negative associations. It referred simultaneously to the angry, dangerous, frequently *ad hominem* content of a work; to its legal status; and to its size (libel coming from the Latin 'libellus' or 'small book'). For some, libels were irrevocably associated with sedition. As art forms supposedly written by lower-class poets and believed to appeal to the political susceptibilities of a volatile populace, verse libels were held to be symptoms of a dangerous 'popularity', rhyming harbingers of political breakdown.[3] 'Libel' was thus a description that any author might wish to contest. I will nevertheless employ the label as the most convenient shorthand for the material under discussion.

Until recently, scholars have paid little sustained attention to verse libels.[4] Partly, this is a result of difficulties of access. Verse libels were not printed; they survive, in the main, in widely dispersed manuscript verse miscellanies, commonplace books, and the like. It is thus quite difficult to gain a sense of the verse libel as a genre. This problem, however, only partly explains the neglect. The Percy Society edition of poems and songs on Buckingham has been available for over a century but has been scarcely utilised. This is probably due to matters of taste – literary, moral and historical. Thomas Cogswell, one of the few historians to explore libels as sources, notes that 'much of this verse has all the delicacy and literary merit of modern graffiti'.[5] Many, though by no means all, of the libels lack any redeeming aesthetic qualities. Occasional flights of poetic language are more than counterbalanced by legions of excruciating puns enlightening us on the double meanings latent in such events as the impeachment of Francis *Bacon* at the hands of Edward *Coke*. Many libels are also unpleasantly obscene. Frederick Fairholt, the Percy Society editor, deemed it wise in 1850 to excise some of the ruder lines from his collection, while Beatrice White, in the 1960s, decided that one ballad on the Essex divorce scandal was mostly 'unquotable'.[6]

Neglect may also stem from value judgements of a different kind. Many verse libels, even when not explicitly obscene, focus extensively on the sexual and scandalous sides of Stuart politics. John Morrill has argued that although provincial gentry received a good amount of political news and comment, it was trivial in content and quality, concentrating on what was 'distasteful and unpleasant about the Court' at the expense of discussing 'the real constitutional issues'.[7] Morrill's distinction rests on a presumption that court scandal was not the stuff of 'real' politics. Certainly, verse libels written in 1628 say far more about the vices of Buckingham and his family than about threats to habeas corpus or to the subject's liberties, but it may be presumptuous to assume that the latter are more important than the former, or that contemporaries might not have seen links between them.

Historians should not let their own tastes blind them to material their subjects found fascinating enough to write, copy and collect in large numbers, or frightening enough to attack and prosecute. This chapter argues that the verse libel was, in Cogswell's words, 'a remarkable vehicle for the dissemination of political attitudes'.[8] The first section of the paper examines the verse libel as a 'vehicle for dissemination', looking at form, circulation and readership. The second section considers the 'political attitudes' present in the libels and in the Stuart response to them.

I

Politically charged illegal verse was by no means a new phenomenon in the early seventeenth century. When Lewis Pickering was tried in 1605 for a crude verse libel attacking the late Archbishop Whitgift, his judges referred to a precedent from Richard III's reign.[9] Under Henry VIII, politically delicate prophecies were circulated in verse form, and leading ministers such as Wolsey and Cromwell became the butt of libellous ballads. One minstrel recalled having been physically intimidated in a Westmoreland alehouse by an audience eager for an anti-Cromwell song.[10] In 1537 a Dominican was executed for composing a seditious ballad popular in Yorkshire during the Pilgrimage of Grace, a ballad avowedly modelled on others then in circulation.[11] Verse libels so concerned Mary Tudor that she revised the libel statute to combat the flow of 'heinous seditious and slanderous Writings, Rhymes, Ballads, Letters, Papers and Books', mostly consisting of attacks on her popish religious policies. Two Norwich apprentices were arrested in her reign for singing snatches of anti-Catholic songs learned from a wandering minstrel.[12] Verse libels continued to appear during Elizabeth's reign. In the aftermath of the Essex

Revolt of 1601, poems and ballads circulated in praise of the rebellious earl.[13]

As significant as this chronological pedigree is the close kinship between political verse libels and 'mocking rhymes'. Originally part of the charivari rituals against those who had violated local sexual norms, mocking rhymes were often sung to the tunes of popular ballads or pinned up in public places. The form evolved into a useful vehicle for expressing local political and religious disputes. Verses and mocking songs on national personalities may thus have seemed a natural extension of a traditional local genre.[14]

Verse libels took many different forms, and the form of the verse often, but not always, determined the means of circulation and the potential audience.

The simplest form was the terse rhyming couplet, such as these notorious lines circulated after the lynching of Buckingham's astrologer in June 1628, two months before the Duke's own murder:

> Let Charles and George do what they can
> Yet George shall die like Doctor Lambe.

Rhythm, rhyme and economy meant this squib was easily remembered and circulated without being written down. George Willoughby, a scrivener under investigation in 1628 for his connection to the assassin Felton, was confronted with a copy of these ostensibly incriminating lines discovered among his papers. Under questioning, Willoughby described the passage of this couplet from the street to his desk. Lawrence Naylor, an illiterate baker's boy, had heard the rhyme several times and had memorised it, and then passed it on to one Daniel Watkins, who in turn related it orally to Willoughby.[15] The Suffolk cleric John Rous received a variant version of the couplet in conversation: 'About September 3, I had related to me this foolish and dangerous rhyme, fruit of an after wit.'[16] The brevity and form of the couplet allowed it to circulate across social and literacy boundaries, and in a variety of social settings. Willoughby heard the couplet through contact with tradesmen. Simonds D'Ewes recalled being told a slightly lengthier verse libel against Sir Nicholas Hyde during the 1627 Bury Lent Assizes, though he was not certain he remembered the exact words.[17] The same libel was told to one of Joseph Mead's news sources, but 'being committed to a scholar's fickle memory, he dropped two verses by the way, only bringing their sense in prose.' Mead was only able to pass the libel on properly after receiving 'a fuller copy'.[18] Longer verses made oral communication less reliable.

Other libels were ballads clearly intended to be sung. In 1627, three fiddlers from Middlesex were arrested for singing ballads against the Duke of Buckingham, one of which employed the traditional refrain 'The clean contrary way' to subvert the apparently sympathetic messages of the rest of the verse:

> And when that death shall close up his eyes,
>> Come love me where as I lay;
> God take him up into the skies
>> The clean contrary way.
>> O the clean contrary way.[19]

One obscene ballad on the Essex divorce was set to the tune 'O the wind, the wind and the rain,' another 'to the tune of Oh do me no harm good man'.[20] Ballad-singers performed political material on popular demand. 'When he gets but some Songs or Sonnets patched up with Ribaldry, or interlarded with anything against the state,' noted one contemporary, 'they are many helps to him, and he will adventure to sing them though they cost him a whipping for his labour.'[21] The 'Clean Contrary Way' libel was popular enough that for some it became Buckingham's signature song. Libellers reminisced after his death that,

> What fiddlers sung, now all may freely say,
> The Duke is gone the clean contrary way.[22]

> And now thou art dead, we will rejoice,
>> And merely spend the time both night and day.
> The fiddler's boy that hath the loudest voice
>> Shall sing thy song the clean contrary way.[23]

Performed at fairs and markets and sung in alehouses, ballads such as 'The Clean Contrary Way' could potentially reach a large and diverse audience. After a performance, ballads could be retransmitted in sung snatches or in versions eventually committed to paper.

In contrast to those forms that could circulate orally, other types of libel functioned visually. Chronograms, for example, matched numerical values to letters, uncovering deep, even prophetic, significance in famous names. Both John Rous and Simonds

D'Ewes recorded a popular 1628 chronogram predicting Buckingham's death:

1	5	500	5	10	5	100	1		1000	1	
GEORGI	VS	D	V	X	BV	C	K	I	NGHA	M	I	AE

mdcxxviii

...

Thy numerous name with this year doth agree
But twentie-nine, Heaven grant thou never see![24]

Anagrams, like chronograms, were visual libels that found political significance in the letters of a name. D'Ewes recalled two anagrams that were circulated at the time of the Essex divorce and Overbury murder scandals of 1613–16, commenting on Essex's wife's relationship with royal favourite Carr, and on the fate of the man who tried to thwart that relationship:

F r a n c i s   H o w a r d e
Car finds a Whore

T h o m a s   O v e r b u r i e
O! O! A busie murther[25]

Acrostic verses, in which the first letter of each line spelled out the name of the subject of the poem, also depended on visual transmission.

Between forms comfortably suited to oral transmission and those that actually precluded it lie the vast majority of verse libels. They are not easy to categorise, for they are of various lengths and verse forms; some are simple, some complex; some demanded little detailed knowledge, while others presupposed an extensive familiarity with court personalities. Some libels were parodies of more respectable poems. A few verses were in Latin, sharply restricting the audience. Most verses, however, had at least the potential to reach a broad audience. Verses could be read out loud by a literate person to a group of illiterates, while higher literacy rates in London and among the apprentice classes created a potentially broad pool of individual readers. What varied was the degree to which a reader or listener could decode the more allusion-heavy libels, and the varied tastes and cultural conditions that determined a libel's appropriation.

These poems depended chiefly on manuscript circulation, and although it is impossible to trace the chain of circulation for each particular poem, a general pattern is discernible. Libels, like mocking rhymes, were often left in public places to be picked up, read and copied. William Rider, mayor of London at the turn of the century, kept Robert Cecil informed of libels picked up 'upon the stairs of the Royal Exchange' or 'in the Old Bailey where it was fixed on a door, with another of the same on a post nearby.'[26] In 1623 a lengthy verse libel addressed to the late Queen Elizabeth was placed in the hand of her statue in Westminster Abbey.[27] In 1628, a prose libel on Buckingham and Lambe was found on a post in Coleman Street. Some verses appear to have been left around court, one claiming to have been 'pinned to the court gates, May 1627'.[28] It is likely that libels were also read and copied at such major London news distribution hubs as the Royal Exchange or Paul's Walk (the naves and aisles of St Paul's Cathedral), that 'great exchange of all discourse'.[29]

From London, copies of libels could reach the provinces along developing channels of information distribution. Far from being cut off from London, provincial gentry received plenty of information bringing them into contact with material and ideas originating in the metropolis. Professional and amateur newsletters helped to spread these verses into the provinces. John Rous in Suffolk, Walter Yonge in Devon, William Whiteway in Dorset, and William Davenport in Cheshire all received libels which they copied into news diaries or commonplace books. Rous's diary is full of poems that were 'delivered me', that 'I received', or that 'came to men's hands in these times'.[30] It is possible that some verses may have been copied out and sold by those stationers who specialised in selling manuscript copies of banned works like Thomas Scott's *Vox Populi*.

The distribution of news and libels also occurred in regular sociable contact. Jonson, we may recall, was visiting Sir Robert Cotton's house when he was shown Townley's verse libel lying on the table after dinner.[31] Friends established informal reading groups, circulating amongst themselves what news and comment they could find. In 1628 a Council investigation into charges of subversive speech made against Alexander Gill (junior) uncovered a cache of libels on Buckingham that Gill and his Oxford friends had copied out and collected.[32] William Davenport of Cheshire copied into his commonplace book news material that he shared with his friends. Sometimes a commonplace book itself could be circulated, each friend writing in anything he had received, or adding verses of his own.[33]

II

Clearly, then, libels took many forms and were circulated across a broad social and geographical range. Thus, as Richard Cust has noted, they are evidence of a spatially and socially broader degree of interest in national political issues than some revisionist histories of the period allow. But the mere fact of bulk and circulation takes us only part of the way towards complete appreciation. It has to be shown that what verse libels said mattered, that they did not trivialise politics.

Few contemporaries readily dismissed verse libels as trivial. John Rous frequently described the libels he received as the product of 'vulgar rumour', but nevertheless he felt compelled to transcribe them into his news diary. Of one of the many mock epitaphs for Buckingham, Rous noted that 'light scoffing wits, not apt to deeper reach, can rhyme upon any the most vulgar surmises'. Yet he was unable to reason the libels away, because Parliament's attacks on Buckingham in 1626 and 1628 seemed to lend them credence.[34] Verse libels were thus only part of the news that men such as Rous had available. This news often made libellous allegations more credible. Libels in commonplace books were often interspersed with other related documents. Next to poems on the Essex divorce and Overbury murder were copies of accounts of the trials. Next to poems lamenting the royal appeasement of Spain and the prospects of a Spanish bride for Prince Charles were illicit manuscript copies of the anti-Spanish *Vox Populi*, or Archbishop Abbot's supposed speech against the match.[35] After the well-publicised trials of the Overbury murderers in 1615–16, even the wildest speculations of libellers may have gained increased plausibility. Even those who thought libels unreliable could use their existence as thermometers of public interest. Letter-writer John Chamberlain considered the circulation of ballads a sign of continued public interest in Walter Raleigh after his execution.[36] The pious and learned Sir Simonds D'Ewes considered verse libels fitting illustrations for the historical context to his autobiography.

The Stuarts also paid attention, especially during periods of heightened political tension, when traditional associations of libel with sedition seemed especially pertinent. In his 'Of Seditions and Troubles', Francis Bacon reasoned that

> Libels, and licentious Discourses against the State when they are frequent and open; And in like sort, false News, often running up and down, to the disadvantage of the State, and hastily embraced; are amongst the Signs of *Troubles*...[T]hey are...the preludes of *Seditions* to come. Howsoever, he noteth it right, that *Seditious Tumults*, and *Seditious Fames*, differ no more, but as Brother and Sister, Masculine and Feminine.[37]

In 1604–5, in the midst of controversy over ceremonial conformity in the Church, the officers of the king seized upon a puritan libel against Whitgift as proof of the seditious intent lurking behind puritan religious qualms. The ensuing Star Chamber trial prompted a vigorous restatement of the law of seditious libel. Edward Coke and the other judges argued that in a society so permeated by notions of honour, libelling someone – impugning his honour – threatened to rend the fabric of respect that stabilised social and political relations in an orderly hierarchical society. Libelling a minister of the crown was tantamount to libelling the king himself, and dishonouring the monarch was a sure way of weakening the ties of respect that supported hierarchy and monarchy. This line of reasoning can be viewed as part of widespread sensitivity among the élite in this period to issues of honour and insult.[38]

In this 1605 case and in the 1621 proclamations against comment on the Spanish match, James refused to acknowledge that attacks on his policies or his ministers were not meant as attacks on his person, however flatteringly he himself was portrayed. This attitude became central to Charles's political mentality, taking the form of a heightened sensitivity to issues of royal honour and an increasing willingness to interpret attacks on his ministers as attacks on his person. In his important study of the politics of the forced loan, Richard Cust argues that Charles's concern for honour and his sensitivity to criticism led him into a potentially dangerous mistrust of his people's loyalty. The plethora of verse libels attacking Buckingham must have contributed to this state of mind. The judges in the Staines fiddlers' case in 1627 castigated libels as 'base and barbarous', threatening to alienate 'affection of the subjects from the sovereign'. Like the 1626 remonstrance of Parliament against Buckingham, libels on the duke were means 'whereby, through the sides of a Peer of this Realm, they wound the honour of their Sovereigns'.[39]

The royal reaction to negative comment on the Spanish match reveals another side to the Stuart distaste for libels. James frequently interpreted opposition to his foreign policy as an unwarranted intrusion of the lower orders into the mysteries of state, in which they had no competence. The continued circulation of anti-Spanish verses through 1623 was perceived by James as another example of irreverent meddling in the *arcana imperii*. He responded to one verse libel by penning a poem of his own:

> Be corrected for your pride
> that kings' designs dare thus deride
> By raylinge rhymes and vaunting verse
> which your king's breast should never pierce.

He questioned the people's fitness to handle politics best suited to divine right kingship: 'God and kings do pace together, / but vulgars wander light as feather.' He commended obedience and silence: 'Hold your prattling, spare your pen / be honest and obedient men.' Responding to libellous criticism of his favourite, James did not stoop to debate policy; rather, he insisted that his choice of advisers concerned him alone: 'Content yourself with such as I / Shall take near, and place on high.'[40] James's sentiments were echoed by another poet writing in 'distaste of England's licentious libellers', those men who sought to 'countermand / the Godlike Actions of his soul and hand' and dared to 'confine / The will of Princes to their crooked line / As if, by frighted reason things should run / And make a Father Pupil to the son.'[41]

The existence of verse libels could very easily reinforce the royal perception that seditious and 'popular' elements were at work destabilising the kingdom. Court drama portrayed libellous poets pandering to the lower classes, and, by 1630, a number of major trials had helped forge a link between the crime of libel and puritanism.

It is possible to argue that the Stuart fear of libel rested on a basic misperception that, by dint of insistent repetition, became a self-fulfilling prophecy.[42] What the Stuarts branded as seditious was often intended as loyal criticism. But although many verse libels were not as radical as they were perceived to be, they were by no means innocuous. The rest of this chapter attempts a preliminary dissection of the ideological content and function of verse libels. A more complete study would require a detailed reading of each poem in its context and a more nuanced consideration of the different audiences at which the verses were aimed; what follows is of necessity a selection of general observations, focusing mainly on Buckingham's career and assassination as seen through the libels.

In his important study of news in early Stuart England, Richard Cust has suggested that circulation of news couched in conflictual terms helped create a perception of politics as an adversarial rather than a consensual process.[43] Verse libels can also be studied as evidence of the existence and creation of political perceptions. At a time when religious standards of morality were tightening, libels reflected and transmitted representations of the court and its courtiers as sexually, politically and religiously corrupt. These representations acquired added meaning as part of a political language that linked corruption to a sinister popish threat to religion and liberty and argued for Protestant, patriotic, parliamentary policies as a defence against this corruption. Verse libels sometimes explicitly operated within this paradigm, connecting the sins of courtiers to the master deviance of religious innovation. Libels that did not make the links explicit could nevertheless be read within the terms set by that paradigm. Cries of popish conspiracy might make greater sense given the libels' circulation of evidence of corruption.[44]

As Pauline Croft intimates in her recent study of attacks on Robert Cecil, it is important to stress the religio-political significance of what appear at first to be merely scandalous allegations. For instance, there was a religio-political overtone to accusations that Cecil, Frances Howard and Buckingham suffered from syphilis. Susan Sontag has argued that dreaded and ill-understood diseases often become entangled with metaphor, 'awash with significance' and general 'feelings about evil', and are then used to judge the state of society.[45] Raymond Anselment has recently described some of the metaphorical significance syphilis acquired in seventeenth-century England, noting how its polemical value was enhanced by an 'association of moral degradation and sexual pollution with the foreign or alien'.[46] This association with the alien was expressed most commonly by the use of 'the french' as a synonym for the disease, although, interestingly enough, at the height of fears about the Spanish match, Edward Coke emphasised in Parliament that a Spaniard was in fact responsible for the initial spread of the disease.[47] The link between syphilis and

Catholicism, another 'foreign' element, was made in an obscene
poem on one Lucy Morgan, who after a life of promiscuity,

> At last some vestal fire she stole,
> Which never went out in her hole,
> And with that zealous fire being burned
> Unto the popish faith she turned,
> And therein died. And is't not fit
> For a poor whore to die in it:
> Since that's the true religion
> Of the great whore of Babylon.[48]

Thus when verse libels alleged that Cecil had died of the pox, or
that Frances Howard's 'tinder-box is full of French matches', more
than 'distasteful' information was conveyed. These allegations
could be intended and read as evidence of serious moral, political
and religious corruption close to the king.[49]

This analysis can be repeated for nearly all the 'distasteful'
allegations made regularly in the libels. Sodomy, for example, was
commonly perceived as a symptom of a general state of sinfulness
that could include religious and political corruption.[50] Sexual
promiscuity, poisoning, and witchcraft were all commonly associated both with each other and with popery. As the puritan
Alexander Leighton put it, Buckingham's 'Masses, Murders,
Poisons, Treasons, Venery, & Venifices' were 'his Jesuited tricks'.[51]

Thus sexual and other apparently apolitical allegations contained in the verse libels could carry powerful political meanings,
constructing a representation of the court that meshed with the
worst fears of popish corruption theorists. The effect of the creation of this powerful negative image was exacerbated by the fact
that James, and especially Charles, withdrew increasingly from the
traditional royal rituals – touching for the evil, the royal progress
and entry – that in Elizabeth's reign had enhanced royal and
court charisma.[52] Along with the withdrawal from public ceremonial came the beginnings of a withdrawal from public relations.
Thomas Cogswell has noted that Charles I increasingly believed
that he did not have to give his subjects explanations for his
actions. He thus left the field dangerously open to explanations
circulated in newsletters, rumours and libels – explanations that
frequently contradicted his own intentions. Both Cust and
Cogswell cite the progressive disaffection of John Rous as an
example of the effects of negative representations on a reader

starved for positive information.[53] Even when Charles and Buckingham did try to present their version of events, they had to contend with counter-representations circulated by libels.

These processes are best illustrated through a detailed case study. The rest of this essay examines libellous representations of Buckingham, and the contest between king and libeller to establish an interpretation of the assassination of the duke.

When John Felton fatally stabbed George Villiers in his Portsmouth lodgings on 23 August 1628, the Duke was, in the words of even his most sympathetic biographer, 'without doubt the most unpopular man in England...he aroused a hatred among the public at large that was without precedent'.[54] One self-referential libeller put into the mouth of the late duke a prediction of the torrent of libels that would follow his murder:

> all did
> Hate me, though at sometimes close they hid
> The rancour of their malice, yet now at last
> They let their sluices ope, which runs at waste.
> I know each letter of my name shall be
> A theme for their inventions, to let flee
> Abroad to all the world, even my black deeds,
> Which from their black pens shall receive black weeds.
> My deeds on seas, in country, court and city,
> Shall be unto their song the final ditty.[55]

From the earliest years of his ascendancy, verse libels had represented Buckingham as a symbol of corruption and political danger. His rapid ascendancy, his shameless nepotism and his manifest venality were regularly denounced. Sometimes the libels cut close to the king himself. They aired suspicions of the homosexual nature of the favourite's relation with James, most commonly through allusions to the myth of Jove and Ganymede. One poet, writing early in the 1620s, represented the court as a disgruntled Greek pantheon:

> Love's queen's so disaffected
>   To what she hath seen
> Or to what suspected,
>   As she in spleen
> To Juno hath protested;
>   Her servant Mars

> Shall scourge the arse
> > Jove's marrow so hath wasted.
>
> The chaste Diana by her quiver
> > And ten thousand maids
> Have sworn that they will never
> > Sport in the shades
> Until the heaven's creator
> > Be quite displaced
> Or else disgraced
> > For loving so 'gainst nature.

Jove's 'vice' had political consequences also, seducing him from proper attention to the needs of the people, into a life of careless drunken debauchery:

> Still Jove with Ganymede lies playing,
> > Hears no triton's sound,
> Nor yet horses neighing:
> > His ears are bound.
> The fiddling god doth lull him,
> > Bacchus quaffs
> And Momus laughs
> > To think how they can gull him.[56]

Another libel associated Buckingham's Ganymedean charms with the lures of political and religious corruption. In the 'King's Five Senses' (a parody of a Jonson song), the poet warns of the danger of bad counsel, the seductive lure of Spanish treaties and the threat from the false religion of Catholicism. The perceived danger of sexual perversity is juxtaposed with the dangers of unorthodox religion:

> Where myrrh and frankincense is thrown
> And altars built to Gods unknown,
> Oh let my sovereign never smell!
> Such damn'd perfumes are fit for hell,
> Let no such scent his nostrils stain;
> From smells that poison can the brain
> Heaven still preserve him; next I crave
> Thou wilt be pleased, great God, to save
> My sovereign from a Ganymede,

> Whose whorish breath hath power to lead
> His excellence which way it list;
> Oh let such lips be never kissed.

The seduction of the royal senses has direct political consequences: a pretty face might lure the king to resign his powers to
a 'skill-less and unsteady hand' which 'May prove the ruin of our
land'; the poet prays that the sportsman king might still hear 'the
sounds / As well of men as of his hounds' and might yet be given
a taste 'Of what his subjects undergo'. Already, in the early 1620s,
the violent removal of Buckingham could be envisioned:

> great Jove, down from the sky
> Beholding earth's calamity,
> Strike with his hand that cannot err
> That proud usurping charioteer,
> And cure...our woe.[57]

God's righteous violence could purge the seductive corruptions
from the court and restore the king to good government.

One of the more impressive verse libels of the early 1620s medi-
tated at length on the spiritually weak condition of a Protestant
nation standing idle as religious war erupted on the Continent.
The nation's unstable condition was epitomised by the rapid rise
and fall of favourites on the Jacobean court's wheel of fortune.
Buckingham, whose rapid rise was the perfect emblem of the
destabilising turbulence of court politics, was linked to the dangerous policies of a pro-Spanish faction of courtiers:

> By this time Europe hurried is in arms,
> But what have I to do with war's alarms,
> I homeward came unto our country peace
> And find a Spanish faction to increase.
> For great king James, would not have us complain
> That he intends to match the prince with Spain
> Thus Buckingham, and Arundel combine
> And many others to the sort incline.

He was thus complicit with the sinful state of the nation:

> O times of sin, so full of frantic passions:
> O strange unheard of changes in a state,

> So full of pride, lust, avarice, and hate.
> Where is Religion's purity? where is
> God's word? a touchstone to try what's amiss.[58]

An obscene poem of about the same period alleging adultery, sodomy and idiocy among Buckingham's kin could surely have been read as a dismayingly plausible account of what accompanied pro-Spanish policies.[59]

As Cogswell has shown, Buckingham's adoption of a patriotic, Protestant, parliamentary and anti-Spanish policy in 1624 helped temporarily to reverse some of these perceptions of the duke. Political poets and anti-popish pamphleteers alike saw the new Buckingham as a force for good. For a while, Buckingham was portrayed in glowing terms. One poet celebrated the return of Buckingham and Charles from Spain by declaring

> I love the prince and every name
> That honours noble Buckingham.[60]

The attempt by Spanish ambassadors to create a breach between James and Buckingham by alleging that the Duke had engaged in treasonable conspiracy was met by an outraged libeller:

> Durst they...demand
> The head of any subject in this land?
> No: Raleigh's blood did flesh their first desire,
> And now they dare to higher heads aspire...
>
> . . . .
>
> let not that head satisfy the thirst
> Of Moorish pride, which was the very first
> Of all thy favourites who undertook
> His country's cause, and thus did overlook
> Spanish deceivings; for he hath done more
> Than twenty of thy favourites before.
> Give him but force his own head to maintain,
> And like brave Scipio he will sack proud Spain.

Instead of being identified as the moral and political opposite of charismatic Protestant heroes such as Raleigh or classical worthies such as Scipio, Buckingham was here associated with, even placed above, these figures. Buckingham's change in policy had separated him from his former cohorts among the 'Jesuited English, drunk with propery, / That view your country with a Spanish eye.'[61]

Buckingham's career as a charismatic exemplar of Protestant military virtue was short lived, however. From 1625 to 1627 a succession of verse libels presented him as the focal point of moral and political corruption, the cause of military embarrassment abroad and religious innovation at home. By 1626 Buckingham was accused of wrecking the harmony between king and parliament and of interrelated sexual and religious corruption:

> An art sprung from a blacker seed
> Than that which he poured in that need
>   Whom we call Guido Fawkes,
> Who if he fired had his vessel
> Of sulphur standing on bare tressel
>   In his sepulchral walks,
> Could not so have dispersed our state
> Nor opened Spain so wide a gate
>   As hath his graceless grace.
> For till time comes which is at hand
> That all speak Spanish in our land,
>   We are bound to rue his fate.
> And yet I guess we need not do it,
> For France has sent one to undo it,
>   Her countryman the pox,
> A hungry Monsieur who will vate
> His joints past cure of any sweat
>   That Poe's great art unlocks.[62]

Pox jokes were also used to deflate Buckingham's attempts during his 1627 military campaigns against the French to reassociate himself with militaristic Protestantism through a sympathetic news journal and the patronage of patriotic works such as Drayton's *Battle of Agincourt*.[63] One libel opened with the misleading raising of hopes:

> Rejoice, brave English gallants,
>   Whose ancestors won France;
> Our Duke of Buckingham is gone
>   To fight and not to dance,

only to playfully mock them by dissociating Buckingham from the tradition of English military strife against the French, making him instead the champion of syphilitic courtiers:

> they, and every man
> Are glad, that loves a wench,
> That since he's gone, he's gone to kill
> His enemies the French.[64]

Officially sponsored campaign reports from the Île de Rhé tried to make the most of Buckingham. Reports were spread of his escape from a Jesuit-inspired assassination. The 30 August issue of *A Continued Journall* included an insert with a life-size illustration of the intended murder weapon carried by the 'Jesuited Villain' from whom the duke escaped under 'God's Providence'.[65] An earlier report used the incident to associate Buckingham with a more famous victim of Jesuit assassination, Henry IV of France, describing the murder weapon as 'a long Ravaillac-like knife poisoned,' and contrasting the perfidy of the French with Buckingham's honourable conduct of the war and humane treatment of prisoners. He was praised as the image of combined 'Religion, Fortitude, and Clemency; being the true Characters of a noble General'.[66]

These positive images were countered in 1627 and 1628 by a series of libels that searched for the causes of the failure of the Rhé expedition. A typical example was the libel 'And Art returned again with all thy faults', which replaced Buckingham's self-fashioned trinity of religion, fortitude and clemency with the opprobrious triad of 'treachery, neglect and cowardice'.

This libel is a catalogue of negative representations of the duke. Military defeat was pinned squarely on Buckingham's unfitness for command:

> Venus pavilions do befit thee best,
> Periwigs with helmets are not to be pressed.
> To o'errun Spain, win Cales, and conquer France,
> Requires a soldier's march, not courtier's dance.

Buckingham's cowardice in the face of battle was held responsible for the loss of an advantageous military position and the deaths of many worthier and more valiant Englishmen. 'How comes this voyage t'have such bad effect', the libeller asked, 'Without close treachery or great neglect?'

Tied to these allegations were allusions to other scandals. In 1626, a tract written by James I's physician, George Eglisham, alleging that Buckingham had poisoned the king and several nobles, aroused considerable interest. By 1628 one MP could privately assume that 'all the realm suspects [him] to have poisoned King James'.[67] Discussing the failures at Rhé, the poet of 'And art thou returned' invoked

> thy potion [which]
> Torture[d] the noble Scot, whose manes tell
> Thy swoll'n ambition made his carcase swell.

The discussion of military failure continued with references to Buckingham's patronage of Arminian clerics, his mother's acknowledged Catholicism, and the suspicions of black magic involving her and the astrologer John Lambe:

> Could not thy titles scare them? and thy Lambe's
> Protection safeguard thee from the French rams?
> Could not thy zealous Cambridge pupils' prayers,
> Composed of Brownist and Arminian airs,
> Confound thy foes?
>   .   .   .   .
> Could not thy mother's masses, nor her crosses,
> Nor yet her sorceries prevent these losses?

It is important to recognise how these allegations worked in tandem to create the powerful impression of deep moral corruption at work. It was not surprising to contemporaries that popery might be accompanied by witchcraft, that the sexually lax might favour Arminians, that the enemy of Parliaments might poison his rivals. All were recognisable symptoms of the corruption associated with the alien, and especially with popery. Clearly, such a catalogue of sins might anger God:

> Happy success then great attempts attends,
> When they command whom virtue still commends.
> Thy sins, God's justice, and the kingdom's curse,
> Makes me admire thy fortunes were no worse.

The libel's anger with Buckingham eventually spilled over into a barely veiled threat to

> Reclaim thyself, be govern'd by the state.
> For if but one year more thou lord it thus,
> Thou'lt bring confusion on thyself and us.

The libel also felt it necessary to warn Charles:

> God's deaf to kings that will not hear the cries
> Of their oppressed subjects' injuries.[68]

As one writer opined, the libel was 'guilty of people-pleasing, which is the worst flattery'.[69]

Other libels also dared to implicate the king in Buckingham's offences. The king was implicitly blamed as the neglectful captain of the ship of state, sleeping while 'one doth rule and guide the ship / That neither card nor compass knew before'.[70] Libellers did not flinch from imagining, even advocating, a violent purging of Buckingham from the body politic:

> Since thou hast guilt of all the blood Rhee spent;
> Must thou still live to break a Parliament!
> Hath no witch poison? Not one man a dagger?
> Or hath our coward age forgot to swagger?[71]

> To hunt the doe I have refused,
> Which is a sport by great men used.
> Yet shall I love to hear a cry
> Of hounds, when Buck-in-game shall die.[72]

Libels reflected and created a moral universe in which Buckingham's assassination became both imaginable and desirable. It is hard to avoid the conclusion that their circulation must have contributed, along with the parliamentary remonstrance against the duke, to the tide of real and mimetic violence that eventually culminated in the murder of the favourite. John Lambe, Buckingham's astrologer, who had served time in prison for witchcraft and had recently been tried for rape, had been frequently demonised by libels. In June 1628 Lambe was lynched by a London mob that threatened to do the same to the duke.[73] Libels celebrated the lynching and warned Buckingham that he would be next. Whether Felton read any of these libels we cannot know. Most historians assume he killed Buckingham out of a mixture of personal and political reasons, a blocked promotion compounded by reading Parliament's remonstrance against the duke. The privy council, at least, thought it significant that the man who lent Felton the copy of the Remonstrance also had on his desk the rhyming threat that 'George shall die like Dr Lambe.' Felton's widely circulated self-defence aired themes common to the libels of 1627 and 1628 – themes of God's displeasure, of a coward age, of Buckingham as enemy to the public good.[74]

The libellous reputation of Buckingham ensured that his death was popularly welcomed and that his assassin could plausibly be represented as a hero. The libels circulating after the assassination established a dichotomy between the alien, feared Buckingham and the patriot-hero Felton. The assassination was represented as a purgative, a chance to put the country on a new course:

> Awake, sad Britain, and advance at last
> Thy drooping head: let all thy sorrows past
> Be drowned and sunk with their own tears, and now
> O'erlook thy foes with a triumphant brow.
> Thy foe, Spain's agent, Holland's bane, Rome's friend,
> By one victorious hand receiv'd his end.
> Live ever, Felton, thou hast turned to dust
> Treason, ambition, murder, pride and lust.[75]

Felton was uniformly hailed as 'stout' and brave, the opposite of the effeminate, foppish coward Buckingham. Representations of Felton as the hero of the 'Country', the exemplary patriot, were reiterated in a deluge of libels. Zouch Townley, addressing his 'confined friend', urged Felton to 'Enjoy thy bondage' in the knowledge that he had liberated his country:

> Let the Duke's name solace and crown thy thrall:
> All we by him did suffer, thou for all.
> And I dare boldly write, as thou dar'st die,
> Stout Felton, England's ransom, here doth lie.[76]

To another poet, Felton was a champion, an

> Immortal man of glory, whose brave hand
> Hath once begun to disenchant our land
> From magic thralldom.

He had rescued 'ancient English liberty' from the corruption of the law, had shattered the illusions of grandeur that had been created around the duke:

> Antwerpian Rubens' best skill made him soar,
> Ravish'd by heavenly powers, unto the sky,
> Opening and ready him to deify

> In a bright blissful palace, fairy isle.
> Naught but illusion were we, till this guile
> Was by thy hand cut off, stout Machabee.

Felton was a match for all the Israelite, Greek, Roman and British heroes:

> In spite of charm
> Of witch or wizard, thy most mighty arm
> With zeal and justice arm'd hath in truth won
> The prize of patriot to a British son.[77]

Treating Felton as a common murderer, the government worked to create a representation of the assassin and his crime that would undercut popular sympathy. At his trial, Felton's judges openly declared that 'it was either Popery or Atheism put that malice into his heart to commit so barbarous a murder', and compared him to Ravaillac, the Jesuit assassin of Henry IV of France.[78] Newsletter accounts of Felton's execution referred to a penitent and humble last speech, quickly put into print, that disavowed his crime as a 'horrid and vile sin... seduced by the Devil'.[79] After Felton was hanged, Charles apparently changed his mind about the disposal of the corpse and ordered it transported to Portsmouth, 'there to be hanged up in chains upon the highest tower', as a dire warning to others.[80]

These official representations of the assassin and his crime were challenged by alternative representations circulated in verse libels. Felton's suffering and execution were portrayed as a martyrdom, directly contesting the royal version of the crime as a common murder.

One libeller placed different last words in Felton's mouth:

> Sorrow and joy at once possess my breast:
> How can such contraries together rest?
> I grieve my friends and country thus to leave;
> I joy I did it of her foe bereave.
> My grief is private, as of flesh and blood;
> My joy is public: 'tis a public good.[81]

Two libels rhapsodised that Felton's uninterred body, far from shaming him or declaring the revenge of the state, was in fact glorified by a tomb resplendent with natural glory,

Arched o'er with heaven, set with a thousand fair
And glorious diamond stars. A sepulchre
That time can never ruinate, and where
Th'impartial worm, (which is not brib'd to spare
Princes corrupt in marble), cannot share
His flesh.[82]

[His] carcase far from crawling worms too good
Doth gorge the eagle's or the falcon's brood;
Here Felton hangs, a spectacle of dread,
A pendant sword o'er proud ambition's head,
Whom here the winds embalm with fragrant scents,
To whom sad clouds contribute their laments,
And time each night upon his tomb presents
A thousand lights, which burn till day appears,
And then his requiem's sung by winged quires.[83]

So powerful were these sentiments that one poet was moved to circulate a response meditating on Felton's 'cursed corpse... besmeared in [the duke's] faultless blood...shrouded in clouds black as his sepulchre', the food not of noble birds of prey but of 'harpies foul'.[84]

Attempts through punitive ritual and poetic responses to portray Felton as a murderer, or at least to raise the issue of the morality of the crime, were subverted by libels which ignored the moral issues of assassination to ruminate instead on the public good that had resulted. Other libels vigorously defended Felton's deed as an act of justice or excused him as a vehicle for the judgement of God against the sinful Buckingham. One libel, a sophisticated moral and psychological account of Buckingham's first taste of, and then enmeshment in, a life of sin, represented the assassination as an act of inevitable divine justice for the one sin that could not be forgiven, the plotting of

            the ruin of heaven's favourite,
        Reform'd religion. Oh! my Sinon's art,
        To seem to be, and not to be in heart;
        Of all impieties superlative.
        Had this sin not been mine, perhaps alive
        I had been still, and to old age remained,
        Although my honour was most foully stained
        With other crimes.[85]

'The bold pious petition of free bound Felton' had the prisoner present himself as 'Christ's freeman' and one of the greatest of God's instruments of justice, a second David to slay a new Goliath:

> I did hear, and see, and know, too well,
> What evil was done our English Israel:
> And I had warrant sealed, and sent from heaven,
> My work to do: and so the blow is given.[86]

Another libel echoed this Biblical perspective, representing Buckingham's assassination as a judgement of God, pruning from the vineyard the 'branch that did of late o'ertop the rest', a sign that God still cared for 'This land of ours, this vineyard of thine own, / This England's Eden.[87] One audacious libel warned that God's judgement against Buckingham should stir his master to change, for 'God's sickle spares not either King or crown', an astonishing proto-republican sentiment.[88] Another noted that the 'will of justice' had killed Buckingham for his crimes of murdering 'right, religion, piety', and now therefore 'the law's in force again'. The final wish was for Charles to change, 'that our prince those laws would foster more, / Then should we flourish as we did before.'[89]

Many libels assumed that the assassination heralded a new and better political future. Felton's 'petition' notified the king that 'I your servant...have set you free.' The new vision of political harmony ushered in by Felton included the unity of king and Parliament. Felton had served the country's cause by ridding the court of the source of the corruption that had prevented king and Parliament from working together in patriotic unity. Felton had endeavoured 'by one stroke to make / The King and commons (by him put asunder) / Join all in one, and resolution take / To mend all things unto the world's great wonder.'[90]

These hopes were to be dashed. The libels' challenge to Charles's representation of the assassination was perceived as a dangerous continuation of disloyalty and 'popularity'. Poems were circulated to stem the flood of support for Felton. One poet warned that 'He that doth bless a murder, kills a King' and, casting Felton as a 'slave', urged the reader to 'believe two Kings before one slave'.[91] The pursuit of Zouch Townley and the prosecution of Alexander Gill are evidence of the concern that libels caused Charles after Buckingham's murder. The epitaphs mocking the dead Duke were presumably taken by Charles as attacks on his royal person and honour. For a king so unnerved by the threat of disloyalty, the actions of Felton and the chorus of popular support that he received in verse invective and drunken toasts must have confirmed his worst fears of seditious 'popularity' in the kingdom. The circulation of verse libels hoping for restored unity merely distanced Charles still further from his people. A clash of political world-views was taking place. For the writers of verse libels, the harmonious political process had broken down because of creeping corruption at court. The libellers assumed that the removal of the centre of that corruption would restore the harmony between king and people. For Charles, however, political breakdown was the result of 'popular' spirits, puritan demagogues encouraging disloyalty in the kingdom. Buckingham's murder, and the popular rejoicing that followed, merely confirmed Charles's fears, giving him reason to withdraw further from parliamentary government, and contributed to the state of mind that launched him on eleven years of personal rule.

Christopher Hill has recently suggested that to understand the range of political opinion in early Stuart England, historians must exploit those sources that escaped the 'conventions of political discourse' imposed by censorship.[92] Verse libels – surreptitiously circulating, uncensored texts – are precisely such sources. Their language suggests a considerable degree of political discontent in this period. Their wide distribution among regions and classes allowed them an important role in politicising the nation, expressing and creating discontent, and eroding political legitimacy. They circulated representations of deep corruption at court, corruption that was particularly unnerving in the context of widely held beliefs about the dangers of Catholic conspiracy. When John Pym and his allies publicly invoked popish conspiracy in 1641–2, libels had played (and were to play) their part in structuring the ways people might respond.

Representations of corruption at court maintained importance during the years of civil war and interregnum, eventually becoming part of the defence of republicanism. George Eglisham's tract on the poisoning of King James was reprinted in 1642. Verse libels from 1627–8 on the Rhé expedition and Buckingham in Hell were finally printed in 1644. John Milton countered attempts to glorify Charles's character after the regicide by invoking, among other things, Charles's and Buckingham's sexual vices. To make their case against the Stuart dynasty, interregnum histories of the Jacobean court dwelled at length on sexual and financial scandal.

Even during the exclusion crisis, the relationship between James I and Buckingham could still be cited as proof of the Stuarts' moral turpitude.[93]

Much work remains to be done on verse libels, their circulation and cultural spheres, their precise function in specific political contexts and within other paradigms of corruption. This work needs to be conducted with an increased sensitivity to the cultural nature of politics, and particularly to questions of perception. How people perceived reality affected the way they chose to act. However distasteful or simplistic we may think them, libellous perceptions need to be integrated into any account of the ideological origins of the civil war. Robert Darnton has written, of sexual 'libelles' circulated against the court in eighteenth-century France, that 'this was more dangerous propaganda than the *Contrat Social*'.[94] Only further study will enlighten us as to whether 'raylinge rymes' were of equal importance in the origins of the English Revolution.

Bibliography

1. COURT-CENTRED POLITICS AND THE USES OF ROMAN HISTORIANS *Malcolm Smuts*

The study of early Stuart political thought has been dominated by a concern with formal constitutional issues and by legal and theological questions. As a result relatively little has been written about the sort of analysis of political processes and behaviour examined in this essay. The situation is very different with respect to continental European societies, for which a broad and sophisticated historiographical literature exists dealing with topics like Machiavellianism, Taciteanism and concepts of statecraft. Two good introductions to European Taciteanism are Kenneth Schelhase, *Tacitus in the Renaissance* (Chicago, 1976) and Gerhard Oestereich, *Neostoicism and the Early Modern State,* tr. David McLintock (Cambridge, 1982). Quentin Skinner, *Foundations of Modern Political Thought,* vol. ii (Cambridge, 1978) provides a more general guide, with bibliographical references to particular topics. Donald Kelley, *The Beginnings of Ideology* (Cambridge, 1981) is less systematic in coverage, but interesting and suggestive. J.H.M. Salmon, *The French Religious Wars in English Political Thought* (Oxford, 1959) remains useful on the reception of European political ideas in England.

The mental outlook of the English court and high nobility has received considerable attention of late. For the Elizabethan period see, in particular, Mervyn James, 'English politics and the Concept of Honour, 1485–1642' and 'At a crossroads of political culture: the Essex revolt, 1601', both in *idem, Society, Politics and Culture* (1986); Richard McCoy, *The Rites of Knighthood* (Berkeley and Los Angeles, 1989) and F.J. Levy, 'Francis Bacon and the Style of Politics', in Arthur Kinney and Dan Collins (eds), *Renaissance Historicism* (Amherst, Ma., 1987). These may be profitably compared to a French study stressing broadly similar themes, Arlette Jouanna, *Le devoir de revolte: La noblesse Francaise et la gestation de l'Etat moderne, 1559–1661* (Paris, 1989). The best starting point for examining the outlook of the Jacobean ruling elite is Linda Levy Peck (ed.), *The Mental World of the Jacobean Court* (Cambridge, 1991).

For attitudes toward history in Tudor and Stuart England see F.J. Levy, *Tudor Historical Thought* (San Marino, 1967); *idem* 'Hayward, Daniel and the Beginnings of Politic History in England', *Huntington Library Quarterly* (1987); and D.R. Woolf, *The Idea of History in Early Stuart England: Ideology and the Light of Truth from the Accession of James I to the Civil War* (Toronto, 1991). An historiographical landmark of the 1590s has recently appeared in a modern edition, John J. Manning (ed.), *The First and Second Parts of John Hayward's The Life and Reigne of King Henrie iiii,* Camden Society Publications, (1991). Kevin Sharpe, *Sir Robert Cotton* (Oxford, 1979) examines the political career of an important Jacobean antiquarian.

David Womersley, 'Sir Henry Savile's Translation of Tacitus and the Political Interpretation of Elizabethan Texts' *Review of English Studies,* n.s. 42 (1991) pp. 313–42 sheds light on the origins of English Taciteanism. It is not entirely convincing on politics. The two best essays on Taciteanism and related issues in the Jacobean period are Alan T. Bradford, 'Stuart Absolutism and the "utility" of Tacitus', *Huntington Library Quarterly,* 45 (1983) pp. 127–55 and J.H.M. Salmon, 'Stoicism and Roman Example: Seneca and Tacitus in Jacobean England', *Journal of the History of Ideas,* 50 (1989) pp. 199–225. Blair Worden, 'Classical Republicanism and the Puritan Revolution', in Hugh Lloyd Jones, Valerie Pearl and Blair Worden (eds), *History and Imagination: Essays in Honour of H.R. Trevor Roper* (1981) is also relevant.

Several recent works have dealt with the political implications of Stuart drama. Albert Tricomi, *Anticourt Drama in England 1603–1642* (Charlottesville, 1989) is dated in its approach to politics, but provides a useful overview of the plays. Rebecca Bushnell, *Tragedies of Tyrants: Political Thought and Theater in the English Renaissance* (Ithaca, 1990) is good on traditional images of tyranny but less persuasive on how these might have been applied under the Stuarts. More convincing is Martin Butler, 'Romans in Britain: *The Roman Actor* and the Early Stuart Classical Play' in Douglas Howard (ed.), *Philip Massinger: a Critical Reassessment* (1985). The bibliography on Shakespeare continues to expand rapidly. Alexander Legatt, *Shakespeare's Political Drama: the history plays and Roman plays* (1987) and Phyllis Rackin, *Stages of History: Shakespeare's English Chronicles* (Ithaca, 1990) both attempt to relate the plays of the 1590s to the politics of the age. Although both afford insights into particular plays, neither is sufficiently well grounded in late Elizabethan history to provide a convincing picture of Shakespeare as a fully political thinker.

2. LUCAN, THOMAS MAY, AND THE CREATION OF A REPUBLICAN LITERARY CULTURE   *David Norbrook*

For an introduction to English republicanism, see Blair Worden, 'Classical Republicanism and the Puritan Revolution' in Hugh Lloyd-Jones, Valerie Pearl and Blair Worden (eds), *History and Imagination: Essays in Honour of H.R. Trevor-Roper* (London, 1981) pp. 182–200. See also Jonathan Scott, *Algernon Sidney and the English Republic 1623–1677* and *Algernon Sidney and the Restoration Crisis, 1677–1683* (Cambridge, 1988–91). On republicanism in political theory see J.G.A. Pocock, *The Machiavellian Moment: Florentine Political Thought and the Atlantic Republican Tradition*

(Princeton, 1975) and Quentin Skinner, *The Foundations of Modern Political Thought*, 2 vols (Cambridge, 1978). Renaissance commentaries on Latin literary texts offer a huge, and largely unexplored, body of evidence about ways of reading politically in the Renaissance; for general studies see J.E. Sandys, *A History of Classical Scholarship*, II (Cambridge, 1908) and R.R. Bolgar, *The Classical Tradition and its Beneficiaries* (Cambridge, 1954). Lisa Jardine and Anthony Grafton, '"Studied for Action": How Gabriel Harvey Read His Livy', *Past and Present*, 129 (November 1990) 30–78, give a ground-breaking case study in the history of reading classical texts, to be developed in a forthcoming book; see also their *From Humanism to the Humanities* (London, 1986). On Lucan see O.A.W. Dilke, 'Lucan and English Literature' in D.R. Dudley (ed.), *Neronians and Flavians: Silver Latin 1* (Greek and Latin Studies: Classical Literature and its Influence) (London and Boston, 1977) pp. 83–112 and Gerald M. MacLean, *Time's Witness: Historical Representation in English Poetry, 1603–1660* (Madison, 1990) pp. 26–43. The literary republican who has been most studied is of course Milton; for possible links with Lucan see William Blissett, 'Caesar and Satan', *Journal of the History of Ideas*, 18 (1957) 221–32; see also Charles Martindale, 'The epic of ideas: Lucan's *De bello civili* and Milton's *Paradise Lost*', *Comparative Criticism* 3 (1981) pp. 133–56. On republicanism and literary culture see also Blair Worden, 'Milton's Republicanism and the Tyranny of Heaven' in Gisela Bock, Quentin Skinner and Maurizio Viroli (eds), *Machiavelli and Republicanism* (Cambridge, 1990) pp. 225–45; Blair Worden 'Andrew Marvell, Oliver Cromwell, and the Horatian Ode' in Kevin Sharpe and Steven N. Zwicker (eds), *Politics of Discourse: The Literature and History of Seventeenth-Century England* (Berkeley, Los Angeles and London, 1987) pp. 147–80; and David Norbrook, 'Marvell's "Horation Ode" and the Politics of Genre' in Thomas Healy and Jonathan Sawday (eds), *Literature and the English Civil War* (Cambridge, 1990) pp. 147–69. Christopher Hill, *Milton and the English Revolution* (London and New York, 1977), gives a wide-ranging survey of Milton's political contexts, though not specifically of his republicanism. Other republican poets have received far less attention. The only full-length study of May is Alan Griffith Chester, *Thomas May: Man of Letters, 1595–1650* (Philadelphia: 1932), a useful introduction which by now needs replacing. On the emergence of a poetic 'opposition' under James I, see David Norbrook, *Poetry and Politics an the English Renaissance* (London and Boston, 1984).

3.   BEN JONSON AMONG THE HISTORIANS   *Blair Worden*

The standard edition of Jonson's works is C.H. Herford, P. Simpson and E. Simpson (eds), *Ben Jonson*, 11 vols (Oxford, 1925–52). There is a good recent edition of *Sejanus his Fall* by Philip Ayres (Manchester, 1990), and there are useful modern editions of Camden and of Hayward: William

Camden, *The History of Princess Elizabeth*, ed. Wallace T. MacCaffrey (Chicago, 1970: an abridged version); and John J. Manning (ed.), *The First and Second Parts of John Hayward's The Life and Reigne of King Henry IIII* (London: Royal Historical Society, Camden 4th ser., 49, 1991).

On the historians with whom Jonson associated, three works stand out: Kevin Sharpe, *Sir Robert Cotton 1586–1631* (Oxford, 1979); Hugh Trevor-Roper, 'Queen Elizabeth's First Historian: William Camden' in Trevor-Roper's *Renaissance Essays* (London, 1985); D.R. Woolf, *The Idea of History in Early Stuart England* (Toronto, 1990), which has a long chapter on Selden.

Three works are especially illuminating on Jonson's relationship to ancient Rome and to its poetry: Richard Peterson, *Imitation and Praise in the Poetry of Ben Jonson* (New Haven, 1981); Howard Erskine-Hill, *The Augustan Idea in English Literature* (London, 1983); Katherine E. Maus, *Ben Jonson and the Roman Frame of Mind* (Princeton, 1984). For the influence of Tacitus on Jonson's generation, see the numerous studies listed in J.H.M. Salmon, 'Seneca and Tacitus in Jacobean England' in Linda Levy Peck (ed.), *The Mental World of the Jacobean Court* (Cambridge, 1991), pp. 321–2. The Tacitean features of late Elizabethan politics are graphically documented by Lacey Baldwin Smith, *Treason in Tudor England: Politics and Paranoia* (London, 1986).

4.   BEN JONSON AND THE LIMITS OF COURTLY PANEGYRIC
  Martin Butler

The two most influential modern books on the Stuart masque have been Stephen Orgel's literary study, *The Jonsonian Masque* (1965) and D.J. Gordon's volume on masque iconography, *The Renaissance Imagination* (1975). There are several useful surveys and collections of essays: see especially Graham Parry, *The Golden Age Restor'd: The Culture of the Stuart Court* (1981); David Lindley (ed.), *The Court Masque* (1984); and Roy Strong, *Henry, Prince of Wales, and England's Lost Renaissance* (1986). The masque designs are edited by Stephen Orgel and Roy Strong as *Inigo Jones: The Theatre of the Stuart Court* (2 vols, 1973), and the masque music is edited by Andrew Sabol as *Songs and Dances from the Stuart Masque* (1959; expanded 1978).

About the first serious attempt to address the politics of the masques was Stephen Orgel's short, seminal book, *The Illusion of Power* (1975). Politics have loomed much larger more recently. About the best of the politicised studies is R. Malcom Smuts's *Court Culture and the Origins of a Royalist Tradition in Early Stuart England* (1987), which explores the ideological structures of court culture in the period. Leah Marcus's *The Politics of Mirth* (1986) links the masques with ideas of revelry and refor-mation. Kevin Sharpe's *Criticism and Compliment: The Politics of Literature in the England of Charles I* (1987) argues that the Caroline masques constituted a vein of criticism from within Whitehall. Patricia Fumerton's *Cultural Aesthetics: Renaissance Literature and the Practice of Social Ornament* (1991) situates the masques within the preoccupations of 'New Historicism'.

Specifically on Jonson: Jonson's career has been recently described by David Riggs in *Ben Jonson: A Life* (1989), a book which pays some attention to the politics of writing at court. For essays that deal with the politics of his masques, see Sara Pearl, '"Sounding to present occasions": Jonson's masques of 1620–5', in David Lindley (ed), *The Court Masque* (1984) pp. 60–77; David Lindley, 'Embarrassing Ben: The masques for Frances Howard', *English Literary Renaissance*, 16 (1986) pp. 343–59; John Peacock, 'Jonson and Jones collaborate on *Prince Henry's Barriers*', *Word and Image*, 3 (1987) pp. 172–94; and two essays by Martin Butler, '"We are one mans all"': Jonson's *The Gipsies Metamorphosed*', *Yearbook of English Studies*, 20 (1991) pp. 253–73, and 'Ben Jonson's *Pan's Anniversary* and the politics of early Stuart pastoral', *English Literary Renaissance* (forthcoming).

5. THE KING'S WRIT: ROYAL AUTHORS AND ROYAL AUTHORITY IN
    EARLY MODERN ENGLAND   *Kevin Sharpe*

There has been surprisingly little discussion of Elizabeth's devotional works. See W.P. Haugaard, 'Elizabeth Tudor's *Book of Devotions*: a neglected clue to the Queen's life and character', *The Sixteenth Century Journal*, XII (1981). The only commentary on her translations is in the introduction to C. Pemberton (ed.), *Queen Elizabeth's Englishings* (1899). On Elizabeth's education in general see the recent biography, A. Somerset, *Elizabeth I* (1991).

James's poetry and some of his devotional works have been largely neglected. However, there are brilliant insights into James I and the relationship of his writing to authority in J. Goldberg, *James I and the Politics of Literature* (Baltimore, Md and London, 1983). See also K. Sharpe, 'Private conscience and Public Duty in the Writings of James VI and I', in J.S. Morrill, P. Slack and D. Woolf (eds), *Public Duty and Private Conscience in Seventeenth Century England* (Oxford, 1993).

On Charles I and his preference for silence, see P. Thomas, 'Charles I: the tragedy of absolutism', in A.G. Dickens (ed.) *The Courts of Europe 1400–1800* (1977) and K. Sharpe, *The Personal Rule of Charles I* (New Haven and London, 1992).

There has been a great deal written about the Eikon Basilike (for example, F. F. Madan, *A New Bibliography of the Eikon Basilike* (Oxford, 1950), but little examination of its ideological or rhetorical strategies. We await Steve Zwicker's brilliant discussion in *Lines of Authority: Politics and Literary Culture 1649–1689* (Ithaca, NY, 1993).

See too in general, T.A. Birrell, *English Monarchs and Their Books* (1986).

6.   POLITICS AND PASTORAL: WRITING THE COURT ON THE
     COUNTRYSIDE   *Leah S. Marcus*

Robert Herrick, ed. Ann Baynes Coiro, special double issue of *George Herbert Journal*, 14, nos 1–2 (fall 1990, spring 1991) pp. 1–20.

Christopher Hill *Society and Puritanism in Pre-Revolutionary England*, 2nd edn, (New York, 1967).

David Lindley (ed.), *The Court Masque*, (Manchester and Dover, New Hampshire, 1984).

Anthony Low *The Georgic Revolution* (Princeton, 1985).

David Norbrook, *Poetry and Politics in the English Renaissance* (London, Boston, and Melbourne, 1984).

Stephen Orgel *The Illusion of Power* (Berkeley and London, 1975).

Annabel Patterson *Pastoral and Ideology: Virgil to Valery* (Berkeley and Los Angeles, 1987).

Buchanan Sharpe *In Contempt of All Authority: Rural Artisans and Riot in the West of England, 1586–1660* (Berkeley and London, 1980).

Kevin Sharpe *Criticism and Compliment: The Politics of Literature in the England of Charles I* (1987 paperback edition, Cambridge, 1990).

David Underdown *Revel, Riot, and Rebellion: Popular Politics and Culture in England 1603–1660* (Oxford, 1985).

Don Wayne, *Penshurst: The Semiotics of Place and the Poetics of History* (Madison and London, 1984).

Raymond Williams *The Country and the City* (1973 paperback reprint, London and New York, 1975).

7.   CHIVALRY AND POLITICAL CULTURE IN CAROLINE ENGLAND
     J.S.A. Adamson

The study of the relations between politics and culture in the England of Charles I is still in the early stages, and this fact is reflected in its historiography. There are, however, a number of works which open up the terrain. A general introduction to the period is provided by R.M. Smuts, *Court Culture and the Origins of a Royalist Tradition in Early Stuart England* (Philadelphia, 1987); however, a full-length study of chivalric ideas during the seventeenth century has yet to be written. In the mean time, there are a number of important studies of the subject for earlier periods. Sydney Anglo's edited collection, *Chivalry in the Renaissance* (Woodbridge, 1990), is largely devoted to sixteenth-century chivalry, but contains an essay by the editor which offers insights, and suggests approaches, which could be pursued fruitfully for the chivalric culture of the seventeenth century. A.B. Ferguson, *The Chivalric Tradition in Renaissance England* (Washington, 1986), is a useful survey of Tudor and some early Jacobean chivalric literature, but is rather too ready to write off post-Jacobean chivalry as decadent and moribund.

On specific subjects which have a chivalric dimension: the decline of the tournament is dealt with in Alan Young's *Tudor and Jacobean Tournaments* (1987) – a work which is lavishly and intelligently illustrated, Malcom Smuts offers a perceptive and lucidly argued account of the changing place of the royal entry in court ceremonial in R. Malcom Smuts, 'Public Ceremony and Royal Charisma: The English Royal Entry in London, 1485–1642' in A.L. Beier, David Cannadine and James M. Rosenheim (eds), *The First Modern Society: Essays in English History in Honour of Lawrence Stone* (Cambridge, 1989). And more generally, the structures of the 'honour culture' – with which chivalric ideas were closely related – are examined in two essays by Mervyn James, 'English Politics and the Concept of Honour, 1485–1642' and 'At a Crossroads of the Political Culture: The Essex Revolt, 1601', reprinted in his *Society, Politics and Culture: Studies in Early Modern England* (Cambridge, 1986).

The politics of portraiture is a subject which awaits its historian; some of the subject's possibilities, however, are suggested in Sir Roy Strong's *Van Dyck: Charles I on Horseback* (1972), which offers an imaginative (if at times highly speculative) approach to the interpretation of one of the most famous images of monarchy produced by the Caroline court. Some of the political implications of Van Dyck's use of iconography are persuasively demonstrated in a brilliant case study by Jeremy Wood, 'Van Dyke's pictures for the Duke of Buckingham: The Elephant in the Carpet and the Dead Tree with Ivy', *Apollo,* 136 (July 1992) 37–47. On the Caroline court masque the best study remains Kevin Sharpe, *Criticism and Compliment: The Politics of Literature in the England of Charles I* (Cambridge, 1987) pp. 179–264. In the masque, of all theatrical genres, the visual element is paramount, and no masque text can be considered outside of the set and costume designs that complemented it. These are most conveniently found in the massive study of Inigo Jones's work for the court masque by Stephen Orgel and Sir Roy Strong, published as *Inigo Jones: The Theatre of the Stuart Court,* 2 vols (Berkeley and London, 1973). For the popular stage, the most useful introduction remains Martin Butler, *Theatre and Crisis, 1632–1642* (Cambridge, 1984).

8.   THE POLITICS OF PORTRAITURE   *John Peacock*

John Pope-Hennessy, *The Portrait in the Renaissance* (London and New York, 1966).

Lorne Campbell, *Renaissance Portraits* (New Haven and London, 1990).

318   BIBLIOGRAPHY

Nicholas Hilliard, *A Treatise concerning the Art of Limning*, ed. R.K. Thornton and T.G.S. Cain (Ashington, 1981).

Roy Strong, *The English Icon. Elizabethan and Jacobean Portraiture* (London and New York, 1969); *The English Renaissance Miniature* (London, 1983); *Van Dyck: Charles I on Horseback* (London, 1972).

Oliver Millar, *The Age of Charles I* (London, 1972); *Van Dyck in England* (London, 1982).

Malcolm Rogers, *William Dobson 1611–1646* (London, 1983).

John Murdoch, 'Painting from Astraea to Augustus', *The Cambridge Guide to the Arts in Britain*, vol. 4, *The Seventeenth Century* (Cambridge, 1989) pp. 234–65.

Lucy Gent and Nigel Llewellyn (eds), *Renaissance Bodies. The Human Figure in English Culture c.1540–1660* (London, 1990).

9. INIGO JONES AND THE POLITICS OF ARCHITECTURE
   J. Newman

J. Webb, *The Most Notable Antiquity called Stone-Heng* (London, 1655).

N.G. Brett-James, *The Growth of Stuart London* (London, 1935).

P. Palme, *Triumph of Peace: a Study of the Whitehall Banqueting House* (London, 1957).

J. Summerson, *Inigo Jones* (Harmondsworth, 1966).

R. Strong, *Britannia Triumphans: Inigo Jones, Rubens and Whitehall Palace* (London, 1980).

R.M. Smuts, *Court Culture and the Origins of a Royalist Tradition in Early Stuart England* (Philadelphia, 1987).

J. Harris and G. Higgott, *Inigo Jones: Complete Architectural Drawings* (London, 1989).

10. DEEDS AGAINST NATURE: CHEAP PRINT, PROTESTANTISM AND MURDER IN EARLY SEVENTEENTH-CENTURY ENGLAND
    Peter Lake

K.V. Thomas, *Religion and the Decline of Magic* (London, 1970); N.Z. Davis, 'Printing and the people' in her *Society and Culture in Early Modern France* (London, 1975); T. Watt, *Cheap Print and Popular Piety, 1550–1640* (Cambridge, 1991); P. Collinson, *The Birthpangs of Protestant England* (London, 1988); S. Clark, *The Elizabethan Pamphleteers: Popular Moralistic Pamphlets, 1580–1640* (London, 1983); L.B. Wright, *Middle Class Culture in Elizabethan England* (Ithaca, N.Y., 1958); J. Sharpe, '"Last dying speeches": Religion, Ideology and Public Execution in Seventeenth Century England', *Past and Present*, 107 (1985); T. Lacqueur, 'Crowds, Carnival and the State in English Executions, 1604–1868' in A. Beier, D.

Cannadine and J. Rosenheim (eds.), *The First Modern Society* (Cambridge. 1989); P. Lake, 'Puritanism, Arminianism and a Shropshire Axe-murder', *Midland History*, 15 (1990).

11. 'RAYLINGE RYMES AND VAUNTING VERSE': LIBELLOUS POLITICS IN EARLY STUART ENGLAND   *Alastair Bellany*

There has been, as yet, little systematic study of verse libels in this period. Pauline Croft explores libels against Robert Cecil in 'The Reputation of Robert Cecil: Libels, Political Opinion and Popular Awareness in the Early Seventeenth Century', *TRHS*, 6th ser., 1 (1991), and literary critic Gerald Hammond examines a small selection of the Felton–Buckingham libels of 1628 in his *Fleeting Things: English Poets and Poems 1616–1660*, (Cambridge, 1990). The most successful attempt to integrate libels into a larger political narrative can be found in Thomas Cogswell's *The Blessed Revolution: English Politics and the Coming of War, 1621–1624*, (Cambridge, 1989). This monograph, and the same author's 'Politics and Propaganda: Charles I and the People in the 1620s', *Journal of British Studies*, 29 (1990), along with Richard Cust's 'News and Politics in Early Seventeenth Century England', *Past and Present*, 111 (1986), provide an excellent starting point for any serious consideration of 'public opinion' and politics in early seventeenth-century England. These works, together with Clive Holmes, 'The County Community in Stuart Historiography', *Journal of British Studies*, 19 (1980), offer serious and persuasive modifications to localist and revisionist arguments about political awareness in the provinces, such as can be found in John Morrill's important *The Revolt of the Provinces*, 2nd edn, (London, 1980), and 'William Davenport and the "Silent Majority" of early Stuart England', *Journal of the Chester Archaeological Society*, 58 (1974), and which form part of the basis for Conrad Russell's powerful opening chapter in *Parliaments and English Politics, 1621–1629*, (Oxford, 1979).

Issues of ideology have recently been resuscitated after a prolonged historiographical coma. Religion and politics are interlinked, and anti-Catholic and anti-popularity fears are brilliantly discussed, by Peter Lake, 'Anti-Popery: The Structure of a Prejudice' in Richard Cust and Ann Hughes (eds), *Conflict in Early Stuart England*, (London, 1989). Essays in the same volume by Cogswell, Cust, Hughes and Sommerville offer an equally promising prognosis for ideology's future historiographical health. Charles I's political mentality is best approached through Richard Cust, *The Forced Loan and English Politics, 1626–1628*, (Oxford, 1987), and in Conrad Russell, *The Causes of the English Civil War*, (Oxford, 1990).

Much literature on court scandal prefers the sensational to the scholarly approach. Any serious reconsideration should start with the classic statement, too summarily dismissed in recent years, of the importance of scandalous images of the court in an evolving political crisis given by Lawrence Stone in *The Causes of the English Revolution 1529–1642*, (London, 1972). The same author's *The Crisis of the Aristocracy*, abridged edn (Oxford, 1967) looks at the role of scandal in undermining the prestige of the aristocracy. Linda Levy Peck's *Court Patronage and Corruption in Early Stuart England*, (Boston, 1990) offers a perceptive account of financial corruption at the Stuart court.

Historians of early modern England are all too often heedless of comparisons with other countries. Any student of libels, however, would be well served by Robert Darnton's seminal collection of essays on illegal literature in pre-Revolutionary France, *The Literary Underground of the Old Regime*, (Cambridge, Mass, 1982).

When all is done, however, students can do no better than read the libels for themselves. It is to be hoped that Thomas Cogswell's plans for an edition come to fruition. Until then, the best introduction would be to look at Frederick W. Fairholt (ed.), *Poems and Songs Relating to George Villiers, Duke of Buckingham* (London, 1850).

Notes and References

INTRODUCTION

1. For not altogether favourable comment on this development see L. Stone, 'The Revival of Narrative: Reflections on a New Old History', *Past and Present*, 85 (1979). Narrative is not, of course, a distinctively revisionist mode. Some of the most powerful recent critics of revisionism have adopted a densely narrative approach, albeit not one limited to the traditional terrain of high politics. See R.P. Cust, *The Forced Loan and English Politics, 1626–1628* (Oxford, 1987) and T. Cogswell, *The Blessed Revolution* (Cambridge, 1989).

2. The phrase is J.H. Hexter's and is the title of a series of collaborative studies being published under his aegis by Stanford University Press.

3. The first systematic presentations of this view of the period were contained in C.S.R. Russell, *Parliaments and English Politics, 1621–9* (Oxford, 1979); M.A. Kishlansky, *The Rise of the New Model Army* (Cambridge, 1979); and K. Sharpe (ed.), *Faction and Parliament* (Oxford, 1978). For some critical remarks on the revisionists' obsession with manuscript sources see R.P. Cust and A.L. Hughes (eds), *Conflict in Early Stuart England* (London, 1989) pp. 12–13.

4. See the now famous description of Russell *et al.* as 'antiquarian empiricists' in Stone, 'Revival of Narrative'; for more measured criticism along the same lines see T.K. Rabb, 'The Role of the Commons' and D. Hirst, 'The Place of Principle' both in *Past and Present*, 92 (1981).

5. Notable exceptions to this are the works of Kevin Sharpe and Mark Kishlansky. Sharpe has often returned to the interplay between politics and ideas. See Sharpe, *Sir Robert Cotton* (Oxford, 1979), *Criticism and Compliment* (Cambridge, 1987) and in particular the first chapter of his collected essays *Politics and Ideas in Early Stuart England* (London, 1989). Mark Kishlansky's book *Parliamentary Selection* (Cambridge, 1986) is best seen as an attempt to reconstruct from the political theatre of parliamentary s/election and the rhetorical and personal posturing and manoeuvre that preceded and attended it the norms and assumptions of 'consensus politics'. Kishlansky was here defending and refining a view of the political culture of the period first advanced in his 'The emergence of adversary politics in the Long Parliament', *Journal of Modern History*, 49 (1977). While Professor Russell's reading of the political culture of the day has remained implicit it can be relatively clearly discerned in chs I and VI of his *Parliaments and English Politics* and ch 6 of his *The Causes of the English Civil War* (Oxford, 1990). Also see his early article of 1967,

NOTES AND REFERENCES

'Arguments for religious unity in England, 1530–1650' now reprinted in Russell's *Unrevolutionary England* (London, 1990).

6. We are gesturing here towards and rather summarily glossing the school of literary criticism often referred to as 'new historicism'. For some works representative of this approach see S. Greenblatt, *Renaissance Self-Fashioning* (Chicago, 1980) or *idem.*, *Shakespearian Negotiations* (Berkeley and Los Angeles, 1988). Also see J. Goldberg, *James I and the Politics of Literature* (Baltimore, Md., 1983); S. Greenblatt (ed.), *Representing the Renaissance* (Berkeley and Los Angeles, 1988); L.A. Montrose,'"Eliza, Queen of Shepherdes" and the Pastoral of Power', *English Literary Renaissance*, 19 (1980). The quote from David Norbrook comes from his article 'The life and death of Renaissance Man' *Raritan*, 8 (1989).

7. See ch. 8 of Russell's *Causes of the English Civil War*, for other versions of Charles's style based on very different sources see R. Strong, *Charles I on Horseback* (London, 1972); S. Orgel, *The Illusion of Power* (Berkeley and Los Angeles, 1975); M. Smuts, *Court Culture and the Origins of a Royalist Tradition in Early Stuart England* (Philadelphia, 1987); K. Sharpe, *Criticism and Compliment* and K. Sharpe, *The Personal Rule of Charles I* (New Haven and London 1992).

8. D. Norbrook, 'Renaissance Man' and his 'Absolute Revision', a review of Goldberg's *James I and the Politics of Literature*', *English*, 33 (1984).

9. One central strand of revisionist interpretation was based on the opposition between a national political sphere and an apolitical or prepolitical vision of the localities. The 'localist' sentiments imputed by some revisionists to the 'county communities' of the English shires were seen as a product of the natural social solidarity of the gentry, united in defence of the financial interest and social unity of their 'countries', against the demands of an intrusive central government. See J.S. Morrill, *The Revolt of the Provinces* (London, 1976) and Russell, *Parliaments and English Politics*; for the extension of this approach into the cultural sphere see J.S. Morrill, 'William Davenport and the "silent majority" of Early Stuart England', *Journal of the Chester Archaeological Society*, 1974. For critiques of this approach stressing the complex interactions between the 'political' and the 'administrative', on the one hand, and the ideologically and polemically constructed nature of 'localism', on the other, see P. Lake, 'The collection of ship money in Cheshire during the 1630s: a case study of relations between central and local government' *Northern History*, 17 (1981) and A.L. Hughes,'Militancy and localism: Warwickshire politics and Westminister politics', *Transactions of the Royal Historical Society*, 5th ser., 31 (1981) and *idem*, 'The King, Parliament and the localities during the English Civil War', *Journal of British Studies*, 24 (1985).

10. P. Zagorin, *The Court and the Country* (New York, 1969); P. Thomas, 'Two cultures? Court and country under Charles I' in C.S.R. Russell (ed.), *The Origins of the English Civil War* (London, 1973).

11. M. Smuts, 'The political failure of Stuart cultural patronage' in G. Fitch Lytle and S. Orgel (eds), *Patronage in the Renaissance* (Princeton, NJ,

1981); *idem*, 'Cultural diversity and cultural change at the court of James I' in L.L. Peck (ed.), *The Mental World of the Jacobean Court* (Cambridge, 1991); also see his *Court Culture*, especially ch. 3. More generally on the same theme see James Robertson, 'Caroline Culture: Bridging Court and Country?' *History*, 75 (1990).

12. P. Collinson, *The Birthpangs of Protestant England* (London, 1988), ch. 4; M. Aston, *England's Iconoclasts* (Oxford, 1988); for the dominance of the writings of even conformist divines by a view of Protestantism as a religion of the word, but also for the observation that Elizabethan England contained cultural materials enough to allow Richard Hooker to produce a compelling revaluation of symbol, ritual and worship, see P. Lake, *Anglicans and Puritans: Presbyterianism and English Conformist Thought from Whitgift to Hooker* (London, 1988).

13. For a fascinating case study of a considerable concern for church fabric and indeed church (re)building in a parish dominated by a word-centred hot Protestantism, see Julia Merritt, 'Religion, government and society in early modern Westminister', PhD(London University, 1992).

14. Lucy Gent, *Picture and Poetry, 1560–1620: Relations between Literature and the Visual Arts in Renaissance England* (Leamington Spa, 1981).

15. T. Watt, *Cheap Print and Popular Piety, 1550–1640* (Cambridge, 1991).

16. D. Underdown, 'The taming of the scold' in A. Fletcher and J. Stevenson (eds), *Order and Disorder in Early Modern England* (Cambridge, 1985); also see his *Revel, Riot and Rebellion* (Oxford, 1985) and M. Ingram, 'Ridings, rough music and "the reform of popular culture" in early modern England', *Past and Present*, 105 (1984).

17. Of course, the status of these pamphlets, poems and libels as constructed commodities and of many of their authors as in some sense cultural mediators renders them, on one view, a tainted source for the reconstruction of genuinely or autonomously 'popular' attitudes. Until we have a good deal more research on the marketing and appropriation of cheap print, of the sort being pioneered by Dr Watt, there will always be a distressing element of circularity about such arguments. For an acute but inconclusive discussion of these issues in France see N.Z. Davis, 'Printing and the People' in her *Society and Culture in Early Modern France* (London, 1975). Certainly, the precise relations between the élite and the popular in this period remains a subject of debate. See for instance D. Rollison, 'Property, ideology and popular culture in a Gloucestershire village', *Past and Present*, 93 (1981), to which Ingram, 'Ridings, rough music' is in many ways a reply.

18. The social composition of London theatre audiences is a matter of controversy, usefully summed up in M. Butler, *Theatre and Crisis, 1632–1642* (Cambridge, 1984), appendix II.

19. W. Hunt, 'Civic chivalry and the English civil war' in A. Grafton and A. Blair (eds), *The Transmission of Culture in Early Modern Europe* (Philadelphia, 1990); also see L.C. Stevenson, *Praise and Paradox:*

Merchants and Craftsmen in Elizabethan Popular Literature (Cambridge, 1984) for more on the continuing hold of chivalric culture on the literate middling sort.

20. M. Spufford, *Small Books and Pleasant Histories* (London, 1981).

21. Ingram, 'Ridings, rough music'; Underdown, 'Taming of the scold'; P. Lake, 'Anti-popery: the structure of a prejudice' in Cust and Hughes (eds), *Conflict in Early Stuart England.*

22. Cust and Hughes (eds), *Conflict in Early Stuart England*, pp. 17–18; D.G. Hale, *The Body Politic: A Political Metaphor in Renaissance English Literature* (The Hague, 1971); J. Daly 'Cosmic harmony and political thinking in early Stuart England', *Transactions of the American Philosophical Society*, 69 (1979); S. Clark, 'Inversion, misrule and the meaning of witchcraft', *Past and Present*, 87 (1980).

23. See D.J. Gordon, 'Poet and Architect: the intellectual setting of the quarrel between Ben Jonson and Inigo Jones' in S. Orgel (ed.), *The Renaissance Imagination* (Berkeley, Calif., 1975). The quotation is at p. 90.

24. See L. Marcus, *The Politics of Mirth* (Chicago, 1986) which sets Jonson's concern with popular pastimes in the high political, courtly context provided by James I's book of sports.

25. R.S. Peterson, *Imitation and Praise in the Poems of Ben Jonson* (New Haven, Conn., 1981).

26. On Jonson's *Works* of 1616 see R.C. Newton, 'Jonson and the (Re)Invention of the book' in C.J. Summers and T-L. Rebworth (eds), *Classic and Cavalier: Essays on Jonson and the Sons of Ben* (Pittsburg, Pa., 1982); generally for Jonson's career see D. Riggs, *Ben Jonson: A Life* (Cambridge, Mass., 1989).

27. See J.G.A. Pocock, *The Ancient Constitution and the Feudal Law* (Cambridge, 1987, a reissue of the original edition of 1957 with a lengthy retrospect) and *idem, The Machiavellian Moment* (Princeton, NJ, 1975). For a more recent statement see his 'Texts as events' in K. Sharpe and S. Zwicker (eds), *Politics of Discourse* (Berkeley and Los Angeles, 1987). Also see J. Tully (ed.), *Meaning and Context: Quentin Skinner and his Critics* (Oxford, 1987).

28. For one such slippage see K. Sharpe, 'The foundation of the Chairs of History at Oxford and Cambridge: an episode in Jacobean politics' in his *Politics and Ideas.*

29. P. Lake, 'Anti-popery' and his 'Constitutional consensus and puritan opposition: Thomas Scott and the Spanish Match', *Historical Journal*, 25 (1982).

30. J.P. Sommerville, *Politics and Ideology in England, 1603–1640* (London, 1986). This is not a reading of his work with which Dr Sommerville is likely to agree, since he wishes to stress the very different theories of government that some contemporaries constructed from the ideological materials available to them. The extent of the theoretical divisions amongst contemporaries upon the subject of the derivation and nature of royal power remains controversial. For the revisionist position see Sharpe, *Politics and Ideas*, ch. 1; Russell, *Causes of the English Civil War,*

ch. 6 and his *Unrevolutionary England*, p. xxx; also see P. Christianson, 'Royal and parliamentary voices on the ancient constitution, *c.*1604–21' in Peck (ed.), *Mental world of the Jacobean Court.*

31. Arguably, at least in its earlier rescensions, the Pocockian view of the languages or discourses available to contemporaries for broadly political purposes was too narrow in the number of discourses it posited, in the range of sources in which it assumed those discourses could be located and in its conception of the ways in which contemporaries could combine and thus modify and indeed transform the ideological materials available to them. In part, that foreshortening of view was a product of the very long period over which the discursive structures and paradigm shifts described in both the *Ancient Constitution* and the *Machiavellian Moment* were conceived. For scholars operating in a more densely political, short-term, narrative mode, things must inevitably appear both more complex and more fluid. Cf. Sharpe, *Politics and Ideas*, chapter 1.

32. See F. Raab, *The English Face of Machiavelli* (London, 1964).

33. P. Lake, 'Anti-popery' and his 'Conformist clericalism? Richard Bancroft's analysis of the socio-economic roots of Presbyterianism' in W.J. Sheils and D. Wood (eds), *Studies in Church History* (Oxford, 1987). This, of course, is the view of puritanism taken by Jonson through such characters as Zeal-of-the-Land-Busy in *Bartholomew Fair* and Ananias in *The Alchemist.* More generally on the concern with dissimulation, hypocrisy and casuistry produced by an age of vicious confessional conflict see P. Zagorin, *Ways of Lying* (Cambridge, Mass., 1990).

34. On the highly moralised language of patronage, projects and corruption see L.L. Peck, *Court Patronage and Corruption in Early Stuart England* (London, 1990).

35. This is a rushed and rather crude rendition of the argument of ch. 1 of Sharpe's *Politics and Ideas* and *Criticism and Compliment.*

36. For a version of the religious history of the period refracted through the self-perceptions and polemic of William Prynne see W. Lamont, *Godly Rule* (London, 1968), building on his earlier *Marginal Prynne* (London, 1963).

37. On the rapid circulation and potential polarising effect of news see R.P. Cust, 'News and politics in early seventeenth century England', *Past and Present*, 112 (1986).

1. COURT-CENTRED POLITICS AND THE USES OF ROMAN HISTORIANS *Malcolm Smuts*

1. *Nugae Antiquae* (1804) I, pp. 343.

2. Alexander Grosart (ed.), *Complete Works in Prose and Verse of Samuel Daniel* (1896) II, p. 23.

3. For two recent surveys of treatments of tyranny in early Stuart drama see Albert Tricomi, *Anticourt Drama in England 1603–1642*

(Charlottesville, 1989) and Rebecca Bushnell, *Tragedies of Tyrants: Political Thought and Theater in the English Renaissance* (Ithaca, 1990). For general accounts of historiography in this period see, esp., F.J. Levy, *Tudor Historical Thought* (San Marino, 1967) and D.R. Woolf, *The Idea of History in Early Stuart England: Ideology and the Light of Truth from the Accession of James I to the Civil War* (Toronto, 1990).

4. As James I put it, 'by reading of authentic histories and chronicles, ye shall learn experience by Theoric, applying the past things to the present estate.' Charles McIlwain (ed.), *Political Works of James I*, (Cambridge, Mass., 1918) p. 40. On this topic see, esp., F.J. Levy, 'Hayward, Daniel and the Beginnings of Politic History in England', *Huntington Library Quarterly*, 50 (1987) pp. 1–3.

5. It is unclear whether the *Richard II* play revived by Essex was Shakespeare's.

6. For this work see J.J. Manning (ed.), *The First and Second Parts of John Hayward's The Life and Reigns of King Henri the IIII* (Camden Soc 4th Ser. xlii 1991). On the connection of Hayward's history to Essex and the revolt see Levy, 'Hayward, Daniel and the Beginnings of Politic History', pp. 16–21 and Mervyn James, *Society, Politics and Culture: Studies in Early Modern England* (Cambridge, 1986) pp. 418–23.

7. Levy, 'Politic History', *passim; idem, Tudor Historical Thought*, ch. 6; S.L. Goldberg, 'Sir John Hayward, "Politic" Historian', *Review of English Studies*, n.s. VI (1955) pp. 233–44; Edwin Benjamin, 'Sir John Hayward and Tacitus', *Review of English Studies* n.s. 8 (1957) pp. 275–6.

8. PRO SP12/274/61. The features of Hayward's history I have recited derive from this document, containing the charges drawn up against him.

9. For a discussion of how fear of persecution led to strategies of veiled and indirect communication see Annabel Patterson, *Censorship and Interpretation: The Conditions of Writing and Reading in Early Modern England* (Madison, 1984), esp. ch. 2.

10. For a systematic discussion of this point in the context of French politics see Arlette Jouanna, *Le Devoir de revolte: La noblesse francaise el la gestation de L'etat moderne, 1559–1661* (Paris 1989). Ronald Asch and Adolf Birke (eds), *Princes, Patronage and the Nobility: The Court at the Beginning of the Modern Age c.1450–1650* (Oxford, 1991) provides a panoramic survey. The best general discussion for England remains Wallace MacCaffrey, 'Place and Patronage in Elizabethan Politics' in S.T. Bindoff, Joel Hurstfeld and C.H. Williams (eds), *Elizabethan Politics and Society: Essays Presented to Sir John Neale* (London, 1961). See also Geoffrey Elton, 'Tudor Government: The Points of Contact III: The Court', *Transactions of the Royal Historical Society*, 26 (1976) pp. 211–28.

11. Here I disagree with the emphasis in an otherwise valuable collection: David Starkey (ed.), *The English Court from the Wars of the Roses to the Civil War* (London, 1987). For an expansion of my argument see Malcolm Smuts, 'Cultural Diversity and Cultural Change at the Court of

James I' in L.L. Peck, *The Mental World of the Jacobean Court* (Cambridge, 1991) pp. 102–6. This is supplemented by Pauline Croft, 'Robert Cecil and the Early Jacobean Court', ibid., pp. 134–47.

12. For a discussion see ibid., pp. 99–112 and Malcolm Smuts, *Court Culture and the Origins of a Royalist Tradition in Early Stuart England* (Philadelphia, 1987) pp. 16–18 and ch. 3. Richard McCoy, *Rebellion in Arcadia* (New Brunswick, 1979) provides a generally persuasive analysis of the political ambiguities inherent in Sidney's works, that can be generalised to apply to the use of neo-chivalric culture by courtiers like the Earls of Leicester and Essex.

13. Two published collections of letters illustrate the efforts of young men seeking to train themselves for the court. Logan Pearsal Smith, *Life and Letters of Henry Wotton*, vol. I, and James Spedding (ed.), *Bacon*, vols. I and II.

14. For an interesting general treatment see Donald Kelley, *The Beginning of Ideology* (Cambridge, 1981).

15. For a brief but valuable discussion of this topic see J.H.M. Salmon, *The French Religious Wars in English Political Thought* (Oxford, 1959) pp. 181–6. Cf. Fulke Greville's account of his unsuccessful efforts to become directly involved in the French wars of religion in Alexander Grosart (ed.), *Works in Verse and Prose of Fulke Greville* (1870) IV, pp. 147–9. John Bossy, *Giordano Bruno and the Embassy Affair* (London, 1991) provides a fascinating glimpse into the Elizabethan world of international espionage.

16. In this connection see the extensive list of French publications translated into English between 1560 and 1598, in Salmon, *French Religious Wars*, pp. 171–80. Historians have in the past greatly exaggerated the insularity of English political thought, ignoring substantial evidence of cosmopolitan reading habits.

17. On this subject see esp. Quentin Skinner, *The Foundations of Modern Political Thought*, 2 vols (Cambridge, 1978) II, pp. 308–9; Donald Kelley, *The Beginning of Ideology*, ch. 5 and pp. 294, 330–1; *idem*, 'Murd'rous Machiavel in France', *Political Science Quarterly*, 85 (1970) pp. 545–59; Robert Brierley, *The Counter-Reformation Prince*, (Chapel Hill, 1990). The most important Huguenot attack on Machiavellianism, Innocent Gentillet's *Anti-Machiavel* (1576), was translated into English in 1602 and reprinted in 1608. Machiavelli's views were often distorted and caricatured by writers in this tradition.

18. *Politicorum, sive civilis doctrinae libri sex* (1589), translated as *The Six Books of Politics* (1594). For a discussion see Gerhard Oestereich, *Neostoicism and the Early Modern State*, ed. Brigitta Oestereich and H.G. Koenigsberger, tr. David McLintock (Cambridge, 1982), ch. 3. For an introduction to the extensive secondary literature on European Taciteanism see Kenneth Schelhase, *Tacitus in the Renaissance* (Chicago, 1976).

19. See Levy, *Tudor Historical Thought*, pp. 249–51. An interesting discussion of the Taciteanism of the Sidney family, beginning as far back as the late 1570s, is Blair Worden, 'Classical Republicanism and the

Puritan Revolution' in Hugh Lloyd-Jones, Valerie Pearl and Blair Worden (eds), *History and Imagination: Essays in Honour of H.R. Trevor-Roper* (1981) pp. 181–200.

20. *The Ende of Nero and Beginning of Galba, Fower Bookes of the Histories of Cornelius Tacitus. The Life of Agricola.* (Oxford, 1591). An Italian translation of *The Agricola* had been published in London six years earlier with a dedication to Robert Sidney, *La Vita di Giulio Agricola Scritta Sincerissamente da Cornelio Tacito Suo Genero messa in volgare da Giovan Maria Manelli* (1585).

21. C.H. Herford, P. Simpson, and E. Simpson (eds), *Ben Jonson* , 11 vols (Oxford University Press, 1925–52) I, p. 142.

22. The following discussion attempts to build upon the important findings of Womersley, 'Savile's Tacitus'. Womersley is especially suggestive on *The Ende of Nero and Beginning of Galba*. D. Womersley, 'Sir Henry Savile's Translation of Tacitus and the Political Interpretation of Elizabethan Texts', *Review of English Studies* n.s. 42 (1991), pp. 313–42.

23. Tacitus reports rumours that Domitian had poisoned Agricola, without taking a stand on their accuracy.

24. *Ende of Nero* (1591) p. 13.

25. Ibid., p. 37; Womersley, 'Savile's Tacitus', p. 318, argues that this is an extraordinary stance for a Tudor writer.

26. *Ende of Nero*, p. 1.

27. Manelli's dedicatory epistle is suggestive as to the reasons for English interest in *The Agricola*. He describes it as an account by an historian 'tanto celebrato' of 'uno de piu valorosi capitani che militasse sotto il gloriosisimo Imperio Roma': in other words, a tale of military heroism. *Vita di Agricola*, n.p.

28. For which see esp. James, *Society, Politics and Culture*, chs. 8 and 9.

29. See R.C. McCoy, *Sir Philip Sidney* (Hassocks, 1979) chs. 5 and 6, esp. p. 140.

30. Womersley, 'Savile's Tacitus', pp. 316, 321–9.

31. A.B. emphasised the importance of repeated rereadings of Tacitus. For a discussion of habits of reading in sixteenth-century England see Lisa Jardine and Anthony Grafton, 'How Gabriel Harvey Read his Livy', *Past and Present*, 129 (1990) pp. 30–78.

32. Oestereich, *Neostoicism*, ch. 5.

33. Savile, *Ende of Nero*, p. 18 of notes. Essex explained his decimation in a letter to the Council of July 1599, Folger Library (Washington) Mss. V.b. 214, fo. 264.

34. Printed in John Nichols, *The Progresses and Public Processions of Queen Elizabeth* (1823), vol. III, pp. 161–7.

35. For Savile's travels see *DNB* and Womersley, 'Savile's Tacitus', pp.313, 329–30.

36. Womersley seems to me to overlook this point, assuming a domestic context and telescoping the 1590s so that Essex's position at the decade's end is read back into the very different situation of 1591: ibid., pp. 330–42.

37. Savile, *Ende of Nero*, p. 3 of notes (separately paginated).

38. Ibid., p. 48 of notes.

39. Ibid.

40. F.J. Levy, 'Francis Bacon and the Style of Politics' in Arthur Kinney and Dan S. Collins (eds), *Renaissance Historicism: Selections from English Literary Renaissance* (Amherst, 1987) pp. 150–3.

41. See, for example, William Camden, *Annals*, trans. R.N. (1635) p. 504.

42. *Ende of Nero*, tr. Savile, p. 2.

43. James, *Society, Politics and Culture*, ch. 9, esp. pp. 419–23.

44. The short fifth book of *The History* and the *Dialogue on Oratory* were the only works that remained untranslated.

45. Levy, 'Bacon', p. 151 and *passim*.

46. For a particular example see Ronald A. Rebholz, *The Life of Fulke Greville First Lord Brooke* (Oxford, 1971) pp. 124–40.

47. Herford *et al.* (eds), *Ben Jonson*, V, p. 115. For another discussion of this poem see Jonathan Goldberg, *James I and the Politics of Literature* (Baltimore, 1983) pp. 120–4.

48. *Ben Jonson his part of King James his Royall and Magnificent Entertainement through...London* (1604), D2v [16].

49. For an overview of the play with references to the extensive secondary literature see the introduction to the Revels edition, Philip J. Ayres (ed.), *Sejanus his Fall* (Manchester, 1990).

50. Jonas Barish (ed.), *Ben Jonson's Sejanus* (New Haven, 1965) pp. 115, 129.

51. Ibid., p. 133.

52. Jonas Barish, *The Anti-Theatrical Prejudice* (Berkeley, 1981). Cf. Alexander Legatt's discussion of Jonson's mistrust of 'false creations' in *Ben Jonson, His Vision and His Art* (London, 1981) ch. 1., esp. pp. 1–5. Several critics have remarked that Jonson presents both Sejanus and Tiberius as consummate actors, e.g. Anne Barton, *Ben Jonson, Dramatist* (Cambridge, 1984) p. 104.

53. On the rhetorical basis of humanist political thought see Kelley, *Beginning of Ideology*, pp. 134–42.

54. *The Works of Francis Bacon (1860–1864)*, ed. J. Spedding, R.L. Ellis and D.D. Heath, VI (1861), p. 711.

55. Herford *et al.* (eds), *Ben Jonson*, VIII, p. 636.

56. Ibid., p. 113.

57. Levy, 'Francis Bacon'.

58. Grosart (ed.), *Works of Fulke Greville*, vol.I, p. 5.

59. On this see Annabel Patterson, 'Roman-cast Similitude: Ben Jonson and the English Use of Roman History' in P.A. Ramsey (ed.), *Rome in the Renaissance* (1982). Patterson seems to me, however, to exaggerate the transition and the distinctions between Tacitean and other historical models.

60. Quoted in Gregory Wheare, *The Method and Order of Reading both*

Civil and Ecclesiastical History, trans. Edmund Bohun (London, 1698) p. 108. On the anti-Tacitean reaction at the Jacobean court see Alan T. Bradford, 'Stuart Absolutism and the "Utility" of Tacitus', *Huntington Library Quarterly*, 45 (1983) pp. 127–55.

61. Thomas Birch, *The Life of Henry Prince of Wales* (1760) p. 121.

62. On this see esp. R.P. Cust, 'News and Politics in Early Seventeenth Century England', *Past and Present*, 112 (1986); F.J. Levy, 'How Information Spread Among the Gentry, 1550–1640', *Journal of British Studies*, 21 (1982) pp. 11–34; Thomas Cogswell, *The Blessed Revolution* (Cambridge, 1989), pp. 20–36.

63. E.g. British Library Egerton Mss. 2026, 'Observations in the Earl of Essex's example that it is exceeding dangerous to a favorite to be long absent from his Prince.' Cf. Greville's comments on Essex's fall in Grosart (ed.), *Works of Fulke Greville*, IV, pp. 157–8.

64. On this see Neil Cuddy, 'Anglo-Scottish Union and the Court of James I', *Transactions of the Royal Historical Society*, 5th ser., 39 (1989) pp. 107–24.

65. Holles to Lord Norrice, August 1614, in P.R. Seddon (ed.), *Letters of John Holles 1587–1637*, Thoroton Society Record Series, 31 (Nottingham, 1975) p. 57. I wish to thank Linda Peck for calling this collection to my attention.

66. Ibid. p. 85.

67. Ibid. p. 118.

68. Ibid. p. 66.

69. Ibid. p. 71.

70. J.H.M. Salmon, 'Stoicism and Roman Example: Seneca and Tacitus in Jacobean England', *Journal of the History of Ideas*, 50 (1989) p. 209. This essay is reprinted in Peck, *Mental World*.

71. As is well known. For two examples of this mentality see *Works of Fulke Greville*, iiii, p. 45, on the relationship of Catholic spiritual subversion to Spanish goals, and John Holles's comments on the European situation in Seddon (ed.), *Letters of John Holles*, I, pp. 67 and 72.

72. Nichols, *Progresses of Queen Elizabeth*, III, p. 162.

73. *An Apologie of the Earle of Essex* (1603) p. Eiiii.

74. On this see esp. Linda Peck, *Court Patronage and Corruption in Early Stuart England* (London, 1990), esp. p. 11, ch. 1 and pp. 173–81, 203–15.

75. Lambeth Palace Archives Ms. 292. This unattributed treatise appears to be a fair copy of Cotton's tract in B.L. Sloane Ms. 3073.

76. Ibid., 10R.

77. Ibid. fo. 23V.

78. McIlwain (ed.), *Political Works of James I*, p. 55.

79. Stephen Orgel (ed.), *Ben Jonson: The Complete Masques* (New Haven, 1969), p. 149.

80. Pauline Croft (ed.), 'A Collection of Several Speeches and Treatises of the Late Lord Treasurer Cecil', *Camden Miscellany* 29, Camden Society Publications, 4th ser., 34 (1987) p. 298.

81. For the context of this book see David Norbrook, below, pp. 56–7; A.T. Bradford, 'Stuart Absolutism and the "Utility" of Tacitus' *Hunt. Lib. Quart.*, 46, (1983) p. 139.

82. Edmund Bolton, *Nero Caesar or Monarchy Depraved* (1623) p. 69.

83. Ibid.

84. Ibid., p. 74.

85. I have used Savile's translation: *Ende of Nero*, p. 251.

86. The latest and most impressive example is Johann Sommerville, *Politics and Ideology in England 1603–1640* (London, 1986).

87. J. Rushworth, *Historical Collections* (1659), i, 359.

88. For an expression of both views see Sir John Eliot's Negotium Posterorum reprinted in Maija Jansson (ed.), *Proceedings in Parliament, 1625* (New Haven, 1987) pp. 485–569.

89. Ibid., pp. 20–2.

90. Ibid., pp. 123–4.

91. Thomas May, *A Continuation of the Subject of Lucan's Historical Poem till the Death of Julius Caesar* (1633). This work is not without its ambiguities, however, which space does not permit us to discuss here.

92. *The Tragedy of Julia Agrippina* (1639). This play was staged in 1628. M. Butler, 'Romans in Britain, *The Roman Actor* and the Early Stuart classical play' in Douglas Howard (ed.), *Philip Massinger: A Critical Reassessment* (Cambridge, 1985) pp. 148–9 provides a discussion.

93. This is especially clear in an unpublished record of the Star Chamber proceedings against Prynne, Bedford Estate Office Mss. 240.

2.   LUCAN, THOMAS MAY AND THE CREATION OF A REPUBLICAN LITERARY CULTURE   *David Norbrook*

I am indebted to Peter Lake and Nigel Smith for comments on earlier drafts of this article and to James Shapiro for information on Tudor translations.

1. J.L. Chester (ed.), *Westminster Abbey Registers* (London, 1876) pp.521–3.

2. 'Tom May's Death' may be by Andrew Marvell, but there are doubts about the attribution and date; the question requires separate study. May is known to have associated with the freethinking republicans Thomas Chaloner and Henry Marten, and the suspicion of religious heterodoxy may have been a major factor in attacks on this character; his admiration for the freethinking Lucan would then have taken on a particularly dubious cast in the eyes of the godly.

3. Alan Griffith Chester in *Thomas May: Man of Letters, 1595–1650* (Philadelphia, 1932), long ago attempted a rehabilitation, but May remains little studied.

4. *Behemoth: The History of the Causes of the Civil Wars of England*, in William Molesworth (ed.), *The English Works of Thomas Hobbes of Malmesbury*, 11 vols (London, 1839–45) VI, p. 193.

5. See Howard Erskine-Hill, *The Augustan Idea in English Literature* (London, 1983). Erskine-Hill makes little mention of anti-Augustan currents, on which see Howard D. Weinbrot, *Augustus Caesar in 'Augustan' England: The Decline of a Classical Norm* (Princeton, 1978).

6. John Aubrey, *Brief Lives*, ed. Andrew Clark, 2 vols (Oxford, 1898) II, p. 56. Aubrey noted this point down twice at different times.

7. For an exemplary study of the significance of classical reading for Renaissance politics, see Lisa Jardine and A.L. Grafton, '"Studied for Action": How Gabriel Harvey Read His Livy', *Past and Present*, 129 (November 1990) pp. 30–78.

8. The following brief discussion draws heavily on Frederick M. Ahl, *Lucan: An Introduction* (Ithaca and London, 1976); see also O.A.W. Dilke, 'Lucan's Political Views and the Caesars' in D.R. Dudley (ed.), *Neronians and Flavians: Silver Latin 1* (Greek and Latin Studies: Classical Literature and its Influence) (London and Boston, 1972) pp. 62–82, and the same author's 'Lucan and English Literature', ibid., pp. 83–112. I retain the form *Pharsalia* – from the name of the poem's climactic battle – since it was generally current in the Renaissance; Ahl, *op. cit.*, pp. 327ff, defends *Pharsalia* as title. *Lucan*, trans. J.D. Duff (Cambridge, Mass. and London, 1988).

9. On this debate in the Renaissance, see Gerald M. MacLean, *Time's Witness: Historical Representation in English Poetry, 1603–1660* (Madison, 1990) pp. 26ff.

10. Ahl, *Lucan: An Introduction*, p. 56.

11. From the preface to Googe's translation of Palingenius's *The Zodiac of Life*, in Judith M. Kennedy (ed.), *Eclogues, Epitaphs, and Sonnets* (Toronto, Buffalo and London, 1989) p. 127.

12. George Turbervile, *Tragical Tales* (London, 1587) sigs. Avivff. The vision is dated about 1570 by C.H. Conley, *The First English Translators of the Classics* (New Haven, 1927) p. 50.

13. On the European reception see Walter Fischli, *Studien zum Fortleben der Pharsalia des M. Annaeus Lucanus* (Luzern, n.d.) pp. 45ff.

14. On the Elizabethans and Lucan see William Blissett, 'Lucan's Caesar and the Elizabethan Villain', *Studies in Philology*, 53 (1956) pp. 553–75; Christopher Hill, *Intellectual Origins of the English Revolution* (Oxford, 1965) p. 130; George M. Logan, 'Lucan-Daniel-Shakespeare: New Light on the Relation between *The Civil Wars* and *Richard II*', *Shakespeare Studies*, 9 (1976) pp. 121–40, and Emrys Jones, *The Origins of Shakespeare* (Oxford, 1977) pp. 125ff, 273–7.

15. Roma Gill, *Complete Works of Christopher Marlowe, I: The Translations* (Oxford, 1987) p. 89. James Shapiro, '"Metre meete to furnish Lucans style": Reconsidering Marlowe's *Lucan*' in Kenneth Friedenreich, Roma Gill and Constance B. Kuriyama (eds), *'A Poet and a filthy Play-maker': New*

Essays on Christopher Marlowe (New York, 1988) pp. 315–25, argues against the common view that the translation was written early in Marlowe's career.

16. Bodleian MS. Casaubon 28, fol. 127r, cited by Jardine and Grafton, '"Studied for Action"', p. 75 n.144. The exact passage at issue is not clear from Casaubon's account.

17. *Lucan's Pharsalia*, trans. Sir Arthur Gorges (London, 1614) sig. A3v. The translation seems to have been popular, going through three issues in the same year.

18. See Barbara K. Lewalski, 'Lucy, Countess of Bedford: Images of a Jacobean Courtier and Patroness' in Kevin Sharpe and Steven N. Zwicker (eds), *Politics of Discourse: The Literature and History of Seventeenth-Century England* (Berkeley, Los Angeles and London, 1987) pp. 52–77; Paul R. Sellin, *So Doth, So Is Religion: John Donne and Diplomatic Contexts in the Reformed Netherlands, 1619–1620* (Columbia, 1988) pp. 114ff.

19. On humanist reading and the art of war see Jardine and Grafton, '"Studied for Action"', p. 69ff; on Lucan as military poet see Fischli, *Studien zum Fortleben der Pharsalia*, pp. 47, 49.

20. Letter to Daniel Heinsius, 20 April 1614, in P.C. Molhuysen and B.L. Meulenbrock (eds), *Briefwesseling van Hugo Grotius* (The Hague , 1928), I, p. 307. While in England Grotius visited Sir Henry Savile, the translator of Tacitus, on whom see R.M. Smuts's article (pp. 25–6). For Grotius's influence on English republicanism, see Jonathan Scott, *Algernon Sidney and the English Republic 1623–1677* (Cambridge, 1988) pp. 56ff.

21. A.D.B., *The Court of the Most Illustrious and Magnificent James, the First* (London, 1619), dedication to Buckingham and sig. A3r.

22. 'Feltons epitaph', in David Norbrook and H.R Woodhuysen (eds), *The Penguin Book of Renaissance Verse,* (Harmondsworth, 1992) pp. 148–9. This poem is also discussed in Alastair Bellany's article (pp. 305–7). See also Gerald Hammond, *Fleeting Things: English Poets and Poems, 1616–1660* (Cambridge, Mass. and London, 1990) pp. 49–66, and James Holstun, '"God bless thee, little David": John Felton and His Allies', *Journal of English Literary History,* 59 (1992) pp. 513–52.

23. From the version in British Library MS Sloane 826, fol. 197r; this manuscript, compiled in the Caroline period, is a comprehensive assembly of material relating to Buckingham in which the Lucan epigraph stands as the last word. The Lucan tag is also found in Bodleian MS. Malone 23, p. 210.

24. *HMC Earl Cowper*, II, pp. 65–6, letter to Sir John Coke, 1634.

25. Alan R. Bradford, 'Stuart Absolutism and the "Utility" of Tacitus', *Huntington Library Quarterly*, 46 (1983) pp. 127–55 (139).

26. [Edmund Bolton], *Nero Caesar, or Monarchie Depraved* 2nd edn. (London, 1627) sig. A3v.

27. Ibid., 1624 edition, pp. 8ff, 233ff, 65, 193ff, 240ff.

28. Ibid., pp. 236, 241.

29. James Craigie (ed.), *The Poems of James VI of Scotland*, I (Edinburgh and London: Scottish Text Society, 1955), pp. 61–3. The poem was published in 1584. Caesar's speech had attracted much commentary, e.g. by the influential rhetorician Rudolphus Agricola in *De Inuentione Dialectica* (Louvain, 1515) sigs. Cvir-v.

30. Anon., *The Tragedy of Nero* (London, 1633) sigs. C4v, B4r. For this and other Roman plays – including May's *Tragedy of Julia Agrippina* – see Martin Butler, 'Romans in Britain: *The Roman Actor* and the Early Stuart Classical Play' in Douglas Howard (ed.), *Philip Massinger: A Critical Reassessment* (Cambridge, 1985) pp. 139–70.

31. Thucydides, *The Peloponnesian War: The Complete Hobbes Translation*, ed. David Grene (Chicago and London, 1989) pp. 572–3. Hobbes received help from Ben Jonson, who contributed commendatory verses to May's translation in 1627.

32. Thomas May, *Lucans Pharsalia: or The Ciuill Warres of Rome* (London, 1627) sigs. a3r-v.

33. PRO SPD 16/68/74, calendared under June 1627. Samuel Rawson Gardiner, *England under the Duke of Buckingham and Charles I*, 2 vols (London, 1875) II, pp. 130–1, links the lines with the Rhé campaign; R. Malcolm Smuts, *Court Culture and the Origins of a Royalist Tradition in Early Stuart England* (Philadelphia, 1987) p. 250, stresses the poem's links with the Caroline cult of peace and takes it to be referring to `an uneventful expedition'. Buckingham is known to have staged a masque for the king in his own and his fleet's defence on 15 May 1627, and the speech perhaps had some relation with that masque; further research may perhaps help to unravel the complexities of May's allegiances at this time.

34. It was to a history of the battle of Nieuwpoort that the Tacitean scholar Isaac Dorislaus devoted his scholarly labours after the collapse of his Cambridge history lectures: P. Alessandra Maccioni and Marco Mostert, 'Isaac Dorislaus (1595–1649): The Career of a Dutch Scholar in England', *Transactions of the Cambridge Bibliographical Society*, 8 (1981–84) pp. 419–70 (432).

35. For the peers' resistance see Richard Cust, *The Forced Loan and English Politics 1626–1628* (Oxford, 1987) pp. 102ff, 170–5, 229ff.

36. Roger Lockyer, *Buckingham: The Life and Political Career of George Villiers, First Duke of Buckingham, 1592–1628* (London and New York, 1981) p. 304.

37. The pamphlet, which was circulated in manuscript, anticipated central themes of the Parliamentarian literature of 1640–2 (Cust, *The Forced Loan*, p. 174).

38. May, *Lucans Pharsalia*, facing frontispiece.

39. The engraving was by Frederick van Hulsen, whose other work was devoted to anti-Catholic and anti-Arminian works by George Carleton, Daniel Featley, Christopher Lever and Michael Sparke: Margery Corbett and Michael Norton (eds), *Engraving in England in the Sixteenth and Seventeenth Centuries, Part III: The Reign of Charles I* (Cambridge, 1964) pp. 213–5.

40. May, *Lucans Pharsalia*, sig. T7v.

41. That is the suggestion made by F.B. Williams, *Index of Dedications and Commendatory Verses in English Books Before 1641* (London, 1962) p. 241. In the copies I have been able to examine, the dedications to Mulgrave, Essex and Lindsey are those most frequently excised; a full bibliographical study is called for. I am grateful to D.F. McKenzie and Katherine Pantzer for help on this matter.

42. Maccioni and Mostert, 'Isaac Dorislaus', p. 425. See also Kevin Sharpe, "The Foundation of the Chairs of History at Oxford and Cambridge: An Episode in Jacobean Politics' in *Politics and Ideas in Early Stuart England: Essays and Studies* (London and New York, 1989) pp. 207–30 (221–2).

43. Thomas May, *A History of the Parliament of England: which began November the Third, MDCXL* (London, 1647) I, p. 7.

44. Thomas May, *A Continuation of Lucans Historicall Poem until the Death of Ivlivs Caesar* (London, 1630) sig. H6r.

45. Ibid., sig. J5r.

46. Ibid., sig. H6v. Howard Erskine-Hill, *The Augustan Idea in English Literature*, pp. 184–5, notes the Augustan tone of the *Continuation*.

47. Smuts, *Court Culture*, p. 272.

48. Thomas May, *History of the Parliament of England*, I, p. 12.

49. Ibid., I, p. 21.

50. Ibid., I. p. 19.

51. Ibid., I, pp. 14, 18.

52. BL Add. MSS 25, 303, fol. 186v, cited by Chester, *Thomas May* p. 56.

53. Ibid., I, p. 27.

54. R.T. Bruère, 'The Latin and English Versions of Thomas May's *Supplementum Lucani*', *Classical Philology*, 44 (1949) pp. 145–63.

55. Thomas May, *Supplementum Lucani* (Leiden, 1640) sigs. *3r-4r, *5r-v, *6ff. May signed himself 'Subditus & Servus humillimus'. Fanshawe had been educated by Thomas Farnaby, who had published a Latin edition of Lucan in 1618.

56. Cowley, *The Civil War*, in Thomas O. Calhoun, Lawrence Heyworth and Allan Pritchard (eds), *The Collected Works of Abraham Cowley* (Newark, 1989), I, pp. 377ff.

57. Ibid., I, p. 29.

58. May, *History of the Parliament*, I, p. 20.

59. On the Tacitist element in May I am indebted to an unpublished lecture by Professor J.G.A. Pocock.

60. [Thomas May], *A Discourse Concerning the Success of Former Parliaments* (London, 1642) pp. 2–3; cf. Harold Laski (ed.), *A Defence of Liberty Against Tyrants* (London, 1924) pp. 136–7.

61. Ibid., I, p. 12.

62. May did not, however, reject masques altogether, suggesting that Charles's masques would not have provoked such hostility had they not been performed on the Sabbath (*History of the Parliament*, I, p. 24).

63. Ibid., III, p. 47.

64. [Thomas May], *A Breviary of the History of the Parliament of England* (London, 1650) p. 215.

65. The brilliant description of the devastated landscape of monarchical peace in Italy (*Discourses concerning Government*, II, p. 26) seems to me to echo Lucan's portrayal of imperial Italy, *Pharsalia*, I, pp. 24ff).

66. Chester, *Thomas May* p. 74 (Gorges's funeral monument had also presented him as reviving Lucan's spirit); Nedham translated the phrase in *Mercurius Politicus*, 13–20 November 1651, p. 1206.

3.   BEN JONSON AMONG THE HISTORIANS   *Blair Worden*

1. C.H. Herford, P. Simpson and E. Simpson (eds), *Ben Jonson*, 11 vols (Oxford, 1925–52, hereafter *Jonson*), I, pp. 38–9, 140, 193–200; II, pp. 37–8. (Jonson appears not to have written the offending passage of *Eastward Ho!*, and seems to have given himself up to the authorities in solidarity with his fellow authors.)

2. Hope Mirrlees, *A Fly in Amber* (London: Faber, 1962) p. 48; Kevin Sharpe, *Sir Robert Cotton 1586–1631* (Oxford, 1979) pp. 199–207; British Library, Cottonian MS. Julius C. III, fo. 199.

3. Mirrlees, *Fly in Amber*, p. 20.

4. *H&S*, VII, p. 92; x, p. 390.

5. Hugh Trevor-Roper, 'Queen Elizabeth's First Historian: William Camden', in his *Renaissance Essays* (London, 1985) pp. 145–6.

6. Thomas Fuller, *The Worthies of England*, ed. John Freeman (London, 1952) p. 500.

7. William Camden, *Remaines concerning Britain* (London, 1614) p. 8.

8. Trevor-Roper, *Renaissance Essays*, p. 138; D.R. Woolf, *The Idea of History in Early Stuart England* (Toronto, 1990) p. 262.

9. Joseph A. Bryant, jr., 'The Significance of Ben Jonson's First Requirement for Tragedy: "Truth of Argument"', *Studies in Philology*, 49 (1952) 204.

10. G. Giovanni, 'Historical Realism and the Tragic Emotions in Renaissance Criticism', *Philological Quarterly*, 32 (1953); Joseph A. Bryant, jr., 'Catiline and the Nature of Jonson's Tragic Fable', *Proceedings of the Modern Language Association*, 69 (1954); Bryant, 'Significance of Ben Jonson's First Requirement'; Jonas A. Barish (ed.), *Ben Jonson: Sejanus* (New Haven, 1965) p. 3.

11. Ben Jonson, *Sejanus his Fall*, ed. Philip Ayres (Manchester, 1990) p. 9.

12. *Jonson*, IV, p. 324.

13. *Journal of the House of Commons*, I, 148; quoted by Howard Erskine-Hill, *The Augustan Idea in English Literature* (London, 1983) p. 130.

14. *Jonson*, I, pp. 138, 162.

15. Ibid., VIII, p. 207 (*Underwood*, 43), XI, pp. 78–9. It looks as if the work, like Camden's (and Tacitus's) *Annals*, was (i) written in Latin and (ii) organised on the regnal principle.

16. Ibid., VIII, p. 31 (*Epigrams*, 14).

17. Ibid., IV, pp. 4–5, 31.

18. Ibid., III, p. 301.

19. Ibid., I, p. 143.

20. Ibid., I, p. 260.

21. John Selden, *Titles of Honour* (London, 1614), ep. ded.; J.M. Hebel (ed.), *The Works of Michael Drayton*, 5 vols (Oxford, 1961) iv, p. 160.

22. *Jonson*, VII, pp. 83, 177, 250; x, pp. 453, 487.

23. Ibid., I, pp. 139–40; VIII, p. 41 (*Epigrams*, 45).

24. Ibid., I, p. 48.

25. Sharpe, *Sir Robert Cotton*, p. 206n.

26. *Jonson*, XI, p. 57.

27. Ibid., VIII, p. 53 (*Epigrams*, 79).

28. Ibid., IV, p. 292 (*Poetaster*, v. i. 94).

29. Ibid., VIII, p. 597.

30. Ibid., VIII, pp. 158–61 (*Underwood*, 14).

31. William Camden, *Britannia*, trans. Philemon Holland (London, 1610) p. [iii].

32. Richard Peterson, *Imitation and Praise in the Poems of Ben Jonson* (New Haven, 1981) pp. 56, 61.

33. Camden, *Britannia*, pp. [iii], 634.

34. William Camden, *The History of... Princess Elizabeth*, ed. Wallace T. MacCaffrey (Chicago, 1970) p. 7; cf. Tacitus, *Annals*, III, 65.

35. *Jonson*, VIII, p. 70 (*Epigrams*, 109; cf. VIII, p. 262, *Underwood*, 78).

36. John Selden, *Titles of Honour* (London, 1614) pp. 38–41.

37. *Jonson*, XI, p. 595.

38. Ibid., VIII, p. 282; Selden, *Titles of Honour*, preface.

39. Camden, *Britannia*, pp. 169, 190.

40. Ibid., pp. 38, 444.

41. Thomas Smith (ed.), *V.Cl. Gulielmi Camdeni... Epistolae* (London, 1691: hereafter Smith, *Camden*), 'Annales', 15 March 1604.

42. Camden, *Remaines*, p. 154.

43. Camden, *Britannia*, pp. 76, 167.

44. *Jonson*, V, p. 95 (*Volpone*, IV. ii. 29–30), 321 (*Alchemist*, II. ii. 86–7), IX, p. 723; cf VIII, p. 42 (*Epigrams*, 46).

45. Camden, *Britannia*, p. 176.

46. Smith, *Camden*, p. 188.

47. Ibid., p. 247.

48. Camden, *Remaines*, p. 56; repeated in Selden, *Titles of Honour*, p. 123.

49. Selden, *Titles of Honour*, pp. 61–2, 67.

50. Ibid., pp. 9, 12, 46–7, 148.

51. *Jonson*, VIII, p. 31 (*Epigrams*, 14), p. 175 (*Underwood*, 24), p. 591.

52. Ibid., VIII, pp. 61–2 (*Epigrams*, 95).

53. The work is edited, together with a supplement which Hayward did not publish, by John J. Manning: *The First and Second Parts of John Hayward's The Life and Raigne of King Henry IIII*. (London: Royal Historical Society, Camden 4th ser., 49, 1991).

54. S.L. Goldberg, 'Sir John Hayward, "Politic" Historian', *Review of English Studies*, new ser., 6 (1955); F.J. Levy, 'Hayward, Daniel and the Beginnings of Politic History', *Huntington Library Quarterly*, 50 (1987); David Womersley, 'Sir John Hayward's Tacitism', *Renaissance Studies*, 6 (1992).

55. Edwin B. Benjamin, 'Sir John Hayward and Tacitus', *Review of English Studies*, new ser., 8 (1957), pp. 275–6; Womersley, 'Sir John Hayward's Tacitism'.

56. Woolf, *Idea of History*, p. 160.

57. Camden, *Britannia*, pp. 369–71, 577.

58. *Jonson*, VII, pp. 51–62. Anne Barton, in *Ben Jonson, Dramatist* (Cambridge, 1984) pp. 338–40, prefers a later dating of *Mortimer his Fall*.

59. J. Max Patrick (ed.), *Style, Rhetoric and Rhythm* (Princeton, 1966) p. 152.

60. The seminal works on this subject (even though their findings have been modified by subsequent studies) are George Williamson, *The Senecan Amble* (London: Faber, 1951), and the material by Morris Croll in Patrick (ed.), *Style, Rhetoric and Rhythm*.

61. Camden, *History* (ed. MacCaffrey) pp. 13, 213, 330; William Camden, *The History of the... Princesse Elizabeth... Composed by way of Annals*, trans. R. Norton (London, 1630: hereafter *Annals*), pt. ii, p. 80; Trevor-Roper, 'Queen Elizabeth's First Historian', pp. 142–3. (Camden and his friends drew on medieval and English traditions of typology as well as on Roman models.)

62. Pauline Croft, 'The Reputation of Robert Cecil', *Transactions of the Royal Historical Society*, 6th ser., 1, 55–6.

63. *Jonson*, I, p. 33.

64. Laurence Michel (ed.), *The Tragedy of Philotas by Samuel Daniel* (New Haven, 1949) p. 61; Camden, *Annals*, pt. iv, pp. 180, 183; *Times Literary Supplement*, 10 May 1928, p. 85.

65. Compare James Spedding *et al.* (eds), *The Works of Francis Bacon*, 14 vols (London, 1857–74), IX, p. 248, with Tacitus, *Annals*, IV. 2.

66. Camden, *Annals*, pt. iv, p. 189.

67. Benjamin, 'Sir John Hayward and Tacitus', p. 276.

68. For the mentality of Essex's party see Mervyn James, *Society, Politics and Culture* (Cambridge, 1986) ch. 9.

69. Manning, *Hayward*, p. 202; Tacitus, *Annals*, IV. 35.

70. *Jonson*, IV, p. 408 (*Sejanus*, III. 473–4), IX, p. 615.

71. Ibid., IV, p. 299 (*Poetaster*, V. iii. 65).

72. Ibid., I, p. 141.

73. Manning, *Hayward*, pp. 28–9, 31–2.

74. *Jonson*, IV, p. 205 (*Poetaster*, Prologue).

75. Ibid., IV, p. 350 (*Sejanus*, 'To the Readers').

76. The preoccupation of Jonson's contemporaries with that subject is discussed vividly by Lacey Baldwin Smith, *Treason in Tudor England. Politics and Paranoia* (London, 1986), and briefly by me in 'Shakespeare's Politics' in Stanley Wells (ed.), *Shakespeare Survey 44* (Cambridge, 1991), xi, 14–15.

77. *Jonson*, IV, pp. 382, 390, 401–2 (*Sejanus*, II. 216ff., 444–9, III. 273–85).

78. Ibid., XI, p. 21.

79. Ibid., VIII, p. 65 (*Epigrams*, 101).

80. David Norbrook, *Poetry and Politics in the English Renaissance* (London, 1984) p. 187.

81. Camden, *Remaines*, p. 49.

82. *Jonson*, VIII, p. 99 (The Forest, 2).

83. Camden, *Britannia*, 'Ireland', p. 118.

84. *Jonson*, VIII, p. 600.

85. Camden, *Remaines*, p. 173.

86. *Jonson*, VIII, p. 594.

87. Ibid., I, pp. 33, 181.

88. Ayres (ed.), *Sejanus his Fall*, pp. 9, 41.

89. Rebecca W. Bushnell, *Tragedies of Tyrants* (Ithaca, 1990) p. 1.

90. Woolf, *Idea of History*, pp. 110, 292.

91. Alan T. Bradford, 'Stuart Absolutism and the "Utility" of Tacitus', *Huntington Library Quarterly*, 46 (1983) p. 131.

92. Daniel Boughner, 'Jonson's use of Lipsius in *Sejanus*', *Modern Language Notes*, 73 (1958) 248.

93. *Jonson*, VIII, p. 37 (*Epigrams*, 35).

94. Ibid., V, p. 446 (*Catiline*, I. 347).

95. Camden, *Britannia*, p. 578; *Cottoni Posthuma* (London, 1651) p. 351.

96. Camden, *Remaines*, p. 155; Selden, *Titles of Honour*, p. 125.

97. *Jonson*, VIII, pp. 177, 180 (*Underwood*, 25).

98. Ibid., IV, p. 424 (*Sejanus*, IV. 165–6).

99. Camden, *Annals*, pt. iv, p. 127.

100. Ibid., pt. iv, p. 222; *Jonson*, IV, p. 436 (*Sejanus*, IV. 520). The phrase 'the rising sun' had long been current to describe Elizabeth's likely heir: first Mary Queen of Scots, then James I.

101. Smith, *Camden*, pp. 347–8.

102. Camden, *Annals*, pt. iv, p. 105.

103. Ibid., pt iv, pp. 139, 178.

104. *Jonson*, VIII, pp. 40, 47–8 (*Epigrams*, 43, 63–5); Ian Donaldson (ed.), *Ben Jonson. Poems* (Oxford, 1975) p. 35n.

105. *Jonson*, VII, p. 156.

106. *Harleian Miscellany*, 8 vols (London, 1744–6) III, p. 510.

107. *Jonson*, IV, pp. 398, 423 (*Sejanus*, III, 168–71. IV. 140–1), VII, pp. 102–3.

108. For the possibility that the new king was expected to favour the

study of Tacitus, see Kenneth C. Schellhase, *Tacitus in Renaissance Political Thought* (Chicago, 1976) p. 159.

109. *Jonson*, VII, pp. 98, 100, 102, 108 (cf. VII, pp. 126–7).

110. Erskine-Hill, *Augustan Idea*, pp. 99, 103.

111. *Jonson*, IV, pp. 210, 220, 224, 225, 227, 235, 262–5, 281, 284–5, 288, 301. (*Poetaster*, I. ii. 47; II. i. 4, 9, 127–155, II. ii. 27; III. i. 51; IV. i. 3–11; IV. ii. 2–13, 56, IV. vi. 56; IV. vii. 38, 45; IV. viii. 1ff.; IV. ix. 69, V. iii. 132.)

112. Ibid., IV, 355, 356, 361, 362, 383, 393, 423, 430, 434, 446, 455–6 (*Sejanus*, I, 13–14, 47–50, 178–90, 220–3; II, 262–3; III, 16–17; IV, 138–9, 359–61, 457–9; V, 256–8, 490–7).

113. Ibid., VIII, 579 (cf. VIII, 582).

114. Sir William Monson and Heywood Townshend, *Megalopsychy* (London, 1682) p. 178.

115. J.E. Neale, *Elizabeth I and her Parliaments*, 2 vols (London, 1956 edn) ii, pp. 241–5, 257–8, 269, 278–9, 370–1. For Morice (who was protesting against ecclesiastical grievances) see also Jennifer Loach, *Parliament under the Tudors* (Oxford, 1991) pp. 107–8.

116. Manning, *Hayward*, p. 113; Henry Savile, *The Ende of Nero and the Beginning of Galba* (London, 1604 edn) p. 184. Cf. *Jonson*, IV, 358 (*Sejanus*, I. 87–9).

117. Sharpe, *Sir Robert Cotton*, pp. 29–30.

118. Ibid., pp. 36, 82–3.

119. *Jonson*, V, 447 (*Catiline*, I. 392–3). (Sallust's *Catiline War*, XX, 12, says that the nobility pulled down new houses.)

120. Camden, *Annals*, pt. ii, pp. 51, 69; Selden, *Titles of Honour*, p. 61.

121. *Jonson*, VIII, pp. 93, 95 (*The Forest*, 2).

122. Camden, *Annals*, pt. ii, p. 69.

123. Camden, *Remaines*, pp. 230–7.

124. *Jonson*, VIII, p. 564, XI, p. 214; Camden, *Britannia*, p. [iii].

125. *Jonson*, VIII, p. 593.

126. For Arundel see Kevin Sharpe, 'The Earl of Arundel, his Circle, and the Opposition to the Duke of Buckingham, 1618–1628' in Sharpe (ed.), *Faction and Parliament* (Oxford, 1978); Sharpe, *Sir Robert Cotton*, pp. 208ff.; Barton, *Ben Jonson*, pp. 303–4; Camden, *Britannia*, p. 310.

127. *Jonson*, IV, pp. 93, 132 (*Cynthia's Revels*, III. iv. 107; V. i. 37), 427 (*Sejanus*, III. 278–9); V, p. 484 (*Catiline*, III, 480); viii, p. 116 (*The Forest*, 13).

128. Camden, *Annals*, pt. iv, p. 187.

129. E. Sawyer (ed.), *Memorials... from the Original Papers of Sir Ralph Winwood*, 3 vols (London, 1725) II, pp. 198, 216.

130. Barish (ed.), *Ben Jonson: Sejanus*, pp. 11–15.

131. *Jonson*, VIII, p. 66 (*Epigrams*, 102); Peterson, *Imitation and Praise*, p. 60.

132. Camden, *Annals*, pt. iv, p. 128 (cf. p. 172).

133. *Jonson*, I, p. 151.

134. Justus Lipsius, *Six Bookes of Politickes*, trans. William Jones (London, 1594) p. 2.

135. Blair Worden, 'Constancy', *London Review of Books*, 3 February 1983.

136. *Jonson*, IV, p. 428 (*Sejanus*, IV. 294–6).

137. Ibid., IV, p. 404 (*Sejanus*, III. 359–65).

138. Ibid., IV, pp. 384, 408 (*Sejanus*, II. 299, III. 462).

139. Ibid., IV, pp. 219–20, 228 (*Poetaster*, I. iii. 60–78; II. ii. 53–63), 402 (*Sejanus*, III. 286).

4. BEN JONSON AND THE LIMITS OF COURTLY PANEGYRIC
Martin Butler

A version of this essay was read at a colloquium on Ben Jonson at the Woodrow Wilson Center, Washington DC, in 1991, and I am grateful to the participants for the comments I received on that occasion. I am also especially indebted to Ted Leinwand and David Lindley for their detailed responses to an earlier version of this piece.

1. The most substantial recent discussion along these lines is Malcolm Smuts' *Court Culture and the Origins of a Royalist Tradition in Early Stuart England* (Philadelphia, 1987).

2. C.H. Herford, P. Simpson and E. Simpson (eds), *Ben Jonson*, 11 vols (Oxford, 1925–52) VIII, p. 209. All quotations from Jonson refer to this edition.

3. On this topic, see O.B. Hardison, jr., *The Enduring Monument* (Chapel Hill, 1964); and E.W. Talbert, 'The Interpretation of Jonson's Courtly Spectacles', *Proceedings of the Modern Language Association*, 61 (1946) 454–73.

4. K. Sharpe, *Criticism and Compliment: The Politics of Literature in the England of Charles I* (Cambridge, 1987). I have responded to this book in a review essay, 'Early Stuart Court Culture: Compliment or Criticism?'. *Historical Journal*, 32 (1989) 425–35; and at greater length in 'Reform or Reverence? The Politics of the Caroline Masque' in R. Mulryne and M. Shewring (eds), *Theatre and Government under the Early Stuarts* (forthcoming, Cambridge University Press).

5. The best account of Jonson's career is David Riggs's *Ben Jonson: A Life* (Cambridge, Mass., 1989).

6. Herford *et al.* (eds), *Jonson*, I, p. 141.

7. 'An Epistle to Master John Selden', ll. 19–22 (*Jonson*, VIII, p. 159).

8. *Jonson*, VIII, pp. 217, 384. Compare also the astonishingly sweeping disclaimer in the 1616 preface to *The Epigrams*: 'Amongst whom, if I have praysed, vnfortunately, any one, that doth not deserue; or, if all answere not, in all numbers, the pictures I have made of them: I hope it will be forgiven me, that they are no ill pieces, *though they be not like the persons'* (*Jonson*, VIII, p. 26, my emphasis).

9. 'An Expostulation with Inigo Jones', *Jonson*, VIII, pp. 403–4.

10. Jonson's problems with Prince Henry are brilliantly explicated by John Peacock in 'Jonson and Jones collaborate in *Prince Henry's Barriers*', *Word and Image*, 3 (1987) pp. 172–94.

11. N.E. McClure (ed.), *The Letters of John Chamberlain*, 2 vols (Philadelphia, 1939), I, p. 561.

12. See D.B.J. Randall, *Jonson's Gypsies Unmask'd* (Durham, NC, 1975). For a rather different review, see M. Butler, '"We are One Mans All": Jonson's *The Gipsies Metamorphosed*', *Yearbook of English Studies*, 21 (1991), pp. 253–73.

13. Chamberlain, *Letters*, II, p. 333; and see M. Butler, 'Ben Jonson's *Pan's Anniversary* and the Politics of Early Stuart Pastoral', *English Literary Renaissance* 22, (1992) pp. 369–404.

14. Chamberlain, *Letters*, II, p. 473.

15. *Jonson*, X, pp. 658–9.

16. S.R. Gardiner, *History of England... 1603–42* 10 vols (London, 1883–4), II, p. 108.

17. The only dancers whose names we definitely know are John Livingstone (a groom of the bedchamber), Abraham Abercromby, and Sir Henry Bowyer (son of an Exchequer official). See note 20 below.

18. Chamberlain, *Letters*, I, p. 325.

19. See Gardiner, *History*, II, pp. 134–65; and R. Strong, 'England and Italy: The Marriage of Henry Prince of Wales' in R. Ollard and P. Tudor-Craig (eds), *For Veronica Wedgwood These* (London, 1986) pp. 59–87.

20. Unfortunately Chamberlain's eye-witness account survives only as a fragment: '... 200 li geven and equally distributed among ... gallants chosen out of the Kings and Princes men to ... of masque on Twelfth Night. They were most ... Scotts as Leviston, Abercrummit, and I know not ... n else saving Sir W. Bowiers son and two ... When they came to take out Ladies, beginning ... of Essex and Cranbourn, they were refused ... example of the rest, so that they were fain ... alone and make court one to another, whe ... was exceedingly displeased and spake low ... pacified with a borrowed excuse: though at ... saide he repented that he had not intreated ... and his daughter to daunce and grace the ... ' (*Letters*, I, p. 328). Jonson describes the masque as performed by 'Gentlemen the KINGS *Seruants*', but Chamberlain makes it clear that the dancers came from both the King's and Prince's gentlemen, and in the Revels accounts it is described as 'The Princes Mask' (*Jonson*, X, p. 531).

21. *Calendar of State Papers, Venetian* [hereafter *CSPV*], *1610–1613*, pp. 264–5.

22. *CSPV 1610–1613*, pp. 328, 300–1.

23. In J. Orrell, 'The London Stage in the Florentine correspondence 1604–1618', *Theatre Research International*, 3 (1977–8) pp. 173–4.

24. *CSPV 1615–1617*, pp. 61–2, 79.

25. *CSPV 1615–1617*, pp. 53, 57.

26. *Jonson*, X, p. 547. The circumstances of this masque are discussed in full detail in a forthcoming essay by Martin Butler and David Lindley.

27. See, for example, P[ublic], R[ecord], O[ffice], SP 14/82/72, 14/82/80, 14/83/35. (I am grateful to David Lindley for these references.)
28. For example, Jonson's epigram to Somerset (*Jonson* VIII, p. 384).
29. C.H. Mcllwain (ed.), *The Political Works of James I* (Cambridge, Mass., 1918) p. 320.
30. *CSPV 1617–1619*, p. 87.
31. PRO SP 14/94/52, 55, 57, 73; 14/95/12.
32. M. Prestwich, *Cranfield* (Oxford, 1966) p. 179.
33. PRO SP 14/94/52.
34. *CSPV 1617–1619*, pp. 113–4.
35. *Jonson*, X, pp. 576–7.
36. *Jonson*, VIII, p. 200.
37. *Jonson*, VIII, p. 220.

5. THE KING'S WRIT: ROYAL AUTHORS AND ROYAL AUTHORITY IN EARLY MODERN ENGLAND   *Kevin Sharpe*

1. M. Foucault, *Power/Knowledge*, ed. C. Gordon (New York, 1980); D. Macdonnell, *Theories of Discourse* (Oxford,1986); G. Kress and R. Hodge, *Language as Ideology* (London, 1979) especially ch. 4; J.G.A. Pocock, *Politics, Language and Time* (London, 1972); S. Greenblatt (ed.), *The Forms of Power and the Power of Forms in the Renaissance* (Norman, Oklahoma, 1982).
2. On the increasing importance of the word, E. Eisenstein, *The Printing Press as an Agent of Change* (Cambridge, 1980); cf D. Katz, 'The Language of Adam in Seventeenth Century England' in H. Lloyd-Jones, V. Pearl and B. Worden (eds), *History and Imagination* (1980) pp.132–46.
3. *Richard II*, Act 1, Scene III, ll. 213–15.
4. Ibid., Act IV, Scene I. Cf *Henry V* Act I, Scene I, ll.36 ff. for a comparison of Henry's discourse with his authority.
5. S.W. Hull, *Chaste, Silent and Obedient: English Books for Women 1475–1640* (San Marino, 1982); A. Fraser, *Weaker Vessel: Woman's Lot in Seventeenth Century England* (London, 1984).
6. Machiavelli, *The Prince*, ed. Q. Skinner (Cambridge, 1988) pp. 61–3; *Richard III*, Act III, Scene VII, ll. 141–74.
7. Cf. M. Walzer, *The Revolution of the Saints* (Cambridge, Mass., 1965).
8. The epistle dedicatory is politically explicit, speaking of the need to tread between 'popish persons and self-conceited brethren who run their own ways'.
9. Elizabeth I, *A Godly Medytary on the Christian Soule* (1548) ff. 15–17, 19–19v. 21v, 22v, 24, 25v, 26v–27, and *passim*; *idem*, *The Mirror of the Sinful Soul* (1897) pp. 12, 15, 23–5, 31, 43, 63. *Christian Prayers and Meditations* (1569) sigs cii, ki; BL. MS facs 218; W.P. Haugaard, 'Elizabeth Tudor's

Book of Devotions: A Neglected Clue to the Queen's Life and Character', *The Sixteenth Century Journal*, 12 (1981) pp. 79–105, 83.

10. *The Queenes Prayers* (1571), sig. D3v; cf. sig. C4v.

11. Ibid., sig. B.

12. *Christian Prayers and Meditations* (1569) sigs Fiii, Kiii, Niv, piiv–iii. This compilation, known as 'Queen Elizabeth's prayerbook' (see sigs Kiiii, piiv), is published with the queen's arms at the front and back and a frontispiece woodcut of Elizabeth at prayer. It underlines the ambiguity of 'authoring' and 'authorizing' in sixteenth century usage. I shall explore this in a fuller study of royal texts.

13. *Precationes Private Regiae* (1563).

14. Haugaard makes too little of this, 'Elizabeth Tudor's Book of Devotions', pp. 80–1.

15. BL MS facs 218 f 34v. The 1569 *Christian Prayers* contains a section of 'Certain Sentences taken out of Promises, Admonitions and Counsels to good kings...'

16. *Christian Prayers*, sig. Ee iiv.

17. Haugaard, 'Elizabeth's Devotions', p. 92; *Christian Prayers*, sigs Gg i–ii; Elizabeth uses the familiar 'tu' when discoursing with God.

18. *The Argument Against Transubstantiation with Queen Elizabeth's Opinion Concerning the Erroneous Doctrine* (1735) p. 30. Haugaard refers to the queen's 'priestly function', p. 103.

19. The prayers begin the process of constructing Elizabeth and her people as God's chosen. *Christian Prayers*, sigs Kiiii, Kkiv, Ggi. See *Queen Elizabeth's Opinion Concerning Transubstantiation* (1688).

20. C. Pemberton (ed.), *Queen Elizabeth's Englishings* (1899), introduction, esp. pp. viii–xiii, 140, 149. *De Curiositate* is in Elizabeth's own hand.

21. PRO SP Elizabeth 289; Pemberton, *Queen Elizabeth's Englishings*, pp. 101, 141, 149.

22. Pemberton finds it hard to explain how a busy queen found time for these translations (p. xii). See A Somerset, *Elizabeth I* (1991) p. 12.

23. Pemberton *Queen Elizabeth's Englishings*, pp. 18, 53.

24. Ibid., p. 32.

25. Ibid., pp. 66.

26. Ibid., p. 79, 104.

27. Ibid., p. 20.

28. K. Sharpe, *Politics and Ideas in Early Stuart England* (London, 1989), pp. 28–31.

29. Pemberton, *Queen Elizabeth's Englishings*, p. 44; cf p. 96.

30. Ibid., pp. 107, 120.

31. Ibid., p. 102.

32. Ibid., pp. 136, 140–1. Elizabeth read Cicero's *De Officiis* in prison at Woodstock: Haugaard, 'Elizabeth Tudor's *Book of Devotions*', p. 88.

33. See A. Kernan, *The Cankered Muse* (New Haven, 1959).

34. Pemberton *Queen Elizabeth's Englishings*, p. 137.

35. *Encyclopaedia Britannica* (1973) XVIII, p. 70.

36. Horace, *On The Art of Poetry*, in T.S. Dorsch, *Classical Literary Criticism* (Harmondsworth, 1965) pp. 90–1.

37. Pemberton, *Queen Elizabeth's Englishings*, p. 143.

38. Ibid., p. 146.

39. Ibid., pp. 144–5.

40. J. Nichols, *The Progresses and Public Processions of Queen Elizabeth* 3 vols (1823) II, p. 627.

41. Ibid., I, p. 177.

42. T.A. Birrell, *English Monarchs and Their Books* (London, 1986) p. 30.

43. H.R. Trevor-Roper, *Queen Elizabeth's First Historian* (1971); W. Notestein, F. Relf and H. Simpson, *Commons Debates 1621*, 7 vols (New Haven, 1935) IV, p. 71.

44. J.O. Halliwell (ed.), *Letters of the Kings of England* 2 vols (1848) II, pp. 146–7.

45. C.H. McIlwain (ed.), *The Political Works of James I* (Cambridge, Mass., 1918) p. 169.

46. Ibid., p. 65.

47. J. Craigie (ed.), *The Basilikon Doron of King James VI*, 2 vols (Scottish Text Soc., Edinburgh, 1844), I, p. 184.

48. *The Workes of the Most High and Mighty Prince James* (1616) preface.

49. Ibid., p. 19.

50. Ibid., p. 11.

51. Ibid., p. 65.

52. Ibid., p. 81.

53. Ibid., p. 82.

54. Ibid., p. 87.

55. Ibid., p. 83.

56. Ibid., p. 86.

57. James I, *A Meditation Upon the … XXVII Chapter of St Matthew* (1620) pp. 12, 35–6, and *passim*. Cf K. Sharpe, 'Private Conscience and Public Duty in the Writings of King James VI and I' in J. Morrill, P. Slack and D. Woolf (eds), *Public Duty and Private Conscience in Seventeenth Century England* (Oxford, 1993) pp. 77–100.

58. James I, *A Meditation Upon the Lords Prayer* (1619), p. 18

59. Ibid., pp. 14, 22.

60. Ibid., pp. 116–19.

61. *Workes of Prince James*, p. 361.

62. Ibid., pp. 365, 368, 371–2.

63. J. Craigie (ed.), *The Poems of James VI of Scotland*, 2 vols (Scottish Text Soc. Edinburgh, 1955–8), II, pp. 11, 34.

64. 'The Furies' in Ibid., I, p. 98.

65. Ibid., I, p. 126.

66. Ibid., I , p. 134.

67. Ibid., I, pp. 184, 190.

68. Ibid., I, p. 194.

69. Ibid., I, p. 176.

70. 'The Lepanto of James the Sixth', ibid., I, p. 198.

71. Ibid., I, p. 218.

72. Ibid., II, p. 172.

73. Ibid., II, pp. 179–82.

74. 'King James His Verses Made Upon a Libell...', ibid., II, pp. 182–91.

75. P. Sidney, *An Apology for Poetry*, ed. G. Shepherd (Manchester, 1973) p. 104; James wrote an epitaph on Sidney, *Poems*, II, p. 104. The Scottish tradition of the 'flytinge' may help explain James's decision to contest in verse. I would like to thank Greg Walker for this point.

76. Craigie, *Poems of James VI*, II, p. 68.

77. James VI, *The Essayes of a Prentise in the Divine Art of Poesie*, ed. E. Arber (1869) p. 29.

78. I. Donaldson (ed.), *Ben Jonson Poems* (Oxford, 1985) p. 223.

79. James VI, *Essays of a Prentise*, p. 31.

80. Ibid., pp. 54–6, 63–4.

81. Craigie (ed.), *Basilikon Doron*, I, p. 104.

82. James VI, *Essays of A Prentise*, p. 9.

83. *Workes of Prince James*, dedication to Prince Charles; James I, *Meditation Upon St Matthew*, dedication. J. Goldberg, *James I and the Politics of Literature* (Baltimore and London, 1983) p. 94.

84. *The Works of Charles I* 2 vols (1662) I, pp. 357, 377; K. Sharpe, *The Personal Rule of Charles I* (New Haven and London, 1992) pp. 179–80.

85. Sharpe, *Politics and Ideas*, pp. 47–8.

86. M. Pickel, *Charles I as Patron of Poetry and Drama* (London, 1936) pp. 20–2. I have seen the Aristotle and Shakespeare in the Royal Library.

87. Sharpe, *Personal Rule*, pp. 198–205.

88. Pickel, *Charles I*, pp. 14, 177–8; BL Ms Add 24195.

89. *Works of Charles I*, I, pp. 357, 361, 365.

90. *Bibliotheca Regia* (1659) part II, pp. 355ff.

91. Ibid., p. 385.

92. Ibid., pp. 394–417.

93. J.F. Larkin (ed.), *Stuart Royal Proclamations II: Royal Proclamations of King Charles I 1625–46* (Oxford, 1983) pp. 226–8.

94. Charles I, *A Form of Common Prayer* (1625, 1636).

95. P. Thomas, 'Charles I. The tragedy of Absolutism' in A.G. Dickens (ed.) *The Courts of Europe 1400–1800* (London, 1977) p. 195.

96. Larkin, *Proclamations*, pp. 662–7, 664.

97. [W. Balcanquall], *A Large Declaration* (1639).

98. *Works of Charles I*, II, p. 73.

99. *His Majesty's Answer to a Declaration of Both Houses 5 May 1642* (E148/13) pp. 1–2.

100. *Works of Charles I*, II, p. 134.

101. *A Form of Common Prayer Appointed by His Majesty* (Oxford, 1643) pp. 3, 13–14; *A Collection of Prayers...used in His Majesty's Chapel and His Armies* (1643), pp. 3–4 and *passim*.

102. *His Majesty's Declaraton to Ministers and Freeholders of the County of*

York, 3 June 1643 (E149/27).

103. *His Majesty's Last Speech to ...Privy Council* (E83/44) pp. 4, 7; *A Joyful Message* (E109/1) p. 3.

104. *His Majesty's Speech to the Gentlemen of Yorkshire, 4 August 1642* (E109/26), pp. 1–2.

105. C. Petrie (ed.), *The Letters, Speeches and Proclamations of King Charles I* (London, 1935) p. 166; *Works of Charles I*, I, p. 246.

106. R. Sanderson, *De Juramento...*'Revised and approved under his Majesty's hand' (1655).

107. *Works of Charles I*, I, pp. 430–5, 455.

108. For bibliographical analysis see F.F. Madan, *A New Bibliography of the Eikon Basilike* (Oxford, 1950).

109. *Eikon Basilike* (1876 ed.) pp. 32, 114.

110. Ibid., p. 141.

111. Ibid., pp. 23, 106, 187.

112. Ibid., pp. 10, 88, 157.

113. Ibid., p. 174.

114. W.H. Haller (ed.), *Eikonoklastes*, in *The Works of John Milton*, V (New York, 1932) p. 309. See too *Eikon Basilike* ed. P.A. Knachel (Ithaca N.Y. 1966), introduction.

115. Ibid., pp. 84–9, 125; Cf p. 162.

116. S. Zwicker, *Lines of Authority: Politics and Literary Culture 1649–1689* (Ithaca, 1993). I am grateful to Steve Zwicker for a chance to read this brilliant book in typescript.

117. Hobbes, *Leviathan*, ed. R. Tuck (Cambridge, 1991) pp. xvii, 39.

6.   POLITICS AND PASTORAL: WRITING THE COURT ON THE
     COUNTRYSIDE   *Leah S. Marcus*

1. Svetlana Alpers, *The Art of Describing: Dutch Art in the Seventeenth Century* (Chicago and London, 1984) pp. 119–68.

2. In a recent article, Alastair Fowler has contended that country house poetry needs to be understood as georgic rather than pastoral, 'Country House Poems: The Politics of a Genre', *The Seventeenth Century*, 1 (1986) 1–14. For our purposes here, however, the broader term *pastoral* is more useful, in that it allows us to group together, and recognise connections between, different kinds of Stuart literature supporting an idealised country life.

3. For two recent interpretations of the political significance of seventeenth-century Spenserianism, see Richard Helgerson, 'The Land Speaks: Cartography, Chorography, and Subversion in Renaissance England' in Stephen Greenblatt (ed.), *Representing the English Renaissance* (Berkeley and London, 1988); and David Norbrook, *Poetry and Politics in the English Renaissance* (London, Boston, and Melbourne, 1984) ch. 8.

4. Stephen Orgel, *The Illusion of Power* (Berkeley, 1975) pp. 49–50.

5. Here and throughout, Jonson's masques are cited from Stephen Orgel (ed.), *Ben Jonson: The Complete Masques* (New Haven and London, 1969).

6. James Craigie (ed.), *The Poems of James VI of Scotland*, 2 vols (Edinburgh, 1955–8) II, p. 179 (Scottish Text Society, 3rd ser., vol. 26). For a more elaborate interpretation of the poem and masques in praise of the policy, see Leah S. Marcus, 'City Metal and Country Mettle: The Occasion of Ben Jonson's *Golden Age Restored*' in David M. Bergeron (ed.), *Pageantry in the Shakespearean Theater* (Athens, 1985) pp. 26–47; and Marcus, *The Politics of Mirth: Jonson, Herrick, Milton, Marvell, and the Defense of Old Holiday Pastimes* (Chicago and London, 1986) ch. 3.

7. Cited in modernized form from Richard Fanshawe, *Shorter Poems and Translations*, ed. N.W. Bawcutt (Liverpool, 1964) pp. 5–9.

8. Annabel Patterson, *Pastoral and Ideology: Virgil to Valéry* (Berkeley and Los Angeles, 1987) pp. 148–49. Patterson also discusses several other Stuart pastoral poems, among them verses by James I defending Prince Charles and the Duke of Buckingham at the time of their sudden 1623 trip to Spain to woo the Infanta.

9. Cited in modernized form from Thomas Randolph, *Poems*, ed. G. Thorn-Drury (London, 1929) pp. 79–82.

10. See A.L. Rowse's reprint, *The Poems of Shakespeare's Dark Lady: Salve Deus Rex Judaeorum by Emilia Lanier* (New York and London, 1979) pp. 137–43. For discussion of the poem, see Elaine V. Beilin, *Redeeming Eve: Women Writers of the English Renaissance* (Guildford, Surrey and Princeton, 1987) ch. 7.

11. Don Wayne, *Penshurst: The Semiotics of Place and the Poetics of History* (Madison and London, 1984) p. 62.

12. Wayne, *Penshurst*, p. 64. Here and subsequently in the essay, Jonson's poetry is cited in modernised form from C.H. Herford, P. Simpson and E. Simpson (eds), *Ben Jonson*, VIII (Oxford, 1947).

13. Norbrook, *Poetry and Politics*, p. 190. For a more detailed discussion of the poem, see Norbrook's excellent political treatment, pp. 190–4.

14. Cited, in modernised form, from *The Poems of Thomas Carew*, ed. Rhodes Dunlap (Oxford, 1949).

15. See Kevin Sharpe's revision of Dunlap's information in *Criticism and Compliment: The Politics of Literature in the England of Charles I* (Cambridge, 1990) p. 128n.

16. Michael P. Parker, '"To my friend G. N. from Wrest": Carew's Secular Masque' in Claude J. Summers and Ted-Larry Pebworth (eds), *Classic and Cavalier: Essays on Jonson and the Sons of Ben* (London and Pittsburgh, 1982) pp. 171–91.

17. Cited in modernised form from C.H. Wilkinson (ed.), *The Poems of Richard Lovelace* (1930; reprinted Oxford, 1963).

18. For a more detailed reading, see Marcus, *Politics of Mirth*, pp. 240–63.

19. *The King's Majesty's Declaration to His Subjects, concerning Lawful Sports to be Used* (London, 1618) pp. 6–7.

20. J.A.W. Bennett and H.R. Trevor-Roper (eds), *The Poems of Richard Corbet* (Oxford, 1955); see also Corbett's satire against puritan

condemnation of the maypole, pp. 52–6.

21. Herrick's poems are cited in modernised form from L.C. Martin (ed.), *The Poetical Works of Robert Herrick* (1956; reprinted London, 1965).

22. There is a more extensive discussion of the play's political and ecclesiastical resonances in Marcus, *Politics of Mirth*, pp. 158–65; Jonathan F.S. Post has disputed the interpretation in 'Robert Herrick: A Minority Report' in Ann Baynes Coiro (ed.), *Robert Herrick*, special double issue of *George Herbert Journal*, 14, numbers 1–2 (fall 1990, spring 1991): pp. 1–20.

23. Cited by Amy Charles from BL Add MS 22084 in *A Life of George Herbert* (Ithaca, 1977) pp. 228–32.

24. Raymond Williams, *The Country and the City* (London and New York, 1973; Oxford, 1975); see also Peter Stallybrass, '"We Feast in Our Defense": Patrician Carnival in Early Modern England and Robert Herrick's "Hesperides"', *English Literary Renaissance*, 16 (1986) pp. 234–52.

25. Ann Baynes Coiro, *Robert Herrick's 'Hesperides' and the Epigram Book Tradition* (Baltimore and London, 1988).

26. See Marcus, *Politics of Mirth* on Jonson and Milton, pp. 106–39, 169–212; David Norbrook, 'The Reformation of the Masque' in David Lindley (ed.), *The Court Masque* (Manchester and Dover, New Hampshire, 1984) pp. 94–110; Norbrook, *Poetry and Politics*, pp. 215–85; and, for other recent political readings of *Comus*, John Creaser, '"The Present Aid of This Occasion": The Setting of *Comus*', in Lindley (ed.), *The Court Masque*, pp. 94–110; and Cedric Brown, *John Milton's Aristocratic Entertainments* (Cambridge, 1985).

27. Cited from Thomas Dekker, John Ford and William Rowley, *The Witch of Edmonton*, ed. Simon Trussler and Jacqui Russell (London, 1983).

7. CHIVALRY AND POLITICAL CULTURE IN CAROLINE ENGLAND
J.S.A. Adamson

1. I am grateful to Professor Sydney Anglo, Dr Simon Adams, Mr John Kerrigan, Dr John Morrill, Professors Conrad Russell and Malcolm Smuts and Dr Blair Worden for reading and commenting upon drafts of this essay. Earlier versions of this paper were presented at the early modern history seminars at Oxford and Harvard; I am grateful to the conveners and members of those seminars for their comments and suggestions.

2. R.M. Smuts, *Court Culture and the Origins of a Royalist Tradition in Early Stuart England* (Philadelphia, 1987); A.B. Ferguson, *The Chivalric Tradition in Renaissance England* (Washington, 1986) pp. 139–52; Alan Young, *Tudor and Jacobean Tournaments* (1987) pp. 43–73.

3. D.M. Bergeron, *English Civic Pageantry, 1558–1642* (1971) pp. 105–21; idem, 'Charles I's Royal Entries into London', *Guildhall Miscellany* III (1970), pp. 91–7; R. Malcolm Smuts, 'Public Ceremony and Royal Charisma: the English Royal Entry in London, 1485–1642', in A.L. Beier, David Cannadine and James M. Rosenheim (eds), *The First Modern*

Society: Essays in English History in Honour of Lawrence Stone (Cambridge, 1989) pp. 89–93. The rarity of the Caroline formal entry is relative: English monarchs did not, in general, employ the entry as often as their continental counterparts – an observation I owe to Professor Anglo.

4. *The Wasp or the Subject's Precedent*, ed. J.W. Lever (Malone Soc., Oxford, 1976); for the dating see pp. xv–xvi; March 1640 is the *terminus ante*. Except for titles of contemporary publications, spelling has been modernised in all quotations.

5. For a subtle and perceptive introduction to the spectrum of chivalric culture, see Sydney Anglo (ed.), *Chivalry in the Renaissance* (Woodbridge, 1990).

6. Young, *Tudor and Jacobean Tournaments*, pp. 74–122.

7. Ibid., p. 208.

8. [Miguel de Cervantes], *The History of the Valorous and Wittie Knight-Errant, Don-Quixote*, trans. Thomas Shelton (1612).

9. Francis Beaumont, *The Knight of the Burning Pestle*, ed. S.P. Zitner (Manchester, 1984); the play enjoyed a revival during the 1630s and was performed at court by 'Her Majesty's servants' on 28 Feb. 1636 (ibid., p. 43).

10. It should be stressed, however, that this Elizabethan heyday was itself a revival, and that the skills cultivated in the accession-day tilts bore little direct relation to the realities of war.

11. PRO, SP 14/155, fo. 82.

12. PRO, SP 14/155, fo. 31v: Chamberlain to Carlton, 6 Dec. 1623.

13. PRO, SP 14/155, fo. 82.

14. PRO, SP 14/155, fo. 84: list of Giants belonging to the 'Order of the Blue'; undated, but almost certainly part of the series of documents collected by the privy council in December 1623.

15. B.L., Trumbull MS VII/136; VII/140. PRO, SP 14/155, fo. 32. G.E. C[ockayne], *The Complete Peerage*, ed. V. Gibbs (12 vols, 1910–59), '4th Lord Vaux of Harrowden', *s.v.* Vaux had been suspected of complicity in the Gunpowder Treason, and had refused the Oath of Allegiance.

16. PRO, SP 14/155, fo. 82.

17. [John Reynolds], *Vox Coeli or, Newes from Heaven* (1624) pp. 4–55 (*STC* 20946.4). Only the papist Queen Mary takes the Spanish side. Reynolds's authorship of this pamphlet is established in Simon Adams, 'The Protestant Cause: Religious Allegiance with the West European Calvinist Communities as a Political Issue in England, 1585–1630' (D. Phil. dissertation, Oxford, 1973) p. 460.

18. [Reynolds], *Vox Coeli*, sig. B[v].

19. [Thomas Scott], *Robert Earle of Essex his Ghost, Sent from Elizian* (1624) pp. 1–4; *idem, A Post-Script, or, A second Part* (1624) pp. 5–8. The work was largely a compilation drawn from Essex's *Apologie* (Adams, 'The Protestant Cause', p. 458); by 1622 at the latest Scott was in the pay of the exiled King and Queen of Bohemia (ibid., p. 454). 'Elizian' may well be a pun on Eliza[beth] (a suggestion I owe to Professor Conrad Russell).

20. *A Lamentable Dittie Composed upon the Death of Robert Lord Devereux Late Earle of Essex* (1603), *STC* 6791, 6791.5, 6791.7, 6792; reprinted in *The Roxburghe Ballads*, ed. Charles Hindley (2 vols, 1873–4) II, pp. 202–11. During the 1620s, a new ballad commemorating Essex was added to the repertory. Like the Welladay ballad of 1603, this new ballad depicted Essex as a paragon of chivalric virtue. It was reprinted at least twice, in the mid-1620s and again in the mid-1630s. *A Lamentable New Ballad upon the Earle of Essex Death* [c.1620, reprinted c.1625, 1635], *STC* 6792.3, 6792.7, 6793; printed in *Roxburghe Ballads*, I, pp. 394–8; quote on p. 394. For the Artillery Company's associations with the militant godly, see Valerie Pearl, *London and the Outbreak of the Puritan Revolution* (Oxford, 1961), pp 170–2, 278–9; Robert Ashton, *The City and the Court 1603–1643* (Cambridge, 1979) pp. 173–5.

21. Samuel Ward, *Woe to Drunkards* (1622), title page. Further editions were published in 1622, 1624, 1627, 1635. For Ward see Patrick Collinson, *The Religion of Protestants: the Church in English Society 1559–1625* (Oxford, 1982) pp. 153–4, 175–6; *DNB*, 'Samuel Ward', *s.v.* Ward had been briefly imprisoned in 1621 for a caricature of the Spanish ambassador, Gondomar.

22. For this image, cf. Thomas Moffet, *Nobilis or a View of the Life and Death of a Sidney [1593]*, ed. V.B. Heltzel and H.H. Hudson (San Marino, 1940) p. 87.

23. [Reynolds], *Vox Coeli*, p. 37.

24. Fulke Greville, 'A Dedication to Sir Philip Sidney', in *The Prose Works of Fulke Greville, Lord Brooke*, ed. John Gouws (Oxford, 1986) p. 126.

25. S.R. Gardiner, *The History of England from the Accession of James I to the Outbreak of the Civil War*, 10 vols (1887–91), VI, p. 10. The story of Essex's taking of Cadiz had been recently retold in G[ervase] M[arkham], *Honour in his Perfection* (1624) p. 30.

26. Thomas Cogswell, *The Blessed Revolution: English Politics and the Coming of War, 1621–24* (Cambridge, 1989) p. 314.

27. Francis Bacon, *Essays* ed S.H. Reynolds (Oxford, 1980) pp. 268–71; quoted in Ferguson, *The Chivalric Tradition*, p. 140.

28. Kevin Sharpe, *Criticism and Compliment: the Politics of Literature in the England of Charles I* (Cambridge, 1987) pp. 179–264.

29. James Shirley, 'The Triumph of Peace', in S. Orgel and R. Strong, *Inigo Jones: the Theatre of the Stuart Court* (2 vols, Berkeley and London, 1973) II, p. 540; (also printed in Clifford Leech (ed.), *A Book of Masques in Honour of Allardyce Nicoll* (Cambridge, 1967) p. 285.) For the cost of the masque, at £15 000, see Tucker Orbison and R.F. Hill (eds), 'The Middle Temple Documents relating to James Shirley's *The Triumph of Peace*', *Collections*, XII (Malone Soc., Oxford, 1983) pp. 31–84, and esp. p. 42.

30. Shirley, 'The Triumph of Peace' in *Inigo Jones* II p. 543; F.P. Wilson and R.F. Hill (eds), 'Dramatic Records in the Declared Accounts of the Office of Works, 1560–1640', in *Collections*, X (Malone Soc., Oxford, 1977) pp. 45–6.

31. Sharpe, *Criticism and Compliment*, pp. 179–82, 207–9.

32. [Cervantes], *The History of Don-Quixote*, trans. Shelton (1612 edn); for the windmills, pp. 52–61 (part I, ch. 8).

33. Shirley, 'The Triumph of Peace' p. 550; (in the edition by Clifford Leech, p. 295).

34. *Britannia Triumphans* (1637), printed in James Maidment and W.H. Logan (eds), *The Dramatic Works of Sir William D'Avenant*, 5 vols (Edinburgh, 1872–4) II, p. 282. Inigo Jones's drawings of the knight and squire from *Britannia Triumphans* are reproduced in Orgel and Strong, *Inigo Jones*, II, p. 698. See also, the 'four antique cavaliers, imitating a manage and tilting' in Davenant's *Salmacida Spolia* (1640), in ibid., II, pp. 732, 772.

35. John Kerrigan, 'Thomas Carew', *Transactions of the British Academy*, 74 (1988) p. 313. Thomas Carew, *Coelum Britannicum*, ll. 21–2, printed in Rhodes Dunlap (ed.), *The Poems of Thomas Carew* (Oxford, 1949) pp. 151–85; (references are to the line numbers of this edition).

36. Sharpe, *Criticism and Compliment*, pp. 109–13.

37. Giordano Bruno, *Spaccio de la Bestia Trionfante* (Paris, 1584); reprinted in Bruno, *Opere Italiane*, eds Giovanni Gentile and Vincenzo Spampanato 3 vols (Bari, 1923–7) II, pp. 1–230; English translation by Arthur D. Imerti, *The Expulsion of the Triumphant Beast* (New Brunswick, 1964); for the epistle to Sidney, see ibid., pp. 69–88.

38. On Sidney's posthumous reputation, see J. van Dorsten, D. Baker-Smith and A.F. Kinney (eds), *Sir Philip Sidney: 1586 and the Creation of a Legend* (Leiden, 1986).

39. Carew, *Coelum Britannicum*, ll. 106–7.

40. [Scott], *Robert Earle of Essex his Ghost*, p. 1; [Reynolds], *Vox Coeli*, pp. 3, 54.

41. Carew's reference back to the anti-Spanish polemic of the mid-1620s was certain to have been noticed by at least one of the *Coelum Britannicum*'s masquers, for in 1623 the author of *Vox Coeli* had been the travelling companion of and tutor to the young Lord Feilding – now one of the 'British Heroes' of Carew's masque. *Coelum Britannicum*, 1146; cf. [Reynolds], *Vox Coeli*, p. 54; Warwickshire RO, CR 2017/C2/188 (Denbigh papers), and CR 2017/C7/1: Reynolds to the first Earl of Denbigh, 29 May and 10/20 June 1624.

42. Carew, *Coelum Britannicum*, ll. 423–49.

43. Ibid., ll. 426–7, 431–3.

44. The tapestries, which were destroyed in the fire of 1834, are reproduced in John Pine, *The Tapestry Hangings of the House of Lords* (1739); reprinted in Henry Y. Thompson, *Lord Howard of Effingham and the Spanish Armada* (Roxburghe Club, 1919); for the cost, p. 12.

45. PRO (Kew), AO 1/2353/72 (Removing Wardrobe acc.). They were later removed to the Tower (by 1644): LJ, VI, p. 554.

46. Carew, *Coelum Britannicum*, ll. 949–53.

47. Ibid., ll. 1080–6; and see also Sharpe, *Criticism and Compliment*, pp. 233–43.

48. Carew, *Coelum Britannicum*, ll. 1031–4. In a work dedicated to Charles I, Peter Heylyn went so far as to argue that St. George, Sir Guy of Warwick, and Beavis, Earl of Southampton (the Saxon noble who was supposed to have defeated the Normans at Cardiff in 1070) were probably all historical figures: Peter Heylin, *The Historie of that Most Famous Saint and Souldier of Christ, St George of Cappadocia* (1631) pp. 70–2. From the perspective of some of Carew's audience, the ancient heroes, Guy, Beavis and St. George, were possibly viewed as only scarcely less historically 'real' than more recent Elizabethan heroes such as Sidney and Essex.

49. Hatfield House, Herts, Cecil MS 197/115; calendared in *HMC Salisbury (Cecil) MSS*, xxii (1971) p. 210.

50. Kevin Sharpe, 'The Image of Virtue: the Court and Household of Charles I, 1625–42', in David Starkey (ed.), *The English Court: from the Wars of the Roses to the Civil War* (1987) pp. 241–2.

51. Elias Ashmole, *The Institution, Laws and Ceremonies of The Most Noble Order of the Garter* (1672) pp. 570–2. Ashmole drew much of his account from a MS 'compiled ... about the year 1631' by Bishop Matthew Wren, who was then Register of the Order, in which Wren had set out in detail the 'alteration there hath been in the Law of the *Garter*' and its ceremonies up to the accession of Charles I. The paper was possibly prepared to complement the king's efforts during 1631–2 to reform the statutes of the Garter.

52. Ashmole, *The Garter*, p. 572. For contemporary evidence of the number of canopy bearers: BL, Add. MS 37998 (Sir Edward Walker papers), fos. 50v, 51. (I owe my knowledge of this MS to Dr David Smith.)

53. Heylyn, *The Historie of St George*, ep. ded. to Charles I.

54. Heylyn, *The Historie of St George*, p. 314; Pierre Boitel, *La Relation des ... Ceremonies Observées à la Reception des Chevaliers de l'Ordre du Sainct Sprit* (Paris, 1620) BL, 9930. b. 7; Ashmole, *The Garter*, p. 122. Cf. Van Dyck's painting of James Stuart, Duke of Richmond, in which the aureole and badge are prominently displayed on the sitter's cloak (Metropolitan Museum of Art, New York).

55. Ortwin Gamber, 'Armour made in the Royal Workshops at Greenwich: Style and Construction', *Scottish Art Review*, xii (1969), no. 2, pp. 1–13; Roy Strong, *Van Dyck: Charles I on Horseback* (1972) p. 20. (Strong's essay is a detailed and stimulating account of the intellectual context in which these paintings were produced.)

56. Andreas Alciatus, *Emblemata cum Commentariis* (Padua, 1621) pp. 852–3: 'Quercus symbolum erit illius qui multa gessit praeclara facinora, sed iam nomine tantum et fama durat'; and see also the claim, 'Quercus enim primo salutis est symbolum, quia qui Romanum ciuem in bello seruabat, coronam quercam accipiebat, quae Ciuica vocabatur'. Alciati's emblem book had first appeared in 1531, and was widely influential during the sixteenth and early seventeenth centuries.

57. Roy Strong, *The English Icon: Elizabethan and Jacobean Portraiture* (1969) p. 63 (pl. 52), for the anonymous Elizabethan portrait of *Sir George*

Somerset; cf. Robert Peake the elder (attrib.), *Henry Prince of Wales and the 3rd Earl of Essex, c.*1605 (in ibid., p. 246, pl. 222); and Geffrey Whitney, *A Choice of Emblemes, and Other Devises* (Leiden, 1586; rep. Aldershot, 1989) p. 126; and Hilliard's portrait of Cumberland in R. Strong, *Artists of the Tudor Court: the Portrait Miniature Rediscovered, 1520–1620* (1983) pp. 134–5 (pl. 216).

58. BL, Add. MS. 10112 (Van der Doort's catalogue), fo. 4 (foliation in top right-hand corner); printed in Sir Oliver Millar (ed.), *Abraham van der Doort's Catalogue of the Collections of Charles I* (Walpole Soc., XXXVII, 1960) p. 62.

59. Smuts, *Court Culture*, p. 206.

60. BL, Department of Manuscripts, Seal LXXX, 43–44; described in W. de G. Birch, *Catalogue of Seals in the Department of Manuscripts*, 6 vols (1887–1900), II, pp. 332–3. For a comparison with earlier seals, BL, Seal XXXIV.33 (Richard Neville, Earl of Warwick, c.1449–71); and the late 13th century seals of Richard Fitz-Alan, seventh Earl of Arundel (BL, Seal LXXIX.2) and Gilbert de Clare, seventh Earl of Hertford and Gloucester (BL, Seal L.F.C. XII.5).

61. Henri Estienne, *The Art of Making Devises*, trans. Thomas Blount (1646) sig. A2[v].

62. BL, Seal LXXX.44.

63. Edward Bysshe (ed.), *Nicholai Uptoni de Studio Militari Libri Quatuor* (1654), 'In Nicholaum Uptonum Notae', p. 43.

64. Francis Quarles, *Argulus and Parthenia* (1629) ep. ded.; reprinted in the edition of David Freeman (Cranbury, NJ, 1986). For Quarles's relations with Holland, see Karl Josef Höltgen, *Francis Quarles, 1592–1644* (Tübingen, 1978) pp. 58–61.

65. *The Ancient, Famous and Honourable History of Amadis de Gaule*, 4 vols (1618–9).

66. *Amadis de Gaule*, ep. ded. to Pembroke (then Earl of Montgomery), Book I, sig. A2. Gilbert Saulnier, *The Love and Armes of the Greeke Princes* (1640) title page.

67. [Sir Thomas Malory], *The Most Ancient and Famous History of the Renowned Prince Arthur King of Britaine* (1634).

68. BL, Add. MS. 37998 (Sir Edward Walker papers), fo. 50. V.F. Snow, 'An inventory of the Lord General's library, 1646', *The Library*, XXI (1966) pp. 115–123, entries 53, 27, 33 respectively.

69. Margaret Spufford, *Small Books and Pleasant Histories: Popular Fiction and its Readership in Seventeenth-Century England* (Athens, Georgia, 1982) pp. 224–44.

70. Martin Butler, *Theatre and Crisis, 1632–1642* (Cambridge, 1984) pp. 198–9, and see pp. 199–210.

71. Ann Barton, *Ben Jonson, Dramatist* (Cambridge, 1984) pp. 262, 300–2.

72. [The Earl of Newcastle], *The Varietie* (*c.*1641; printed 1649), cited in Butler, *Theatre and Crisis*, pp. 197–8.

73. [Newcastle], *The Varietie* (1649) p. 41.

74. Thomas Rogers, *Leicester's Ghost*, ed. Franklin B. Williams (Chicago, 1972) p. xi.

75. Another tradition, also current in Caroline England, viewed Leicester's magnificence in a more sinister light, regarding him as the cynosure of the over-mighty subject who sought to monopolise power within the state: the tradition of *The Copie of a Leter, Wryten by a Master of Arte of Cambridge* (Paris, 1584), a work better known as *Leicester's Commonwealth*. The work was extensively copied in MS throughout the early seventeenth century and reprinted in 1641.

76. David Piper, *Catalogue of the Seventeenth-century Portraits in the National Portrait Gallery 1625–1714* (Cambridge, 1963) p. 175 and plate 5(d).

77. Smuts, *Court Culture*, p. 206.

78. Sir Anthony Wagner, *Heralds of England: a History of the Office and College of Arms* (1967) p. 255.

79. J.S.A. Adamson, 'The Baronial Context of the English Civil War', *Transactions of the Royal Historical Society*, 5th series, XL (1990) pp. 102–3.

80. [Thomas Spencer], 'The Genealogie, Life and Death of the Right Honourable Robert Lord Brooke', ed. P. Styles, *Miscellany I* (Publications of the Dugdale Society, Oxford, 1977) p. 178.

81. *A Declaration of … the Earle of Newcastle* (York, Feb. 1642[3]) p. 9. I am grateful to Dr Lynn Hulse for a discussion of Newcastle's chivalric ideas.

82. BL, Sloane MS 5247 (Banners of the parl. armies) fo. 36.

83. College of Arms, MS M.6, fo. 56v; and cf. [Paulo] Giovio, *Dialogo dell'Imprese Militari et Amorose* (Lyons, 1574) p. 112.

84. BL, Sloane MS 5247, fo. 37v.

85. Young, *Tournaments*, p. 133; Estienne, *The Art of Making Devises*, trans. Blount, ep. ded., sig. A3[1]; Henry Peacham, *Minerva Britannia* (1612) p. 114.

86. BL, Sloane MS 5247 (Banners of the parl. armies) fo. 2 (*comes* in Latin signifies both 'companion' and 'earl').

87. Estienne, *Devises*, sig. A3[1].

88. Sir William Davenant, *Gondibert: an Heroick Poem* (1651) preface, p. 35.

89. Sir John Suckling to [?], [May–June 1639]: printed in Thomas Clayton (ed.), *The Works of Sir John Suckling: the Non-Dramatic Works* (Oxford, 1971) p. 144; cf. *Henry IV, Part I*, III, i, 96–100 (where the river is the Trent). I owe this reference to Mr John Kerrigan.

90. Scottish RO, Hamilton MS, GD 406/1/1419: Essex to Hamilton, 30 August 1641. Cf Shakespeare, *Henry IV: Part I*, II, iii.

91. Waller to Sir Ralph Hopton, 16 June 1643; the most accurate text of this letter is printed in Mary Coate, *Cornwall in the Great Civil War and Interregnum*, 2nd edn (Truro, 1963) p. 77.

92. BL, Sloane MS 5247 (Banners of the parl. armies) fo. 22v; Saulnier,

The Love and Armes of the Greeke Princes, III, p. 44; cf. 78, 82. I am grateful to Dr Ian Roy for pointing out to me the allusion to Agincourt in this banner.

93. *The Answer of Ferdinando Lord Fairfax to a Declaration* (3 Mar. 1642[3] p. 8. See also the *Observations upon the Earle of New-Castles Declaration* (1643) p. 15.

94. Ben Jonson, *The New Inn* (1631) I. vi. 125. For Newcastle's relations with Jonson, see Barton, *Ben Jonson*, pp. 300–2.

95. *The Earle of Essex his Desires to the Parliament* (15 Aug. 1642) p. 3 (BL, 101, b. 49).

96. *The Resolution of ... the Earl of Essex his Excellencie* ([9 Sept.] 1642) pp. 1–2.

97. *The Life and Death of the Right Honourable, Robert, Earle of Essex, the Noble Branch of his Thrice Noble Father* ([12 Oct.] 1646) BL, 669 f. 10/93. Cf. William Rowland's *Epitaph* ([23 Oct.] 1646): 'that Essex is/ the man, an earl renown'd by his/ Most noble birth: whose father Queen/ *Eliza* had in great esteem' (BL, 669 f. 10/97).

98. Wenceslaus Hollar, 'The Manner and Forme of the Arch-Bishops Trial', frontispiece to William Prynne, *A Breviate of the Life of William Laud* (1644). PRO (Kew) AO 1/2353/72 (Removing Wardrobe acc.). *LJ*, VI, p. 554 (15 May 1644).

99. *The Great Champions of England: being a Perfect List of the Lords and Commons that have stood right to this Parliament ... under the command of His Excellency Sir Thomas Fairfax* (1646) BL, 669 f. 10/69.

100. Cf. William Rowland's *An Elegie upon the Death of ... Robert Devereux, Earle of Essex and Ewe* ([23 Oct.] 1646), which opens 'Can England's noble Champion (ESSEX) die?' (BL, 669 f. 10/97).

101. Young, *Tudor and Jacobean Tournaments*, pp. 58–71.

102. Bodl. Lib., MS Gough misc. antiq. 8 (Le Neve papers) fo. 6. (I owe this reference to Mr Jeremy Maule.)

103. Roy Strong, *Henry, Prince of Wales and England's Lost Renaissance* (1986) figs. 44–5. The pose of the horse also provided the equestrian pattern for the warhorse in Robert Peake's portrait of Henry, Prince of Wales. The 'Henri II' pose was also adopted during the 1650s, probably *via* the Fairfax woodcut of 1646, for the anonymous portrait of Cromwell, now in the Cromwell Museum, Huntingdon (reproduced on the cover of J.S. Morrill (ed.), *Oliver Cromwell and the English Revolution* [1990]).

104. Even the great Duke of Buckingham had been interred at night by torchlight, without elaborate ceremonial and expense. Roger Lockyer, *Buckingham: the Life and Political Career of George Villiers, First Duke of Buckingham, 1592–1626* (1981) pp. 457–8.

105. [William Ryley], *The True Mannor and Forme of the Proceeding to the Funerall of the Right Honourable Robert Earle of Essex and Ewe* (1646) pp. 15–17, 19–20; on the decline of the elaborate aristocratic funeral in the early seventeenth century, see Lawrence Stone, *The Crisis of the Aristocracy* (Oxford, 1965) pp. 572–81.

106. [Ryley], *The True Mannor and Forme*, woodcut facing p. 18. For criticism of the scale and extravagance of the funeral, see Bodl. Lib., MS Douce 357 (Verse anthology) fo. 12v: 'Rithmes made In a Belcony by one who Impatiently Exp[e]cted the shews att the E[arl] of E[ssex] his funerall'.

107. Christ Church Muniment Room, Oxford, Browne Letters, Box D-L: Sir Kenelme Digby to Sir Richard Browne, Rome, 31 July [new style?] 1645.

108. H.R. Trevor-Roper, 'Milton in Politics', in *idem, Catholics, Anglicans, and Puritans: Seventeenth Century Essays* (Chicago, 1987) p. 247.

109. Davenant, *Gondibert* (1651 edn) preface, p. 6.

110. Davenant, *Gondibert* (1651 edn), 'The Answer of Mr Hobbes to Sir William Davenant's *preface* before Gondibert', p. 59; reprinted in J.E. Spingarn (ed.), *Critical Essays of the Seventeenth Century*, 3 vols (Oxford, 1908) II, p. 61.

111. Samuel Butler, *Characters, and Passages from Note Books*, ed. A.R. Waller (Cambridge, 1908) p. 469.

112. Sir William Waller to Sir Ralph Hopton, 16 June 1643; printed in Coate, *Cornwall*, p. 77.

113. Butler, *Characters, and Passages from Note Books*, ed. Waller, p. 469.

114. Butler, *Hudibras*, part I, canto ii, ll, 321–3.

8.   THE POLITICS OF PORTRAITURE   *John Peacock*

1. *Calendar of State Papers Venetian* (*CSPV*) X, 1603–7, 9–10.

2. Exodus 20: 4–5, *The Geneva Bible. A facsimile of the 1560 edition*, intro. Lloyd E. Berry (Madison, Milwaukee and London, 1969).

3. Hastings Robinson (ed.), *Original Letters Relative to the English Reformation*, 2 vols (Cambridge, 1846) I, pp. 184–95, 192.

4. Robert McNulty (ed.), *Ludovico Ariosto's 'Orlando Furioso' Translated ... by Sir John Harington* (Oxford, 1972) p. 385.

5. William Perkins, *A Reformed Catholike* (Cambridge, 1598) p. 172, quoted M. Aston, *England's Iconoclasts* (Oxford, 1988) p. 451.

6. Henry Peacham, *The Art of Drawing With The Pen, And Limming In Water Colours* (London, 1606) p. 1.

7. Ibid., p. 8.

8. Henry Peacham, *Graphice Or The Most Auncient And Excellent Art of Drawing and Limming* (London, 1612) pp. 11–12.

9. Ibid., p. 7.

10. Ibid., p. 12.

11. Oliver Millar, *The Queen's Pictures* (London, 1977) pp. 11–12.

12. Erna Auerbach, *Nicholas Hilliard* (London, 1961); Nicholas Hilliard, *A Treatise concerning the Arte of Limning*, ed. R.K.R. Thornton and T.G.S. Cain (Ashington, 1981).

13. John Pope-Hennessy, 'Nicholas Hilliard and Mannerist Art Theory', *Journal of the Warburg and Courtauld Institutes*, 6 (1943) 89–100.

14. Hilliard, *Treatise*, p. 65.

15. Ibid.

16. Ibid., pp. 85–7.

17. Ibid., p. 89.

18. Ibid., pp. 33–6.

19. Franciscus Junius, *De Pictura Veterum*, Amsterdam, 1637; *The Painting of the Ancients* (London, 1638; facsimile Farnborough, 1972, reprinted 1982).

20. Cecil Grayson (ed.), Leon Battista Alberti, *On Painting and on Sculpture* (London, 1972); Gaetano Milanesi (ed.), *Le opere di Giorgio Vasari*, 9 vols (Florence, 1906, reprinted 1981); Giovanni Paolo Lomazzo, *Trattato Dell' Arte Della Pittura, Scoltura, Et Architettura* (Milan, 1584) trans. Richard Haydocke: *A Tracte Containing The Artes of curious Paintinge Carvinge Buildinge* (Oxford, 1598, facsimile Amsterdam and New York, 1969).

21. Junius, *Painting of the Ancients*, p. 2.

22. Aristotle, *Poetics*, IV. 3, in S.H. Butcher, *Aristotle's Theory of Poetry and Fine Art* (New York, 1951) p. 15; cf. Junius, *Painting of the Ancients*, p. 79.

23. Oliver Millar, *The Age of Charles I* (London, 1972) p. 56, no. 84 (reprod. frontispiece).

24. *Poetics*, IV. 8, in Butcher, p. 15.

25. *Poetics*, XV. 8, in Butcher, p. 57.

26. Plutarch, *Life of Pericles*, III. 2; see Alberti, *On Painting*, pp. 79–81.

27. Milanesi (ed.), *Opere di Vasari*, IV, pp. 462–3; also quoted Anthony Blunt, *Artistic Theory in Italy 1450–1600* (Oxford, 1956) p. 89.

28. Milanesi (ed.), *Opere di Vasari*, VII, pp. 271–2; Robert J. Clements, *Michelangelo's Theory of Art* (London, 1963) pp. 152–5.

29. Margaret Whinney, *Sculpture in Britain 1530 to 1830*, (Harmondsworth, 1964) pp. 26–7, plate 20.

30. Vincenzio Danti, *Il primo libro del trattato delle perfette proporzioni* (Florence, 1567) in Paolo Barocchi, *Scritti d' arte del Cinquecento*, 3 vols (Milan and Naples, 1971–77) II, pp. 1570–1.

31. Sir Philip Sidney, *An Apology for Poetry*, ed. Geoffrey Shepherd (London, 1965) p. 102.

32. Excerpted in Barocchi, *Scritti d'arte*, III, pp. 2737f.

33. Ibid., p. 2737.

34. Ibid., p. 2739.

35. Ibid., p. 2740.

36. Ibid., pp. 2742–3.

37. Roy Strong, *The English Icon: Elizabethan and Jacobean Portraiture* (London, 1969) p. 29.

38. Roy Strong, *Artists of the Tudor Court: The Portrait Miniature Rediscovered 1520–1620* (London, 1983) p. 64, no. 61; Oliver Millar (ed.),

Abraham van der Doort's Catalogue of the Collections of Charles I (Walpole Soc., XXXVII, 1960) p. 111.

39. Ibid., p. 196.

40. Ibid., p. 197.

41. Steffen Heiberg (ed.), *Christian IV and Europe* (the 19th Art Exhibition of the Council of Europe) (Copenhagen, 1988) pp. 45–6 (nos. 109–11), 98 (no. 302), 104 (no. 231), 238–9 (no. 1067).

42. Roy Strong, *Henry, Prince of Wales and England's Lost Renaissance* (London, 1986) p. 114, plates 42–3; Walter L. Strauss (ed.), *The Illustrated Bartsch. 3. Netherlandish Artists. Hendrik Goltzius* (New York, 1980) pp. 100, 102 (nos. 5, 7). Goltzius dedicated the prints to the Emperor Rudolph II.

43. Livy, VII. ix. 3–x. 14.

44. Livy, VII. v–vi.

45. Guy de Tervarent, *Attributs et Symboles dans l'art profane 1450–1600*, 2 vols (Geneva, 1958–9) I, p. 91.

46. G.W. Groos (ed.), *The Diary of Baron Waldstein* (London, 1981) p. 85.

47. 'The Journal of Sir Roger Wilbraham', *Camden Society*, 3rd ser. vol. IV, *Camden Miscellany* x (London ,1902) p. 23.

48. Groos (ed.), *Diary of Baron Waldstein*.

49. Lindsay Boynton (ed.), *The Hardwick Hall Inventories of 1601* (London, 1971) p. 23.

50. Ibid., pp. 26–7, 29.

51. Millar (ed.), *Van der Doort's Catalogue* pp. 2–7. For an account of the Whitehall pictures from a different point of view see Francis Haskell, 'Charles I's Collection of Pictures' in Arthur MacGregor (ed.), *The Late King's Goods* (London and Oxford, 1989) pp. 204–6.

52. Gregory Martin, *National Gallery Catalogues. The Flemish School* (London, 1970) pp. 116–125.

53. Millar (ed.), *Van der Doort's Catalogue*, pp. 41–61.

54. Oliver Millar, *Van Dyck in England* (London, 1982) pp. 46–7, no. 7.

55. Millar (ed.) *Van der Doort's Catalogue*, pp. 20–2.

56. Ibid., pp. 35–6.

57. Strong, *English Icon*, pp. 5f.

58. R. Strong, *Gloriana: The Portraits of Elizabeth I* (London, 1987), *passim*.

59. Strong, *English Icon*, pp. 225–54, 259–68.

60. Strong, *Henry, Prince of Wales*, p. 91.

61. Millar, *Age of Charles I*, p. 13, nos. 1–2; David Howarth, *Lord Arundel and His Circle* (New Haven and London, 1985) pp. 57f., gives a more complicated explanation of the pictures.

62. Howarth, ibid., pp. 77–96; D.E.L. Haynes, *The Arundel Marbles* (Oxford, 1975).

63. Arthur K. Wheelock *et al.*, *Anthony van Dyck* (Washington, 1990) pp. 53–8; Millar, *Van Dyck in England, passim*.

64. Milanesi (ed.) *Opere di Vasari*, IV, pp. 11–14.

65. Millar, *Van Dyck in England*, p. 21.

66. For the protruding elbow see the so-called portrait of Ariosto, and for the figure superimposed on a distant landscape see Bacchus and Ariadne, both in the National Gallery: Harold E. Wethey, *The Paintings of Titian*, 3 vols (London, 1969–75) II, pp. 103–4, no. 40, and III, pp. 148–51, no. 14.

67. Millar, *Van Dyck in England*, pp. 50–2, no. 11.

68. *Mercurius Aulicus* (16–22 June 1644), p. 1040, quoted in Jacqueline Eales, *Puritans and Roundheads: The Harleys of Brampton Bryan and the outbreak of the English Civil War* (Cambridge, 1990) pp. 182–3.

9. INIGO JONES AND THE POLITICS OF ARCHITECTURE
J. Newman

1. Stephen Wren, *Parentalia: or Memoirs of the Family of the Wrens*, (London, for T. Osborn and R. Dodsley, 1750; facsimile reprint Farnborough, 1965) p. 351.

2. Aristotle, *Nichomachean Ethics*, book IV, ch. 2. This passage is discussed by John Onians, *Bearers of Meaning* (Princeton, 1988) pp. 123–6.

3. Fifty books survive from Jones's library, almost all at Worcester College, Oxford. The quotations given here are from his marginal notes.

4. John Webb, *The Most Notable Antiquity of Great Britain, vulgarly called Stone-Heng on Salisbury Plain, Restored by Inigo Jones Esq.* (London, 1655).

5. Ibid., p. 13. See the discussion of this passage in R. Malcolm Smuts, *Court Culture and the Origins of a Royalist Tradition in Early Stuart England* (Philadelphia, 1987) p. 266.

6. H.M. Colvin (ed.), *The History of the King's Works*, vol. IV (London, 1982) pp. 320–5.

7. Per Palme, *The Triumph of Peace: A Study of the Whitehall Banqueting House* (London, 1957) p. 120.

8. Ibid., pp. 7–13.

9. Colvin (ed.), *History of the King's Works*, IV, p. 330.

10. Rudolf Wittkower, *Architectural Principles in the Age of Humanism* 3rd edn (London, 1962) pp. 143–4.

11. Andrea Palladio *I Quattro Libri dell' Architettura* (Venice, 1601; facsimile Newcastle, 1970) vol. III, pp. 38–9.

12. Ibid., vol. II, pp. 41–2.

13. Mark Girouard, 'Elizabethan Architecture and the Gothic Tradition', *Architectural History*, 6 (1963) pp. 23–40.

14. Stephen Orgel and Roy Strong, *Inigo Jones: The Theatre of the Stuart Court* (London and Berkeley, 1973) vol. I, plate 37.

15. Ibid., II, plates 191–2, 279.

16. Henry Wotton, *The Elements of Architecture* (London: John Bill, 1624; facsimile Farnborough, 1969) pp. 82–3.

17. Colvin (ed.), *History of the King's Works*, IV, p. 332.

18. Palme *Triumph of Peace*, p. 78.
19. R. Strong, *Britannia Triumphans: Inigo Jones, Rubens and Whitehall Palace* (London, 1980).
20. Ibid., p. 20.
21. Norman E. McClure (ed.), *The Letters of John Chamberlain* 2 vols (Philadelphia, 1939).
22. I here follow the discussion in John Peacock, 'Inigo Jones's catafalque for James I', *Architectural History*, 25 (1982) pp. 3–4.
23. For this and what follows see N.G. Brett-James, *The Growth of Stuart London* (London, 1935).
24. J. Alfred Gotch, *Inigo Jones* (London, 1928, reissued New York, 1968) p. 118.
25. J.F. Larkin and P.L. Hughes, *Stuart Royal Proclamations*, I, 1603–25 (Oxford, 1973) nos. 186, 204, 234.
26. T. Rymer, *Foedera*, 3rd edn (London, 1741) xvii, pp. 119–21, quoted in Brett-James.
27. *The Survey of London*, XXXVI, *The Parish of St Paul Covent Garden* (London, 1970).
28. John Newman, 'Nicholas Stone's Goldsmiths' Hall: Design and Practice in the 1630s', *Architectural History*, 14 (1971) pp. 33–4.
29. Howard Colvin, 'Inigo Jones and the Church of St Michael le Querne', *London Journal*, 12:1 (1986) pp. 36–9.
30. Margaret Whinney, 'John Webb's Drawings for Whitehall Palace', *Walpole Society*, 31 (1946) p. 46.
31. Ibid., p. 106.
32. Whinney, 'John Webb's Drawings' p. 46.
33. John Harris and Gordon Higgott (eds), *Inigo Jones, Complete Architecture Drawings* (London: A. Zwemmer, 1989) p. 252.
34. *The Survey of London*, XXXVI, p. 99 and note.
35. Rudolf Whittkower, 'Inigo Jones – "Puritanissimo Fiero"', *Burlington Magazine*, 90 (1948) pp. 50–1.
36. John Newman 'Italian Treatises in Use: The Significance of Inigo Jones's Annotations' in J. Guillaume (ed.), *Les Traités de la Renaissance* (Paris, 1988) pp. 439–40.
37. John Williams, *The Holy Table Name & Thing* (London, 1637) p. 38.
38. The monument perished in the Fire of 1666, but a sketch of it is preserved in Oxford, Bodleian Library, MS Aubrey 8.
39. Webb, *Stone-Heng Restored*, p. 108.

10. DEEDS AGAINST NATURE: CHEAP PRINT, PROTESTANTISM AND MURDER IN EARLY SEVENTEENTH-CENTURY ENGLAND
   Peter Lake

1. C. Haigh, 'The continuity of catholicism in the English reformation' and 'The recent historiography of the English reformation' both in

C. Haigh (ed.), *The English Reformation Revised* (Cambridge, 1987); also see his 'Puritan evangelism in the reign of Elizabeth I', *English Historical Review*, 92 (1978) and his 'The Church of England, Catholics and the People' in C. Haigh (ed.), *The Reign of Elizabeth I* (London, 1984); J.J. Scarisbrick, *The Reformation and the English People* (Oxford, 1984). There is, of course, a counter narrative of the Reformation which, while admitting the strength and longevity, in some areas, of popular conservatism and conceding that everywhere the Reformation was a contested event, still stresses that Protestantism, in particular early Protestantism, could be 'popular'; that is, it could draw support from the relatively humble, women and the young and draw on genuinely popular genres and cultural forms to gets its message across. See, for instance, S. Brigden, 'Youth and the English reformation' *Past and Present*, no. 95, 1982 and her *London and the Reformation* (Oxford, 1989); P. Collinson, *The Birthpangs of Protestant England* (London, 1988), espec. chapter 4 and now T. Watt, *Cheap Print and Popular Piety, 1550–1640* (Cambridge, 1991). It is as a contribution to and extension of this second approach that the present essay is intended.

2. C. Hill, *Puritanism and Society in Pre-revolutionary England* (London, 1964); K. Wrightson and D. Levine, *Poverty and Piety in an English Village: Terling, 1525–1700* (London, 1979); W. Hunt, *The Puritan Moment* (Cambridge, Mass., 1983).

3. J. Marshburn, *Murder and Witchcraft in England, 1550–1640* (Norman, Okla., 1972); T. Watt, *Cheap Print and Popular Piety*. In terms of genre, the murder pamphlets were really a subset of the highly providentialised news and prodigy pamphlets of the period, laced with elements of Dr Watt's cheap godlies and sometimes of the contemporary crime and cony-catching pamphlets. Indeed, examples of the three genres often appeared within the same compilation. For instance, see Anthony Munday, *A View of Sundry Examples, Reporting, Many Strange Murders* (London, 1580) or *A World of Wonders: A Mass of Murders a Covy of Cosonages* (London, 1599). See Sandra Clark, *The Elizabethan Pamphleteers: Popular Moralistic Pamphlets, 1580–1640* (London, 1983). Cheap providentialist news and prodigy pamphlets are currently the subject of important research by Alex Walsham of Trinity College, Cambridge. I should like to thank Ms Walsham for many discussions on this subject.

4. *The Most Cruel and Bloody Murder Committed by an Innkeepers Wife called Annis Dell and her Son George Dell* (London, 1606) sigs. A3v., Bv.–B2r.; also see another pamphlet on the same subject, *The Horrible Murder of a Young Boy of Three Years of Age* (London, 1606).

5. *The Manner of the Cruel Outrageous Murder of William Storr... Minister...* (Oxford, 1603) sig. A3r.

6. *Two Notorious Murders. One Committed by a Tanner on his Wife's Son... The Other on a Grasier near Aylsbury ...* (London, 1595) p. 5; *Three Bloody Murders* (London, 1613) sig.C3 r.–v.

7. *The Bloody Book, or the Tragical and Desperate End of Sir John Fittes* (London, 1605). For another similar rake narrative see *Two Most*

Unnatural and Bloody Murders (London, 1605) reprinted in J.P. Collier, *Illustrations of Early English Popular Literature* (London, 1863) vol. I.

8. *Deeds Against Nature and Monsters by Kind* (London, 1614), quote from sig.4v.

9. Henry Goodcole, *The Adulteress's Funeral Day in Flaming, Scorching and Consuming Fire* (London, 1635), quote at sig.Bv. Henry Goodcole, *Heavens Speedy Hue and Cry* (London, 1635), sig. C2r. Also see Goodcole's *Nature's Cruel Stepdames* (London, 1637)

10. *The Crying Murder, Containing the Cruel and Most Horrible Butcher of Mr Trat, Curate of Old Cleave* (London, 1624) reprinted in J. Marshburn (ed.), *Blood and Knavery* (Rutherford, NJ, 1973) pp. 40–57; *A Horrible, Cruel and Bloody Murder, Committed at Putney in Surrey* (London, 1614), quote at sig.Bv.; *The Examination, Confession and Condemnation of Henry Robson, Fisherman of Rye* (London, 1598).

11. *A True Report of the Horrible Murder, which was Committed in the House of Sir Jerome Bowes* (London, 1607) sig.A2r; H. Goodcole, *Heaven's Speedy Hue and Cry after Lust and Murder* (London, 1635) preface. Gilbert Dugdale, *A True Discourse of the Practises of Elizabeth Caldwell* (London, 1604) sig.A3v.; Arthur Golding, *A Brief Discourse of the Late Murder of Master George Sanders* (London, 1577) sig.A2v.

12. M. Ingram, 'Ridings, Rough Music and "the reform of popular culture" in early modern England', *Past and Present*, 104 (1984); D. Underdown, 'The taming of the scold' in A. Fletcher and J. Stevenson (eds), *Order and Disorder in Early Modern England* (Cambridge, 1985); F. Laroque, *Shakespeare's Festive World* (Cambridge, 1991) esp. pt. 1.

13. *A Most Horrible and Detestable Murder Committed by a Bloody Minded Man upon His Own Wife* (London, 1595) sig.A2 r.

14. *Deeds Against Nature and Monsters by Kind* (London, 1614); H. Goodcole, *Nature's Cruel Step-dames or Matchless Monsters of the Female* (London, 1637); *A Pitiless Mother, that Most Unnaturally at One Time Murdered Two of Her Own Children* (London 1616); *The Arraignment and Burning of Margaret Ferneseed for the Murder of Her Late husband* (London, 1608) *passim*. With the figure of Ferneseed we are close to a rather different universe of pamphlet debate on the nature of women for which see Linda Woodbridge, *Women and the English Renaissance: Literature and the Nature of Womankind, 1540–1620* (Urbana, Ill., 1984).

15. *News from Perin in Cornwall of a Most Bloody and Unexampled Murder* (London, 1618); the ballad *Murder upon Murder*, reprinted in Marshburn (ed.), *Blood and Knavery*; *A Brief Discourse of Two Most Horrible Murders Committed in Worcestershire* (London, 1583).

16. John Taylor, *The Unnatural Father or a Cruel Murder Committed by one John Rouse ... upon Two of His Own Children* (London, 1621), reprinted in *Early Prose and Poetical Works* (London, 1888) pp. 243–58. Both Caverly's and Fitz's crimes are in the pamphlets cited in note 7.

17. It is worth noting here that the pamphlets never told stories about the sort of armed affrays or fights between equals (men) which often produced

33364

---

violent death. They were concerned only with those often intra-household crimes which appeared most directly to threaten the cause of social and moral order and could serve most easily to catch the attention of a half fascinated and half horrified readership and provide occasion for the sort of moralising which, as we have seen, both framed and legitimated some of the most violent and titillating narratives. In this the pamphlets mirror the assumptions which Philippa Maddern has recently discerned beneath the conduct of the late medieval courts. Murder and violence perpetrated between equals seldom led to conviction but killings of husbands or masters that 'offended the hierarchical principles of right violence' did. 'Culpable homicide was not only defined by the law, but recognised by the juries as radically offensive to the principles of social hierarchy.' Here, at least, the pamphlet narratives were building on and developing long established social practice and popular assumption. See P. Maddern, *Violence and Social Order; East Anglia 1422–1442* (Oxford, 1992), chapter 4, quotes on pp. 122, 128.

18. Goodcole, *Heavens Speedy Hue and Cry* sig. A3r; Goodcole, *Nature's Cruel Step-dames*, p. 5; *The murder of Page of Plymouth* from A. Munday, *Sundry Strange and Inhumane Murders Lately Committed* (London, 1591) reprinted in Marshburn, *Blood and Knavery*, p. 59; for other examples of the tragic consequences of marriages arranged against the wife's wishes see Goodcole, *The Adulteress's Funeral Day* and Dugdale, *A True Discourse of the Practises of Elizabeth Caldwell*, sig.A4r. As Dr Ingram has pointed out (in his *Church Courts, Sex and Marriage in England, 1570–1640* (Cambridge, 1987) pp. 134–42) the relationship between parental authority and personal preference in marriage formation was a complicated area, in which the theoretical right of the parents to an absolute authority had to be balanced against the interests and rights of the child. Here was a perfect image for the proper exercise of authority in early modern England which, even at the highest level, depended on a proper balance being struck between the rights and liberties of the subject and the powers and prerogatives of the crown. Should either side fail to play its part, chaos and anarchy, tyranny or subversion would result. Sir John Fitz and Margaret Ferneseed had their equivalents in élite political theory. The language of order in the murder pamphlets was clearly very similar to the language of order operative at more exalted social and theoretical levels.

19. *A Most Horrible and Detestable Murder*, sig.A2r.–v.

20. *A Pitiless Mother*, sig.A3v.; *A Horrible, Cruel and Bloody Murder Committed at Putney in Surrey*; on the devil and Cain see T. Kyd, *The Truth of the Most Wicked and Secret Murdering of John Brewen* (London, 1592) reprinted in Collier, *Illustrations*, I, p. 5; on the devil as the murderer's master see *The Apprehension, Arraignment and Execution of Elizabeth Abbot* (London, 1608) sig.Bv.

21. *News from Perin*, sig.B4r.; *Murder, Murder or a Bloody Relation how Ann Hamton ... by Poison Murdered Her Dear Husband* (London, 1641) reprinted in *The Old Bookcollectors Miscellany* (London, 1872) vol. 2, p. 4; *The Life, Confession and Hearty Repentance of Francis Cartwright* (London,

1621) sig. A3v.; *A True Relation of the Most Inhumane and Bloody Murder of Master James Minister ... at Rockland in Norfolk* (London, 1609), sig.A3 v.; John Taylor, *The Unnatural Father*, p. 245; *A True Report of the...Murder...in the house of Sir Jerome Bowes*, sig.C r.–v.; *A Most Horrible and Detestable Murder Committed by a Bloody Man upon His Own Wife* (London, 1595) sig.A2r; *The Examination, Confession and Condemnation of Henry Robson*, sig.A3r.

22. *A True Report of the Late Horrible Murder Committed by William Sherwood* (London, 1581); Golding, *A Brief Discourse*, sig.A3r.

23. *A True Relation of the...Murder of Master James, minister ... at Rockland in Norfolk*, passim.

24. *The Horrible Murder of a Young Boy*, pp. 3, 7, 9; *The Most Cruel and Bloody Murder*, sigs. Cv., B3v.

25. *Two Cruel Murders Lately Committed* (London, 1591) sig.A4 r.

26. *News from Perin*, sig.Cr.; *A True Relation of the murder of Master James minister ... at Rockland*, sig.Br.; *The Murder of Page of Plymouth*, reprinted in Marshburn, *Blood and Knavery*, p. 64.

27. *A True Report of the...murder in the House of Sir Jerome Bowes*, sig.C2r.; *The Most Horrible and Tragical Murder of ... Lord John Bourgh* (London, 1592) reprinted in Collier, *Illustrations*, I, pp. 9–10; Henry Goodcole, *A True Declaration of the Happy Conversion, Contrition and Christian Preparation of Francis Robinson* (London, 1618) sig.Br–B2r.

28. Thomas Cooper, *The Cry and Revenge of Blood* (London, 1620) p. 56; *The Crying Murder*, reprinted in Marshburn, *Blood and Knavery*, p. 53; *Two Horrible and Inhumane Murders Done in Lincolnshire by Two Husbands upon Their Wives* (London, 1607) reprinted in J. Foster (ed.), *Reprints of English Books, 1475–1700* (Claremont, Calif., 1948) I, no. 4, pp. 8–9; *Two Most Unnatural and Bloody Murders* (London, 1605) reprinted in Collier, *Illustrations*, I, p. 37.

29. Maddern, *Vidence and Social Order* p. 80. Thus the Protestant and puritan providentialism which Keith Thomas sees wearing away the 'magical' elements in medieval popular belief systems is perhaps better conceived as appropriating and merging with existing notions and expectations rather than simply displacing and destroying them. See K.V. Thomas, *Religion and the Decline of Magic* (London, 1970) esp. chs 3 and 4.

30. *Two Cruel Murders Lately Committed* (London, 1591) sig.A2v.; *A True Report of the...murder in the House of Sir Jerome Bowes* (London, 1607) sig.A4r.; Goodcole, *Deeds against Nature*, sig.A2v.; *Three Bloody Murders* (London, 1613) sig.C2v.

31. Cooper, *The Cry and Revenge of Blood*, p. 58.

32. Golding, *A Brief Discourse*, sig.A7r.; *The Manner of the Death and Execution of Arnold Cosby* (London, 1591) reprinted in Collier, *Illustrations*, I, pp. 15–17; *A True Report of the Arraignment, Trial, Conviction and Condemnation of a Popish Priest named Robert Drewrie* (London, 1607) sig. B5r.–v.; for an example of the efforts of magistrates and ministers to bring felons to repentance and of considerable popular interest in the performance of the murderer on the gallows see Golding, *A Brief*

Discourse, sig.A6 r.–v. and sig.A7r. Prison writings and prayers allegedly said at the execution by the accused were reprinted at the end of the pamphlet. Also see *The Apprehension, Arraignment and Execution of Elizabeth Abbot* (London, 1608) sig.C3r.–v. On this subject see J.A. Sharpe, ' "Last dying speeches": religion, ideology and public execution in seventeenth-century England', *Past and Present,* 107 (1985).

33. T. Lacqueur, 'Crowds, Carnival and the State in English Executions, 1604–1868' in A. Beier, D. Cannadine and J. Rosenheim (eds), *The First Modern Society* (Cambridge, 1989). The structure of assumptions discerned here in the pamphlets parallels and develops that found underlying the workings of medieval justice by Dr Maddern. On her account 'the courts operated to oversee cases of violence: to bring them within the scope of constituted authority and distinguish the allowable from the totally unjustifiable'. In the latter cases 'the hanging verdicts of the law overwhelmed offence and restored order to real life as surely as did the righteous swords of the knights of romance in literature. If hierarchy was to be upheld, servants and wives who killed their masters... had to be eliminated from the system with exemplary public disgrace'. Maddern, *Violence and Social Order,* pp. 117, 128. Again, the pamphlets operated by adopting and developing the cliches of previous social discourse and practice.

34. Golding, *A Brief Discourse,* sig.B3r.–B4r.

35. Ibid., sig.B4r.

36. Ibid., sig.A8r.; sig. Br.; sig.B3r.

37. Taylor, *The Unnatural Father,* p. 252; Goodcole, *Natures Cruel Step-dames,* sig.A2. and p. 9.

38. *The Lives, Apprehension, Arraignment and Execution of Robert Throgmorton, William Porter, John Bishop* (London, 1608) sig.C3r.; Dugdale, *A True Discourse of the Practises of Elizabeth Caldwell,* sig.B2r.–v, B4r.–v, B4v.–C5v.

39. *A True Report of the...murder...in the House of Sir Jerome Bowes* (London, 1607) sig.E4v.; H. Goodcole, *A True Declaration of the... Conversion of ... Francis Robinson* (London, 1618) sig.C3v.; Goodcole, *The Adulteress' Funeral Day,* sig.C2r.

40. *The Lives...of Robert Throgmorton, William Porter, John Bishop,* sig.Bv.; *A True Report of the...murder...in the House of Sir Jerome Bowes,* sig.Dr.–D3v, quote at sig.D3v.

41. Dugdale, *A True Discourse of the Practises of Elizabeth Caldwell,* sig.B2r.–v., Cv.; Golding, *A Brief Discourse,* sig.B7r.

42. *A Horrible Cruel and Bloody Murder Committed at Putney in Surrey,* sig.A4r.; *Deeds against Nature,* sig.A2r.; Goodcole, *A True Declaration of the ... Conversion...of Francis Robinson* (London, 1612) sig.Br.; Cooper, *The Cry and Revenge of Blood,* pp. 56–7 and *passim.*

43. See for instance, R. Yearwood, *The Penitent Murderer being an Exact Narrative of the Life and Death of Nathaniel Butler* (London, 1657). I hope to return to this subject elsewhere.

44. On the background and content of Studley's pamphlet see P. Lake, 'Puritanism, Arminianism and a Shropshire Axe Murder', *Midland History*, 15 (1990).

45. J.A. Sharpe, 'The History of Violence in England: Some Observations', *Past and Present*, 108 (1985) and J.S. Cockburn, 'Patterns of Violence in English Society: Homicide in Kent, 1560–1985', *Past and Present*, 130 (1991).

11. 'RAYLINGE RYMES AND VAUNTING VERSE': LIBELLOUS POLITICS IN EARLY STUART ENGLAND   *Alastair Bellany*

I would like to thank the following: Julian Mitchell, without whose collection of libel transcripts this project could not have been conceived; Lawrence Stone, Peter Lake, and Tom Cogswell for comments and references; the Graduate History Association Colloquium at Princeton for providing a sounding board for an earlier version of this chapter; and my wife, Deborah Yaffe, for policing my prose.

1. 'The Examination of Benjamin Jonson', printed in W. Douglas Hamilton (ed.), *Original Papers Illustrative of the Life and Writings of John Milton* (Camden Society: vol. 75, 1859) pp. 72–3; Thomas Birch (ed.), *The Court and Times of Charles I* (1849), I, p. 427; for the poem's Jonsonian style, Anne Barton, *Ben Jonson, Dramatist* (Cambridge, 1984) pp. 315–17.

2. E.g. Sara Pearl, 'Sounding to Present Occasions: Jonson's masques of 1620–1625' in David Lindley (ed.), *The Court Masque* (Manchester, 1984); Martin Butler, '"We are one man's all": Jonson's *The Gipsies Metamorphosed*', *The Yearbook of English Studies*, 21 (1991).

3. See below; I plan to deal more extensively with perceptions of libel and libellers in a forthcoming article.

4. Pauline Croft, 'The Reputation of Robert Cecil: Libels, Political Opinions and Popular Awareness in the Early Seventeenth Century', *TRHS*, 6th ser., 1 (1991). Richard Cust, 'News and Politics in Early Seventeenth Century England', *Past and Present*, 111 (1986) pp. 66–9; Derek Hirst, *Authority and Conflict: England 1603–1658* (Cambridge, Mass., 1986) p. 151, and Ann Hughes, *The Causes of the English Civil War* (1991) p. 72, briefly incorporate libels into their surveys.

5. Thomas Cogswell, *The Blessed Revolution: English Politics and the Coming of War, 1621–1624* (Cambridge, 1989) p. 325.

6. Frederick W. Fairholt (ed.), *Poems and Songs Relating to George Villiers, Duke of Buckingham* (Percy Society, 1850) pp. 1–2; Beatrice White, *Cast of Ravens: The Strange Case of Sir Thomas Overbury* (New York, 1965) p. 222.

7. John Morrill, *The Revolt of the Provinces* (1980) pp. 22–3.

8. Cogswell, *Blessed Revolution*, p. 325.

9. William Paley Baildon (ed.), *Les Reportes del Cases in Camera Stellata (1583–1609)* (1894) p. 225.

10. Charles Firth, 'The Ballad History of the Reigns of Henry VII and Henry VIII', *TRHS*, 3rd ser., 2 (1908) pp. 35–40; Alistair Fox, 'Prophecies and Politics in the Reign of Henry VIII' in Alistair Fox and John Guy (eds), *Reassessing the Henrician Age* (Oxford, 1986).

11. Allan G. Chester, 'The Authorship and Provenance of a Political Ballad in the Reign of Henry VIII', *Notes and Queries*, 195, no.10 (1950).

12. Charles Firth, 'The Ballad History of the Reigns of the Later Tudors', *TRHS*, 3rd ser., 3 (1909) pp. 64–5; *Statutes of the Realm*, IV: I (1819), pp. 240–1.

13. Frederick J. Furnivall (ed.), *Ballads from Manuscripts, II* (Hertford, 1876).

14. See Martin Ingram, 'Ridings, Rough Music and Mocking Rhymes in Early Modern England' in Barry Reay (ed.), *Popular Culture in Early Modern England* (1985).

15. SPD 16/114/30,31,32.

16. Mary Green (ed.), *The Diary of John Rous* (Camden Society: vol.66, 1856) p. 26.

17. J.O. Halliwell (ed.), *The Autobiography and Correspondence of Sir Simonds D'Ewes* (1845) II, p. 49.

18. Birch (ed.), *Court and Times*, I, p. 199.

19. BL Add. MSS 48057, fo.77r. Fairholt (ed.), *Poems and Songs*, pp. 10–13; Claude M. Simpson, *The British Broadside Ballad and Its Music* (New Brunswick, 1966) p. 109, prints the tune.

20. White, *Cast of Ravens*, p. 222; Commonplace Book of William Davenport 1613–1650, City of Chester Record Office (CCRO) CR 63/2/19, fo.13v.

21. R.M., *Micrologia* (1629) sig. C8v.

22. Bod. Tanner MSS 465, fo.104.

23. Bod. Dodsworth MSS 79, fo.158.

24. Halliwell (ed.), D'Ewes, *Autobiography*, I, p. 389. Green (ed.), *Diary of John Rous*, p. 26.

25. Halliwell (ed.), D'Ewes, *Autobiography*, I, p. 87.

26. *Historical Manuscripts Commission, Salisbury MSS*, XI, pp. 156, 321–2.

27. Bod. Malone MSS 23, fo.32.

28. Birch (ed.), *Court and Times*, I, p. 368; CCRO, CR 63/2/19, fo.58r.

29. John Earle, *Microcosmographie* (1628; reprint, 1897) p. 104. Cust, 'News and Politics', p. 70.

30. Green (ed.), *Diary of John Rous, passim*; Yonge and Whiteway, see V.L. and M.L. Pearl, 'Richard Corbett's "Against the Opposing of the Duke in Parliament, 1628", and the Anonymous Rejoinder, "An Answere to the Same, Lyne for Lyne": The Earliest Dated Manuscript Copies', *Review of English Studies*, 42 (1991) p. 32; Davenport, CCRO, CR 63/2/19; for the circulation of information in the provinces, see Clive Holmes,

'The County Community in Stuart Historiography', *JBS*, 19 (1980); F.J. Levy, 'How Information Spread Among the Gentry', *JBS* 21 (1982); Cust, 'News and Politics'.

31. Hamilton (ed.), *Original Papers*, p. 72.
32. SPD 16/117/10, 16/118/77.
33. John Morrill, 'William Davenport and the "Silent Majority" of Early Stuart England', *Journal of the Chester Archaeological Society*, 58 (1974) p. 121. Norman K. Farmer, Jr., 'Robert Herrick's Commonplace Book? Some Observations and Questions', *Papers of the Bibliographic Society of America*, 66:1 (1972) p. 30; the verse libels from this commonplace book are reproduced in facsimile and with transcripts by Norman Farmer in *Texas Quarterly*, 16:4 (1973), supplement, (hereafter cited as *TQ*).
34. Green (ed.), *Diary of John Rous*, pp. 22, 30.
35. *TQ*, introduction; CCRO, CR 63/2/19.
36. Norman E. McClure (ed.), *The Letters of John Chamberlain* (Philadelphia, 1939) II, p. 185.
37. Michael Kiernan (ed.), *Sir Francis Bacon: The Essayes or Counsels, Civill and Morall* (Cambridge, Mass., 1985) p. 43.
38. I will deal with the 1605 case in much greater detail in a future article; for élite sensitivity, see Lawrence Stone, *Crisis of the Aristocracy* (Oxford, 1965) p. 750; Keith Thomas, 'The Place of Laughter in Tudor and Stuart England', *TLS*, 21 January 1977, p. 79.
39. James F. Larkin (ed.), *Stuart Royal Proclamations* (Oxford, 1983) II, p. 94; BL Add. MSS 48057, fo.77v, 78r; Richard Cust, *The Forced Loan and English Politics, 1626–1628* (Oxford, 1987).
40. James Craigie (ed.), *The Poems of King James VI of Scotland* II (Edinburgh, 1958), pp. 183ff.
41. Bod. English Poetry MSS e.14, fo.52v.
42. As is argued for the 1630s by Stephen Foster, *Notes from the Caroline Underground* (Hamden, 1978).
43. Cust, 'News and Politics', *passim*.
44. For this language or paradigm, see Richard Cust and Peter Lake, 'Sir Richard Grosvenor and the Rhetoric of Magistracy', *BIHR*, 54 (1981); Peter Lake, 'Constitutional Consensus and Puritan Opposition in the 1620s', *HJ*, 25 (1982); Peter Lake, 'Anti-Popery: The Structure of a Prejudice' in Richard Cust and Ann Hughes (eds), *Conflict in Early Stuart England* (1989).
45. Susan Sontag, *Illness as Metaphor* (Toronto, 1988) pp. 58, 73.
46. Raymond A. Anselment, 'Seventeenth-Century Pox: The Medical and Literary Realities of Venereal Disease', *The Seventeenth Century*, 4:2 (1989) pp. 197, 198.
47. Wallace Notestein *et al.* (eds), *Commons Debates 1621* (New Haven, 1935) v, p. 219.
48. *TQ*, pp. 36–7.
49. For Cecil, Bod. Tanner MSS 299, fo.11; for Frances Howard, BL Add. MSS 15476, fo.92r.

50. Alan Bray, *Homosexuality in Renaissance England* (1982) ch.1.

51. Alexander Leighton, *An Appeal to the Parliament: or Sion's Plea against the Prelacie* (Amsterdam?, 1629) p. 162.

52. Judith Richards, '"His Nowe Majestie" and the English Monarchy: the Kingship of Charles I before 1640', *Past and Present*, 113 (1986); Malcolm Smuts, 'Public Ceremony and Royal Charisma: The English Royal Entry in London, 1485–1642' in A.L. Beier *et al.* (eds), *The First Modern Society: Essays in Honour of Lawrence Stone* (Cambridge, 1989).

53. Thomas Cogswell, 'Politics and Propaganda: Charles I and the People in the 1620s', *JBS*, 29 (1990); Cust, 'News and Politics'.

54. Roger Lockyer, *Buckingham* (1981) p. 463.

55. Fairholt, *Poems and Songs*, pp. 59–60.

56. *TQ*, pp. 129–33.

57. Ibid., pp. 136–41.

58. Bod. English Poetry MSS c.50, fo.5r, 6v.

59. Cogswell, *Blessed Revolution*, pp. 47–8.

60. Bod. Rawlinson Poetry MSS 26, fo.22.

61. Bod. English Poetry MSS c.50, fo.21r.

62. Bod. English Poetry MSS c.50, fo.14r–v; Poe was a doctor associated with the court (and the treatment of syphilis) since Cecil's time.

63. See Cogswell, 'Politics and Propaganda', pp. 201–2.

64. Fairholt, *Poems and Songs*, pp. 14, 15.

65. *A Continued Journall of all the Proceedings of the Duke of Buckingham his Grace, in the Isle of Rhee* (1627), 30 August issue, insert.

66. Ibid., 17 August issue, pp. 14–15, title page.

67. George Eglisham, *The Forerunner of Revenge Upon the Duke of Buckingham* ('Frankfurt', 1626); Mary F. Keeler *et al.* (eds), *Proceedings in Parliament 1628* (New Haven and London, 1977–1983) VI, pp. 132–3.

68. Fairholt, *Poems and Songs*, pp. 19–24.

69. BL Add. MSS 22591, fo.315.

70. Fairholt, *Poems and Songs*, pp. 33–4.

71. BL Add. MSS 29492, fo.55r.

72. Bod. Ashmole MSS 36–37, fo.174v.

73. Birch, *Court and Times*, I, pp. 364–5; Leba M. Goldstein, 'The Life and Death of John Lambe', *Guildhall Studies in London History*, 4:1 (1979).

74. CCRO, CR 63/2/19, fo.69r.

75. Fairholt, *Poems and Songs*, pp. 66–7.

76. Ibid., pp. 75–6.

77. Ibid., pp. 69–70.

78. Birch, *Court and Times*, I, pp. 438, 445.

79. *The Prayer and Confession of Mr Felton, word for word as he spoke it immediately before his execution November 29, 1628* (1628), p. 4; Birch, *Court and Times*, I, pp. 441–2, 446.

80. Birch, *Court and Times*, I, p. 442.

81. Fairholt, *Poems and Songs* p. 76.

82. Ibid., p. 78.

83. Bod. English Poetry MSS e.14, fo.76v.
84. BL Add. MSS 15226, fo.28r–v.
85. Fairholt, *Poems and Songs*, p. 42.
86. Ibid., p. 73.
87. BL Sloane MSS 1199, fo.70v.
88. Fairholt, *Poems and Songs*, p. 54.
89. Bod. English Poetry MSS c.50, fo.13v.
90. Fairholt, *Poems and Songs*, p. 77.
91. Bod. Ashmole MSS 38, fo.142.
92. Christopher Hill, 'Political Discourse in Early Seventeenth-Century England' in *A Nation of Change and Novelty* (1990).
93. *Hell's Hurlie-Burlie, or a Fierce Contention betwixt the Pope and the Devill* (1644); Martin Dzelzainis (ed.), *John Milton: The Political Writings* (Cambridge, 1991) p. 137; Sir Walter Scott (ed.), *The Secret History of the Court of James I*, 2 vols, (Edinburgh, 1811); Stone, *Crisis*, p. 668.
94. Robert Darnton, *The Literary Underground of the Old Regime* (Cambridge, Mass., 1982) p. 204.

Notes on Contributors

J.S.A. ADAMSON is a Fellow of Peterhouse, Cambridge, and Editor of the *History of Parliament: 1640–1660* for the History of Parliament Trust.

ALASTAIR BELLANY was educated at Lancaster Royal Grammar School, and at Balliol College, Oxford, where he took a first in Modern History in 1989. He is currently a graduate student in the Department of History at Princeton University, researching a dissertation on the Overbury murder, court scandal and political culture in early Stuart England.

MARTIN BUTLER is a Lecturer in the School of English, University of Leeds. He is the author of *Theatre and Crisis 1632–1642* (1984) and *Ben Jonson's 'Volpone': A Critical Study* (1987), and he has edited *The Selected Plays of Ben Jonson*, volume 2 (1989).

PETER LAKE is Professor of History at Princeton University. The author of a number of studies on politics and religion under Elizabeth and the early Stuarts, he is currently working on *English Conformist Thought from Hooker to Laud* and the rise of the funeral sermon and godly life in the period down to 1660.

LEAH S. MARCUS teaches English at the University of Texas, Austin. She is the author of *Childhood and Cultural Despair* (1978), *The Politics of Mirth* (1986), *Puzzling Shakespeare* (1988) and *Unediting the Renaissance* (forthcoming).

J. NEWMAN is a Reader in the History of Art at the Courtauld Institute of Art, University of London. He specialises in seventeenth and eighteenth century British architecture. His latest article is an extended study of Inigo Jones's early annotations.

DAVID NORBROOK is Fellow and Tutor in English at Magdalen College, Oxford. His publications include *Poetry and Politics in the English Renaissance* (1984) and *The Penguin Book of Renaissance Verse* (with Henry Woudhuysen, 1992).

JOHN PEACOCK is a Lecturer in English at Southampton University, where he teaches Renaissance literature. His research has focused on Elizabethan, Jacobean and Caroline court culture. His book *Inigo Jones's Masque Designs: the European Context* is to be published by CUP.

KEVIN SHARPE is Reader in History at the University of Southampton. Among his books are *The Personal Rule of Charles I* (1992), *Politics and Ideas* (1989) and *Criticism and Compliment* (1987, 1990). He is currently working on representations of authority and images of power in early modern England.

MALCOLM SMUTS is Associate Professor of History at the University of Massachusetts in Boston. He is the author of *Court Culture and the Origins of a Royalist Tradition in Early Stuart England* (Philadelphia 1987) and is currently working on historiography and political ideas in England, 1580–1640.

BLAIR WORDEN is Fellow and Tutor in Modern History at St Edmund Hall, Oxford. He is the author of *The Rump Parliament 1648–1653* (Cambridge 1974), and of a series of essays on the religion, politics and literature of early modern England.

Index